**Published by:**

*National Association for Public Safety*

**please visit us on the web at:**
www.napsusa.org
www.cafepress.com/manning
shermanmanning.blogspot.com

**or contact us at:**
hallopeter@sunrise.ch

**© Copyright 2004 Sherman D. Manning**


**ISBN 0-9743260-0-3**

Other Books by **Sherman Manning:**

*Reach Beyond the Break and Hold On*
*Dream and Grow Rich*
*If It Doesn't Fit, You Must Acquit*
*Through the Valley of the Shadow of Death (Columbine High School)*
*Teens Are Dying/Parents Are Crying: Where Do We Go From Here?*
*American Dream, A Search for Justice Vol. 1*

## HarperCollins

*HarperCollins* books may be purchased at local bookstores or over the Internet. The author encourages readers to purchase books in bulk by writing to: Special Markets Department, HarperCollins Publishers, Inc., 10 East 53$^{rd}$ Street, New York, NY 10022.

*Newly Revised and Updated* **American Dream, A Search For Justice**

This newly revised issue includes powerful new chapters, entries and data on Kobe Bryant, Lynn Stewart, Johnnie Cochran, Willie Gary, Beverly Ann Monroe and more . . .

***Read on!***

# Table of Contents

**Author's honorees': Christopher Gardner, Earl Graves, P. Diddy, Attorney Willie Gary, Attorney Van Jones, F. Lee Bailey and Senator Ted Kennedy**

# Special Dedication

Paul and Jan (husband and wife) Crouch are to Christian television as Ted Turner is to cable news. They have done with T.B.N. (Trinity Broadcasting Network), what CNN did for news internationally. They've done for the church what the Wright Brothers did for transportation. Any pastor, church or ministry that wants to spread their message to the four corners of the earth should try to get airtime on T.B.N. It is absolutely mind boggling and mesmerizing to watch the impact that Trinity is having on North America and in many other countries across the world. Juanita Bynum, Paula White, Bishop T. D. Jakes, Bishop Eddie Long and Gilbert Patterson (to name a few) have all catapulted their local ministries into worldwide ministries because of the power of T.B.N.

I have never met Paul and Jan Crouch but I am absolutely certain that God is pleased with the work that they are doing via T.B.N. and I feel like they are my personal friends, role models and partners in ministry.

I'm not sure if Paul and Jan know how many men and women in prison would commit suicide or homicide; would die and go to hell if it were not for the ministry that they receive via T.B.N.

Many people in prison never get a letter in the mail or a visit from a chaplain. Many who are trapped behind the concrete walls would get no word, no church, no revelation or inspiration if there were not a T.B.N. I applaud Paul and Jan Crouch for the marvelous work they are doing to bring Christian television behind these walls and the third world countries all over the earth.

Peter said, "You should tell Mr. And Mrs. Crouch to offer this book over television to all prisoners and the families of prisoners. And you should allow forty percent of the profits to go to T.B.N. to keep Christian television up and running. Hundreds of thousands of inmates watch T.B.N. and perhaps millions of prisoners' family members watch T.B.N. I am certain they could raise a lot of money with a book like American Dream/A Search For Justice."

Well, I want to *one up* Peter by telling Paul and Jan and any ministry, which is on T.B.N. that you may offer this book to your viewers and you can keep *fifty* percent of the profits. (Log on to CafePress online...Sherman Manning and/or email hallo peter@freesurf.ch or call the Avid Reader Bookstore in Davis, California to arrange for more copies of this book). I encourage every person who is holding this book in your hands right now to subscribe to T.B.N. and contribute to T.B.N. They need your prayers and your financial support. Paul and Jan cannot continue to take Jesus to the world without money. So we must all do what we can to support T.B.N. You should sit down today and write out a check to T.B.N. at P.O. Box "A" in Santa Ana, CA 92711. I thank God for T.B.N. and I thank God for Paul and Jan Crouch. I hope they will continue to spread the word that Jesus Christ is Lord through their networks and over their satellites.

Dr. E. V. Hill went on home to glory but Paul and Jan have committed T.B.N. to continue airing messages preached by E. V. Hill over the airwaves of T.B.N. How can we not support them and help them?

Jasper Williams, Leroy Elliott, Jesse Jackson and Rev. Cecil Murray ought to be lining up to buy time on T.B.N. If they did, they would see their ministries grow beyond all imagination. And when I get my miracle and get out of prison, I will work tirelessly to get I-May, a weekly program on T.B.N. As I salute the dedication and determination of Paul and Jan Crouch, I hope you (the reader) will take out time and help T.B.N. with a check today. For it is more blessed to give than it is to receive . . .

**November 2003**

# <u>Opening argument by Peter Andrist</u>

"This is Sherman's best writing ever. I'm totally convinced that trial experts such as Murray J. Janus, Roy Black, Anthony Brooklier and Gerry Spence will call this book a classic. There are numerous new entries spread out all over the book and you'll find a powerful Kobe Bryant chapter near the end of this book. I sat glued to this book for seven hours. I was mesmerized and amazed by many of the new details contained herein. I suggest that each reader grab a cup of coffee, take off your shoes and prepare for *lift off*. Simply stated, *this* is one of the greatest books I've ever read in my entire lifetime . . . Now get ready for a powerful, concise and skillfully written update by Sherman himself. Peace be with you all . . ."

*Peter Andrist*
*Vice President & CFO*
*A&M Enterprises*
*Zürich Switzerland*

# Rush (to judgment?) Limbaugh

Is Rush Limbaugh really a big fat liar? Is Rush really a drug addict and hypocrite? Does he really know "the way things ought to be"? Perhaps it would be pragmatic to advise you (the reader) to refer to the book by Al Franken in order to form an opinion concerning Mr. Limbaugh. Possibly I should not risk potentially frustrating or alienating some of my core readers by taking any position on the Limbaugh fiasco. A large majority of my advisors have expressed to me, in no uncertain terms, their negative and potent critiques of this talk show mogul. Many people think that Mr. Limbaugh has "talent on loan from the devil"!

Rush was born in Cape Girardeau, Missouri, a mid-western small town. He became a top forty deejay in the mid-1960s and held numerous other jobs prior to discovering his "true" calling as a radio talk show host in Sacramento. In 1980 his radio show went national and it is now heard in more than five hundred and twenty markets across America. Rush is definitely a media celebrity with a strong, sound following. The vast majority of Mr. Limbaugh's listeners are God-fearing, decent, successful and hardworking Americans. Many of his fans and supporters believe (as I do) in the basic idea that the "American Dream" is still a possible dream. They believe that if you give a man a fish, you'll feed him for a day but if you teach him how to fish you'll feed him for a lifetime. Quite frankly, I take issue with anyone who can't find logic, truth and reality in the aforementioned adage. Studying, schooling, hard work and self-reliance are (in my humble opinion) necessary ingredients for success and accomplishment in this great country.

Some of Rush's rhetoric is used as a divisive tool by liberals including civil rights leaders, pastors and politicians. My guess is that Rush uses sensational and (sporadically) explosive monologue as shock factors and attention grabbers. I think Rush is perhaps a brilliant talk show host. It is also obvious that Rush is an avid, omnivorous reader. He prepares well and definitely knows how to stir up a debate. Mr. Limbaugh comes across as insensitive, arrogant, pompous and a "liar, liar, big fat liar" if one does not take the time to really analyze his political positions.

Arguably, there are some people in the world who specialize in *excuse making*. When it comes to failure, they always have an *excuse*. They blame these failures on their skin color, their parents or their poverty. Yet, one cannot dispute the fact that many people have been able to overcome seemingly insurmountable obstacles and climbed over humongous hurdles to succeed and grow rich in America. Many of those minorities who have achieved success in America are profiled in my book, "Dream and Grow Rich".

Some people just don't seem to understand Rush. They allege that he is racist and a bigot. There are some of us who are tired of hearing every failure, in minority America, being blamed on racism and (to me) it is obvious that a portion of the so-called leaders on the left have become wealthy by capitalizing on so-called racism in America. Please understand that Rush admits there is still racism in America. Mr. Limbaugh has made it crystal clear that slavery was wrong. Slavery was a sin; a crime against humanity and Blacks will continue to suffer the after effects of slavery for a long, long time. Slavery was absolutely horrible. A brilliant psychologist by the name of Dr. Na'im Akbar explains many of the psychological effects of this tragedy in his book, "Breaking the Chains of Psychological Slavery".

My opinion is that Rush is not a racist. I believe he has biases as we all do. He may be prejudiced and possibly a classicist. But I'm pretty much convinced that one needs to not worry about Mr. Limbaugh burning a cross on anybody's lawn. I guess what I enjoy most about Rush is that he seems to genuinely believe what he preaches. I think that he thinks he's right and, of course, I concur with Rush on many, many issues. I am ridiculously impressed with the personal success (es) of many of his callers/listeners. Rush has energy, passion and confidence. He's a self-made multi-millionaire. But, Mr. Limbaugh needs to dig a lot deeper, study a lot longer and explore the ideas of scholars who also proved to be brilliant and credible.

The problem I have with Rush is that I think he's sort of a zealot at times and he seemingly refuses to study or entertain any school of thought or pool of knowledge, which does not corroborate his views. I have learned to read books I don't like, study other languages, cultures and philosophies, which doesn't always support or bolster my political paradigms. I have come to understand that sometimes one need not only study the writings, thoughts and ideas of great men, it is also advisable to study the books that scholars studied in order to try to understand the ingredients, which were utilized in order to cause these scholars to think what they thought and know what they know.

In some instances, when I've read the tomes, which writers read, I've ended up questioning some of the positions which they took after having read what they read. "How could she have gotten this out of that?" I've sometimes ended up asking. One needs to go beyond or beneath this surface level of pseudo intellectualism if one desires to gain a solid and well-rounded set of core beliefs.

If a Black kid likes the speeches and oratory of Malcolm X, I have no problem with that. I do have a major problem with anyone deciding that all White people are blue-eyed devils or all republicans/conservatives are racist and bigoted. But an authentic student of Malcolm X needs to do more than read an article or two about Malcolm in some magazine or newspaper. One may be mesmerized when one discovers that Malcolm read the entire dictionary and hand copied it while sitting in a cold jail/prison cell. Malcolm read books about the Jewish people, masonry, legal law, science, politics, and racism. If I wish to know him, I need to know what books he read, etc. in order to more adequately comprehend why he believed as he believed and did the things that he did.

Maybe Mr. Limbaugh ought to read a book or two by Cheikh Anta Diop, Dr. Cornel West or Andrew Young. Maybe he ought to read some of the writings of Langston Hughes, James Baldwin and Marcus Garvey.

It seems only logical (to me) that Phil Jackson should do more than study the Lakers' film footage from their last game. If Mr. Jackson plans to win the prize, it would be advisable or should I say we would expect Mr. Jackson to study film from the opponent's games. Show me what you *eat* and I'll understand why you weigh what you weigh and how your body became the body (size, shape and weight) which it is.

"Has Limbaugh read a single book by a Black author in the past few years?" an activist asked me. Mr. Randall Robinson could elucidate some issues, which Rush discussed from time to time.

Obviously none of us agree on everything and diverse opinions, differing views and beliefs make for a greater America. I started listening to Rush years ago just because it was entertainment to me and I wanted to debate him. I thought I would disagree with him on almost every single issue; I was wrong. I thought he was an airhead and full of hot air; I was incorrect. Rush knows exactly what he's doing (on the radio) and he is one of the best.

So far as drugs are concerned, I think a man must be presumed innocent. Yet Rush need not request this entitlement or right because he admits to being addicted. Being addicted to any kind of drug is sad and terrifying. Since Rush has been so hard on drug addicts, etc. on his show, it's obviously embarrassing and hypocritical for him to abuse drugs. It's quite disturbing to learn he was obviously using a poor maid to buy the drugs. Mr. Limbaugh ought to be ashamed of himself. He lacks discipline and no matter how much some of us may like listening to his show or concur with his belief in

9

self-reliance, we must stand up and announce Rush was wrong, wrong, wrong.

We must not be afraid to debate Mr. Limbaugh on critical issues if we disagree with him. This is America and Rush has an intelligent, intellectual and mostly well-educated audience. None of Mr. Limbaugh's fans are going to hate, fight or kill because someone disagrees. His listeners are above that. So I admit that Rush disappointed me with this drug addiction. This is not some plot or just left wing conspiracy at work here. He is or was addicted to drugs, plain and simple. A drug addict by any other name is still a drug addict. Rush knows "the way things ought to be" so he must take responsibility, get treatment and then he ought to go on a speaking tour to help other drug addicts by telling them his story.

I'm also disappointed with Mr. Limbaugh's lack of accurate information and obvious ill preparation on the subject of multiculturalism. On this issue, it seems that Mr. Limbaugh just does not really get it. Rush says a series of things that seem to be accurate and sensible on the surface. Yet, it appears he needs to dig a bit deeper and study more meticulously some of the issues, which he chooses to elaborate upon. One of the closest associates to me in North America stated, "I find it disturbing to know that you agree with Rush on so many issues. Rush Limbaugh is a narrow-minded, fat, pseudo intellectual. He's racist, classicist and a bigot."

I strenuously disagree with that critique and I respect each person's right to believe whatever he or she wants to believe. I am also cognizant of the fact that Mr. Limbaugh makes it easy for some to dislike him. If I were a poor minority living in the slums and I heard Rush discussing multiculturalism (for example) I'd become disenchanted.

At this juncture, I want to elucidate a few points on which I tend to disagree with Mr. Limbaugh. Rush believes that most advocates and/or spokesmen for multiculturalism are attempting to revise history. In fact, they are simply attempting to correct history. Rush said, "Some kids are being taught the ideas of the American Constitution were really borrowed from the Iroquois Indians and that Africans discovered America by crossing the Atlantic on rafts hundreds of years before Columbus . . . and made all sorts of other scientific discoveries and inventions that were later stolen from them . . . Ancient Greeks and Romans stole all of these ideas from the Egyptians and that the Egyptians were Black Africans."

Anyone who implies that the Ancient Greeks and Romans stole "all" of their ideas (I believe) is incorrect. Yet, there is much empirical and credible data, which clearly proves many ideas were indeed stolen. I will not attempt to utilize this tome to dispute in any expansive manner the details or the facts on which I think Rush is partially incorrect. I will, however, suggest that Rush needs to become more open-minded and to broaden his own mental horizons by studying historical data (which is indisputable) written by and about Cheikh Anta Diop, Dr. Al Mansour, Dr. Cornell West and many others. Quite often it has been my personal experience that we tend to limit ourselves by studying one school of thought and subconsciously deciding that this school is right and everybody else is wrong. If we decide not to even entertain the possibility that one group of scholars or historians could be wrong on a particular point, we limit our own understanding and our potential for growth and development. Rush said that there is a fallacious premise out there that minority children suffer low self-esteem because they don't have any roots. Rush does not think it is necessary to teach Black kids the origins of their history and the facts that many of them are in the lineage of kings and queens. Basically Rush believes that if you want to get a job at IBM or Xerox, you need to acquire the skills necessary to compete and to work in those companies. I agree with the latter but take issue with the former. Any psychologist or specialist in human behavior will tell us that before you learn skills, which are adequate to compete on any level, etc., you must have a basic, fundamental and elemental belief in yourself. You must believe that you are somebody and it is absolutely absurd to assume that kids in school (i.e. minorities) who are taught with history books that never mentions the factual, credible and successful contributions, which have been made by their ancestors . . . will indeed stunt the mental growth of those children. If you study books written by people who don't look like you, with stories about the roots, origins and contributions of everybody except you, it will contribute to low self-esteem. I'm not going to argue the Hippocratic oath and Imhotep or who built the pyramids or who designed the city of our nation's capitol, etc. Yet, I will suggest that no child should have their history robbed or stolen from them.

Rush said, "And if kids have been taught learning these things means compromising themselves and conforming to White values, how on earth can they be expected to succeed?" Mr. Limbaugh goes on to point out that, "If they want to prosper in America, if they want access to opportunity in America, they must be able to assimilate - to become part of the American culture." Quite frankly, on the surface, Rush is making a valid point. Yet, from a psychological aspect, it's deeper than this surface statement. Perhaps Rush actually means well and maybe his intentions are positive. Yet, without an in-depth knowledge of what it means and how it is to be Black in America or Brown or Indian, etc., Rush does not seem to fully appreciate the improbability of properly assimilating into a culture which routinely discriminates against you. To think that one should not place major importance on one's roots, beginnings and history is not sensible. Simplistically, people need to know where they came from and how/why they got where they are. If all they've been taught is their slave history and about the traumas and tragedies of their blackness or brownness and not about the kings and queens in Africa, etc., their ability to assimilate and prosper in a culture will be extremely difficult. If you don't know who you are, you won't know what you're capable of accomplishing. Blacks, Browns and all other minorities definitely need to assimilate into the American culture. Rush is absolutely correct on that. Yet, there must absolutely be an inclusion (not necessarily a revision) to their cultures, contributions and past in that history. Mr. Limbaugh is an extremely intelligent man and I don't believe that Rush is incapable of comprehending the effects of the psychological torture, physical abuse, kidnapping and lynching that Blacks have suffered here in North America. To imply that one should merely "forget it" and move on may be (indeed) the way things ought to be. But it is "not" the way things are. Gumption tells us that the poverty, crime and hopelessness, which is running rampart in epidemic proportions in many Black (Latino and White) ghettos in North America has a cause. What we see in those communities is a direct result of what was done to the people in this country. I agree that they, which know not their history, are destined to repeat it. Yet, they who dwell on their history are also destined to remain stuck. I want Blacks to *get over it*. That is "the way things ought to be". I understand that merely sitting around talking about slavery in a redundant fashion will not pull minorities out of poverty or put food on the table. I also know we must deal with our past in order to understand our present and improve our future. Rush wants us all to strive for self-reliance. So do I! That is "the way things ought to be". We should all fend for ourselves.

I'm not interested in seeing people who are depending on welfare checks forever. I am cognizant of the fact that there are many trapped in our slums that pay more for their red party lights than they do for their white reading lights. They pay more for their liquor and reefer than they do for their books. This must be changed if we are to ever eliminate poverty and failure in this country. I also agree that many Blacks in this country have been able to pull themselves up by their own bootstraps and achieve remarkable success. Yet, one can't pull oneself up by the bootstraps if one has no boots. We must deal with facts and not just dream about "the way things ought to be". When the dream is over, we are still faced with the way things are.

If you hold a man back for four hundred miles of an eight hundred mile run, you can't just decide, oh well, that was then and this is now. "The way things ought to be" is you fend for yourself. You are now allowed to participate (equally) in the race, that's the way it ought to be and we are not going to do you any favors. This is America and we are all equal.

"Sir, may I ask you what do I do to catch up? How am I equal when you've got four hundred laps or four hundred miles on me?"

I know many of us who have moderate and conservative views don't like to hear things like "leveling the playing field". We don't want to give a hand out but what about a hand up? When you methodically kick a man down, should you not be decent enough to help him to get up? Can we totally pretend that racism is over in America? Do we really, really believe that things are equal? Do we believe that there is equality, liberty and justice for all? Since we know that's not true, what must we do about it? Overlook it? Rush and I both know better.

Blacks "will" be able to make it when playing by the same rules. But those rules must be applied equally and where there is bias and prejudice, there is no equality. If there were a rule stating - a man had to weigh at least two hundred pounds in order to play basketball - I would want that rule applied equally. It would not be right to allow one or two White guys who only weighed one hundred and eighty-five pounds to play just because of their skin color. This would be reverse discrimination! But on closer scrutiny, if it were proven that Blacks systematically and strategically stunted the growth and physical development of Whites (i.e. by withholding food, vitamins and nutritionally robbing them) I would have no problem making allowances and modifying the rules for Whites. The entrance rules must be modified in order to let them in. Yet, in order to stay in, those Whites who weighed only one hundred and eighty-five pounds would need to play the game of basketball by the same rules as everybody else in the game. There should and could be no acceptable excuses for not showing up for practice or not staying and learning the variety of plays. The White player should not be allowed to use the fact that food was withheld to justify a turnover or fumble in the game. I believe (adamantly) he should and can play by the same rules. But we must all be given equal access to the throne of opportunity.

13

Many claim to wonder how boatloads of Vietnamese came to this country and have assimilated and accomplished success in America. This is an example of the fact that Blacks can make it in America!

Mr. Limbaugh titled his tome, "The Way Things Ought To Be". Yet in the book, he admits you must deal with things the way they are. Ditto! I want Rush to know that the way things are in this country is not equal, not just and the Vietnamese, how/why and when they came to America is an entirely different thing. It's like mixing apples with oranges. Mr. Limbaugh failed to mention the special (rule modification) tax breaks given to these Vietnamese business upstarts, which is not given to Blacks in America who wish to start businesses.

There are various other things, which have been done and are being done to especially accommodate foreigners who come to America and open new businesses. Blacks are not given these special accommodations. So we don't only need to dwell on the forty acres and a mule, which Blacks were cheated out of. We can focus on the special tax breaks and incentives given (daily) to Vietnamese and Korean entrepreneurs yet withheld from Blacks entering businesses. So then it is quite easy and simplistic to speak comparatively about the accomplishments of various groups who arrived here in America with nothing and point out what Blacks have not achieved. It is quite easy to paint everything with a broad stroke; to speak in nebulous and ambiguous terms or generalities, etc. but one must deal in the reality of how things are! I don't know many people claiming we should "punish the wealthy" and reward the poor. Nor do I hear Reverend Jesse Jackson or others claiming that equality means everybody in America ought to have the exact size house or the exact amount of insurance, etc. Yet, Mr. Limbaugh takes pains to imply that "all liberals" want everybody to have the exact same amount of money, insurance and even food.

Quite frankly, that smacks of pandering and sensationalism. The very bottom line is Rush has a lot of good points and he's a smart guy. But on many issues, Rush is flat wrong. That does not make him a bad guy.

In my humble opinion, it is absolutely wrong to penalize the wealthy and/or punish the rich. It is also appropriate to teach self-help, self-reliance and self-worth to the poor. One of the ways you teach self-worth to anybody is to empower him or her with the detailed specifics of their authentic history.

Mr. Limbaugh also takes pains in his tome, "The Way Things Ought To Be", to explain how our country was founded on faith in

God, the Ten Commandments and the power of the Holy Bible. I concur. Without engaging in any controversies involving denominational or theological diversities, etc., I suggest that Mr. Limbaugh re-read the entire Book of Isaiah in the Bible. He will clearly see that if we, the church, we America or we the people wish to continue prospering and being blessed, it is our Christian duty to feed the hungry, clothe the naked and take care of the least of these our brethren. Then, perhaps, Mr. Limbaugh should consider perusing the 25th Chapter of St. Matthew in our Holy Bible. We must strive to be open-minded and not zealots. It is absolutely ridiculous to engage in fanaticism or to subscribe to an idea whose time has not come merely because a republican has initiated the idea. Likewise, those who support any and everything advocated by liberals are also pragmatically unsound.

One of the dangers of lifting groups or individuals up as heroes or heroines and supporting any and every idea, which comes out of their mouths, is that when and if those superstars fall from grace, our spirits and very often our political beliefs are shattered.

We cannot ignore the fact that Mr. Limbaugh has lambasted drug addicts and even "prescription" drug addicts for years. He's called them immoral, crazy and spoiled. Now we discover that the man with "talent on loan from God" has (for years and years) articulated many of his extreme ideas while high, stimulated an inebriated by drugs. That's not "the way things ought to be". I'm praying for Mr. Limbaugh and I would hope he would pray for himself.

I am also praying for Michael Jackson. Michael Jackson has been charged with molestation, lewd acts on a child and giving alcohol to a minor. He too is presumed innocent. In the eyes of the law, he is absolutely innocent until proven guilty beyond a reasonable doubt. Mike is eccentric. Michael should not be sleeping with children. In my opinion, he needs help. "If" he is a pedophile he needs help and prison, period. Even if he's innocent (which a part of me really believes he's not a pedophile) he needs help. I believe it would do Mr. Jackson well to obtain therapeutic counseling from the likes of Dr. Na'im Akbar and Tony Robbins.

Michael is one of the most brilliant and skilled entertainers the world has ever seen. He is the king of pop and we hate to see his legacy tarnished by the implications of his eccentricities. We cannot legislate eccentricity and I would hope, believe and pray that Michael is found to be innocent of the crimes. Perhaps, maybe and hopefully after Michael is exonerated and vindicated, he will be persuaded to help others who are in similar situations.

15

Michael said he was mistreated, manhandled and roughed up by Santa Barbara Sheriff's authorities. (Author's note: The Santa Barbara Sheriff has unequivocally denied these accusations). Well, if this is true, I feel sorry for Michael. I want Michael to remember the pain, injustice and trauma he felt and to do something to help somebody else. Michael has always expressed a desire to "heal the world" and I think that is laudable and applaudable. But we must now recognize the fact that prisoners (too) are a part of the world. There are many wrongly convicted, indigent, innocent inmates trapped in the bowels of prisons across this great nation. Guys such as Mr. Limbaugh, Mr. Bryant, P. Diddy, Mr. Jackson, etc. could help these guys with lawyers. I know it sounds like a pipe dream but I still believe in the milk of human kindness.

At some point (why not now?) we must come together (as people) since we are sharing the planet and breathing the same air. We need to feel good about each other and not a single one of us should feel good about an innocent man or woman languishing in a cold jail or prison cell for a crime he or she did not commit.

We should demand law and order. We should be extremely tough on crime and it's time (also) for a pragmatic toughness on crime. We need to rid our streets of rapists, murderers and violent predators. We must protect the safety of the public. Our senior citizens and our children must be safe and secure. We won't accomplish either of those goals by putting the wrong men in jails or letting the wrong guys out of prisons.

Someone should remind Mr. Jackson, Mr. Bryant, Rolando Cruz and Geronimo Pratt that the universe sometimes allows horrible things to happen (to us) so that we will never let it happen to somebody else!

The wealthy, educated and prominent very rarely go to prison and we have empirical data that proves it's not just because rich folk don't commit crimes. Often true crime takes place in corporate suites, not in the streets. But poor folks get poor lawyers and inadequate legal representation. Very, very often they go to prisons for crimes of which they are clearly innocent.

For much of the short time that I've been on the planet, I have thought that all the guys in jails and prisons were violent, vicious predators. Yet, experience has shown me that many in prisons are nonviolent, petty violators who are taking up space and wasting taxpayers' money. We are on the verge of bankrupting our economy by incarcerating petty thieves, weed smokers and bad check writers. America must begin to demand a more pragmatic spending of her tax dollars. With the enormously high rate of recidivism in this country, she must also demand a better return on her investment. To say the system is not working is an understatement.

Brilliant, well-versed and learned men such as Tony Brown are cognizant of these facts. Yet, Tony Brown gets only thirty minutes airtime on Sunday mornings and most of the guys in jails and prisons are watching cartoons at that time. It is inexcusable to not get behind Tony Brown and help him educate the public concerning the sham of a system, which we call crime and punishment here in North America.

The public ought to know that despite empty promises, reform has eluded prisons across America. Let us take California for example: Five years ago, after state prison scandals gripped California with tales of officers conspiring against and setting up prisoners in human cockfights and then shooting them dead, the Department of Corrections vowed to transform its ways. They claimed whistleblowers would be protected, not punished. Internal investigations were to be encouraged to pursue corrupted guards. The correctional officers union no longer would have a hand in dictating policy. This new day never came. C.D.C. remains riddled with allegations that rogue cops still go unpunished, union bosses continue to exercise strong power and the wardens still thwart whistleblowers. It is a sad fact that "corrections" in California need "correcting".

Senator Gloria Romero (D - Los Angeles) who heads the prison oversight committee said, "We intend to start the New Year off with a bang and take a hard look at everything. We have a great opportunity with the new administration to make some real changes." One would expect that a guy such as Rush Limbaugh would be willing to add his voice and influence to the call to clean up C.D.C. Especially since Rush worked in Sacramento for a number of years. Since Rush's hypocrisy is obvious by his admitted addiction to drugs, etc. he could redeem himself by helping expose the evils of C.D.C. The brilliant entertainer, Michael Jackson, who is arguably one of the most philanthropic artists alive, should also join the fight.

Michael said the deputies at Santa Barbara abused him physically. He said they bruised his arm and locked him in a bathroom with human feces all over the walls. If this actually occurred, it is sick, illegal and immoral. If this transpired, then Michael should have no problem believing that inmates, trapped in prisons across America, are set up, beat, abused and attacked on a daily basis in these prisons. Michael has lived an insulated, pampered and upscale life for the past thirty plus years. I am a personal witness that when one lives a life of opulence and has limited or no contact with the police, prisons, etc., it is quite easy to become disconnected by *those* people who are trapped in jails and prisons. The atmosphere and subculture inside prison walls is foreign, unique, terror-filled and horrendous. It is quite easy to assume that tales of abuse at the hands of authorities, etc. are spurious and mendacious.

But experience is the best teacher and I would hope Mr. Jackson's abuse at the hands of jail and law enforcement authorities will cause the fire of justice and equality to burn in his belly. I was moved to tears when Michael declared years ago his desire to "heal the world". Prisoners would suggest to Michael that, "we (too) are the world". I would hope Michael is now propelled to help "heal the world" of guys trapped in jails and prisons. Michael is smart enough to know that just as he claims he's innocent and falsely accused of this horrible crime, there are others. These people did/do not have the wealth of Michael Jackson. If one of the most famous citizens in this world can be wrongly accused, who can't be? The authorities "know" that Michael has the money to hire a "dream team" of defense lawyers. They are cognizant of the fact that (to many) he is considered an untouchable celebrity and famous, opulent and influential in every sense of the word. Yet, they charged him! According to Michael, he is innocent.

Donald Trump stated, "Michael is a wonderful person. I believe he is innocent and they're just looking for a *payday*. People always take advantage of Michael."

It would be fantastic to win the interest of someone as brilliant as Mr. Trump in the fight to correct wrongful convictions and prison corruption in this country. If America is ever to adequately right these wrongs and truly correct the evils of a judicial system which is apparently out of control, we need to bring forth a pragmatic mindset such as that which is utilized by Donald Trump in the business world.

Prisons are big business! Prisons cost an enormous amount of money to run. Entire communities are built off the backs of prisoners. One of the difficulties is that we have wardens who barely read and write overseeing ninety million dollar budgets.

I don't envy the "governator" in California (Schwarzenegger). Arnold has a mess on his hands. He has been catapulted into the midst of a cesspool of sin, shame, torture and corruption. I have confidence that Arnold is basically a good human being who means well and intends to do no harm. But if he is going to clean up the California "department of corruption", he may need to appoint a prison czar. Unfortunately, protests, marches and emotionalism won't correct C.D.C. It needs a catharsis.

As much as I admire Rod Q. Hickman, I must state that I don't think Rod can/will clean up C.D.C. Rod has been in the system for twenty-five years. He certainly knows the system. But is he willing to risk everything including the wrath of the CCPOA by doing what it takes to put the system in check?

I hope that one day soon a Don King, Donald Trump, Jackson, Bryant or P. Diddy Combs will come forward and take an interest in corrections in California.

Michael Jackson fired Frank Dileo years ago in a "power" struggle. Yet, even though Michael *fired* Frank, Frank calls Michael the most giving and altruistic person he knows. "I don't believe Michael would molest a child," Frank said. Frank explains how insulated and isolated superstars like Michael are. He said the staff is afraid to speak out or criticize anything their boss (the superstar) says or does. Ipso facto nobody had the gall to tell Michael, "It's kinda weird to sleep with eleven-year-old boys." To be fair, Michael now claims he would sleep on the floor. I'm not so sure this is true (but I'm not a judge. I was not there).

I do believe Donald Trump, perhaps, has it right. These people are looking for a *payday*. I shall reiterate that it is sick and shameful to molest a child. Child molesters should be (while being treated for their sickness and perversion) put away for a very, very long time. It's unthinkable and unspeakable to harm a child!

It is also unthinkable to falsely accuse a man (Michael or anyone else) of child molestation. Calling Michael "Jacko" and "whacko", etc. is also mean, foolish and unfair. Michael deserves justice!

Mike Tyson did not get justice! Tyson (I'm convinced from reading the actual transcripts and from the writings of brilliant Attorney Alan Dershowitz) was wrongly and falsely convicted of rape. No matter how troubled (mentally speaking) Tyson may be, he was mistreated by the judicial system! Wrong! Wrong! Wrong!

It would appear that superstar Kobe Bryant may be headed in the same direction as Mr. Tyson (more on Kobe in other sections of this tome). We need to clear our minds as Americans. After the media hype has cleared the air and after we negate all of the sensationalism and perhaps yellow journalism, it is extremely difficult to believe Kobe committed rape.

The evidence (says insiders closely familiar with the facts) does not support the charge. Kobe was foolish. Kobe is young, gifted and Black. Kobe should probably have his butt kicked for numerous reasons. I love Kobe's basketball skills. I am a Laker fan! I love the brilliance and wizardry of Phil Jackson. I am also rooting for Mr. Mailman Malone to finally get that ring. Setting aside all fan loyalty, I am livid that Kobe allowed *any* situation to seemingly turn him at odds with his parents. I adamantly oppose that foolishness. I also oppose adultery from a Christian paradigm. I am also critical of the fact that Mr. Bryant, Tim Duncan, Michael Jordan and many, many, other rich sports superstars don't give a damn or a dime for the least of these/those in prisons who are wrongly convicted, poor, busted, broke and disgusted. Shame on them!!

But Kobe probably did *not* commit rape. Something in the milk is not clean. Was/is the sheriff a friend of the alleged victim's family? The alleged victim has a checkered past. She has been a drug abuser? Suicidal? Had semen on her panties, which did not belong to Kobe? Kobe seems to be factually and actually innocent. I've not heard Mr. Limbaugh speaking out against the Kobe prosecution. There is something inconsistent about Mr. Limbaugh believing that he (himself) is supposedly being singled out by a left wing conspiracy and a witch-hunt. Yet, he simultaneously refuses to believe that a Kobe or a Jackson could also be innocent. Rush wants us to believe that although he has admitted to being a drug addict, etc., he did not shop for doctors and pay his housekeeper to buy drugs, etc. Yet, Rush refuses to believe that although Michael admits to sharing his bed with kids, he is innocent of molestation. Likewise, Rush does not believe that Kobe is authentic when he admits to adultery but denies rape.

There appears to be a pattern here. Rush seems to assume that he is the only celebrity who can be a victim of embellished, exaggerated and blown out of proportion criminal accusations.

Rush is blessed to have Roy Black, a brilliant lawyer, as his attorney. I suggest Rush ask Roy how often men are falsely accused of rape.

I'm tired of people who think, "It's only me"! They will lambaste, criticize and ridicule others when others are accused or charged with a crime. They will imply that the judicial system is perfect and never errs. Yet, the moment their (prescription) drug addiction is uncovered or their personal crimes come to light, (all of a sudden) they want the public to believe that the accusations are embellished . . . "Everybody else is guilty! R. Kelly? Guilty! Absolutely no way anyone would fabricate these kinds of allegations against an innocent man. Kobe? Of course, he's guilty and so is Michael Jackson. We ought to lock the three of them away and never allow them to see the light of day. They are predators, thugs, vicious miscreants and they cannot be allowed to play the race card either.

Lock 'em up and throw away the key." That's what Rush would say. It is what many of us say when we have never been charged with or accused of a crime. Yet, what is seriously disturbing is to see a person accused who dares to look straight into a camera and claim, "I'm wrongly accused but they're not." That smacks of elitism and perhaps delusional thinking.

Not a single person who is perusing this tome at this juncture was there with Mr. R. Kelly, Mr. Michael Jackson, Mr. Kobe Bryant or Mr. Michael Tyson (with the exception of the victims or alleged victims who may be reading this). So no one is capable of stating what transpired to a degree of certainty. We may speculate, assume and surmise but whenever we get finished; we just don't know.

We routinely destroy people's lives, careers and families by jumping the gun and spreading journalistic accusations around the world as if they were fact. The old folks say that a lie will travel all over the world before the truth even gets out of the bed in the morning.

The mere thought of sending people to dangerous prisons across this country for crimes of which they are innocent is frightening. As a matter of fact, when one of our kids has one beer too many and accidentally kills somebody and goes to prison; now what? This teenager, kid or youngster will be (and you can believe it does happen everyday) catapulted into one of these cold and violent prisons and once he gets there; life will never, ever be the same for him again.

Imagine what it would be like in prison for smoking or dealing weed and you are housed with violent sexual predators or you find yourself in a small cell with a killer, pervert or lunatic. Society, in general, would have us assume that you'd be okay because prison authorities will ensure your safety and security. You're in good hands. *Good hands*? If Americans still believe that prisons are safe havens, which rehabilitate humans or correct criminal behavior, etc., one would need to ask - what planet have they been living on? One needs to only peruse California newspapers (in a cursory fashion) such as the L.A. Times to discover how wicked, evil, violent and corrupted the California prison system is. (C.D.C. is not an aberration . . . It is indicative of the conditions of prison across the nation including New York's Riker's Island, Lorton, Reidsville in Georgia, Angola, etc., etc.).

In the last year, for example, the California Department of Corrections has reversed its demotions of two sergeants working at Ironwood Prison in Blythe, California. After a lengthy internal probe, C.D.C. initially decided to terminate Jesse Lara and Glenn Barr for tying up a fellow officer, spray painting him with obscenities and displaying photos of the dastardly hazing. Yet, after both admitted to the misconduct, C.D.C. agreed to demote them instead.

Afterwards, in a move that stunned the Internal Affairs Unit, both officers were given back their sergeant stripes and full back pay. According to C.D.C. spokesman, Ruis Heimerich, the decision to restore Barr and Lara nearly fifteen months of their demotions was made by wardens at their respective prisons. "The promotions send the absolute wrong message that even when you do wrong, it doesn't matter in the Department of Corrections. You'll be quickly forgiven," stated Monroe Mabon, council for the Internal Affairs Unit.

C.D.C. flip-flopped on the Orozco killing at the hands of Officer Bruce Brumana. Twenty-three-year-old Orozco was serving nine years for dealing drugs when he was gunned down by C.O. Brumana during a fistfight at Pleasant Valley Prison. A few months latter C.D.C.'s Shooting Review Board ruled the killing unjustified. It was a murder by a correctional cop. "The fight posed no imminent danger or threat to inmates or staff", stated the report. "The fight could have been stopped without a gunshot".

C.D.C. suspended Brumana for ninety days. He was clearly a murderer. In civilian life, had he not been a C.D.C. officer, he would have been charged with murder! But under the color of authority and hiding behind badges of power, officers are often allowed to cut down inmates like a hunter kills rabbits.

This was the first time a Shooting Review Board had ever ruled against a prison guard. Union representatives were livid, but then C.D.C. Director Cal Terhune stood firm assembling an Executive Review Committee that ratified the finding. Supposedly the case was over and Brumana agreed to his punishment before the State Personnel Board.

Attorney Bob Navarro said, "It was signed, sealed and delivered, (Bob was co-counsel for the Orozco family) it went all the way up to the director."

Yet, late last year, Robert Borg, former warden and longtime corrections analyst, took it upon himself to dig back into the well-worn case. Borg read the case files and decided that the shooting was justified. Borg took his findings to C.D.C. Deputy David Tristan. In an amazing unilateral ruling outside C.D.C. policy, Tristan assigned an internal investigator to re-review the shooting. Five months ago, Tristan reversed the finding. Brumana was awarded back pay. Tristan, not surprisingly, is a friend of the union bosses.

Any careful and pragmatic observer has to admit that the "prison guards own the gates" and they control everything that goes on inside those gates and one major difficulty in correcting corrections is the fact that the guards union spend heavily on wining and dining state legislators and politicians. Basically, the guards union has many powerful state politicians in their hip pockets. So when there is a need for oversight, reprimand or termination, politicians turn a blind eye to prison officials' corruption. For example: powerful State Senator Jim Brulte, (R-Rancho Cucamonga), who is the senate republican leader, has been showered with vacations, trips and more than one hundred and fifteen thousand dollars in campaign contributions. Ipso facto, Brulte is trying to persuade the governor to close the state's last five private prisons - nonunion prisons that the guards union views as a jobs threat. "The guards own the gates". The guards union opposes the training, education and counseling programs that keep communities safer by reducing inmates relapse into criminal activity after their release from prison. Last year, then Governor Gray Davis, who had received $3.4 million from the guards union since 1998, persuaded legislators to shut down four of the state's nine private prisons and cut prison vocational programs. These cuts left more money to raise prison guard's salaries by 37.3 percent over three years, to $73,428 by 2006. That is more than twice the average salary in the next highest paying state. By contrast, the average California teacher's salary is less than fifty-four thousand dollars. The union also undermined oversight by successfully pushing for a large cut in the inspector general's budget. Presently, the union is trying to eliminate college and voc-ed programs statewide. The "governator" must question why the union wants to close all private prisons when the best of them provide drug treatment, counseling and moral education for fifty-five dollars a day - a bargain compared with the eighty-seven dollars a day for only a bed at a minimum security public (union run) prison. Some private prisons provide laboratories for transformation for reforms which public prisons shun.

The ultimate victims of this feudal control of prisons are law-abiding citizens who live and work in the neighborhoods into which prisoners are released, full of hate, anger, devoid of skills and *programmed* to *fail.*

I will not "rush" to judgment but the jury is *not out* (as it is in Limbaugh's situation, R. Kelly, Michael Jackson and Kobe Bryant) on the status of our judicial system nationwide and on the need for corrections in corrections across this country.

Inmates trapped in prisons in Alabama, Texas, Florida and many other states in North America will never be the same again.

The biggest mistake we made in America was to snatch rehabilitation out of the prisons. We would be foolish to coddle prisoners. We don't need to make prisons country clubs or glamorous. Nevertheless, we must do away with the knee-jerk decision to make them rough and tough. Obviously, we have empirical data, which proves conclusively that warehousing inmates does not work. We have empirical data from Reidsville State Prison in Georgia, Pelican Bay in California, Rikers Island in New York and Lorton Penitentiary (to name a few) that locking them down, denying them privileges, incentives, education, etc. does not solve crime, correct behavior or lessen recidivism upon their release. It does not take a rocket scientist, penologist or psychiatrist to know that the prisons as they are - don't work. It's broken and needs to be fixed.

Public outcry, publicity and a taxpayer revolt against prison corruption are a must if we're going to protect safety and security. Small-minded, petty and uneducated thugs out of the woods must no longer be allowed to keep the kept and guard the gates. You can take a man out of the country but you can't take the country out of him is *more* than a cliché.

How can we justify prison guards who rise to the rank of captain, associate warden, chief deputy and warden who can't read, write or spell? It's called the good ole boy (country as it sounds) network. It's called nepotism, bias and prejudice.

Captain Martel, who is at New Folsom State Prison is basically, functionally illiterate. New Folsom Chief Deputy Warden George Stratton reads at a seventh grade level, yet earns ninety-four thousand dollars per year.

At this very moment, I am a living, breathing victim of the combined effects of corruption and retaliation of Mr. Stratton and Mr. Martel. They got rid of me. They coerced Lt. Moreno to lie about a R.V.R. hearing. Lt. Moreno clearly indicated to me, "I'm finding you guilty of this '115' and I'm dismissing the other '115'". He dismissed it. Yet, lo and behold, when I got the paperwork, it stated that I was found guilty of both "115s". Shortly after, Captain Martel took over as the general population captain in New Folsom. He told me that he was going to get rid of me one way or another. Martel pitted an inmate against me - J. G. H. of whom I still have concern for. They manipulated him and at heart he's not a bad guy. They locked me in ad-seg, refused to allow me to call my attorney, withheld all of my incoming and outgoing mail, persuaded Corey McKay to lie to Attorney Comiskey and orchestrated a transfer to Mule Creek Prison. "Oh no, Paul. Sherman is not being transferred."

I'm here! They got me. Mr. Stratton's son works at New Folsom State Prison's A-facility. This young man is described by his co-workers as lazy, arrogant, egotistical and vindictive.

The blood of Gilbert Salazar is on Stratton's hands. Stratton was in the control booth playing dominoes (I've been able to verify) when Salazar was murdered by Frank Christian. Christian had killed a celly before and should have been in single cell status. Since C.D.C. erred, C.D.W. Stratton covered up the murder and coerced New Folsom's investigative unit to rule the homicide as a suicide. The Federal Bureau of Investigations should investigate this cover-up.

My vindictive transfer on December 9, 2003 was clearly retaliation by Captain Martel. He (seriously) claims I'm his enemy. The fact that I mentioned him in a book makes me a threat to him and vice versa. Well, since the C.D.C. director is corrupted and I'm writing it, will they now transfer me out of C.D.C. and send me home to Georgia to finish out my wrongful conviction? I would be glad to go home since I have no family or friends in California. (Any reader interested in true justice is encouraged to contact the F.B.I, the media, politicians, etc. about the Salazar murder/cover-up and/or any other data contained in this tome).

California's prison and parole systems are horrible, miserable and colossal failures that shackle the state with debt and crime, including repeat-offender rates, which are the highest in the nation.

Many prison inmates tell me, "I hate people" and they admit they're on a road to self-destruction. There are more drugs in prisons than there are in most ghettos. Guards smuggle them in and so do visitors. There is a cycle of despair in prison, which feeds violent offenders back into the streets. Experts have warned us that we can't incarcerate ourselves out of crime. Yet, we constantly build more jails and prisons and no schools and colleges.

Ex-inmate, Mike Brady, who was in prison himself three years ago on drug- related offenses, envisioned a treatment centers plan. He prepares the release of fifteen thousand low-risk inmates to centers, which are cost-effective, and reduces addictions. Mike is now deputy secretary of the State of California's Prison Management Agency. Mike knows better than most that success depends not on whether the inmates go to public or private prisons but on whether they end up able to function in society.

Initially, however, California state leaders should utilize some of the $277 million in projected savings from release/transfer to adequately fund treatment. If they fail to do this, the "for profit prisons" will get out of the rehab business and county facilities will end up as glorified drunk tanks, which are respites for crashing a few days after stealing the public's cars and wallets.

Missouri pioneered a no-jargon program called the "Buns Out of Bed" initiative, which requires inmates to participate in school full time, therapy or work. Work is mandatory. Between 1994 and 1999, the amount of Missouri parolees returning to prison on new felony charges dropped from thirty-three percent to twenty percent, the sixth lowest recidivism rate in the nation. California is sixty-nine percent. How could Georgia, California, New York, Alabama or any state argue with these results? Perhaps Mr. Limbaugh will advocate for reform on his radio show?

It is perhaps unthinkable for some to believe that some sworn peace officers are violent, vicious and predatory. Yet, there is an associate warden (Max Lemon) at Folsom State Prison who can attest to the fact that many of them are indeed thugs in uniform.

Max Lemon told KCRA News (in Sacramento) on January 9, 2004, "The cover-up (at Folsom) continues. Chief Deputy Warden Michael Bunnell should not be allowed anywhere near inmates."

On April 8, 2002 there was a riot between Hispanic inmates at Folsom. Captain Pieper had warned Warden Butler not to allow the Hispanics off lockdown. Mr. Pieper stated he feared a riot would break out. Mr. Pieper carried his concerns to C.D.C. Director Alameida and several state senators. No one listened to him and allegedly C.D.W. (Chief Deputy Warden) Bunnell stated to Captain Pieper, "Shut the fu . . up and do as I say. Let them off lockdown." Bunnell and Butler got their wish and as Pieper and A.W. (Associate Warden) Max Lemon had warned; a riot broke out . . . Captain Pieper took the incident so seriously that he shot himself. Yes, (absolutely, not a joke and yes, this book is *non*fiction). Captain Pieper committed suicide. It turns out he even left a suicide note concerning C.D.C. corruption, G. Stratton, Mr. Martel, Billy Mayfield and Director Alameida. He also wrote about Mr. Bunnell. Captain Pieper's widow, Evette Pieper, demands an investigation and wants to know why C.D.C. withheld the missive from her.

Reportedly, Mike Bunnell was fired from Tracy State Prison in 1993 for having personal contacts with inmates. Bunnell allegedly was actually calling "hits" for Hispanic gangs and revealing confidential information to inmates. C.D.C. has telephonic recordings to prove that inmates, while in state prison, were calling Bunnell at home via collect telephone calls. He was apparently involved with perhaps the Mexican mafia. They fired him. Now comes the powerful California prison guards union, which assisted Bunnell in an appeal of his dismissal. They won!! Bunnell was given his job back and moved up the ladder of promotion.

"It is inexcusable that he's still in C.D.C. This creates the image that peace officers are not bound by the same laws as others. No one is above the law," stated Max Lemon.

Ten years and two promotions later, M. Bunnell is (indeed) the Chief Deputy Warden at Folsom and apparently as corrupted as ever. On January 14, 2004 Max Lemon and several other Folsom employees asked the governor and Rod Hickman for protection for their *families*. Max fears that Bunnell may order an attack on his family or himself. One would think that perhaps I'm writing about the mob instead of C.D.C. Yet, this is the California Department of Corrections.

"Lemon will be viewed as some type of plague. Nobody will talk to him anymore. He broke the code. There is nowhere for him (now) in C.D.C.," stated a veteran C.D.C. officer. How strange and unique that a person sworn to "protect and to serve" would feel that Lemon screwed up by blowing the whistle and have no concern about the viciousness, corruption and immorality of the actions of Bunnell.

Captain Pieper was "a punk and went out like a sucker" for killing himself. This statement was made by an inmate? Wrong! An ex-con? Wrong! This foul, vicious statement was made by a C.D.C. staff member. I will repeat (at the risk of tautology) that Associate Warden Max Lemon is presently seeking armed guards to protect him from fellow correctional officers who are also sworn peace officers.

Is it still so difficult to believe tales of abuse, violence, killings, etc., by inmates? If a top administrator at Folsom State Prison is in fear for his life even though he is free, how must an inmate trapped in prison feel? Please understand that officers control every (Remember: The Guards Own the Gates!) moment, action and activity of an inmate. The officers can place an inmate into the hole on a whim and read, withhold, destroy and/or delay his/her mail, etc., deny telephone calls and even lie to lawyers. If they will threaten to kill the family of an associate warden, what will they do to me? I am well cognizant of the fact that Pelican Bay is a place I may visit soon. I've always known there are some who would love to see me in a Shu or full lockdown situation. A counselor recently authorized a chrono (memorandum) stating that I may need to be transferred to a Shu or lockdown program because I filed a grievance!!!

They specialize in doctoring paperwork and utilizing write-ups - C-file data, etc. to portray certain inmates in certain lights. The C-file of President Nelson Mandela, while he was in prison states that

Mr. Mandela was highly manipulative! Ipso facto, when I read in my C-file that I am "highly manipulative" I feel I am in good company. Yet, there are also some statements, writings and claims in my C-file, which are alarming, cruel, spurious and preposterous. However, on any given day, any staff member can document any chrono, which they want to document and place it into the prisoner's file. This data will be utilized at a future time to justify transfers, ad-seg placement, etc., etc.

On any given day, a staff member who is angry with an inmate for filing a grievance or verbally arguing, etc, etc. can pay another inmate to claim "I was raped by inmate so and so" or "I was threatened by inmate so and so". That inmate, so and so, will be placed in the hole. Officer Mansky, C.D.W. Stratton and Captain Martel did it to me.

I'm just thankful that the inmate did not claim I raped him. I thank God that he didn't stoop low enough to make any sexual allegations. My experiences in dealing with C.O. Ferris, (New Folsom R & R) C.O. Zamudio, Macias, Ed Brody and Mansky have taught me to never underestimate their wrath, vindictiveness or ability to retaliate. C.O. Mansky (for example) is a consummate control freak. He attempts to intimidate inmates by his build, size and gesticulations. Mansky is hated by most of his own co-workers. He is racist, vindictive and anti-inmate.

Officer Love is the only co-worker who likes Mansky. Mrs. Love is African American. She is a likable woman who attends church every Sunday. She is Vice Chairman of her usher board and devout in her own mind. Yet, she is a C.D.C. fanatic! In her mind, C.D.C. can do no wrong. Candidly, Mrs. Love is more dangerous than Mansky. The reason? She is the control officer and she has the guns. She is so convinced that backing her co-workers is right (even if her co-workers are committing crimes) that if she saw Mansky walk up to an inmate and take his head off, if she saw Mansky spit on an inmate or slap him, she would claim, "I didn't see anything." It takes a special kind of courage to break the "code of silence".

Sgt. Elsberry did so. She saw Sgt. R. N. Saunders and Sgt. Scarcella beating an inmate viciously and she reported it. Sgt. Scarcella was fired (but knowing C.D.C. Scarcella will probably be back and promoted to Lieutenant) and Sgt. Saunders is on administrative leave. Scarcella and Saunders both threatened and lied on me back in 1998. When I grieved and appealed, they were both cleared. "Mr. Manning's allegations are unfounded and unsubstantiated," stated the reply. Having read this data and being cognizant of the fact that taxpayers are paying Bunnell (a known crook), paying Max Lemon's (a whistleblower) salary and paying to protect Max and his family from Bunnell, Stratton, Martel, Mansky, Steve Vance, G. Wolfe, etc., etc., it becomes crystal clear that "governator/terminator" has his work cut out for him.

I like Arnold and I respect him. He's not a Gray Davis but I pray to God that Arnold will clean up this mess. C.D.C. needs a catharsis. It needs to be cleansed from the director's office all the way down to the ground. Arnold must be firm, he must be fair, pragmatic and he must be courageous. (As an aside, I suggest Arnold get extra security around Maria and his children. And *if* Rod Hickman is really going to clean up C.D.C., he too would be wise to get armed guards for himself and his family). Cleaning up C.D.C. is a job for a tough guy.

I shall remind you that if you have convinced yourself that prisons and prisoners don't affect you, think again. California alone releases one hundred and twenty-five thousand inmates per year. The State's prison and parole cost - $409 million in 1980, bloated to $5.2 billion this year. California's miserable failure is rooted in its erroneous decision, decades ago, to pour money into bricks and mortar and not into the community, prison-based jobs and educational and treatment programs which (in other states) kept inmates from returning to jails and prisons.

A few courageous jail/prison leaders are fighting amidst a culture, which resists inmate rehabilitation. One such leader is Jeannie Woodford, warden of California's oldest penitentiary, San Quentin. Warden Woodford is intent on correcting, not coddling, abusing, pampering or warehousing convicts. She has persuaded volunteers from the community, business groups, motivators, church leaders, etc. to come and tutor her prisoners. She has more volunteers than any prison in California.

Woodford says her goal is to "help inmates change their lives so that we don't create more victims out there. When you ask people whether prisons should have more programs, the knee-jerk reaction is no. But when you explain that the purpose is to hold inmates accountable for their behavior, there's a great deal of support".

This warden should be applauded and emulated. Instead, her efforts are threatened by the prison guards' union.

California has abandoned basic literacy and vocational training as I've pointed out. Even though the Bureau of Prisons reports that inmates who attend school are substantially less likely to re-offend after released. State law requires prisons to provide literacy programs to anyone reading below the ninth grade level. There is widespread condoning of drug sales and abuse in prisons in Texas, California, New

York, Florida and many other states. Almost ninety percent of California inmates are incarcerated for substance abuse connected crimes. Yet, less than six percent of inmates in California are in drug treatment programs. Drugs are smuggled in by prison guards and by visitors.

Recently the State Assembly in California began contemplating taking tobacco out of all California prisons. The reasons are supposedly to save taxpayers money on smoking related illnesses.

On the surface, it seems sensible. Pragmatically it is ludicrous. Drugs are illegal on the streets and in prison! Yet, C.D.C. is full of drugs and thousands of inmates have contracted (i.e. The California inmate hepatitis epidemic) diseases from illegal prison drug use. Tattooing is illegal in prison yet cells are full of tattoo guns and inmates get new tattoos every single day of the week. They catch diseases from this illegal tattooing. Taxpayers pay for the treatment of these diseases. How difficult could it be to stop tattooing in prisons? They strip inmates down to the nude on a regular basis. "Inmate Sanchez has no tattoos", an officer could document on December 1, 2003. Well if Sanchez goes to a visit on February 1, 2004 and (all inmates are strip searched before and after visits) he now has a tiger tattooed on his arm, is it safe to assume somebody tattooed him in prison?

But inmates actually share their newly obtained tattoos with staff. Point being? If it's about saving money for taxpayers, we could save hundreds of millions by merely enforcing the rules already in place. Stop the tattooing, alcohol and drugs in prisons and we'd save (arguably) a half billion dollars.

Three California prisons have already eliminated cigarette smoking for inmates. One such prison is the New Folsom State Prison. I just left (as you well know) New Folsom one month ago. Tobacco was outlawed in New Folsom two years ago and I can report to you with integrity and probity that cigarette smoking is still taking place by inmates in New Folsom right now. New Folsom is filled with tobacco! Prison guards smuggle tobacco in to inmates daily and one can of Bugler ($11.40 at Wal-mart) now costs up to two hundred dollars at New Folsom. I have direct, detailed and specific knowledge of numerous tobacco salesmen (inmate salesmen) at New Folsom. I know numerous New Folsom staff members who bring it in to inmates.

I've also watched inmates become assaultive, combative and suicidal when they didn't have the money to buy tobacco.

So the bottom line is that removing the tobacco from New Folsom was a complete failure and created a new avenue for extortion, assaults and violence. Perhaps the CCPOA should fight against the ban because officers are being tempted into committing more crimes by smuggling in tobacco.

Scientific studies have shown nicotine addiction is more powerful than heroin addiction. New Folsom offered *no* assistance to inmates desiring to stop smoking. Not even nicotine patches or gum. So a man who has been smoking twenty years is all of a sudden (supposedly) told, "You can't smoke anymore. No more tobacco!" Yet, he watches an officer walk right up to him blowing cigarette smoke in his face. It is my opinion that this creates a potential threat to staff's safety and security. It's like telling a crack addict, "No more crack for you beginning at 9:00 a.m. tomorrow." Yet at 9:15 a.m., you walk up to the crack addict and wave crack in his face. The guards at New Folsom absolutely refuse to stop smoking. They also refuse to stop smoking in the presence of inmates. Am I crazy or is there something wrong with this strategy? This is a recipe for extortion, violence and rage. It is clear John Burton and Gloria Romero don't know the specifics of the so-called no smoking for prisoners plan. It is obvious that assembly members have been hoodwinked and shammed. Something is wrong! Something is really wrong!

If Mr. Schwarzenegger or Mr. Hickman would like the names of officers bringing in tobacco at New Folsom State Prison, now they can feel free to contact me. However, since experience has taught me that if a captain such as Martel, does not like what I write in a tome, he will transfer me capriciously, etc. Perhaps they'll need to transfer me to another state. I have no objection to going home to Georgia to serve out my illegal and wrongful conviction.

In January of 2004, C.D.C. ordered its agents who investigate wrongdoing in state prisons *not* to disclose information to legislators, the media or the governor's office. They were told to sign a pledge committing to follow the confidentiality rules or face punishment.

This strange directive was issued as Senators Gloria Romero and Jackie Speier were preparing to hold hearings on cover-ups and misconduct within the corrections department. Senators are also investigating a "code of silence" that often protects rogue guards. "I am deeply concerned that the wording . . .could create a chilling affect on employees who seek to report wrongdoing, waste, corruption or illegal activities," stated Mrs. Romero.

It was "in-artfully written and, from my read, violated individuals' civil rights and the whistleblower statute in this state," said Mrs. Speier.

The memorandum was written by Martin Hoshino, Chief of the department's Office of Investigative Services. At least two agents - both of whom spoke on the condition of anonymity for fear of reprisals - said they viewed the policy as an attempt to silence them at a time of intense scrutiny of the department.

"This obviously is an effort to quiet us down and keep us from coming forward. The hearings are coming up and they want to muzzle us," stated an agent. The hearings were prompted by agents who divulged stories about the code of silence among prison guards and pressure by the guards union to stymie investigations of brutality in California prisons and jails.

"The timing suggests that the department is interested in managing information by suppressing it," stated Attorney Steve Fama of the prison law office.

Former New Folsom Prison Guard Robert Flores stated he was fired for refusing to cooperate with a cover-up and the code of silence. "Keys were smuggled into an inmate and I had to do a report on it. Zamudio, Rosario and Martel changed my reports and when I demanded they be corrected, I was fired," he said.

Former prison guard Sallie Brooks (ex-New Folsom office) states, "I've seen staff commit sexual assault on inmates and fellow staff right on the prison grounds. Staff (to me) is more dangerous than the convicts we were guarding."

One can imagine what would happen to Michael Jackson if he is convicted and sent to the California prison system. Even though my wrongful conviction is bad, I thank God that my conviction does not involve a child. Child molesters are treated as scum of the earth in prison. Staff refuses to believe an inmate can be wrongfully convicted. Michael did well by hiring Carl Douglas and Ben Brafman (two excellent trial lawyers) to join his dream team. I would hope (if he's innocent and the evidence is beginning to look like Michael may indeed be innocent) Carl, Ben and Mark are successful at vindicating his rights. Michael had a *caravan of love* to show up at his arraignment on January 16, 2004 to show support.

As I rode down the highway, exiting the prison at Ione en route to Sacramento, I almost cried. Out of the windows of the sedan, I looked up at the hills. I saw horses and cows. I saw lots of open land. Ione is like the country. My mind went back to those dusty and country roads that I traveled (with my loving grandmother, Dollie Manning, her sister Annette, Lorrie, Terry and Chico) down in the country as a boy preacher. We were going to churches in McDonough, Georgia, Monroe, Winder, Macon and Griffin. I wondered (to myself) what would have happened if I had Ben Brafman, Johnnie Cochran, Carl Douglas or Donald Marks defending me at trial time. "I would not be here." I mumbled to myself.

I thought, "Here I am going to Sacramento Supreme Court to see a woman (Mary Hanlon Stone) who knows I'm innocent. I'm going to watch her lie, fabricate, exaggerate and embellish to try to see to it that I "never, ever" see my family again. I'm not in Russia. I'm not in South Africa but I'm in America. How can this be?" We arrived at Sacramento Court and Hanlon Stone, Deputy D.A. John Pezone and Jan Scully orchestrated a strategic, passionate and sophisticated plan to try to persuade Judge Jane Ure into abolishing the six-year sentence she had given me for the so-called threatening letter, which was supposedly mailed to Mary Hanlon. Mary, John and the entire D.A.'s office demanded a thirty-five years to life sentence in prison for me. I was horrified. So many times, I've watched judges abuse their power and mete out life sentences as if they were giving out water. The enormous pressure, which was on Jane Ure, is unfathomable. I owe Jane Ure an apology. Yes, I believe she should have dismissed the entire case for several reasons and she could have. Yet, in spite of Mary Hanlon Stone's melodramatics and prosecutorial demands, Judge Ure was fair. All any citizen, who is charged with a crime can ask for is fair. Fairness is justice, which is tempered with mercy.

Attorney Comiskey is not an eloquent man but he did his job - finally. "This alleged threatening letter was written after Mr. Manning had been in solitary confinement for more than ten months, Your Honor. Prison authorities had thrown Mr. Manning into ad-seg because they were retaliating against him for writing a book, which named some of them. It was an angry letter by an angry, despondent, wrongly convicted Black man in prison. I urge the court to reinstate the six-year sentence imposed which is more than enough punishment for an idle threat," stated Paul Comiskey.

I cannot repeat all of the vicious statements made by Prosecutor Hanlon Stone and John Pezone demanding a twenty-five or thirty-five year to life sentence. It was horrible.

"I cannot in good conscience send Mr. Manning to prison for twenty-five years to life for a piece of paper," stated Judge Ure. "If a higher court thinks I'm incorrect, they'll have to overturn my sentence. But I think I'm right. Twenty-five years to life would be cruel and unusual under these circumstances. I have the power by law to strike a strike and I am exercising that power within the law and by the law. Mrs. Stone stated in the newspaper today that if I gave Manning six years, he would be getting away with it. I disagree. I must mete out justice. I must follow the law. I've done that to the best of my ability as an officer of the court. I'll sleep well tonight. This court is adjourned," so stated the Honorable Judge Jane Ure.

I unsuccessfully fought my tears. Fortunately, Mr. Comiskey, Pezone and Judge Jane Ure did not notice the tears trickling down my cheeks. Judge Jane Ure is fair, honest, just and the universe will be kind to this woman. I was humbled. All along, I thought she was going to cave in and just go through the motions like many other judges do. "This is a great woman," I thought.

"You should get down on your knees, thank your lucky stars and thank the man upstairs (God)," stated Officer Coleman aka "Juice".

I whispered to Comiskey and inquired, "What newspaper is Mrs. Ure speaking of? Am I in the paper today?"

"Mary Stone planted a vicious article in the Sacramento Bee today to try to sway Judge Ure. It is biased, embellished and one-sided. We should sue reporter Laura MeCoy. MeCoy did not have the decency and ethics to even contact me for comment," he told me.

I shook Paul's hand. "Thank you for a tremendous job. God bless you," was all I could say. "Thank you, Your Honor," I stated as I shuffled out of the courtroom.

Downstairs, I persuaded C.O. Coleman to let me read his newspaper. I read Laura McCoy's story and was amazed and mesmerized. Not one word from our side. Everything written here came from Prosecutor Hanlon Stone. Is this what reporting has come to? Ken Auletta, Helen Thomas and Ed Bradley would call this "biased, one-sided and inadequate" reporting. I decided to send Laura "back story" a book by Mr. Auletta. Mary Hanlon Stone is a *wicked* woman. I am afraid of people like her. If the D.A., who is prosecuting Michael Jackson, is half as vindictive, evil, dishonest and corrupted as Mary Hanlon Stone (as I've heard is true), I fear for Mr. Jackson.

Prior to my contact with Mary, I basically believed that most prosecutors were by the book, honest and fair. But Mary Hanlon Stone proved (to me) conclusively that neither F. Lee Bailey, Johnnie Cochran nor Gerry Spence is lying about the so-called myriad of corrupted prosecutors. Judge Robert Altman proved that judges often lie, cheat and coerce even witnesses into lying or not testifying at all. (Refer to my book, "If It Doesn't Fit, You Must Acquit").

If we could get a federal judge, the F.B.I. or a special prosecutor to take a look at Altman's and Hanlon Stone's actions (on and off the record), I believe Arnold would "terminate" my sentence. And send me back home to Georgia.

It turns out that Attorney Robert T. Burns and Private Investigator Curtis Waite were having secret, in chambers, meetings with Judge Altman. There was judicial misconduct, witness tampering and evidence planting during my trial and it was all done in the name of justice. Believe me, I needed that blessed experience from Judge Jane Ure. It has reminded me that God can still say yes. God can still inspire a Johnnie Cochran, Anthony Brooklier, Barry Scheck, Jimmy Mattocks or even Schwarzenegger to set me free from prison. I don't belong here. I did not commit this crime.

So Jayson Williams' words resonated with this author (me) when he stated, "I'm terrified, horrified and I want to be here with my family," he said this on the possibility of going to prison for a death (of his limousine driver) which Jayson says was "an accident". By the time you're holding this tome in your hands, Jayson's trial will be over. Some would assume that I hope he gets off! Absolutely incorrect. I hope Jayson gets justice! Justice is "innocent" until proven guilty beyond a reasonable doubt to a moral certainty. If this intelligent young man didn't do the crime, he shouldn't do any time and his wish to "come home and hug his wife and children and thank God for everyday with his family", should be granted.

Jayson's wife said, "I have tremendous faith in the will of God." She believes he'll be exonerated. His wife reminds me of Cookie Johnson (Magic Johnson's wife) with her outstanding, unshakeable faith in the divine "creator" of the universe.

I want to tell (write) you as you sit on the airplane, in the car, on the bus, train, on your yacht, boat, in your office or living room reading my words that it is absolutely unconscionable and tremendously painful to live in prison knowing you didn't do the crime. I would not wish a wrongful conviction on even my worst enemy. This prison life can break your spirit, bust your dreams and it has the potential to ruin your entire life.

Quite candidly, I don't think the public has any perception about the mentality (much less the brutality) of the prison subculture. There is an odd, unique and unnatural group mentality which runs rampart in prisons that destroys almost anybody who comes here.

Sigmund Freud explained an aspect of the collective (foolish) mentality of which I'm speaking by stating: "The prison mentality goes directly to extremes; if a suspicion is expressed, it is instantly changed into an incontrovertible certainty. A trace of antipathy is turned into furious hatred".

In prison there are what is called "cars". A car means a clique or group you associate closely with. "I'm in the Bronx car" or "I'm in the San Jose car", etc. One does well to find himself a car to get in so that when one has a problem one can call on the members of one's car to bail one out.

The leaders of these cars often specialize in an elementary (keep in mind that many prisoners are not well-educated) form of psychological warfare or prison "Hitlerism." The big lie. Time after time, I've watched guys who were a bit eccentric or odd and who didn't fit in so the group leaders would invent a "jacket" for him. A "jacket" is a representation or an allegation. An "R" in his "jacket" means he has a rape conviction in his file. Fool is a "Chester" means he has a child molestation charge in his "jacket". So if he's disliked, one can simply claim, Dude is a "Chester" and within hours this unsubstantiated, uncorroborated rumor will be all over the prison. Officers will reply by stating, "I heard that too but don't quote me on it." So the rumormonger has now manipulated the entire mindset of hundreds or even thousands of so-called grown men. We are now isolating ourselves and alienating ourselves from this person because we "heard" he was a child molester. But we can know (for a fact) that he's a fratricidal murderer. We can know he/she emptied a shotgun into the heads of his mother and father. We can know that he laughed as he stood over the bullet-riddled bodies of his own kith and kin. Instead of *isolating* him we end up *celebrating* him.

Dr. Freud went on to state that since a group is in no doubt as to what constitutes truth or error, and it's conscious, moreover, of it's own great power, it's as intolerant as it is obedient to authority. It respects force and can only be slightly influenced by kindness, which it regards merely as a form of weakness. It wants to be ruled and oppressed and to fear its masters.

My inside experience with prison has taught me to treat prison as a snake, a dragon and a monster factory - to never get too comfortable because I'm misplaced, wrongly convicted and this is not my home. I've had to psychoanalyze myself over and over and remain free from the group(s). In prison, the mere fact that a man becomes a part of an organized group or gang, he descends several levels down the ladder of civilization. Isolated, he could/can be a polished, cultivated human being; in a prison crowd/group, he is barbaric, brutal, unthinking - that is, a creature acting by instinct. Neither his left/right brain hemisphere, nor his frontal lobe is of any use to him. He is a raging idiot. A damn fool. He utilizes the spontaneity, the violence, viciousness, the ferocity and also the enthusiasm and heroin of primitive beings. He dwells, lives and operates within the lowered intellectual disability, which individuals experience when their mentality is merged into a group. Most prisoners who are in these cars, cliques or groups are impulsive, changeable and irritable. The impulses that these groups obey may (according to the circumstances) be generous or cruel, courageous or cowardly, yet they are always too imperious that one personal ambition, not even self-preservation, can make itself felt. The masters, the guards, the keepers of the prisoners are like convicts in uniform or prisoners with badges. Most of them (too) are in cars. They promote and demote according to the dictates of the driver or leader of those cars. Ipso facto (i.e.) Lieutenant Jimmy Gaton, Lt. Percy Massey would or could never promote to Captain at New Folsom State Prison because of the bias and perhaps racism of group leader Terry L. Rosario.

Revisiting the subject of Folsom State Prison: Last evening - January 17, 2004 - there was a prayer vigil held at Folsom State Prison for the late Captain Doug Pieper. My level of respect for Associate Warden Max Lemon increased twofold as I watched him speak with power, conviction, emotion and with tears rolling down his cheeks. For a time, I had suspected that perhaps some of Max's anger with C.D.C. was suspect. "I know he's not lying about the corruption and cover-ups but still he may be trying to get a promotion or something. Why speak out now?" I had thought. Not anymore. I am fully persuaded and totally convinced that Max Lemon is absolutely authentic, selfless and true to his convictions. He stood there at the podium, braving the cold winds and said, "On January 15, 2002 Doug Pieper called me and said Max, I've been called by the Investigative Services Unit and they want to talk to me about the Folsom riots. Later that day, I got a call from David Tristan telling me Douglas had taken his life. It's deeper than we know and it is a shame that not *one* uniformed officer is here at this vigil. Their absence speaks volumes about how afraid they are to get involved."

They're afraid for their lives and livelihoods. At this vigil: George Stratton? - Absent! Steve Vance? - Absent! Terry L. Rosario? - Absent! Captain Martel, Lt. Baughman, Kimbrell, Lance Corcoran and David Tristan? - All Absent! How could they not show up?

Doug Pieper's son said, "It was not in my Dad's character to commit suicide." Doug's widow, Evette Pieper said, "Everything has not come out yet. It's deeper than we know."

A prison officer (on the condition of anonymity) alleges that maybe Doug was murdered by an angry officer.

It's chilling to think that these guys are responsible for protecting public safety, charged to serve and to protect the public but their co-workers are so afraid of them that they need armed federal agents to guard their families from fellow officers. I say to Arnold Schwarzenegger, Gloria Romero, Jackie Speier, John Burton, etc., etc., it is time! From C.D.C.'s headquarters downtown all the way to Calapatria, we must clean up the department. Starting at the top we must rid C.D.C. of these vindictive, angry, uneducated supervisors such as Mr. Schievelbein, Stratton, Duane Fidel, M. Todd, Martel, Vance, Bunnell, Janice and Billy Mayfield. They must be fired! If we are to clean up C.D.C., we must bring in new blood.

We need a brand new start. Let's start grading wardens on lessening recidivism. Grade them! "How many inmates got out of Chino or Folsom last year and stayed out?" - is the question. If we adjust warden's paychecks by the success or failure of their inmates, they'd have an incentive to *correct*.

The senate hearings on the corrections cover-up begin this week. I am tempted to delay finishing this update and "Rush to Judgment" Chapter until the hearings are over but my best friend, Peter and numerous others in the publishing field are absolutely insisting that I finish and finish today. Rest assured that I shall begin another book this month and if all goes well, we can have it in your hands by June of this year. I suggest readers begin to e-mail Amazon.com, Barnes & Nobel, B. Dalton Books and CafePress in May of this year to reserve your copies of the upcoming book.

I must reiterate the fact that *you the people* must insist on the governors of these states and our senators clean up these prisons. Almost a million prisoners will get out this year. They will be living in your neighborhoods, shopping in your stores and working (if they're lucky) at your places of employment. The more humane, corrective, sane and rehabilitative their places of incarceration are, the less likely they are to kill, steal, rob, rape and maim when they re-join you in society. Groups such as Critical Resistance in California, CA Prison Focus, FAMM and I-May are making a difference and you should support them. I would hope that Frank Dileo, Donald Trump, Michael Jackson, Rush, Jayson Williams, R. Kelly, P. Diddy and others who have felt the sting and imagined the horrors of an unfair judicial system will join us in the struggle. We all need to pool our resources, give of our money, time and talents to get innocent men out of prison and clean up the corruption in these prisons. I continue to salute, applaud and recognize the tenacious efforts of Barry Scheck, Peter Neufeld and other lawyers who work pro bono on behalf of innocents in prison.

I would hope that sooner rather than later; Ben Brafman, Johnnie, Roy Black, Gerry Spence, Carl Douglas, Dershowitz, Ephraim Margolin, Dennis Riordin and thousands of wealthy and powerful lawyers will step up and help the innocent, indigent and wrongfully convicted who are trapped in the bowels of evil prisons all over America.

Preachers ought to preach about it, teachers ought to teach about it, singers ought to sing about it and mothers ought to pray about those who are here doing the time but did not commit the crime.

I want to make a special appeal here to the former President of the United States of America, The Honorable Jimmy Carter. If President Carter is reading, I need his (your) help. Mr. Carter is my homeboy (he's from Plaines, GA and I'm from Atlanta) and I have the utmost respect for him. I've often stated that the main problem Mr. Carter had was his honesty. The man embodies the authentic definition of Christianity. Politics today require compromise, dishonesty, saying what people want to hear and having few strong convictions. If President Carter had sold out, he would have been re-elected. My only (if I were a politician, I'd delete this because you're only supposed to say what you think people want to hear) disagreement with Mr. Carter was his asking Uncle Andy (Ambassador Andrew Young) to resign as U.N. Ambassador. I think that was a bad decision!

No former president has worked more vigorously for the poor, homeless and the downtrodden than Mr. Jimmy Carter - i.e. Habitat for Humanity, etc. He's not running for office. He's not trying to lobby on behalf of billion dollar corporations. He's not looking for a photo op. The only explanation for Carter's altruism and struggle for the poor is he "loves those people".

When I think of Harriet Tubman and ask myself why did she continue to risk her life going back and forth to free other slaves? She "loved those people". Honorable Martin Luther King, Jr. sacrificed his life as the Black Moses; he "loved those people". My personal mentor, leader, advisor, hero, the late, great Rev. Dr. Hosea Williams - kept on feeding the hungry, clothing the naked and fighting for justice; Hosea "loved those people". Glory to God.

Jimmy Carter, the man who walked all the way from a peanut factory in a country Georgia town to the White House in D.C. He "loves those people".

I'm asking Mr. Carter for two things:

      A. Pray for me. Pray for my justice!

      B. Come and visit me so I can tell you what happened to me.

I need to see Jimmy Carter. If he looks me in my eyes and I tell him that I'm innocent; that I did **not commit this crime**, he will feel my integrity and he'll help me to get my freedom.

If Aaron Goodwin in Oakland, California, Lt. Colonel Samuel Harris, Chris Gardner, President Mandela, Bruce Cutler and Anthony Brooklier get behind me, I'll win my exoneration, soon . . .

They claim I'm one of the best public speakers since Dr. Martin Luther King, Jr. and I hope they're correct. Ipso facto, I'm afraid every time I write a book. My books are arguments! Arguments for justice and about injustice. I'm concerned that my arguments, which have proven to be successful when presented in person and received by the eyes and ears of the people, will appear inadequate and amateurish on the written page. When I speak, I don't try to speak as if what I say will be literally transcribed. When one thinks the linear thoughts of a written speech, one which proceeds from left to right as it takes place, word by word, on a page, the magic is lost, and the raw power which drags from the pit of the soul all the elixir of the oratory dries up.

Although this book is filled with empirical data, which has been carefully researched about a variety of "searches for justice". I really wish I could converse with you right now. I want to talk to you. I need to talk to Mr. Jimmy Carter, Jesse Jackson, Rod Hickman and Governor Arnold. I need to talk to Gloria Romero and John Ashcroft. Because regardless of how well the written (i.e. this tome) argument is delivered, it shall never move the listener, it can't transform a person's mind, it can't win and succeed like something born spontaneously from the soul. But (at present) the only tool I have (this argument) for its exposition is the black words printed linearly by machinery on empty white paper. It isn't easy to explain multi-dimensional magic on mere two-dimensional pages. I would, therefore ask you to (as you read this) imagine Dr. Martin Luther King, Jr. preaching this book to you. Use your imaginative ear and hear Martin saying every word in this book to you.

Hear King telling you that they need to let Marcus Dixon out of prison. Marcus Dixon? He was an "A" student in Rome, Georgia on his way to Vanderbilt University. Marcus is Black and he had consensual sex with a White classmate. When her parents discovered she was messing around with a Black boy, she screamed, "He raped me!" (Kobe Bryant??) But a mostly White jury found Marcus "not guilty" of rape. Jurors believed it was definitely consensual sex. No question. But District Attorney Lee Patterson added a charge of aggravated child molestation and implied to the jury that this was a misdemeanor. Lee persuaded the jury to believe by saying, "If you do believe the evidence proved it was consensual and not rape; well, you ought to send a message about sex between minors so let's slap him on the wrist with this minor charge." He told the jury that even if it was consensual; if a minor receives an injury during consensual sex, then that is aggravated child molestation. The *injury* (he convinced them) was the fact that she lost her virginity!! Gerry Spence would not have lost this trial! Willie Gary, M. Gerald Schwartzbach, Roy Black and Ben Brafman would have won the case out right. But in these little rural towns, quite often juries are hoodwinked and the public defenders are poorly trained and ill prepared. Marcus received a ten-year prison term! Marcus was adopted as a kid by White parents. His adoptive dad (Ken Jones) stated, "When he told me he had sex with a White girl - I just sat down and cried like a baby. Cause (sic) I know what they was going to do to him."

Juror K. Tippet told Dan Rather, "We were sure he was going to go home that day. We were deceived by the prosecutor. Marcus needs to come home."

Think of it, en route to Vanderbilt University an "A" student. Has consensual sex and now he sits in prison serving ten years. Prosecutors deceive jurors everyday of the week. "Prosecutors are not concerned about *justice*. They are concerned about *winning*," said Gerry Spence. Remember, Mr. Spence himself was once a prosecutor.

"Their need for a conviction helps them to look innocence straight in the face and pretend not to see it," stated F. Lee Bailey.

Peter lost the argument! I'm still writing. Still trying to transform my verbal argument into a written argument. Max Lemon testified yesterday before Gloria Romero. Max had tears in his eyes.

"There is corruption and cover-ups at the highest levels of C.D.C.," Associate Warden Lemon testified. "There is a 'code of silence' among C.D.C. employees. I've had to have twenty-four hour protection from the state police since I began speaking out." This testimony was powerful and gut wrenching.

Sgt. Sam Cox testified that he had been ordered to go into the media room and dub out all the audio from the videotape of the Folsom riot so Bunnell couldn't be heard giving orders to let the riot proceed. Mr. Cox refused and has been demoted twice. Bunnell was scheduled to testify but refused to show up.

An audit has shown that C.D.C. overspent its budget by $1.4 billion in the last three years. Much of the money is unaccounted for. Rod Hickman testified and to his credit he admitted that there are problems in C.D.C. - "I'm working aggressively to rectify those problems," he said. I don't envy him and if Rod is really, really going to clean up C.D.C., I encourage (and I'm not being melodramatic) him to get twenty-four hour personal protection. If the CCPOA can run

Senator Richard Polanco out of town, if they can threaten the higher ups to keep Associate Warden Chastain on the job (without a demotion) after he was accused of sexual misconduct, if they got Bunnell's job back . . . what can they do to the first Black corrections chief if he does not tap dance? Rod, if you're reading - get protection.

I don't understand the lack of public outcry and outrage. California is flat broke! When it is proven that C.D.C. has squandered a billion and a half dollars yet they want to cut cigarette smoking in the prisons to save taxpayers a few million dollars, the public should rise up.

I demand that preachers get the heck out of the pulpit and get involved. We all sing the praises of Martin Luther King, Jr. but we don't want to work as he worked.

One (I'm digressing but it's the preacher in me so y'all stay with me) Easter Sunday, Dr. King's dad (Daddy King) was calling Birmingham and urging King, Jr. to come back to Atlanta. He needed to be at Ebenezer for the most important Sunday service (Easter Sunday) of the year. King told his staff, "I've got to go and pray about it." He returned to the room in blue jeans instead of a suit. It was obvious King was bypassing anthems, flowers and ceremonies and would not be in church that Easter Sunday. "I'm going to jail," he told his staff. King continued, "Unmerited suffering is always redemptive." He chose to walk right into the teeth of suffering. The media eviscerates Dr. King's platform. Joe Lowery tells us how . . . "Now that he's safely dead, let us praise him. Because dead men cannot rise up and challenge the images we fashion of them, let us make a monument. It is easier to build a monument than it is to build a movement."

The media's favorite line is "I have a dream". But what of the other parts of that speech? America has written poor people a check or promissory note and the check has come back stamped insufficient funds. But I refuse to believe that the bank of justice is bankrupt. Let us hear that part of the "I have a dream" speech. God has not chosen America to be a messianic messenger or a world police. God has a way of rising up and saying, don't play with me; America you're too arrogant. But I will rise up and break the very backbone of your power and nation. I will put a nation in charge that doesn't even know my name. God will tell America to be still and know I'm God."

John Ashcroft and Mr. Rumsfeld ought to listen to that entire speech. Shortly before King was cut down, he said, "Let me be clear. Integrating lunch counters did not cost America one penny. Giving Black people the right to vote did not cost America one penny. But now America needs to spend billions of dollars and undergo a radical redistribution of wealth and power." I've never seen that speech on ABC, CBS or NBC. Contractor Peter Gaeth, mailroom clerk David Dasky and J. Ashcroft probably never heard it either.

In lieu of all of these wrongful convictions, prison brutality and corruption within the judiciary *somebody* (Eddie Long, Jesse Jackson, T. D. Jakes, Billy Graham?) must rise up and take a stand even if it is an unpopular stand. When Martin spoke out and fought against the war in Vietnam, he was criticized by even his own supporters. "Other preachers, leaders and politicians can choose not to speak out. They may feel, for various reasons that they can't speak out. That's their business! But I must say today that justice is indivisible. Injustice anywhere is a threat to justice everywhere," King said.

Yes, they fought him. During some of his marches, the police and politicians orchestrated planned disruptions. They paid youngsters to disrupt the march to try to make it appear that King's nonviolent methods was not working. Then that good ole boy Senator Robert Byrd asked the public to look at Dr. King in a different light and to not follow him. Police officer cover-ups, corruption and the orchestration of trumped up charges, etc. has been going on forever.

The only time and the only way it can change is when we rise up and fight corruption. The senate hearings on C.D.C. corruption are still going on but what will happen when they end? This is not the first time C.D.C. has been in the media for their corruption, setups and brutality. But what happened the last time? There was great focus for a few weeks, heads rolled, butt was kicked but as Judge Steve White testified before the senate, "In ninety days C.D.C. will be back to normal. The higher ups will continue to obstruct justice and prison guard brutality will march on." Judge White was the inspector general of C.D.C. so he ought to know. He just became a judge (Superior Court) recently. I'm trying (desperately not to be redundant but I've got to repeat (re-write?) that Max Lemon - an associate warden in command at Folsom State Prison, has had to obtain twenty-four hour protection for his family. He's being guarded by the state police at home! He walks amongst convicted murderers and rapists all day long in prison. But he's unsafe (he feels) in the quiet comforts of his own home. When we come to a place where a warden is more afraid of sworn peace officers than he is of convicted killers, the prisons are out of control. This tome is not all about *me*, but I'm gonna reiterate to Jimmy Carter, Chris Gardner, M. L. King, III, Jesse, Sharpton, Dershowitz and Cochran: I need y'all to come get me out of here.

I am misplaced! I don't belong in prison. If you can't exonerate me rapidly, at least (Mr. Carter) call Rod Q. Hickman and Mr. Schwarzenegger and ask them to send me to Georgia's prison system, while we fight this wrongful conviction. It is inhumane, cruel and unusual to keep my mother, grandmother and entire family from seeing me. I have nobody in California - no family and no friends in California at all. Get me out! Please get me home! There are many Rolando Cruzes, Hurricane Carters and Anthony Porters trapped right here.

If Dr. Goudeaux, Charles Blake, Eddie Long and T. D. Jakes were to organize, galvanize and mobilize their congregations, if they committed money toward cleaning up corruption (corrections?) and weeding/seeding the wrongly convicted in prisons, what would happen?

What would happen if they engaged in sustained, organized and publicized efforts on behalf of the least of these? Need I remind you that it's awfully dark and lonely in these prisons? It is a horrible and awful place to be. Especially if you're innocent. We need help. We need to transform these dungeons of despair into havens of hope. We must immediately begin to restore rehabilitations into these prisons. Otherwise, we can't complain about the *monsters* we keep creating. We will either clean up the prisons, save the people together or we will continue to witness the destruction and annihilation of the community at large! Those one hundred and twenty-five thousand California inmates who will get out of prison in California *are coming to get you*! Those seven hundred thousand prisoners leaving prisons (in Georgia, Alabama, Mississippi, New York, Illinois, etc.) this year are coming to your neighborhood!

They will work, reside, deal (drugs), kill, stab, rape and molest right where you are. You cannot keep them in prison forever. With George Bush, John Ashcroft and Rumsfeld in office, we are locking up more and more crack addicts and dope dealers than ever before. Where will we house them? What will we do with them when their time is served?

I hope governors, senators and our congress will overhaul the system at once. We cannot incarcerate ourselves out of poverty! We cannot arrest our way out of crime. Now is the time for pragmatic action. We must fight for real change. We need to fight poverty just as we fight crime. We must fight hunger, homelessness and illiteracy in North America. If we put in one-tenth of the money we put into ousting Saddam Hussein, we will win. Money is power. "The only thing the power structure understands and responds to is money!

White folks will listen to you if you bring them some money!" Rev. Hosea Williams stated to me in late 1994.

Money is power! There are many inequities, etc. There is tremendous poverty in the urban cities but there is also wealth. If ten churches combined their wealth, we're talking hundreds of millions of dollars. Everybody wants to call Oprah. Hell, Oprah can't save the world. She is one person (only) and she can't support everybody. Often times, we just want a "hand-out" not a "hand-up". But if we would take the time to come up with real pragmatic plans that we can show Oprah, Donald Trump, Don King, Bill Gates, Warren Buffett or Chris Gardner, then they would help us.

We can't go begging, "Give us some money, so we can fight poverty." Fight poverty how? Fight poverty with what?

We must have strategic plans, which we can implement at once. To be sure, (on the prisons issue) the more volunteers from the civil community, pastors and church workers, etc. we have working in the prisons, the less likely officers are to abuse and brutalize prisoners.

Presidential candidate Dennis Kucinich (D-Ohio) told me, "We must look at the broader context of the criminal justice in America and the journey that takes people into repeated offense. We need to understand there is a direct link between the hopelessness and despair that causes people to repeatedly break the law and the fact that people don't have jobs, people don't have housing, there is not adequate education - the society fails. Forty-three hundred individuals (in California) mostly people of color are serving this 'three strikes' and you're out law and basically their whole lives have been sacrificed to it. Three strikes and you're out has been a form of capital punishment." Presidential candidate Kucinich went on to explain, "Incarceration can go as high as fifty thousand dollars a year. There are many other charges, depending on where you're housed and at what level, and then the Shu . . . we must let the taxpayers know what's going on. As people become aware that the transfer of wealth also includes the building of new prisons, the building of the criminal justice system that locks people up without any hope of recovery. I think people can understand that they can't separate themselves from what's happening in the criminal justice system."

I concur with those assessments. One way to inform the nation about what's going on is to get them this book. Y'all need to e-mail every congress member, every senator, every governor, mayor, etc. and tell them to log on to the Internet (CafePress.com/Sherman Manning or Amazon.com or HalloPeter@freesurf.ch) and order this book!

Since we know our system is not working and we know politicians (with the exception of a few, i.e. Romero, Speier, Hickman and perhaps the "terminator") are not trying to fix it, we must begin to organize in the communities.

A. Lets do all we can to stop people from ever going to prison. (I shall discuss solutions in the next tome but for now - you develop programs).

B. We must shake up and clean up the prisons. We can't allow officers and wardens to set up fights, riots and killings. When guys come to prison nowadays its like entering into a war zone (literally)! Hell, when they get out on parole we ought to tie a yellow ribbon around them and help them get jobs and to stay out of prison.

C. We have got to convince Rod Hickman and prison directors across the nation to bring rehabilitation back into the penal system. Let's have self-help, motivational seminars and programs to develop the inner man inside out. Let's start "turn around" programs and stop warehousing and creating "monsters" in prison.

I had gotten the famed motivator, Zig Zigler, to agree to provide the prison *free* materials and to collaborate with me on teaching his "I can" course in prison. Director Alameda said, "Hell no." We're talking about a free program! No cost to C.D.C. and they disallowed it. I had convinced famed author Stephen Covey to work with me and develop the "Seven Habits of Highly Effective People/Prisoners". Again free - Alameida? No way! Gloria Romero ought to call Mr. Covey and Zigler and arrange to allow the materials in the prison!

On January 23rd, I spoke with Peter Andrist: "Marc (Peter calls me Marc) I had a dream the other night that you were out preaching and speaking. I believe God was telling me we are on the brink of your miracle." It was an exciting and inspiring conversation. Peter is without a doubt the best friend that I have in this country. He's getting married in September of this year and you all can e-mail wedding congratulations to him at hallopeter@freesurf.ch. Peter went on to state, "What is wrong with the judicial system in America? One thing I know is you do not belong in prison. Should we send Mr. Coronado, (reporter at Sacramento Bee) Dan Rather, Jesse Jackson and Arianna Huffington your book? Do you think we can persuade Michael Jackson to buy twenty thousand copies of this book and donate them to prisons and juveniles across the country? We must get this book to movers and shakers. We need help! We must get you out! And not only that, this book will help many, many people. It will help young men to not go to prison. It will help men in prison to get out."

I concurred with Brother Andrist as he concluded, "Can't Gloria Romero and Jackie Speier get you out? Is there any way possible to get Mrs. Romero or Jackie to merely read your trial transcripts? Because pragmatically, if they would read just Mr. Calvario's testimony they would know that you are innocent all over the world - we in Switzerland, Japan, Spain and France, etc. are usually so impressed with America. Everybody wants to at least visit the land of the free and home of the brave. I'm not criticizing America as a whole; it is a great country but something needs to be done to fix the justice system. It is unthinkable and unimaginable that a country as great as America would allow wrongful convictions to stand up in the face of innocence and keep people incarcerated based upon technicalities, trumped up profiles and propaganda.

Peter went on to state, "Why is it so difficult for many Americans to believe they falsely accuse and wrongly convict men! And that they establish, create and utilize profiles to substantiate their convictions. If the former head of the Federal Bureau of Investigations Chief (F.B.I. Director J. Edgar Hoover) could and would lie on the world famous Martin Luther King, Jr., what won't they do to a normal citizen? Mr. Hoover used propaganda, disinformation and misinformation against Dr. King. He stooped so low as to accuse King of being a homosexual! So prosecutors stand up in court and declare eloquently to jurors that there is a pattern of crime in this man's life. In 1988 he was arrested for this. In 1992 he went to jail for that. In 1996 a woman accused him of this and in 1999 a man accused him of that. But they never tell the whole story, Marc. They will not explain that in many instances once you have been accused of any type of crime you are marked for life. So innocent or guilty, the police will now focus on you for any similar type case. They will tell that woman who is a victim of an assault or rape; that well, you know this guy probably did it because he's done it before and got away with it. Take a hard look at him. Did the assailant look anything like him? There goes his life. He will be arrested and re-arrested. So when he gets in prison and attempts to reach out for help, people look at his criminal record and assume he's guilty or if he didn't commit this crime he still deserves to be in prison for the other crimes. Marc, we must fight! The battle begins with getting you out of there. Should I call Floyd Abrams, Mr. Uelman, Gerry Spence, and Johnnie? Should we ask Mrs. Romero, Speier or Hickman to read your trial transcripts? What must we do?"

I had to calm Peter down. It appears that his dream about me being at home preaching had lit and ignited a fire in his belly. We strategize and I *believe* that we cannot forget the spiritual elements, which are also at work. We won't leave God out of the battle. I am asking every believer who is reading this tome at this juncture, wherever you are today, "pray for me". I'm serious. I want people who know there is a God to pray for my safety and for my freedom. Then, after you pray, get on your telephone and call another believer and tell them to get this book and to also pray! I want you to send e-mails (i.e. to Bishop T. D. Jakes, Eddie Long, Gloria Romero, P. Diddy, Stevie Wonder and Oprah) and announce this book and my need for prayer to them. Do it! Just do it!

If we could get churches to have shut-ins for prisoners and even for prison staff, we'd transform the nation! Many, many guys in prisons need prayer! Guys like Chava, (inmate Ibarra) Johnnie Willie, Mumia Abu Jamal and many others need your prayer and your support.

And let's get the word out to prisoners that true change comes from the inside out. Guys in prisons have a helluva fight if they're going to get out in one piece. It requires discipline, stick-to-it-tiveness and drive to study, plan, dream and visualize while you're incarcerated. But you can't get out until you start seeing out! While you're still in trouble you must have a vision that you're going to get out. You must dream, hope, yearn, visualize and have faith in your God and in yourself. God is not going to do for you what you can do for yourself. Get some nonfiction books and read! Your oppressor can't stop you from reading! Read books by Na'im Akbar, Nathan MeCoy, Malcolm, Dennis Kimbro, Tony Robbins, etc. You ought to turn your prison cell into a classroom! I tell y'all if Mexicans stop fighting these petty butt wars against each other in prisons, if Caucasian brothers turn to each other and not on each other, if the Black on Black prison wars would cease and if we put down our arms and pick up our books, Bibles and Korans . . . if each one would reach and teach one, we could begin to shut down prisons! Let me be clear! There are hundreds of billions of dollars being earned on the backs of prisoners. It's a numbers game as quiet as it's kept; they want you to come to prison. But if prisons became learning centers and universities, etc., they'd start letting folks out of prison. Can you imagine if the guys in jails came out educated, rehabilitated and ready to live, work and succeed? What would happen? We've got to try something different because this prison thing isn't working anymore. Of the one hundred and twenty-five thousand who got out of the California prison system last year; eighty percent of them went in illiterate and came out scholars. They're not committing any more crimes. Let's pump more crack, heroin and acid into their communities. Arrest them and give them fines instead of (prison) time! Do anything except send them to prison, is what they'd say. I'm tired of these cry babies in prison walking around waiting on the man to change a law and let them out of prison. They drink pruno, smoke dope, shoot heroin and gamble (their lives away) while they wait! Think! Plan! Get a strategy! Let's think our way out of this monster factory!

Candidly, if you can't read, write and count and you've got all this time in prison and aren't trying to learn, I don't want to talk to you. You ought to kick your own butt! Let's call a moratorium on violence and stickings. To all prisoners nationwide, I say beginning June 15, 2004, let us stop all prison violence for six months! No stabbings, no assaults, no violence! Let's ask Gloria Romero, Governor Schwarzenegger, Rod Hickman, the Sacramento Bee, New York Times, L.A. Times, Atlanta Constitution, African American Newspapers, Doug Banks, Larry King, Snoop Dogg, Michael Jackson, Kobe, Arianna Huffington, Dennis Kucinich, T. D. Jakes and Eddie Long to put the word out about this moratorium. Are y'all down? Put your money where your mouth is. You claim to be a warrior so out think, out smart, out strategize your opponents and right now your opponents are corrupted government officials who have you oppressed. Fight! Fight the power! Fight physical force with soul force! Fight with the weapons of pen and paper. Call you momma, daddy and your girlfriend. Call your male lover or that woman you're playing out of money and packages and tell them to contact the media, contact their pastor, their fraternity and sorority and tell them to put the word out about this national moratorium. Call, write and e-mail Bishop T. D. Jakes and ask him to send "Bad Boys And The God Who Loves Them" and "A Prince In Egypt". Ask Eddie Long to send "Passion For Life" to your Chaplain. Ask Na'im Akbar to send "Morehouse A Hall Of Transportation" and play these videos on April 15th to prisoners.

We've tried gangs and we're still in prison. We have fought and killed fellow prisoners for years and we're still here! What we have been doing is not working so lets try something new. Call Jesse Jackson, Al Sharpton, Steve Harvey, and Oprah and tell them to put the word out! No violence for six months. Ask Michael Jackson, Magic Johnson, Bill Gates, Donald Trump, Aaron Goodwin, Willie Gary, lawyers, pastors and professors to send this book around the country. We want this announcement, this book, in all thirty-three prisons in California. We want the inmates in Reidsville, Georgia, Alto, Georgia, Valdesta, Georgia, Rikers and every prison in every state in North America to have at least two copies of this book. You all pass it around and you know how to copy it.

It's time for the non-violent revolution to take place. If you e-mail Michael Jackson, he will help! Tell him his dad, Joe Jackson knows me! When I worked with Rev. Hosea Williams, I met Mr. Jackson. Michael has a heart. If you get this book to him (however you need to do it, i.e., via his kid's nanny, his ex-wife, Brian Oxman in L.A., etc.) he will help! We are asking Mr. Jackson to purchase at least twenty thousand copies of this book (or more if possible) and let's arrange to "heal the world" by sending two copies to ten thousand prisons nationwide.

I'm ready to go to war! I am ready to do war! War with our heads and hearts and not our bodies and blood. Write to President Nelson Mandela in South Africa and ask for his support. Ask him to give a press statement to CNN, C-Span, ABC, NBC and CBS supporting our moratorium on prison violence. I know for a fact that President Mandela will do it. He is a compassionate, altruistic, authentic modern day Moses.

You people reading my words who are free must get on your computers, the internet and the telephones to contact Mr. Mandela and ask the Honorable President Mandela to announce our moratorium and pledge his support. If you reach him, he will support it!

I believe Mr. Mandela is one of the greatest men to have ever walked the planet. "Long Walk To Freedom" ought to be required reading for every prisoner in America.

In a perfect world we could/would get Rod Hickman, Schwarzenegger and governors across America to provide inmates incentives to read! Shave six months off the sentences of any inmate who reads (and is capable of proving he or she read it) "Long Walk To Freedom" and "Makes Me Wanna Holler" by Nathan McCall. Actually, just as judges sometimes sentence people to "community service", etc. Granting inmates incentives to read nonfiction books would be a community service per se because books build character, discipline and self-growth! I know I'm correct.

But pragmatism says most politicians are not going to give prisoners a sentence reduction for reading. They want to be hard and tough on crime! It's the only way to get elected! "I'll be tough on crime". Translation? "I'll lock 'em up and throw away the key" and "I'll give them twenty-five years to life for stealing four cartons of cigarettes". I'm not going to waste another page explaining politicians to you. If you don't know them by now, you'll never know them. If we want change, then it shall begin with the "Man In The Mirror"! Though millions of civilians will end up perusing this tome, the plan (goal) is for every one of you out there to reach in here with a book!

I'm not going to beg you! I'm not going to speak (write) in tongues or prophesy, etc. to get you to do it. The bottom line is either you want to make a difference or you don't. If you do, it will help to "heal the world". Our world! When guys find out a book is written by a guy presently in prison they are more inclined to peruse it. If we only get *one* out of ten to "turn around" and get it together, etc. that's one *less* to come out an animal and wreak havoc in your community. One less to get out and shoot, kill, rob and rape.

My pen is a tool and it is a weapon being used to fight corruption, violence and rage. It is a tool being used to educate, elevate, inspire and encourage others.

I've done my part, now it's up to you to call John Burton, the governor's office, reporters and radio stations and ask them have they gotten this book. You must tell them to go on to CafePress and get it.

You get a copy and take it to your pastor. You make sure Rev. Henry B. Lyons, Rubin "Hurricane" Carter and Bruce Cutler get this book. Prisoners need it! Preachers need it. Law professors, law students and politicians need it. Snoop Dogg needs to read this book.

Congressman Janklow was drunk, ran a stop sign, hit a telephone pole and killed a man. The judge sentenced him to one hundred days in prison. Basically three months for recklessly taking a life under the influence of alcohol. But Mike Tyson did not take a life and probably didn't rape anybody and yet served more than three years in state prison!

Hanlon/Stone wanted Judge Jane Ure to give this author twenty-five or thirty-five years to life in prison for a six year old irrational letter! But only one hundred days to the congressman for taking a life! Mr. Bush, Ashcroft, governors, senators are you reading this?

Something Is Wrong! Something about our sentencing laws is unequal. Somebody on the judicial oversight committee needs to examine this one hundred day vehicular homicide sentence. If Michael Jackson is convicted of fondling this kid (and certainly child molestation is a shameful, horrible, dastardly and unspeakable crime! But when you take a life it is the ultimate final crime! A homicide victim can't go get counseling and psychotherapy. Yet, I don't believe Michael will be convicted. If he's innocent, he should not be convicted) I'll betcha Michael won't be let off with a one hundred day sentence! Where is the equity, fairness and equal justice under the law?

I suggest you contact Professor Charles Ogletree at Harvard Law School and Professor David Cole at Georgetown and request their research data on (so called) equality in the justice system.

Let me tell you again that prison is awful, horrible and a dirty place. It took God through (my homeboy) Bishop Eddie Long to remind me that "I am a seed". In case you missed it, I'll repeat it, "I am a seed"! You've never seen a seed grow unless it was in a whole lot of dirt. Sometimes God realizes and recognizes that a *prince* doesn't know he's a *prince*. The *prince* is running around trying to be president of the "willing to fry chicken committee". He's running around wasting his talents and not recognizing his power. God will take a Joseph and snatch him up and throw him in prison. God will let Joseph (and Sherman, Henry B. Lyons, Hurricane Carter, Anthony Porter, Geronimo Pratt?) get charged and convicted of a sex crime. Now Joseph is abandoned because church folks and even preachers don't want to have anything to do with a sex offender. We're too high up to stoop down (that) low and visit a sex offender. Now Joseph is trapped in prison and he spent (you know the Bible and if you don't, go read the Book of Genesis) almost fourteen years in prison isolated and alone. How could he be one of the fellas when they all thought he was a sex offender? Joseph had an "R" in his jacket but God willed it to be, so Joseph would have to talk to God and not men. Some of you reading right now have been abandoned by your family and friends. But get up and stop being sad. Start praising God for your alone time because some things God won't reveal to you until you are alone.

You're down in the dirt but you have to be because you're a seed. Folks on the top (of the ground) think it's all just dirt. But it's hard to understand on top what's going on underground. While you're still in prison, in trouble and in that dirt, God is raising you up!!

Many of you are not wrongly convicted. You did the crime for which you're serving time. But you can still change. You can still transform. Just because you "did it" does not mean you "are it". If I go into a garage it does not make me a car. You may have committed a crime but don't define your future by your past. Don't let your history hinder you from your destiny. You can change who you are and how you are by changing what goes into your mind.

I see a lot of physical workouts and exercising in jail. I see push-ups, sit-ups and burpees but you need to exercise your mind daily. Exercise your vision. You can't be it until you're able to see it. Visualize, imagine, dream and see your future in your mind. What grows in your mind grows (into and with) in time. But I don't see a lot of *vision* in prison.

If you want to leave prison in a body bag with a tag on your toe, just put this book down and keep on doing what you're doing. Smoke that dope, drink that hooch, play cards and watch sports all day long. Prison is and forever shall be your home. But for the guys who are ready to get out, for the few of you who want God, Allah, Buddha (or whoever you believe in) to make a way out of no way, for the few folks who know that what we have been doing ain't working, I say, "Lets break the cycle of despair and choose to go another way!"

I am so glad that God has delivered me from people. Did you miss it? He delivered me from people! I have no desire to be popular. I'm not attempting to get anybody (in here or out there) to "endorse me". I don't need your approval. I know me! I don't give a hoot about what you "think" about me. I know me. So the reason people run from drug to drug, from gang to gang, from man to man, woman to woman trying to get a "Mr. Feel Good" high and to be popular is because they don't know who they are. "Jacob - what is your name?" "My name is trickster. My name is conman. My name is crook. I am who people say I am. They named me so I'm just living up (down) to my name." But God told Jacob (which means trickster) "Your name is not Jacob . . . your name is Israel and Israel means *prince.* You've been a trickster but now you're a *prince*."

Brothers be careful who you allow to name you! You may be in the hood, in the slums or in the prison but the hood, the slums and prisons are not in "you". Get up! You are a *prince!*

Call Ruthie Bolton. She's a star basketball player for the Sacramento Monarchs. Her brother is Rev. L. W. Bolton. I love Rev. Bolton. I met him at Leroy's church (New Greater St. John) in Chicago. You tell Ruthie we want her entire team praying for our moratorium.

I believe it's time for a miracle! It's time to transform these prisons and make the public safer. Listen to me! God can rearrange governments if he has to, to get you out of this. I want some brothers who are trapped in prison right now to reach over and grab your cellmate's hand and tell him "I'm a Prince". He's going to think you're going crazy but it will probably make him curious enough to want to **read this book** when you finish. That is a good thing and every few hours I want you to look up at your celly and tell him something that sounds crazy. Tell him, "I'm getting ready to get up out of here." Since he knows you got a twenty-year sentence, twenty-five to life, etc. he's gonna ask you, "How you gonna get out of here?" I want to you look at your cell partner and tell him, "My *gift* is gonna get me out of here." So the Bible says that your *gift* will make room for you! Joseph got out of prison because of his *gift*! And you have a *gift*. No matter who you are or where you are, you do have a *gift*. My, my, my, I wish you all could get my point. I know I'm talking crazy but it seems crazy because I'm talking like a man. You can't ever become a man until and unless you meet your daddy!

The vast majority of guys in jails and prisons had limited contact (if any) with their fathers. You can't become the success you were supposed to be until your father lays his hands on you and identifies you as a *prince*. I want to let you know that even though you never met your natural daddy and/or even though you met him and he abandoned you, etc., don't worry about "him" right now. Instead, go to your spiritual daddy (God) and ask Him, "Who am I?" God will identify you as a *prince*. You'll have to understand that everybody can't talk to God because God talks crazy! He'll call a poor man rich and a bound man loosed! God calls things that are not as though they already were. If you hadn't gone to prison, you would have never talked to God. God had to let you go to prison in order to "save your life" and now it's time to find out who you are. The reason your fleshly father left you was simply that God didn't trust him. God trusted him to carry (you) the seed. But God knew he was not qualified to nurture (you) the seed. So now that your daddy is gone, get over it. Pick yourself up. You've been running too long. You've played every game you knew how to play. You've manipulated everybody you knew how to manipulate. You've wasted time and farted in the wind too long. You need to "pull yourself together". I want my law professors who are reading this book right now to tell you students "pull yourself together". I want mothers who are at home in Atlanta, New York, Chicago and Los Angeles to put your thumb right here in the book and go tell your husband, son and daughter to "pull yourself together." You guys in juvenile, jails and prisons - go tell your buddy, "Dude you need to pull yourself together." Those of you at home who have a computer, I want you to put your thumb here and log on to the Internet and e-mail T. D. Jakes, Eddie Long and Creflo Dollar and tell them to, "Pray for me Bishop because it's time for me to pull myself together."

It's February 2004 and I'm so excited I can hardly see straight. I'm having trouble sleeping at night because I'm so anxious to wake up and see what God is going to do next. I believe you who are reading are on the brink of a miracle.

I believe you are about to break the curse, which has been spoken over your life. Generational bondages are being loosed as you read this. The spirit of failure is being broken right now.

That's why we must get this book into the prisons because we've got to tell those Brothers that it's not over. It is not over! Your life is not over. These mean, wicked, corrupted and often racist judges are not going to tell prisoners it's time to change. Prison guards depend on those prisoners for job security, so they won't/don't tell them. Prosecutors don't give a darn about them changing their lives.

You must tell them they can, will and must change. You must help them to pull themselves together. You on the outside ought to take a break right now and write a little note to your nephew, son, daughter or cousin in prison and tell them, "Pull yourself together."

A Brother was telling me the other day that when we see Jesus we shall be rich and then we will rule. I had to mess up his theory. I told the brother this - Jesus Christ is Lord. The Bible says, "It does not yet appear what we *shall* be but when He appeared we *shall* be like him". But Brother when you read the Holy Bible you need to really study and pray and ask God for revelation. There were certain words added into the translation and it kind of altered it a bit. There is absolutely no *shall* in there; it was added to make it flow and to sound good. To be candid, it was put in there to sort of keep people in bondage. Just get a Strong's Concordance and you'll see there is no *shall* in it. So we've been singing for years that when Jesus comes back, we *shall* rule and reign but we should be ruling and reigning right now. Read it and eliminate the word *shall*. It does not yet appear what we "be" but when He appeared we "be" like Him. Your prayer ought to be, "God let me see Jesus in the spirit."

I was talking to a young man the other night (Whisper is what we call him) and I dropped a bomb on him. I told him he was a phony. I explained that even his closest buddies didn't know him. His candor and probity in his reply shocked me.

"I've been let down and hurt so many times that I had to develop a façade to keep people from knowing me. I don't let anybody in. To be honest, I don't even know how to be me. I've forgotten how to be me."

Damn! We need to begin to understand why people do what they do and we need to begin to address the cause of crime, racism, anger and rage in order to transform the effect . . .

I shall remind you that politicians aren't going to do it. They make money off of crime. Gloria Romero and Jackie Speier types come far and few between.

It's going to take Deion Sanders, Michael Irving, Eddie Long, etc. to come together and build programs for prisoners such as the Joseph project for prisoners (contact Creflo Dollar in Atlanta, Georgia to find out what the Joseph project is all about). If we want to protect public safety (with tautology, I shall reiterate) we must create an atmosphere of change in the prisons. Otherwise, prisoners will continue to lash out. Eventually they will begin to (I fear; God forbid) lash out at prison guards. They'll riot, hold guards hostage and take over prisons.

Bottled rage and caged loneliness is a recipe for violence. Ipso facto crime continues to skyrocket.

I'm cognizant of the fact that perhaps more civilians are perusing this tome than prisoners are. My advice to you is to do something on the outside to change those on the inside. Order some tapes by Bishop Eddie Long, Noel Jones, Gilbert Patterson, Billy Graham, Na'im Akbar and Malcolm and send them to somebody in prison. What are you waiting on?

Pre-order "Creating Monsters", my next book by logging on to CafePress.com.

More to come . . .

Publishers Note: Some of the following pages appeared in the first edition of this best-selling book . . . Join the national call for a moratorium on prison violence beginning June 15, 2004.

E-mail every pastor, politician, radio station and newspaper which you can think of and ask them to announce the "truce" which is being advanced. Tell the Mexican mafia, northerners, southerners, bloods, crips, bulldogs, 415, nazi low riders, Aryan Brotherhood, etc. to stop all prison violence on June 15, 2004. Encourage prisoners to have their family or chaplain or lawyer to e-mail hallopeter@freesurf.ch and let us know that their gang, their prison is in the truce and will join the moratorium. We challenge Rush Limbaugh to debate prison issues with Ed Schultz. These kinds of debates can help Sherman to reach guys like Woody Rayos, Barney and Chano....

# Prologue

"I feel better when I sleep at night if I've done what I call the three E's - enlighten, encourage, and empower people. Everyday we have a choice as to whether or not we're going to be indifferent or make a difference. We can only make a difference if we get involved," states CNN talk show host Tavis Smiley. Tavis works with teenagers through his "Youth to Leaders" conferences which he holds across the country......

"I stand before you as living proof that the Boys and Girls Clubs work. Everything you've seen or heard about me, in the media and in the movies, began with lessons to live by at the Club. If you listen to the lessons taught there and apply yourself with faith in God, you will succeed," states Denzel Washington. He is now National spokesman for the Boys and Girls Club.

Recently Ray Charles gave two million dollars to Moorehouse College in Atlanta, Georgia. Radio personality Tom Joyner gave thousands of dollars to help kids go to college in Tennessee.... I just wanted to point out a few examples of love and giving in these very hateful and selfish times. In the aftermath of the vicious and dastardly attacks on the World Trade Center and the Pentagon in D.C. a lot of us have a bitter taste in our mouths. When I saw those two planes crash into those towers in New York I wondered how could anybody be that mad. What could possibly make anybody that angry? How could anyone have that much hatred in their hearts? These are times of terror, hurt, pain, and tragedy. But if these are the last days that we are living in then we are the generation, which God has chosen to walk through it.

Brother David said, "Yea though I walk through the valley of the shadows of death I will fear no evil." Later on in that same Psalm, David exclaims that *surely* goodness and mercy shall follow me all the days of my life. I'd like to tell all the family and friends of the victims of the 9/11 (September 11th) tragedy that you are (now) walking through the valley of the shadows of death. It is gut wrenching. It is lonely and painful. You feel empty. You get in bed and hope the sun won't shine again. You are hurting. But I want to tell you to just look over your shoulders and you will see goodness and mercy. You will see that suffering breeds character. Character breeds faith and faith won't disappoint. You will see that the pain will never totally go away, but you can transform pain into power. Nothing just happens. There is a reason for this season in your life and the seeds of love, life, and hope have been planted in your garden. But, it's hard to know what's going on underground when you are standing above the ground. Keep on fertilizing the garden of your life with hope, prayer, faith and love will spring forth. You will rise again. You are too close to your destiny to give up now. Don't allow your history to interfere with your destiny. You have been knocked to your knees, but on your knees you're in a war position.

You are never closer to God than you are on your knees. You may not feel Him, see Him, or hear Him, but he is there all the time. God did not fly those planes into those buildings. He did not cause it but God can use it. He *allowed* it, but let the prayer wheel keep on turning and let the fire keep on burning in your heart. You are not alone. God is there with you. At this very moment He is there. I love you so much.

This book is about wrongful convictions and the Judicial System, but I had to get those thoughts off my chest. I've never been a traditional writer. I write from my heart and not just my head. So, if you find me going back and forth and sort of ricocheting from time to time, so goes the story of my life. Since the book is non-fiction I can't write in a vacuum. What I see, experience, hear, and feel will shape the focus of my writing. So, stay with me as we embark upon the task of telling you the story of a judicial system, which is spinning out of control.

I hear Johnnie Cochran, Gerry Spence, Barry Scheck, Bobby Lee Cook, Alan Dershowitz, and Barry Tarlow echoing down the halls of my mind. I hope I can focus and direct this pen in such a way as to shed some light on the injustice they see in *courtrooms* every day. I want you to literally taste injustice in your mouth and feel corruption in your belly as you turn each page of the book you are now holding in your hands. Most books nowadays begin with an end in mind. Some authors have sold their souls to make money. They write to soothe consciences and to satisfy egos. While I'm quite confident that Gerry Spence, David Cole, Ephraim Margolin, Jay Alan Sekulow and the dedicated lawyers at the A.C.L.U. will have a voracious desire for the contents of this tome; I can not pretend to have written it without being cognizant of the inevitable fact that some folks will read it and love to hate me while reading it. I'm reminded of the fact that the old Folks say if you're not talked about, you're not thought about. No statue has ever been erected to a critic. I received much criticism for part one of this book and I believe I witnessed perhaps one of the most ludicrous, preposterous, and draconian rulings ever rendered within C.D.C. (the California Department of Corrections) as a result of that book. Just three weeks after that book was released C.D.C. orchestrated a conspiracy to transfer me to Mule Creek. Numerous enemies are at Mule Creek such as inmate Christmon and Moreno. C.D.C. absolutely refused to document my enemies at Mule Creek, Lancaster, Corcoran (SATF), and Pleasant Valley. Had I gone to either prison I would have been viciously assaulted and perhaps even murdered. Mentioning murder - we had a murder in this prison in November of 2001. Inmate Anderson was killed.

Let me back up and explain clearly (because I'm cognizant of the fact that law students and constitutional experts are reading this book) what C.D.C. did to *me*. 100 complimentary copies of my book arrived at the prison. These were copies, which I was going to send (gratis) to Tavis Smiley, Tom Joyner, Doug Banks, Tony Brown, Jesse Jackson, etc. C.D.C. withheld all of my books for sixty days. They claimed (and rightfully so) the books were *not* a *threat* to the safety and security, but they claimed if I mailed them out it would constitute operating a *business enterprise* from prison. They clearly alleged "If you make a profit - it's a business", absolutely misunderstanding California Penal Code section 2601. After numerous politicians refuted that foolish argument C.D.C. did an about face and decided, "Upon further review the book is contraband and it is a threat to safety and security". On about the 70th day they gave me one copy of the book and are planning to destroy the remaining 99 copies of my book. They changed their (ludicrous, erroneous, and preposterous) arguments four times over a seventy day period. I do not own, run, or operate a business. I have not profited from a crime. All throughout my tome I clearly maintain my innocence. If I shot someone and pled guilty (for example) and then wrote a book about how I shot them etc.; if I were a notorious bank robber and wrote a book about how I planned and carried out the robberies etc.; that (those) would be books about my crime. I told a fictional tale based upon facts which took up all of two pages in the entire book. Ninety percent of that book was about cases tried by Mr. Cochran, Scheck, Snedeker, and Janus. And there is not a shred of evidence to support any threat to safety and security. I advocate prayer, lawsuits, and nonviolence totally. I have never, ever encouraged any inmate to take up arms and fight. I abhor violence and am totally against it. Violence is never (ever) justified, but the truth of the matter is C.D.C. did not want Tavis Smiley, Tom Joyner, Reverend Al Sharpton or Reverend Jesse Jackson to get that book. They attempted to impugn my constitutional right to *free speech* and *artistic* expression. They think they are (literally) God.

No one has a right in this great country to write anything negative about C.D.C. You can write about the president of our great country. Columnists across the country can write that Mr. Bush was Governor Death. Writers can dig through trash cans and write books about peoples private lives, but (according to C.D.C.) these sworn peace officers who are state workers and paid by the public can not be written about. It is against the law! Who's law? C.D.C.'s law! They specialize in twisting facts to fit whatever out come they desire. I have a pending case in Sacramento and (according to C.D.C.) this is communist China and I have no right to write that I am innocent! If somebody reads my books and says, "This man needs my help, I'm sending him a thousand dollars today" C.D.C. will confiscate it - claiming you sent it for a business and I can't have it because this is not America. It is C.D.C. Well, I'm an American and I have the law on my side.

I say to you who want to help me, send it. One dollar or one million dollars - send the check today. Not for a business. Not for some company but a free will check sent upon your own volition. If they are arrogant enough to confiscate it I'll have the A.C.L.U. and the Center for Constitutional Rights to get a court order to give it to me. I want to tell every evil, corrupted, and ignorant C.D.C. employee who is reading my words that the law is on my side. I will continue (until the day I die) to tell it like it is. If I holler long and loud enough, somebody will hear my cry. There are many corrupted staff members at New Folsom Prison. There are many racist staff members at Mule Creek, Lancaster, Corcoran (SATF) and throughout the Department. My pointing out the fact that there are corrupted people working in these prisons is no more of a threat (to safety and security) than the Sacramento Bee pointing out racism, cover-ups, indifference, and gladiator fights being set up by prison guards. The strategy, which C.D.C. has employed, is a dangerous weapon upon a democracy. They basically say "If we don't like you we will transfer you. Even if we know you will be hurt at the prison we send you to. We will refuse to document your enemies. We will simply say you are manipulating to get out of a transfer. We can also lock you up in Ad/Seg 24 hours per day."

"Sensory deprivation" and the hole is a powerful tool in our arsenal and we will steal, hinder, delay, and sabotage, your incoming and outgoing mail. You cannot fight C.D.C." This is like an unwritten rule. A woman mailed me a registered (certified) letter on August 15, 2001. She then mailed my attorney a copy of the registered mail receipt. As of November I have never seen the mail. C.D.C. rules state they cannot withhold any mail without written notification to the inmate as to why the mail is being withheld. I've not been notified. They have (apparently) stolen the mail.

60

Be not deceived, it is not all staff. We have some good people working in the department. In fact, I am housed on a sensitive yard. I'm very safe (physically) where I am, but there are some angry, vindictive, hillbilly C.D.C. officials who want me to be hurt and they have a choice (they feel). Either make my life so miserable at New Folsom that I'll beg to leave. Conspire against me via setting me up, arbitrarily putting me in Ad/Seg for some trumped up reason, getting some inmate to assault me or transferring me to prisons (i.e. Mule Creek, Corcoran SATF, Lancaster, etc.) where they know I have enemies. What they will choose next, I do not know. They never cease to amaze me. To them I am considered a threat. Not a physical threat, but a threat to expose (at large) their backwards, racist, vindictive, and corrupted ways. They are running scared. Scared of what? Media attention! They are afraid Doug Banks, Tavis, Tom Joyner, Montel, Geraldo Rivera, Jesse Jackson, or Al Sharpton will come looking and asking questions. "How many black captains do you have working in C.D.C.? How many black and Latino Program Administrators do you have at Mule Creek? How many black and Mexican Wardens do you have in California's 33 prisons? Why is this inmate in Ad/Seg? What is his mental status? Who wrote the letter alleging his safety is threatened? Why was this inmate assaulted by staff at Lancaster? Why was this inmate denied medical treatment at Corcoran SATF? Why is there nepotism at Mule Creek and racism at Corcoran SATF? Why is this inmate being singled out and treated arbitrarily?"

These are questions C.D.C. is not ready to answer and if you think C.D.C. has not found another way to punish me for writing this book, think again. Pick up your telephone and call the C.D.C. Director in Sacramento, California and ask if I'm at New Folsom prison (probably not, because I'm safe here) and where did I transfer to. Then when you discover they transferred me ask why am I in Administrative Segregation. Then let the (non-violent) war begin! Call Jesse Jackson, Al Sharpton, the A.C.L.U., the NAACP, Congressmen, Senators, and the news media. Call the F.B.I., I'm surprised that C.D.C. did not try to have Special Agent Jimmy Mattocks arrested when he stated, "C.D.C. is rotten and corrupted at the core." Or was that free speech?

I want to tell the Director of C.D.C. that your prisons (all of them) have some good people working in them, but they also (especially Mule Creek, Corcoran SATF, Lancaster, Pelican Bay, and Pleasant Valley) have some vicious, rogue, renegade, and racist staff working in them. Those that are corrupted within C.D.C. make the LAPD Rampart Division look like sterling characters. I shall never abandon my efforts to see justice roll down like waters and righteousness like a mighty stream. Truth pressed to earth shall rise again. And I want the Governor to tell the Director that illegally allowing staff to withhold books from me is unconstitutional on its face. Even those gross violations of my rights shall never silence me. I will fear no evil no matter how dark it gets. If they send me to Mule Creek, Corcoran SATF, Lancaster - if they trump up a charge to place me in Ad/Seg etc. it shall not stop what can't be stopped. Truth cannot be stopped.

By the time you are reading *this* book *another* one is already being published. It is already in the hands of the legal people who will publish it. It is not contraband. It is my sacred, constitutional right to free speech and artistic expression. It is what makes this country the land of the free and home of the brave. I do not know an attorney who would risk his or her right to practice law by assisting in the transporting of illegal contraband and there is clearly (absolutely) no law prohibiting me from writing or printing or publishing a book, newspaper or newsletter etc. without C.D.C.'s permission. I don't need permission from C.D.C. to write a book for a civilian audience. I don't need C.D.C.'s permission to write anybody in America and if they (the reader) decide to type it, print it, or publish it - they need not call C.D.C. to ask if it is okay to do so. What if I send this to Gerry Spence and say, "It could be a book. I don't know. Just my thoughts and my writings. Do with it what you want." Attorney Spence could throw it in the trashcan or he could have his secretary type it up and get twenty thousand copies printed.

Is C.D.C. going to arrest Attorney Spence, "He's our slave so you should have given it to us." or will they hang me, "Although this is America and you can write any lawyer. We suspect you wanted him to publish it so since it's published you will hang on the gallows." This is my pen. This is my paper. I paid for it. This is my mind. These are my opinions. This is America! I challenge any C.D.C. official to call any constitutional lawyer (Gerald Uelmen, Alan Dershowitz, Ephraim Margolin, etc.) or any law professor (at U.C. Davis, U.C. Berkeley, etc.) and find out if I am within my rights as a U.S. Citizen and political prisoner. My disclaimer is written in stone: I do not own or run a business. I do not advocate any physical violence in any way, shape, form or fashion. Neither this nor any book is about my crime because I did not commit a crime. I am innocent. It doesn't fit, you must acquit!!

Yes C.D.C. (California Department of Corrections) fears exposure. They fear that the good ole boy network of nepotism, racism, and corruption will be found out. My God, my God, I want somebody reading this to get it to former L.A. Mayor Riordin. Mayor Riordin can oust Mr. Davis by exposing this 4.5 billion dollar taxpayer rip off (C.D.C.). Their efforts are to impugn my free speech and to undermine my civil rights. The Supreme Court (in 1995) even protects unpopular individuals from retaliation - and their ideas from suppression. Yet, C.D.C. believes it has an institutional right, which is more powerful than a constitutional law. C.D.C. institutional rules must bow to all protections offered by the First Amendment. C.D.C. can not censor an outside publication and declare it contraband merely because it speaks unfavorably of C.D.C. They have no right to declare an employee's name off limits. These are public employees and their hirings are public record. Have they ever heard of an "Unauthorized Biography"? They are written, published and printed every day in America. I love America. C.D.C. is afraid that Quincy Jones, Ray Charles, Chris Webber, the Prince of Saudi Arabia or Chris Gardner will stumble upon a copy of this book and decide "That boy needs help. Let me send him a few grand." They are afraid that Andrew Bunner, Timothy Goebel, Steven Cozza, Rob Bowen, Aaron Slavin, or Mike Arlen will stumble upon this book and begin discussing it in chat rooms over the Internet. They are mighty afraid that Lucas Guttentag, Larry Bell, Van Jones, and Michelle Alexander will get this book. Oh no, C.D.C. does not want Geraldo Rivera, Jason Read, Jordan Martin, Molly Bell, Chuck D, Jeff Wright, Jacquez Poulin-Denis, David Lynn, David Levine, Rebecca Blood (San Francisco Web Writer), Theo Androus, Steven Champeon, Lance Donovan, Jarold Hayden, Matthew J. Robinson, Igor Stebakova, Mike Gervais, or David Omingo to get this book. They are trying desperately to keep this book out of the reach of Spike Lee, Magic Johnson, and Jim Brown. But since this is America I give you (the reader) my permission to dial up *Blueear.com*. Dial up *Booksurge.com*. Call Jay Rosen at New York University's Journalism Department. Contact Ester Margolis (Nowmarket Publisher), Rodale C.E.O. Stephen Murphy. Call Holloway House in L.A. and give them my permission to contact me about republishing this tome. If they need to reach me and are afraid C.D.C. will steal the mail they can call attorney Paul Comiskey in Sacramento, California. I will not allow C.D.C. to rape the first amendment under a false guise of draconian rules. I have a right to a view, an opinion, ideas and expression. And I will continue to exercise those rights come hell or high water.

I want men who are wrongfully convicted to start exercising their rights. Also don't make a weapon. Don't assault anybody. Do no physical harm to evildoers but take them to court. Expose them. Write Congressmen, news reporters, diaries, and books. Use your mind and your spirit. Don't allow C.D.C. to break your spirit. You are too close to allow your history to interfere with your destiny. They want you to fight, stab and kill. I believe C.D.C. has a vested interest in prison riots and inmate rivalries. But when you rise up and use the tools of nonviolence and the power of the media, C.D.C. will eventually get better. It needs a catharsis. It needs to be cleaned up from top to bottom. Write your congressman. Write your pastor, newspapers, Tom Daschle and the Justice Department. Write California Prison Focus and the A.C.L.U. We literally have some terrorists working in C.D.C. I've seen some of them over the years and I've heard and read about them. Tell the Governor to allow the media into Mule Creek Prison, Lancaster, Corcoran, Pelican Bay etc. Let the truth come out to the people. These people absolutely despise the truth.

"Manning is gonna mess around and get his book to Suge Knight, Mike Tyson, M.C. Hammer or to B.E.T. and somebody is gonna help him get justice in the courts," they fear. Well Doug Banks, Joe Ramirez, Tommy Goss, Tom Joyner, Earl Graves, Susan Taylor, Cathy Hughes, Bobby Lee Cook, Johnnie Cochran, etc. etc. Ladies and gentlemen *here* it is!! I present my thoughts to you uncensored (that's un-American), uncut, straight, from my mind, heart and soul. I solicit your prayers and I encourage your correspondence. And please pray for the victim's families who lost their lives on September 11th of last year. We must not take the pain of their loss for granted. Without a moment's notice their lives were altered. Many dreams were busted on September 11th. Thousands of children went to sleep the night of September 11th wondering "When is mommy or daddy coming home again." I cannot imagine their sorrow nor can I fathom their fear. We as a people must come together. We cannot forget that those planes, which were used as weapons of mass destruction, were not seeking to kill black or white, Jew or gentile. They sought to kill *Americans*. In our flag we find the colors of red, white and blue. In that red, white and blue somewhere there is *you*. We must stay together.

We need Bishop Eddie Long, Reverend Billy Graham, Jeff Wright, Bishop Gilbert Patterson and the church to stay on our knees lifting up holy hands and crying out to God for direction. We need Colin Powell and our military to be like Joshua. They must be brave and be strong. America must deal with the injustices, the poverty and the racism right here in America. God has been good to America. It's time for America to be good to God and to be good to one another. After the bitter struggle for the U.S. Presidency who would have ever thought we'd see Al Gore, George Bush, and Bill Clinton; sitting in the same church singing songs and praying prayers. America is coming together. But we must stay together. I encourage you to get "The Gathering of America" by Bishop T.D. Jakes. Also get "Passion For Life" by Eddie Long in Atlanta, Georgia. I encourage you to share this book with a friend. Share it with pastors, lawyers, politicians, columnists and the media. I believe this book was meant for you......

Sometimes God has to do the almighty through the least likely. If you have read any of my other books you are cognizant of the fact that (love it or hate it) my style is unique, personal and meandering. Peter says, "Your books are like a day at the office. One minute the topic with a coworker may be death; the next minute it is life. One hour you may be engaged in deep dialogue about basketball and the next hour you're discussing politics. This is why one simply cannot skip a single paragraph in any of your books. If so, you are lost." With that in mind I want to revisit the subject of terrorism. For those of you who are anxiously waiting to read about corrupted prosecutors, renegade cops, biased judges, wrongful convictions, and the powerful lawyers who defend them. Keep reading...

Oprah says that one reason God allows horrible tragedies to occur in our lives is so we can "never let it happen to somebody else". That's an awesome task but one in which I totally believe. New York City will rise again as a shining example of triumph over tragedy. I believe the Seinfeld's, Donald Trump, Spike Lee, Elton John, and Rudy Guiliani will help make it happen. On November 12, 2001, a jetliner bound from J.F. Kennedy International Airport to Santo Domingo crashed into Queens. This plane crash appears to have been a mechanical error. Flight 587 was carrying 260 people. This crash jarred a city (and a nation) still scarred and numb from the agony it has already endured. "I've heard the bagpipes 38 times in the last two months," stated Pat Curry Radigan. "Now I'll hear them again, tearing me apart with 'Amazing Grace'. I can't believe that more of my friends and neighbors are dead. When will it end?" How much pain, agony, and hurt can one community take? It is gut wrenching and baffling. The Rockaway community already lost nearly 100 people in the September 11th attack. These 100 included firefighters and police officers who resided in Rockaway. Now this! "I've been to a dozen funerals with my boyfriend, a New York Fire Captain, since September 11th. I've watched the funeral processions of firemen and policemen going into St. Francis de Sales church. I've heard taps and I've watched families pray and grieve. Now we start our mourning all over. How much can we take?" stated Radigan.

At the crash scene Mayor Rudy Giuliani said, "I just passed the church in which I've been to, I think, 10 funerals," speaking of St.

Francis de Sales. "The idea that Rockaway was the victim of this, I mean, any place it happened obviously is awful, but it has real special significance to Rockaway." Fran Rushing, a California resident who was visiting her child in Long Island stated she was devastated by how she digested the news. She indicated that she dreaded the thought, which came next, "That we'd settle in and say, 'Oh thank goodness, it's just a normal old 300-people-dead plane crash' what have I come to?" These are troubling times and I don't know what the future holds. But one thing I do know for sure is who holds the future. I cannot fathom the trauma, hurt, and pain that family members of the victims of September 11th and November 12th are feeling. What I do know is that I cried. "Yesterday, I cried," states Iyanla Vanzant. Yes, I cried. I cried for New York. I cried for America. I cried for the little children who will never see mommy or daddy again. In our maturity we cope with our pain. I want the world to know that America will rise again. Terrorism is dangerous, hurtful, and painful but most of us have (in some sense) been terrorized all our lives. Our Jewish brothers had to survive and overcome the Holocaust and most of them have never let it happen to somebody else. Blacks have had to survive and overcome slavery and are still dealing with the aftereffects of slavery. Most Blacks will never let it happen to somebody else. Life has taught me that there is a reason for every season. I have learned far far more from the tests, tragedies, and terrors in my life than I've ever learned from my success. As a boy preacher in Atlanta, Georgia, I was popular. I had friends in high places. I could call Ambassador Andrew Young at home. I was a close personal friend of the late Reverend Hosea Williams. I was known throughout the city, the state, and the nation. Reverend Hosea Williams called me "The Martin Luther King Jr. of the pulpit." I was riding high but today, while sitting trapped in a cold prison cell for an alleged crime of which I'm innocent, while 3000 miles away from home unable to see or call Andy Young. Unable to pay my respects and attend the funeral of the late, great Reverend Hosea Williams. Trapped here in this cage of loneliness. I can still say through it all I've learned to trust in Jesus; I've learned to depend upon God. Sometimes God will allow you to go so low that you must look up just to see your shoe hills. Sometimes He allows (but he didn't ordain it) terror, tragedy, and alienation to show us who He is. It was the voice of a threat that drove Elijah into the cave but the voice of a promise brought him out of the cave. A threat brought me into this cave (prison). My lifestyle, my ego, my personality defects etc. They were tools being used to threaten my ministry. So, rather than lose me to a coffin, rather than let me die God allowed me to be falsely accused.

The threat on God's destiny for my life drove me into this cave. Elijah didn't go into the cave voluntarily. Jezebel sent Elijah a message, "I will kill you," and God sees what we can't see, knows what we don't know, and hears what we can't hear. I wish God had done it another way. I don't like the fact that God allowed trumped up charges, false testimony, and prosecutorial misconduct to send me to this cave. But in retrospect, this cave has saved my life. My God, my God I wish you could feel what I know now. Some young man or woman reading my words right now the enemy wants you dead. Dead from crack, dead from gang warfare, dead from heroin. God can hide you and save your life. I can't put any sugar coating on my story. I got to tell it like it is. I did a lot of wrong things. I wasted much of my substance with riotous living. There is a prophecy over my LIFE that God has to fulfill. He asked Elijah, "What are you doing here?" in the cave. Later on God told him to "Go back the way you came." I have got to get out of this cave. I can't let my dreams die in this cave. I can't allow my gifts to die with me in this cave. I'm coming out of here. God is going to break the shackles of this wrongful conviction and I'll rise again. I refuse to give up. There is a gift in my soul and spirit that won't allow me to die here. I'll be a better man and a more humble preacher. I cannot forget the lonely nights. The holidays and birthdays I've spent here in this cave. When Jesus got the word that "Lazarus whom thou lovest is sick." He waited. "Lord why are you waiting?" I've been crying! But Jesus waited four days until Lazarus was dead and when the people had given up faith Jesus showed up and showed out. Jesus said, "Show me where you laid him," and one day Jesus will show up in my prison. He will show up through a Johnnie Cochran, Willie Gary, Barry Scheck, Ephraim Margolin, or a F. Lee Bailey. Jesus will show up.

"Show me where you laid my baby boy. Show me where you laid Sherman Manning, Brandon, Mumia Abu Jamal. Show me where you gave up on them. Show me where you stopped praying for them. Show me where you stopped accepting their collect calls. Show me where you put a block on your telephone. Show me where you stopped writing to them in the prison. Show me where you laid them." Jesus is gonna say, "Come forth!" Jail cells can't hold you when Jesus raises you up. I'll come home saying as Hannah said (1 Samuel 2:1-3). My heart will be filled with joy. God has made me strong. I'll tell those in high places who talk about "incorrigible" prisoners. They remind me of Eliphaz and Zophar who tried to blame Job for his sickness. They thought Job caused his heartache and heartbreak. (But read Job 42:7-16). I will tell preachers and politicians "Don't keep talking so proudly. Don't let your mouth say such proud things. The lord is a God who knows everything." I'll tell them He brings people down but He also lifts people up. (1 Samuel 2:7-8) I'll tell the world "He raises poor people up from the trash pile. He lifts needy people out of the ashes. He lets them sit with princes. He gives them places of honor." I'll tell them God is raising up convicts, ex-cons, prostitutes, and dope addicts. He raised up Joseph from being convicted of a sex crime (Joseph too was innocent) because we will tell real people with real issues that there is life after prison. Life after homelessness. We'll say there is life after alcohol and life after crack. There is life after this and life after that. Up above my head I hear music in the air. There must be God somewhere.

It seems that I can hear God saying to me in this cave, "I am with you. I will watch over you everywhere you go. I will bring you back to this land. I will not leave you until I have done what I have promised you." (Genesis 28:15) Deuteronomy chapter 18 tells us to appoint judges and officials, but it says, "They must judge people fairly. Do what is right", and treat everyone the same. These judges whom you shall read about in this book, the Bible says, "Don't take money from people who want special favors. It makes those who are wise close their eyes to the truth." Bribery isn't only illegal it's also sin. Every judge ought to read Deuteronomy chapters 16 and 17. Every preacher ought to re-read St. Mark 2:15-17. Yes, I'm coming out of this cave. I'll tell the world I was hungry and you fed me not. I was in prison and you visited me not. Naked and you clothed me not. I will be able to go to Brooklyn Tabernacle and tell Jim Cymbala that "God is using you." I can tell T. D. Jakes, Eddie Long, Jesse Jackson, and Jamie Jay Bakker that "God used you to reach out and touch me in prison." I will be able to tell Paul and Jan Crouch not to ever stop buying satellites. God is using Trinity Broadcasting Network to reach, inspire and encourage the least of these our brothers. I'll tell the world. I'll never let this happen to somebody else. I will never ever give up on a person in prison, jail or a homeless shelter. My test will be transmogrified into a miraculous testimony. Jail cells, dope, poverty and stigma cannot hold you when God is with you. I want to tell you; yes God is able. So I say to the people of New York City that morning will come. The darkest hour of the night is the hour just before dawn. Your tears may endure for a night, but joy is coming, the sun will shine again. Out of the ashes of debris and devastation will come a new norm of compassion. Crooked places will be made straight and rough places will be made smooth. Out of the cave of loneliness shall come life and life more abundantly. In your valleys of despair you must build a tunnel of hope. Climb the mountains of pain and carry a stone of Faith. You'll rise again. New York City will rise again. America will rise again. I love America. America has been blessed. America is our land. America is God's country and God will continue to bless America. That common ground that all America found at ground zero, that common ground that we find at the hospitals, morgues funeral homes and at the cemetery. We must remind ourselves of that common ground. Ipso Facto, we must feed our hungry, clothe our naked, do justice, love, mercy and walk humbly with our God. I want to ask each of you who is reading this book right now to call, fax, or E-Mail Diane Sawyer, Charles Gibson, Ed Gordon, Larry King, Paula Zahn, Aaron Brown, Barbara Walters, Montel, Tom Joyner, and share this book with them. This book is no **business** for me. This book **can** make a difference if enough of you share it with **real** people who are willing to **make** a **difference**. Please, use your E-Mail, use your telephone, use your life to help somebody else. When Arrianna Huffington, Doug Banks and reporters out at Jet and Ebony magazine get this book I believe they will tell the world about it and I believe that every single individual who reads this entire book will be moved to action in one way or another. Michael Holt, David Omingo, Steven Cozza (Scouting For All), Cathy Hughes etc., please read this book and share it with somebody else. I love you so much.

Although I've already spoken (written) about T.D. Jakes and Eddie Long a few times. I must revisit Jakes for a moment. I want somebody (you) to please get this book to T.D. Jakes at Potter's House in Dallas. And I want to ask Bishop Jakes for two things; (A) Please pray for me. Pray for my speedy deliverance and all the guys in prison, and (B) Stay on television. I'm writing already to Bishop T. D. Jakes right now; God is saving lives through you (T.D. Jakes). There are men who are trapped behind these walls who never get a visit. Bishop, they are trapped in mental darkness and (simultaneously) cutting their own lights off. And your ministry (through T.B.N.) is shedding some light in some mighty dark places. There are men who were about to take some pills, slice their throats with razors and commit suicide. But then they saw Jakes and Jones reviving the Stones. God has used you (Bishop Jakes) in this time and in this place to save lives. Don't stop preaching. Stay on television. You even reached a bitter, despondent, angry and discombobulated preacher like me. God has used you to help keep me alive and to prepare me for my destiny. So many nights I had to walk alone. I didn't think I could make it. Didn't know anybody to turn to. I *felt* like momma was dead and gone. My father was a long way from home. Friends were all gone. Sisters and brothers had all walked away and left me standing. Bishop - I had to drink tears for water. But God used you to remind me that I'm never alone. I began to tell Jesus, "Lord, if you don't help me, I can't stand through the storm." And *you* reminded me that *no weapon formed by the enemy shall prosper*. You reminded me that *nothing just happens*. *You* reminded me that even though Jonah was in the whale, he was still in the will (of God). God is moving through you my brother. He has an anointing and a calling on your life Bishop Jakes. And eyes haven't seen, ears haven't heard, and neither has it entered into the hearts of men the things He will do if you stay with him and keep him first in your life. Bishop Jakes.......

In mid December of 2001, I received a "Letter of Support" from President *Nelson Mandela*. The missive brought tears to my eyes and I trembled as I read it. Mr. Mandela conveyed his best wishes concerning my new book and my struggle for freedom. I got the letter in December; however, it was postmarked September 17, 2001. I suspect that Prison Authorities withheld, copied and delayed it. They probably wanted to steal it but decided not to commit a Federal crime *this* time. I read an article in the Sacramento Bee newspaper the other day which points out CDC Officers have abused overtime to the tune of $2 million dollars. The article was highly critical of the prison system. I believe prison authorities have *disallowed* the newspaper to come in the prison (according to the unconstitutional, draconian and arbitrary rules they are applying to my books) because the article is a threat to the safety and security of the institution. I read an article in the newspaper four months ago which related a lawsuit in which a female officer sued C.D.C. for allowing a Lieutenant to sexually harass her. At the trial, a C.D.C. captain testified that the Warden (at that prison) tried to get him (the Captain) to falsify documents. The Captain indicated that the Warden was afraid that the woman would win the lawsuit and Warden Wilson (pseudonym) would lose his pension and his home. Nevertheless, the woman won the lawsuit and the California taxpayers are being robbed to pay the bill. Now I happen to *know* the Warden (Wilson) whom the Captain alleges tried to get him to commit fraud. I respect this particular Warden and I really *doubt* that this particular Warden would ask any Captain to break the law. Nevertheless, my point is I read the article in the newspaper. Was this article a threat to the safety and security of our institution because *some* of *us* may know this particular Warden? Should the Sacramento Bee be sanctioned because they used the authentic names of the warden, Captain, and the Lieutenant who are being sued? The article even revealed the fact that the Lieutenant had been convicted of *Child Molestation* in the past. What if I write the Lieutenant's *name here*? I would be thrown into solitary confinement and transferred within a week. I would be set up and brutalized merely because I quoted a newspaper article.

F. Lee Bailey *is reading this book* right now. I got a letter from him the other day. Mr. Bailey, is this fair or unconstitutional?

I also read an article in the Sacramento Bee, which profiled my Warden. It described how she's fair and a highly respected person. I concur with that article. Is it legal for me to write (or say) that I agree that Ms. Pliler is a very fair and professional Warden? Well I do! And I also think that every Warden in California is White! I'm sick of C.D.C. nepotism, racism and bigots. We don't have a single Black Program Administrator at this prison. It is racist and I have a right to say and write it. And I shall never submit to arbitrary, capricious and draconian rules designed to impugn my *free* speech. Never shall I allow them to silence me. I have a duty as a Christian, a man, and an American to speak out when I see wrong, racism and evil all around me. A few weeks ago, Janis Besler Heaphy gave a speech at Arco Arena for a college graduation. She spoke against racism, racial profiling and civil rights violations. She was booed off the stage. She is the Publisher of the Sacramento Bee. I applaud her for being willing to exercise her free speech rights. And I would hope more students will rethink their negative behavior via booing her off the stage.

It appears that some of us think we have a right to silence any voice that disagrees with us. No, not in America. This country was built on free speech.

I want David Richardson at Prima Publishing Company in Roseville, Doug Banks, Tavis Smiley, Tom Joyner, Spike Lee, F. Lee Bailey, Susan Smith and Gerry Spence etc., etc., to fight like hell for free speech rights. We cannot allow our civil liberties to be snatched away in knee-jerk reactions to terrorism.

I know Johnnie Cochran, David Boies, Jay Sekulow, F. Lee Bailey and Alan Dershowitz are livid. David Coles, Charles Ogletree and all Lawyers have to be angry at what they see Ashcroft doing. Tapping telephones and listening in on attorney client conversations in America! That is wrong..... I'll end this unintended preface by talking about Preachers (again). I don't care who you are or where you are. I care not what your faith or denomination may be, you have got to get Bishop T. D. Jakes in your home. I'm telling you to get a copy of "What do you do when you don't know what to do?" By T. D. Jakes. You have *got* to *get it*!! And call Bishop Eddie Long in Atlanta Georgia (my home town) and get a copy of "Passion For Life." And I want my readers to pray for Mattie. Oprah did a show with a little crippled boy who wrote a book of poems called "Heart Songs By

Mattie." And Oprah asked Mattie, "I'll give you *anything* you *want* for Christmas. What do you want?" Mattie's reply was, "If it's not too much trouble for you Ms. Winfrey, Just pray for me for Christmas!" I want you all to pray for Mattie. Pray for Mumia Abu Jamal, pray for Brandon Gene Martinez and pray for his mother. Pray that all *my* folks whom I've not been able to really tell *why* I was/am in prison will receive the *truth* with open minds and prayerful hearts. I was wrong. I should have just told everybody the truth; that I was *lied* on. A person's greed, vindictiveness and anger put me in Prison. It doesn't fit, you must acquit. A young lawyer wrote me the other day and suggested that I write to Mr. Victor Benedetto. More on Mr. Benedetto in a moment. Prisoner's in paradise? Where is paradise? I'm speaking of private beaches and private yachts. Lots of rest and recreation. More specifically, I'm speaking of the Virgin Islands. On January 14, 2000, Lois McMillen told her parents she was going to a local nightclub. She never made it back home again. The next day she was found dead in the water. Lois was a warm, gentle and caring person. And I dare not take the pain her parents feel for granted. Four young men, Michael Spicer, Evan George, Alexander Benedetto, and William Labrador were arrested for her murder. Alex and William own a modeling company in New York. Michael Spicer is a Rich Law School graduate from Virginia. Mr. Victor Benedetto was sickened by the arrests. He said it was a frame-up. The police "Don't have the integrity to admit that these guys are innocent," stated Mr. Benedetto. "They are being treated like animals, locked in horrible jail cells for 23 hours per day. The conditions are terrible," he said. Mr. Benedetto hired a retired Homicide Detective (Jay Salpeter) to fly to *Paradise* (the Virgin Islands) and try to set the prisoners free. The four arrests seem to have been a rush to judgment. Jay Salpeter concluded these guys were falsely accused. Now comes the jailhouse snitch. Jeffrey Plante claimed Labrador confessed to the murder to him in Prison.

Mr. Plante was a con man who had been married 11 times. His parole officer told the jury he was incredible and unbelievable. In prison one must "Concentrate on what one needs to do to get out of here. Anger eats at you when you are innocent and there is no way to release it in here," stated William Labrador. "You do not convict innocent human beings," William also said. Defense attorney Sean Murphy (a personal friend of William's) flew in from New York City to fight for his friend and Sean gave it his best, but in the end the jury believed the snitch. Three of the young men were exonerated by the judge in what we in America would call a directed verdict of acquittal. William was convicted and given a life sentence in prison. I hope (like hell) that Evan George, Mike Spicer, and Alex Benedetto will not forget about their friend who is trapped in prison in paradise! I pray that the righteous anger and disgust that Mr. Victor Benedetto felt at the way the judicial system treated his son will move his heart. My god,

I hope Mr. V. Benedetto will help somebody else who's in prison. I salute Mr. Benedetto for the way that he fought for his son. He did what any good man and good father should do. I commend him and I pray that he would help some of the guys right here in America who were also framed up. What if Alex had been poor? He would have died in prison for a crime he did not commit. I don't know whether Mr. Benedetto cares or not but I am innocent. I need help. I don't want to die here for a crime I did not commit. Far too many guys get out and never look back. They need to help others who are trapped here.

Mr. Benedetto would be sickened, shocked, and amazed if he saw the corruption, frame-ups, and racism in C.D.C. If he saw the way staff beat inmates at Mule Creek, High Desert, Lancaster, and Pelican Bay prison. If he saw the way C.D.C. retaliated against me for daring to write a book. My God ...in December of 2001 inmate Anderson was murdered by his cellmate. It has been alleged that a prison guard was standing right outside the cell watching the murder. Inmates report that the officer sprayed no mace, no gun shots were fired, etc. That the officer just screamed while an inmate choked Mr. Anderson to death. Anderson's family should sue C.D.C. It was the first murder I've ever heard of in the E.O.P. program at New Folsom Prison. C.D.C. has a new Director. But I believe he'll continue the status quo. C.D.C. by and large is the most racist, corrupted, manipulative, and crooked group of state workers in the country. I hope John Lydon, Arianna Huffinton, Betty Jeane Allen, Tavis Smiley and Ronald Dellums will demand a change. When Politically Incorrect, Dan Rather, CNN, Peter Jennings, and Ed Bradley begin to talk about the corruption, racism, violence, drugs, and rapes in California's prisons then the Senate will do something to change it. This place is a cesspool of sin and hatred. If anybody reading knows Mr. Victor Benedetto, tell him I respect him and I need him. Get this tome to him and tell him he has my permission to publish it. All I want is justice and the only way I can obtain justice is to get the capital to secure the services of a Johnnie Cochran, Gerry Spence, Alan Dershowitz, or an Ephraim Margolin etc. I want Scott Yates, David Richardson, Tim Goebels, Steve Cox, Edwin Nieves, and Jason Pinch to help me get the word out. We must fight to free Mumia Abu Jamal, Brandon Gene Martinez, and Williams Labrador. Call

Barry Scheck, Johnnie and Mr. Uelmen and tell them that we need help.

The justice system in America is broken. It is biased and it is unfair. We need to weed and seed out vicious, overzealous, and corrupted prosecutors like Mary Hanlon. We must hire more of the fair and honest prosecutors like David Hicks and Aubrey Davis. What kind of system is this in America when judges will look at you and say truth does not matter and it makes no difference if you're innocent. How do these appellate judges sleep at night? God is going to punish them for all of this wickedness in high places. Somebody needs to call attorney William Bernhardt down in Tulsa, Oklahoma and tell him about this cruel justice in California. This justice is deadly and it is wicked. E-mail attorney Bernhardt at Willbern@mindspring.com and tell him about Mary Hanlon Stone. Call T.D. Jakes, Jesse Jackson and Al Sharpton. This system needs a catharsis. We can't let Brandon die in a California prison cell. We can't let Mumia Abu Jamal die in prison. We must demand justice. Call Martin Luther King III and Kweisi Mfume. Lets get together as Americans and cleanse the judicial system from the bottom up...I am appealing to each individual reader right now. We need you. Let me pause and inform you that you have the right book in your hands. Nothing just happens. There is a reason and a purpose for you holding this book in your hands. Don't close this book. You're holding the right book in your hands at the right time. I may not know you and perhaps you don't know me but you are supposed to be reading these words right now. As you sit there in you lazy chair, in your law office, on your yacht, on the airplane or on the beach. I want you to know that I've been waiting for you. I have looked for you all my life and finally we have met through the printed word. The easy part will be finishing this book. This is the kind of book (don't take my word for it; just try to put it down) that you'll be able to read in one or two sittings. But the true test will be what you do after you read it. It is 2:40 a.m. and I feel good. My gums are tingling. I have goose bumps (seriously) on my skin. I feel like I'm sitting on dynamite, which is about to explode. I am excited because something is about to happen! (More on that later because that is a spiritual intuition.) I challenge you to call everybody you know and tell them about this book. Call lawyers, the media, politicians and pastors. I want Ron Dellums, Richard Polanco, John Burton, Tavis Smiley, Muhammad Ali, Will Smith, Spike Lee, Tom Joyner, Mr. T, Ed Bradley and Denzel Washington to know about this book. You who are reading must go on the Internet, call talk radio stations, etc. and get the word out. Put the word out. You tell them "Extra, Extra, read all about it!" You tell Snoop Dogg and Chuck D that I need help. You call information and find Suge Knight in L.A. and tell him I need help. Not just for me, but every innocent man who is trapped in the bowels of these prisons needs help. I want the NAACP, S.C.L.C., and the A.C.L.U. to demand that the Justice Department conduct a full-scale investigation into C.D.C. These prison guards are rogue, renegade, out of control and corrupted. I want Bill at "Politically Incorrect" to talk about it. I want preachers to preach about it. I want professor Cornel West, Charles Ogletree, Chris Gardner, Tony Brown, and Ed Bradley to speak about it. We need to come together as Americans. Can George W. Bush actually tell me that it's okay to convict men for crimes they did not commit? Can the Justice Department justify my conviction? They can not ...Oprah asked everybody to pray for Mattie. Almost 80 thousand people e-mailed Oprah to (and we in prison can't e-mail her, but we were praying too) tell her they were praying for Mattie's healing. On January 15, 2002, Oprah had Mattie's physician on who said, "He's ninety-five percent healed." No medical explanation. It was prayer ...Brooks Brown, Craig Scott, Craig Kielburger, Scott Yates, David Richardson etc. Lets go to work. I need Jamie Kennedy (actor), John Doggett (Wenatchee Washington), Terry Miller and Dan Savage (Seattle) to lets go to work. You should tremble when you think of what it feels like to be in prison but be innocent. If it can happen to Alexander Benedetto, Mr. George, Spicer, Sean P. Diddy Combs etc. and me, it can also happen to you. Tomorrow your son, daughter, brother, or sister could be falsely accused of rape, murder, or robbery. What would that feel like to you? How would you sleep at night if you knew they were innocent? Ask Wen Ho Lee about conspiracies and frame-ups. The F.B.I. told the world that Mr. lee was a spy. The media believed it. After months of stress, innuendo, propaganda, and accusations etc., the judge in the case apologized to Wen Ho Lee for the overzealous U.S. Prosecutor's. Joe Salvati served 32 years in federal prison for crimes he did not commit. I'll repeat; 32 years and the man was innocent! It turns out that the F.B.I. and the Justice Department knew all along (for more than 33 years) that he was not guilty. This was not a case of mistaken identity. This was not a case that the optimists could ameliorate with "We got it wrong. We actually believed we had the right man in prison. We simply erred." Not so. This was an open and shut case of a U.S. Attorney suborning perjury, prosecutorial misconduct and a set up by the F.B.I. and this evil conspiracy had the approval of J. Edgar Hoover. Yes it did. Mr. J. Edgar Hoover knew that Joe Salvati was innocent.

I'm well cognizant that this is a hard pill for some of us to swallow but is it really? Is it so difficult to believe that J. Edgar Hoover could wire tap Dr. Martin Luther King Jr.'s telephones and perhaps cover up his assassination, yet be incapable of burying an innocent minority in prison for a murder he did not commit? Congressman Dan Burton had this to say, "I'm a die hard Hoover fan, yet after seeing the evidence in the Salvati case, I think we should remove J. Edgar Hoover's name from the F.B.I. headquarters." Those are strange, strong, and abrasive words coming from a noted former Hoover fan. The manner in which the F.B.I. methodically, systematically, calculated and set up Joe Salvati is something out of a William Bernhardt or Tom Clancy novel. It is unspeakable, evil, and wicked. Joe Salvati cried, prayed and begged lawyers and politicians to "believe" him for 32 years while he lingered in the bowels of a cold and vicious prison cell for a crime he did not commit. My lord, and my God. Gerry Spence, Dennis Riordin, Alan Dershowitz, Ephraim Margolin, James Brosnahan etc. hear me. This man was innocent. They set him up to try to get the mob. Please understand my fellow Americans that Joe's case was not and is not an anomaly or an aberration. The police set innocent men up every hour of every day of every week. Go talk to Alexander Benedetto, Michael Spicer, Evan George etc. Ask them how it feels. I must remind you that we have some great police officers and F.B.I. agents. We have some honest, authentic and God fearing prosecutors in this country. Many of them serve their country well. We applaud them and support them but we also have many people in law enforcement who are opportunistic, greedy, and corrupt. They consider the average Joe (Salvati, Manning, G. Martinez, Porter, Hurricane, Cruz, etc.) expendable and disposable. They justify their set ups, frame-ups and putting innocent people in prison by saying (amongst themselves) "We're doing the wrong thing for the right reason." They don't care. The pleadings, groanings, and moanings, of the wrongly convicted fails to touch, affect or concern them. People like Mary Hanlon Stone, Judge Robert Altman are sick. That's the only way I know to describe them. I've tried over and over again in my mind to fathom, imagine, comprehend and understand how, why etc. Altman, Winkler, and Hanlon could sleep at night knowing in their hearts and minds that they had set me up.

I guess I can understand dislike, disenchantment and perhaps even racism. These are some people whom I just don't like or trust. I'm not a saint so I won't pretend not to know anything about bias. But I can truly write to you that there is (absolutely) no way I could put a man in prison whom I knew did not commit the crime with which he was charged.... Joe Salvati had a family, children and friends. When you lock any man up you also lock up the hopes, dreams, and visions of all the people who love him. That's why although I hate what Mary Hanlon did to me I could not turn around and do it to her. I would remember that if I sent her away for a crime of which she was not guilty, I'd be busting the dreams of her children, family and her friends. I cannot understand it. Perhaps I'm too optimistic about humanity. Maybe I just see life and people through rose-colored lenses. But I will never, ever understand falsely accusing, abusing, and conspiring against innocent people. This is Taliban justice.

It is unspeakable. They say art imitates life. Sometimes I wish life would imitate art. On "The Practice" Jimmy Berlutti scolded judges at a hearing about truth, injustice, and fairness. "The adversarial system of justice stopped being about truth and fairness a long time ago," attorney Berlutti stated. He went on to say, "And we wonder why society hates us so much. We lie to each other every day. We care nothing about the truth, life, death, and fairness. With us (defense lawyers) and prosecutors it is only about winning. Winning means everything." I am quite cognizant of the fact that the public perception about lawyers is lopsided. By and large we believe the ambulance chasers lie every day. We've been conditioned to somehow believe that prosecutors are cut from a different type of cloth and the media consistently manipulate the images of lawyers to fit and substantiate that erroneous perception. Bernard Goldberg just retired from C.B.S. and has written a runaway best seller titled, "Bias." Goldberg blows the whistle on even his own former employers (C.B.S.). He explains in detail how C.B.S., A.B.C., and N.B.C. moguls manipulate their coverage and reporting of all news to favor their own personal beliefs and allegiances. Goldberg's book (finally) proves that the underground presses and that radicals and so-called militants have been right all along. So next time you hear Al Sharpton, Jesse or Don King stating that the media are biased and racist etc. you must give them the benefit of doubt. Next time you hear a Gerry Spence or a James Brosnahan state that the media have purposely depicted a defendant as a violent thug etc. You must give them a listening ear. I suggest that any serious journalism student and law student read "Bias" as a fundamental tool of the trade.

James Brosnahan is a brilliant intellectual. He was the special prosecutor in Oliver North's hearing. James is now defending the infamous John Walker. But how did John become infamous? It is impossible to become infamous or famous in 2002 without the media. Goldberg gives detailed, inside specifics in his book as to how the media shapes and spins a story. This molding and shaping the image of defense lawyers as used car salesman and prosecutors as the epitomes of integrity has been transpiring in America for decades! The cat is out of the bag now. Many prosecutors are evil, dishonest, conniving, bribing racists and it is time for a catharsis. I want true criminals in prison. I want violent rapists and murderers in prison, but there is no room at the inn. Our prisons are full and running over with nonviolent dope smokers, petty thieves, and falsely convicted men whom police and prosecutors set up or conspired against. I don't want Christopher Dicristo, Jason Henderson, Steve Cox, Edwin Neives, Jason Pinch, or John Doggett to end up in prison because some crooked cop didn't like their sexuality, nationality, or their religious beliefs. And if either of them or your son, niece, nephew, husband or wife goes to jail tomorrow, you can count on the media trying them and convicting them before they ever make their first court appearance. The media can make or break a case. This is why it requires a skilled attorney such as Brosnahan, Spence, Cochran, Dershowitz, Scheck or Uelman to do damage control and provide their own spin for their clients cases.

The problem for the defendant is affording the astronomical legal fees of these preeminent lawyers. The average Joe cannot afford Brosnahan, Johnnie Cochran or Ephraim Margolin. So they end up with an overworked, underpaid, and burned out public (pretender) defender. (You) they usually end up in prison and make no mistake about it, judges know very well who the worst of the worst public defenders are and very often they purposely assign them to certain cases to ensure a conviction. It happens every day. Any lawyer, anywhere can and will tell you "Judges are corrupt, biased and racist. They take their biases and prejudices to the bench with them." One needs only consider the fact that appellate judges affirm convictions in cases every day in which they write "While it appears that the evidence in this case was weak and there is a strong probability that the defendant is innocent - we affirm the conviction." What about what lawyers call secret justice? I'll step away from secret justice because that will be the title of one of my upcoming books. But I assure you that secret justice has a price tag. The price of justice in America is quite high. Guilty men buy freedom every day. Innocent men fill up the jails and prisons because they can't pay the cost to win favor with the boss. The boss is the guy wearing the black robe. You must read "Injustice For All" and "Justice For None" by Attorney Gerry Spence.

The things, which transpire in courtrooms every day, would blow your mind if you could see them. Some of these secret deals etc. are unspeakable. It is shameful and a disgrace to the human race for any judge to sit on his/her exalted platform and knowingly send an innocent man to prison. Yet, study after study has shown that judges, prosecutors, police officers, and even politicians quite frequently are privy to the details of wrongful convictions and do nothing to rectify the conviction...

The District Attorney's and even the Governors of two states signed off on a deal a couple of years ago involving convicted murderer Michael Ronning. Detective Mullins was considered a top-notch homicide cop in Battle Creek, Michigan. Detective Mullins had a hunch that some cops can just feel in the guts of their bellies about a suspect. Mullins thought Michael Ronning was responsible for at least 9 murders. Ronning was already doing time in prison in another state for another murder. Mullins went and interrogated Ronning in the prison. "I think you killed Mrs. Rosansky in Battle Creek, Michigan.. etc., etc." After several interrogations Ronning confessed to the Rosansky murder. He agreed to tell Mullins everything he wanted to know about the Rosansky murder and at least three more murders and rapes he had committed in Michigan. "We have a *Serial* Killer and rapist on our hands," Mullins told his Police Chief. After many strategy sessions and much posturing, two Governors and two D.A.'s signed an agreement. Ronning would be extradited to Michigan, plead guilty to a minimum of 3 murders and provide specific details that no one except the killer would know. In exchange for willingly giving closure to the Rosansky Family and to all the other victim's families. Everybody agreed it was a good deal. And Ronning would receive a Life sentence without the possibility of parole. He'd be spared the death penalty. *But* during the confessions, the prosecutors met a major dilemma. One of the murders RONNING confessed to was already a *Closed Case*. They had already tried and convicted a man in that case. The man? J. Thomas Cress!! And the prosecutors absolutely refused to admit that Thomas was innocent. So as a result of one of Ronning's confessions threatening to undermine the Cress conviction. The prosecutors and the Governors reneged on their signed agreement with Ronning. When Mr. Cress heard about the confession, he filed an appeal and the good news was there was still DNA available that could be tested and proved conclusively *who raped* and killed that woman. When the D.A. found out about the Ronning confession to the murder, the D.A. ordered all evidence in the case, including the DNA and rape kit to be destroyed. Now says the D.A., "*If I had known* Ronning was a suspect in that case, I would have *never* ordered that evidence be destroyed." So says Detective Mullins, "That is a blatant lie. I specifically told the D.A. that Ronning was a suspect in that case and the evidence should be preserved!! And, "That is a lie," says the D.A.. "Ronning was a suspect in the case before the D.A. ordered the evidence destroyed," states the

*Chief Of Police* in Battlecreek. "I am livid, embarrassed and perplexed that we probably have an innocent (Thomas Hess) man in prison and the D.A. obviously ordered the DNA destroyed to protect the cover-up of a wrongful conviction," states Michigan *Senator Carl Levin*. Hess has already served 12 years. Mr. John Moore who was a reluctant witness at Mr. Hess' first trial, ("I didn't think he was guilty. I still think Hess is innocent. I testified at his first trial that I heard him claim he had something to do with the murder. He was really joking. There was no physical evidence linking Cress to the murder. So I felt guilty of helping send an innocent man to prison. So I refused to testify *against* Hess at his motion for a new trial. But I swear to you,' Moore continues, "The D.A. sent two Investigators to my house and they threatened to throw me in jail on trumped up charges if I did not testify!"

The Battlecreek wrongful conviction, railroading, and cover-up now moves into witness tampering, perjury and coercion. "In my opinion they just want to protect their wrongful conviction," states John Moore. Hess' appeal was denied. Although the D.A. claims not to believe Ronning's confession (selectively), they have *never* explained how Ronning told them specific details about this murder, which were unknown to the press and unknown to the public.

For example: "After I raped and killed her, I took her purse and made it look like a burglary," confessed Ronning. "Where is the purse? We never found it?" asked Mullins. "I buried it...." Ronning told Mullins. The next day Ronning led police to the exact place and they dug, and voila, they indeed found the victims' purse exactly where he led them. There are many (I do mean many) other detailed specifics that Ronning gave which proved to be authentic in this case that would lead any man to believe he (Ronning) absolutely committed the murder. When asked *how* he broke into her apartment, Ronning told Mullins. To counter his admission and undermine the integrity of his confession, the D.A. told the judge it was absolutely physically impossible for *any man* to climb up the staircase and enter (Can't reach the window the D.A. stated) the apartment that way. *But* a Reporter for Dateline demonstrated *on camera* that it was indeed possible to climb the staircase and reach the window exactly the way Ronning explained he had entered the apartment. The D.A.'s misconduct, lies and destruction of crucial exculpatory evidence in this case proves absolutely that it didn't fit. But they wouldn't acquit. The bottom line is many prosecutors and judges will do almost anything to protect and safeguard a dangerously unlawful conviction.

A college freshman who attends UC Davis College is one of my pen pals. Read part 1 of this tome and asked me, "How can we change the system Reverend? I want child molesters, rapists and murderers in prison, but I don't want innocent people in there." I replied by explaining that national or global action is always complex and difficult to measure effectively. But one of the ways she (the student) could make an immense impact would be to organize her Sorority Sisters and call a press conference. Perhaps organize a student committee on wrongful convictions to have journalism and law students to screen some of the trial transcripts, police reports etc. of the men in prison in California, and to expose and publicize the cases in which they discovered reversible error, prosecutorial misconduct and judicial misconduct. They might also begin lobbying and petitioning Law Professors on behalf of the innocent and the wrongly convicted and persuade these brilliant Law Professors to take on some appeals Pro Bono. They could also sign petitions and establish phone banks and telephone campaigns to lawyers asking them to take on cases.

"TO: Mr. Brosnahan, Riordin, Margolin, Dershowitz, Greenberg, Uelmen, Cochran, Foley etc. etc., "My name is_____, and I am calling you to tell you about a case that will turn your stomach. My Sorority (or Fraternity) is willing to raise money, handle the media, do leg work etc. if you will please please at least *read this guys* transcripts. *Read this guys* transcripts. He is innocent!"

Another thing people can do is talk! use the gift of gab! Talk to your Pastor, counselor, Mayor, Congressman, Senator etc. about wrongful convictions. In California, students should E-Mail (inundate) House Speaker Herb Wesson, Mr. John Burton and Richard Polanco and demand a change. Write letters to the Editor. Call Talk Shows (Radio Talk Shows) and engage in dialogue about particular convictions you find troubling. Expose judges who are biased and Appeals Courts, which are willing to look a wrongful conviction straight in the face and pretend *not* to see it. Expose them. Call Hugh Hefner, Larry Flynt, Tom Joyner or B.E.T. and ask them to help expose corrupted judges. You don't have to (I do *not* support Mr. Flynt's graphic photos and line of work etc., yet I respect his right as an American to speak, write, and photograph [if you will] his mind as long as it does *not* involve minors.) subscribe to Larry Flynt's magazine in order to join him in his efforts to bolster every American's right to *Free Speech*. As a Christian and one who loves the Lord with all of my heart. I can not *force my* beliefs, religion or faith on Flynt or anyone else. God created us and gave us the **power** of **choice**. You cannot legislate morality.

And quite candidly, I admire Flynt's willingness to stand up and speak out on the free speech issues that were enacted to protect and apply to us **all**.

I think Newt Gingrich learned to respect Flynt. I've heard that when Gingrich attempted to impugn Flynt's free speech rights, Flynt offered **one million** dollars to anyone with dirt on Gingrich. A couple of days later, Gingrich resigned from his job as House Speaker. Not even Rush Limbaugh or Mike Savage could sweep the dirt under the rug. It is high time that the A.C.L.U., S.C.L.C., and all of us to stand up for our rights, to exercise our right to say, think, believe and feel as we choose to do. And let no one; not a prosecutor or a judge denies us our rights to utilize our voice, via typewriter or computer to voice and express our opinion.

I have been very disappointed with some so-called Liberal Democratic politicians who have shocked us all by slowly but surely supporting draconian and misguided rules which have been implemented to limit American's right to exercise free speech.

Former California Governor, Pete Wilson, passed new laws denying the media the right to interview inmates and he also initiated new legislation which ceased the right of inmates to communicate (via missives) in a confidential fashion with members of the media.

There used to be a time when an inmate could write to Dan Rather, Barbara Walters, Oprah, the LA Times, the Sacramento Observer etc. and CDC Officials were prohibited from reading the correspondence. Ipso Facto, now prison guards read the mail and if it contains anything they desire to keep hidden, they steal, sabotage or destroy the letters. This is a well kept secret in C.D.C..

If an inmate writes a letter to a person in the community etc., C.D.C. authorities will literally **call** the person with whom the inmate is corresponding and threaten the person. They'll also discredit the inmate etc.. "You're going to get a letter from inmate＿＿＿＿＿＿＿. If I were you I would **not** write him back. He is a pervert!" Or, "He is a violent killer!" Or, "He is a rapist and a child molester!"

Who does it? Prison guards, Administrators, Public Information Officer's, Counselors etc. everyday. And this kind of illegal, unethical conduct transpires everyday. California inmates need to come together and appeal to Larry Flynt, Connie Rice, Leo J. Terrell, Paul Cambria, James Brosnahan or a law professor and ask them to support a Class Action Lawsuit against C.D.C.....

I want *you* who are reading my words right now to ask *yourself* the question, "What would I do if it seemed like all hope was gone and I had nobody to believe in me?" Ask yourself, "How would I feel if *I knew* for a fact that I was trapped in prison for crimes I did not commit and every time I tried to reach out for help (by writing good people like David Quindt, Scott t-Yates, Jason Pinch, Gregory Cypin, Steve Cox, Tim Goebel, Brooks Brown, Mike Kelly, Gina Fortunate, John Doggett, James Oliver, Joe and Janet Ramirez, Dee Dee Meyers etc.), the prison authorities called them and said nasty things about me? How would I feel being trapped in the bowels of a corrupted prison system and I knew I was innocent?"

(The no media contact rules, denials of family visiting, which I mentioned earlier, were reversed by the California Legislature, but Governor *Gray Davis* vetoed the repeal. Davis the Democrat).

.......Darlie Lynn Routier is presently sitting on Death Row for crimes she says she did not commit in Texas. She was convicted of murdering her own two children. Barbara Davis wrote a book about the case. Barbara was convinced that Darlie did it! And her book concluded the same; however, right *after* the book was published, Barbara got a telephone call that left tears in her eyes. Her *source* stated, "We just convicted an innocent woman." Barbara went and viewed some crime scene photos, which the source had obtained and Barbara left that meeting knowing an innocent woman had been condemned to die on Texas Death Row.

Multimillionaire Brian Pardo heard about the case, and this altruistic, philanthropic man utilized his own money to hire Stephen Losch and Stephen Cooper to mount a vigorous appeal for Darlie. I am proud of Mr. Pardo. And I'll tell you here and now that if I got Mr. Pardo to help me get Gerry Spence, Gerald Uelmen, Dershowitz, Dennis Riordon, Cochran, Scheck or Ephraim Margolin just to *read my* trial transcripts etc., I'd be home in less than a year. But appeals are complex, difficult and extremely complicated work. To get a conviction overturned, the courts must first find error and (next) they must conclude that the error was extremely prejudicial. Only a handful of appeals clear such tall hurdles in the California Appellate System or the California Supreme Court. The California Supreme Court in the past 8 years has ruled that an extraordinary range and variety of trial court errors were (their favorite word) *harmless*. These errors include egregious cases in which crucial evidence was excluded, the improper admission of prejudicial evidence, prosecutorial misconduct, judicial error, juror misconduct, ineffective assistance of counsel, faulty juror instructions and even defense lawyers sleeping in trials or appearing before the jury intoxicated.

A survey concluded that the court considered whether prejudicial errors occurred in a total of 101 cases within 5 years. The court ruled the trial court errors were harmless and affirmed (rubberstamped) the lower courts decisions in 88 cases. In the other 13 cases, the court found at least one prejudicial error, remanded the case and reversed the convictions. That's an affirmation rate of 87% in California; *something* is *wrong*!

The LA Times found that the court affirms 98% of all Death Appeals, which is the highest rate of affirmation in Capital Cases of any State Supreme Court in our great nation.

Upon close examination, it was discovered that the Supreme Court has excused blatant mistakes, which severely compromised the defendants basic rights under the constitutional protections afforded to every American.

I encourage you to read a paper written by Constitutional Law Professor Erwin Chermerinsky who teaches at U.S.C. Law School. The paper is called, "No Harm, No Foul!" Mr. Chermerinsky is a brilliant Law Professor and perhaps has one of the greatest constitutional minds in California. I'd feel extremely confident having my wrongful conviction pled in court by Mr. Chermerinsky, Morgolin or Mr. Uelmen. And the three of them combined would be simply stated, a dream (appeal) team.

Mr. Chermerinsky recently appealed a Three Strikes case for three California inmates. The odds were stacked ruthlessly against the lone Law professor. One must remember that Three Strikes and your out has been touted by many prosecutors and politicians in California as being as American as baseball, Chevrolets and Mom's Apple Pie.

The D.A. in LA thought sending Alan Stark in (Los Angeles) to prison for 25 years to Life for the non-violent crime of stealing 4 cartons of cigarettes was morally and legally the right thing to do. Perhaps Phillip Morris should have hired Alan (Turtle) Starks a Lawyer since addiction to their product led to him stealing them. I want to serve notice on all these politicians, judges, prosecutors and police officers who claim to be Christians that these sweeping and draconian or barbaric laws are immoral and ungodly. The Old Testament is replete with examples of court conduct. Justice and mercy, crime and punishment are all in the Bible.

And so, on February 8, 2002, Professor Chermerinsky presented his case before a three-judge panel. The ruling dealt a blow and weakened California's "Three Strikes" Law by striking down two sentences, which were imposed under the statute, stating that a 25-year-to-life-term for petty theft constitutes cruel and unusual punishment.

This decision by the 9th U.S. District Court of Appeals was unanimous.

The bold ruling now requires that a sentence must be proportionate to the last crime an individual committed.

Under the courts new ruling it would be virtually impossible for defendants to receive a 25-yearto-life term for a non-violent third felony offense.

This ruling will affect 343 individuals now serving 25-year-to-life terms for petty theft in California and it could also affect a number of the other 6400 people in California who have received 25-year-to-life terms under the Recidivist Statute, which was enacted in 1994. "It is a crucial blow to the law," conceded Stephanie Miyoshi, a Deputy Attorney general who argued the issue before the court. The State has just appealed to the nation's highest court an earlier appeals court ruling, which voided the Life Sentence of a convicted shoplifter. Miyoshi said the State might also appeal this latest ruling as well.

The two men who prevailed in this new case are Earnest Bray Jr., who was convicted in 1994 of shoplifting three videotapes from a store in San Joaquin County, and Richard Napoleon Brown, who was convicted in Long Beach in 1995 of stealing a twenty-five dollar steering wheel car alarm. Bray and Brown both had convictions for prior violent behavior.

Judge Marsha S. Beezon wrote in the new decision that Brown and Bray's sentences were "Grossly disproportionate" to the crime and therefore violated the eighth amendment, which prohibits cruel and unusual punishment.

The lengthy terms "were contrary to and unreasonable applications of clearly established Supreme Court Law" on sentencing, Beezon wrote, the court ordered that the two defendants, whose cases were consolidated for appeal, must be re-sentenced within 60 days or released.

This was actually the second ruling in three months where the Appeal Court has overturned a three strikes sentence. In the earlier decision (2½ months ago), the Ninth Circuit ruled 2-1 that a 50-year-to-life sentence imposed on Leandor Andrade for stealing videos was grossly disproportionate to the offense.

The new ruling written in somewhat broader language appears to enhance the prospects that hundreds of inmates serving long terms under the three strikes law will be able to successfully challenge their draconian sentences.

The man who argued the case and won this humongous victory (Professor Chermerinsky) stated, "Thursday's decision stands for the proposition that the punishment has to fit the crime for which the person is sentenced."

Attorney (and professor) Chermerinsky continued, "This means that the 340 people serving 25 to Life for petty theft clearly have a basis for belief. For the question would be what other crimes are so trivial to be treated like petty theft." on a three strikes challenge, Professor Chermerinsky stated.

He indicated that since the Andrade decision was rendered, many attorneys around the State have been citing it during trials and in State Court of Appeals three strikes sentences. Normally, California law treats petty theft as a misdemeanor, punished by six months in County Jail and up to a $1,000.00 fine.

The Bray and Brown decision is also noteworthy because both defendants had been convicted of prior crimes of violence and appeared less sympathetic than Andrade, who had no violent priors. That makes it likely that this ruling will affect more inmates.

Bray was convicted in 1980 on three separate counts of Robbery. There was a gun wielded by Bray's co-defendant. He had another robbery. Brown has a total of 5 serious or violent prior felony convictions, including two counts of assault with a deadly weapon and robbery.

Many prosecutors claim that the statute has been a necessary deterrent to crime, but thousands of high profile critics have indicated it has been used unjustly to hand down severe sentences to folks who have committed minor infractions. The bottom line is that the public was hoodwinked into passing the three strikes law. They were victims of subterfuge and a scandal. My *mother* believes that violent repeat offenders should be sentenced to lengthy sentences in prison. Most law-abiding citizens concur. We have no sympathy for murderers, violent or vicious rapists etc.. But when a priest can receive probation for molesting a little boy, but I can receive 75 years to life for allegedly writing two missives; something is wrong. And Judges in California have been handing out 25, 50 and 75 years to Life in prison like water flowing in Niagara Falls since 1994. Again I call on you to change this. I suggest that every young person (ages 14-42) buy Craig Kielburger's new tome "Take Action" and then mobilize to change the face of the Criminal Justice System in America.

We must not become soft on *crime*. We can never allow prison to become a plush hotel. We must treat and punish criminals. We must put killers away. We must be extremely tough on crime. But we can not take little White boys when we catch them with speed in their pockets and issue them 25years-to-life in prison merely because they've been convicted twice before.

We must stop taking Black boys in Nickerson Gardens who have a rock of crack cocaine and putting them away for 25-years-to-life in prison. We must take some responsibility for repeat offenders. I'm cognizant of the fact that there are those of us who specialize in blaming the victims under the guise of personal responsibility etc.. But when we first caught the kid with crack, speed or weed, if we had *treated* their addiction perhaps we would have *defeated* their condition and they would have never gotten a second conviction - much less a third strike.

But we simply lock em up and throw away the key! We put White boys in LA County jail and they are surrounded by Blacks and Mexicans (no offense to my African and Latino brothers, but I'm just telling it the way it is) who assault, rob and rape them. We put em in jail without treating them. Because Rush Limbaugh, Mike Savage and Pat Buchanan told us that rehabilitation does not work, and when they exit prison, they are still addicted, sometimes afflicted and they end up getting re-convicted. I'm sorry to announce to Mr. Gray Davis (the most right bent left wing Governor in the Country), Rush, Savage and any other Republican Polls, but *lots* of *times* rehabilitation does work. And we need to treat addiction and not merely mistreat the addicted. Drug addiction is a powerful thing and I'll never miss the opportunity to encourage any lawyer, law student, high school teen, etc. to get help if you're using drugs. There is no such thing as recreational drug use. Don't deceive yourself; you need help! Go to a pastor, Counselor, peer, parent or somebody and just tell them, "I'm on drugs and need help!"

I'll also encourage my friends in high places who are perusing this book right know to follow the example which has been set by multimillionaire Brian Pardo and begin hiring lawyers for the wrongfully convicted. I want Mr. Flynt, Mr. Hefner, Mr. V. Benedetto, Don King, Bill Gates and Ted Turner to begin to help the least of these who are innocent. And we need people like Marcus Blaus, Jamie Kennedy, Hunter Garner, Scott Yates, David Quindt, Steve Cox and Michael Kelly to get involved. We need Christopher Dicristo, Francisco Arcila, Bryce Escobar and Edwin Nieves etc. to call, write, fax and E-mail the billionaires of our society and ask them to help. And you (David, Steve, Chris, Bryce etc.) must be strong and committed. I'll warn you (the reader) that prison authorities will try to dissuade you, "He's a pervert, he's a killer, he's a rapist, don't write him, etc.," they will tell you. But don't allow them to destroy your passion or divert you from your mission. No innocent man should die in prison for a crime he didn't commit. Not in America.....

C.D.C. is *livid*, *distraught* and awestruck. On February 21, 2002, The California Supreme Court overturned a draconian, unconstitutional and unfair law, which had disallowed California inmates the right to write books about their crimes. Any profits from such books, movies, etc. had to be turned over to the State of California. And the State would supposedly give the money to victims. C.D.C. had manipulated this law to (in effect) stop prisoners from writing books. Just four months ago, C.D.C. erroneously used the law against me. My books have never been about my conviction, and my conviction is a wrongful conviction. Yet C.D.C. claimed my book was about my conviction and that I used the *names* of several C.D.C. employees in the book; therefore, my book was contraband. If they can't find a way to manipulate the law, they will claim your book is a threat to the safety and security. They remind me of Bull Connie and Jim Crow. Yet, the California Supreme Court just ruled that this law is a *violation of Free Speech*. Ditto. And all good ole boys in CDC are sweating bullets.

I am ecstatic. Larry Flynt, Hugh Hefner, Bob Gucciano, Christy Heffner, Jay Alan Sekulow, Gerald Uelmer, Alan Dershowitz, Mr. Sirkin, Paul Cambria and all of us who are at the forefront of confrontational issues are exited. "We kicked their asses," stated a lawyer working on the case. Bishop T. D. Jakes says, "God will tear up heaven to get you out of this." He says, "God will rearrange Governments if has to save you." I say, "God will overturn laws," if he has to unblock your blessings. Attorney Jonathan Bloum who is a Lawyer for the American Association of Publishers Inc. argued the case.

The unanimous decision was a humongous victory for book publishers and the movie industry and it found that the States 16-Year ban on profiteering from crime was overly broad and violated free speech rights, which are guaranteed by the U.S. and State Constitutions. The U.S. Supreme Court in 1991 had already overturned the original in "Son of Sam" in New York State.

The law was named after the moniker used by serial killer David Berkowitz, who had terrorized New York City in the 1970's.

This ruling stems from a lawsuit filed by Frank Sinatra Jr. over a movie about his infamous kidnapping from a hotel in Lake Tahoe in 1963. He wanted to prevent Barry Keenan, the mastermind of the crime, from earning money from the sale of "Snatching Sinatra" to Columbia Pictures. The movie is now in production, and Barry says he will turn over all proceeds to charity. Yet a Lawyer for Sinatra Jr. griped that the ruling makes it "Open Season" on criminal memoirs for the movie industry and will be a "Death Knoll" for similar laws in other States.

"This is the movie capitol," stated Attorney Richard B. Specter, for Sinatra's estate. "And because more movies are made here than anywhere else, this is extremely significant."

The Court's decision written by Justice Marvin Baxter states the ban on profits from books, movies and magazine articles was overly broad because it could be applied to any book or movie that dealt with a felon's recollections of crimes.

The law gives to crime victims the proceeds from a wide range of works by convicted felons "Simply because those works include substantial accounts of the prior felonies," Baxter wrote. ""A statute that confiscates all profits from works which make more than a passing, non-descriptive reference to the creator's past crimes....." Baxter said, "Sweeps within its ambit a wide range of protected speech."

The court also said such a law discourages the discussion of crimes in even "non-exploitive" contexts. The ruling noted that works by such authors as Martin Luther King Jr. and Emma Goodman could have been subject to the California law if it had been in effect at the time of these writings.

Writers groups and publishers had strenuously urged the court to rule against Sinatra in the case. They had argued that without the incentive of money, many convicted felons would not tell their stories. Volumes of importance to historians, psychologists, criminologists and law enforcement would be lost, they said and they were correct. The question must not be whether or not one can profit from crime. The question must be can blocking a person's right to free speech and artistic expression stand up to the constitution. And we must be cognizant of the fact that the prison authorities misused and misapplied the "Son of Sam" law as it was written. For example, part one of this book dealt with wrongful convictions in general. My personal case was rarely mentioned. And even when it was mentioned, I adamantly maintained my innocence.

I didn't write some glorified or sensationalized account of a personal crime spree. Someone could legitimately argue that the law as it stood should not have affected me. Not the prison authorities. They manipulated the law by claiming that my mere mention of my conviction was profiting from crime. They also claimed my book was illegal because I used the names of several CDC Officers (even in a positive light). The fact that I went out of my way and used partial pseudonyms was irrelevant they said. Even more ludicrous was the fact that my first book never mentioned my (alleged) crime or any crime. It was an inspirational tome, which never informed the reader that I was in prison. Yet according to C.D.C., "Son of Sam" applied to that book and I have no right to profit from that book. In fact, they confiscated a check, which came to me for only $454.00 by the Chase Manhattan Bank, and C.D.C. thought it was related to my book. Again, that book, "Reach Beyond The Break and Hold On" never mentioned that I was in prison.

C.D.C. basically took the "son of Sam" law and extorted me. They committed cruel and unusual punishment. They barred me from raising capital to hire an appellate attorney. They basically interpreted `Son of Sam as stating inmates could not (under any circumstances) write a book.

And when part 1 of *this* book was released, the prison would not allow me to read it. Numerous copies arrived at the prison and I asked to *mail them out*. The prison authorities (I'm being redundant I know but it's my book) claimed it would constitute operating a business from prison. You know the story..... C.D.C. does not want books written which deal with prison conditions, drugs, politics, and prison staff corruption. They fear that the New York review of books might serialize a book like mine. They become livid when folks like Johnnie L. Jones writes me a letter telling me *this book* is "Awesome, Brilliant and Ingenious. Its impact on the mind, heart and soul is indelible. And as an articulation of penal and judicial nightmares, it is compelling." The prison authorities are terrified. They want their dirt swept under the rug and their secrets to remain unknown. I am a thorn in the flesh of C.D.C.. This is why they hinder, delay and even steal my mail. On 3/04/02, I received another missive from the Office of the *President* (The Honorable) Nelson Mandela. The C.E.O. of the Nelson Mandela Foundation (John Samuel) wrote "Rev Manning..... Mr. Mandela appreciates your support. It is from such support that he draws the strength to promote peace, justice and stability. Mr. Mandela loves reading and would *certainly* read *your* book." I received the letter and 4 photos on 3/04/02. Yet the letter was mailed to me in January. Why did it take so long for me to get it? C.D.C., they did not want me to ever get it. That's too much power and too much encouragement to a lowly prisoner. They don't want prisoners to get encouraged. Their chief aim is to break a mans spirit and to bust his dreams. They want to remove your hope and annihilate your dignity. As long as we have no hope, then faith won't work for you. Since *faith* is the *substance* of things *hoped* for - if you have no *hopes*, you render faith useless in your life.

And as I gaze around me in the bowels of C.D.C., I see an enormous amount of hopeless people. Hopeless prisoners and hopeless staff. I see void, hurt and a tremendous amount of anger all around me. I talk to killers, rapists, and child molesters every day of my life in here. I talk with people in here who cut off the heads of (decapitated) people. Men who emptied shotguns into the heads of their own family members. I speak with guys who are *actually guilty*. I watch them live their lives. I listen to them tell their stories, not in an effort to exploit them or to profit from their victim's pain. (Ipso Facto, you won't find their names in this book). I want to know what makes a killer kill. I want to know how/why a fully-grown man can/will and very often does rape women (and sometimes men). I want to know what makes a man molest children. "What was going through your mind when you did it? How could you get turned on by a child?" I asked a child molester. "It is about power, control, and innocence," he told me.

Some way, somehow, this sick, perverted and cowardly man is attracted to the innocence that is represented by childhood. I've found out that by and large these people don't necessarily have a (total) physical attraction to children. Many of them have a perverted mental attraction to children. It would be easy to simply say they are only sick, only perverted and/or only crazy. And if it were my child they molested, they would probably (also) be only dead. Yet, I think one of the reasons we as a society have been so unsuccessful at treating molesters and have failed miserably at *preventing* child abuse and molestation is because we have generalized and routinized the madness. Our stomachs turn when we hear about a child being molested. And those of us who consider *ourselves* normal and have no sexual or intimate affinity for children usually spend no time trying to *figure out* why they do it. We can't (Thank God) fathom it and it sickens us so we don't deal with it. But I come to tell you *we must deal with it*. We must figure out why many Catholic Priests are seemingly prone to raping altar boys. We must examine and identify these abnormal proclivities.

If we examine and identify crime, we can prevent it. I used to wonder why it is that many (I'm not gay bashing, I'm simply saying out loud what most of us think in silence) men who are molested as children by men grow up and become gay. "If you hated being molested by your uncle, then why did you grow up and be with men instead of women? We tend to avoid things that caused us pain and trauma, so why did you revisit it?" I asked a homosexual. "It just happened. The first time Joe raped me it hurt. It was painful and I cried. I bled and I felt so nasty. But eventually it started to fell good and I sort of started thinking that a female could look at me and know I had been with a man. So I decided to be gay, or I felt I was gay." It had become clear to me that in many instances, the gayness becomes a psychological thing. Perhaps psychosis. OOPS, I am not bashing gays. Gays are human beings. I know that they have a right to life, liberty and the pursuit of happiness just like me. I would never, ever mistreat, injure or discriminate against anyone based on their sexuality. We've got to much meanness and too much hatred in the world already. I also do *not* suggest that gays are psychologically ill. I simply believe that *some* of them who were molested as children went on to develop a form of low self esteem. *Some* (we cannot paint every gay person with a broad stroke) of them were destined to love and become attracted to the opposite sex. The process of evolution from maleness, to boyishness to manhood was interrupted by trauma. And they were psychologically anchored and conditioned to believe that either they were not good enough for women or inadequate enough for women. Ipso Facto, they begin to gravitate toward their comfort zone. Although their introduction into the zone was excruciatingly uncomfortable, repeated patterns leave marks on the brain, and a form of psychological immunity begins to transform discomfort into comfort. And some of them begin to identify with the femininity in themselves and refused to acknowledge the masculinity in themselves.

I'm not qualified to cure gays, nor am I attempting to cure gays. Most of them don't want to be cured and don't feel a need to be cured from anything. I'm simply identifying some of the data, which has been shared with me from individuals who are trapped behind these walls and in the belly of the beast.

And if the sharing of such data is successful in helping just one person (who desires a change) to understand why they feel how they feel and to modify their behavior in the way they desire to, then my writing won't be in vain.

I still believe that any man or woman has a right and even a responsibility to design their own lives. I believe we should master self. I always strive to be the best that I can be and to understand me. And I'm cognizant of the fact that the greater my understanding of who I am and what makes me tick; the greater my capacity to understand, accept, and live with others will become. I believe society and the public at large ought to get inside the minds of criminals. It is pragmatic to study the life and mind of a child predator. If I have no idea how a predator chases his prey, and if I'm not clear on what attracts him to his prey or how he determines who to prey on, then I'm not equipped with empirical data which enables me to teach the children how to avoid and/or escape a predator.

Because I have talked and listened and analyzed the minds of murderers, gang bangers and kidnappers, etc. I am equipped with tools, which can lead to prevention, and tactics, which can lead to detection and prevention. I want to prevent child abuse, murder, rape and robberies. And I have a view, which was shaped and molded in the political arenas of civilized life and by the minority. The view was molded and affected in prison and can be refined and developed by society.

Our politicians have failed to protect the public from lawbreakers, and one of the main reasons is our refusal to fix the failing prison system. These prisons are full and running over with misery and woe. These prisoners (by and large) are confused, angry, scared and handicapped. In prison they often lose touch with reality. They begin to engage in escapism. They escape the drudgery and misery of the idle, angry and violent prisons by using alcohol and drugs as an anesthesia for their pain and as a vehicle for their escape. They feel useless and worthless. They become like crabs trapped in a hole. They run around like mice chasing cheese. There is a difference in the way a prisoner walks and talks. He develops and antiestablishment paradigm of life. This grows out of his anger at the **system**. He often feels that society or the **man** owes him something. The feelings of **nobodiness** run rampant throughout the prisons, and often beatings, stabbings, rapes, assaults and murders in the prison are simply idle and deadly attempts to prove to oneself and others that "I'm a man." It is a sick and filthy place to be. There is even an odor or stench, which is unique to the prisons. A smell unlike anything I've ever breathed.

This is a foreign land and an awful place, and the fact is that people get out of here every day. They leave here with these diverse, demented, disgusted and abnormal ideas about life, manhood and living. In prisons you are shunned if you committed child molestation. Nobody likes baby rapers. Can you blame us? If you raped an adult, we will sometimes give you a pass (excuse), and if you committed murder (the worst and most *final crime* on the planet), you are often a *hero* in prison. Can you imagine a group of people who consider a murderer a celebrity? How polluted or demented must an atmosphere become in order to elevate fratricide to the status of heroism? This is prison.

The boys walk around all day long with their chests poked out spewing ignorance, foolishness and aggression. Everybody is afraid and paranoia is the norm. Staff members are just as evil, violent, and thuggish as the inmates they enslave.

"I could write a book about some of the crimes I've been instructed to commit from the higher ups down town," a retiring Captain told me in 1998. "Prison guards make the LAPD look like sterling characters," Attorney Lippsmeyer wrote to me in 1999. "My job is to break you down and take your dignity. I have total control over your life. You belong to me," a prison guard told a prison inmate the other day. "C.D.C. is racist and rotten at the core," stated F.B.I. Special Agent Jimmy Mattocks. "No one has the audacity to try to front C.D.C. They are too powerful. They are rich and mean and racist. They will bomb your house and shoot your family," a Black Sergeant told me two days before he was fired (Sergeant Rainer).

"There are two kinds of people in the world. The caught and uncaught. I have committed more crimes than most inmates. I just don't get caught," stated Correctional Officer Acosta two days before he was fired for smuggling drugs and ordering a hit (a killing) for the Mexican Mafia.

"I'm afraid for you. They are livid. If your book gets out there they will transfer you to a prison where you will get killed. You are safe at New Folsom Prison. You know it and so do they. But they're gonna try to send you up the river and get you killed. They are masters at covering up crime," a disgruntled C.D.C. Officer now working at Tehachapi told me.

This place is absolutely corrupt. Former best selling author (inmate) Jack Henry Abbott was found dead in his prison cell a few months ago. Attorney Michael Kuzma, who was helping Abbot with a lawsuit against the State for a beating he suffered at the prison two years ago, said he doubted that Abbott committed suicide, because he voiced fears for his safety recently. California prison inmate Nicolas Soltys was found dead in his Sacramento County Jail cell in February of this year. Sacramento County Jailers claim he killed himself but his Attorney suspects "something is wrong" when there was a camera in the guys cell and guards were supposedly watching his every move. "The Deputies were watching a football game on the monitor that they were supposed to be watching my client," stated Attorney Tommy Clinkenbeard.... Stranger things than murder have taken place (unnoticed) behind these walls. "Who is gonna believe a convicted criminal over a Peace Officer?" they tell us every day.

This is why I encourage the family members of prisoners to write, fax, call and E-mail members of Congress, Senators, etc. about the conditions of these jails and prisons. "When (if) ever they kill me" I tell my family, "Call the media, the tabloids, a lawyer and a private investigator. If I die in prison, C.D.C. killed me or had me killed. I promise you," I tell my family.

And they often utilize the strategy of placing an inmate in Ad Seg. They lock him away to break him down and make him desperate. They'll let you out of the hole if you stop complaining, writing books or contacting the media.

C.D.C. specializes in neutralizing, containing or destroying a human being. The Bible says that, "Where there is no *vision*, the people perish." They are masters at destroying vision in this place. Prisons in general are racist, mean and tough. Yet, C.D.C. takes that all to another level. California's 33 prisons are literally *the jaws of death* and *the claws of devastation*. (This is not an understatement and I want you to underline the *next sentence in your mind*.) No man who enters a California prison will ever be the same again......

Sooner or later I'm going to turn C.D.C. right side up. These racist, ignorant, illiterate hillbillies (from the Director's Office all the way down to the floor cops) have already turned it upside down.

......A few days after the California Supreme overturned the Son of Sam law, C.D.C. was bold and arrogant enough to (again) deny my appeal.

Based on the fact that the law was overturned, I filed an emergency appeal. It was dismissed and denied out of hand.

C.D.C. still refuses to bow to the Constitution of the United States of America. They refuse to bow to the State Supreme Court. They indicated that I had (absolutely) no right to write a book without C.D.C. screening it (censorship) first. And upon their approval, I still have no right to sell a book. If I ever receive profits from my book on any subject, it constitutes operating a business enterprise in prison. The California prison authorities very often manipulate rules and misapply situational regulations in order to accomplish *their* goals *by any means necessary*.

The real problem is not that they don't understand the law and/or right and wrong. The challenge is that they do not want inmates having contacts with the public at large. As I've stated before - C.D.C. is one of the few States to disallow inmates to write to the media in a confidential fashion. (Again) why? Because they want to screen each letter and any data, which they find, paints them in a bad light - They will sabotage, hinder, delay or counter. And any officer who consistently steals inmate mail, beats inmates, or is known for mistreating inmates is almost guaranteed a promotion. There is a thick (but corrupted) blue line and a strong white clique in the ranks of

C.D.C.. Come to a Warden's meeting at Mule Creek, Lancaster, Corcoran P-C, New Folsom State Prison or any of California's 33 prisons and you will think you are at a K.K.K. rally. You will think these Warden's meetings were Executive Aryan Brotherhood meetings. Time, after time, after time at prison after prison, the all white administrator's (Captains, Associate Wardens, and Wardens). And very often we find out that the Chief Deputy Warden is related to the Warden by marriage, or we'll find the Chief Deputy Warden is the cousin of the Captain or the Captain's niece is an Associate Warden. Nepotism is clearly an accepted practice within C.D.C. and your question must be, "If Sherman is not embellishing these facts etc., how do prison authorities get away with so much racism, nepotism and corruption?" The answer? The Union! It's all about the California Prison Guard's protective lawyer. That protective lawyer is their Union. The California Correctional Peace Officer's Association (CCPOA) is the most powerful (racist, greedy and corrupted) lobby in the State of California. And it is the most generous, donating more to State Legislators than any other entity. In 1998, CCPOA contributed more than two and a half million dollars to aid gubernatorial candidate Gray Davis, who, after winning the office, rapidly approved over a half billion dollars for prison construction. But Davis' political appointees also gave the Union $4 and a half million from the State Treasury.

California prison guards have milked the political system to turn themselves into a blue collared aristocracy, a powerhouse with the senior guards pulling down salaries of $53.000.00 (annually) plus ample overtime. Many California prison guards earn more than some Professors at a University. The CCPOA utilized its political muscle to push through numerous laws to invent or create perpetual full employment for its members. In 1994, this Union led a campaign for the three strikes law, which resulted in life sentences for many relatively petty offenders. This bill necessitates the building of 20 penitentiaries in the next few years. The CCPOA ran a huge media campaign against the common sense and compassionate Proposition #36, which directed the State government to send people convicted of non-violent drug possession to treatment centers rather than prison. Thanks to the CCPOA, California incarcerates drug users at a rate much higher than the national average. Thanks in part to the Prison Union anti-crime juggernaut. California has since 1980 passed more than a thousand bills that impose harsher sentences. The Prison Thugs Union flexed its corrupted muscles to give its members almost unlimited power over prisoners. California District Attorney's almost never prosecute Prison Guards for beating, hurting or killing inmates.

Why? DA's fear the CCPOA's wrath. A local prosecutor who tried to prosecute a prison guard lost his seat to re-election by a candidate whose campaign was funded by the prison thugs union. When legislators tried to transfer the jurisdiction for prison guard brutality to the State's Attorney General, the CCPOA (prison thugs union) torpedoed the bill. The CCPOA also successfully sued the Department of Corrections and the Department of Justice to prevent the questioning of any prison guard without 24 hours notice. The prison thugs union blocked a bill which would required random searches of prison guards for drugs, lest any of there members find themselves on the other side of the bars. Thug Boss Don Novey said that drug trafficking was limited to only five or ten "ignorant guards". Internal Affairs investigations have turned up hundreds of Correctional Officers in the drug business. The union representing New York State Prison guards is the second largest donor to State politicians in the Big Apple. Illinois' prison guards union demanded that the state hire 500 new guards last year. Pennsylvania's prison guards have organized a new union for their 9600 guards and money does corrupt! It corrupts politicians as well as private businessman. And people working in prisons are very often power hungry, control prone and have low morals. (More on CA Prison guards - money and Governor Gray Davis - later.) The war on drugs staggers on only in America! Since 1980 people incarcerated have quadrupled, only in America, to the tune of almost 3 million. A lawmaker in Louisiana observed that things had gotten so terrible in his state that "half the population" was "in prison and the other half watching them". Stories of draconian sentences, of racist, vindictive enforcement policies, of police and prison brutality and violence, of families shattered by the campaign against marijuana and drugs. The grim, perplexing statistics have cause judges, journalists, governors, pastors, police chiefs, mayors, and lobbyists such as Families Against Mandatory Minimums to declare a need to end the war on drugs; to no avail.

One would ask why is there resistance to rethinking the war on drugs? The answer is money and jobs. In the past five years, the federal government has awarded $8 billion dollars to pay for building state penal facilities. It's a bribe. It swells the bank accounts of local coffers and the flow of money to small towns and depressed areas corrupts the public conscience. A prison with 1158 beds is worth $25 million dollars a year and 350 jobs to a community. Prisons invigorate the local economies of rural towns all over America. These jobs are built off the backs of unequal justice, draconian sentences, and prisons that are filled with non-violent and very often wrongly convicted prisoners.

Prison profiteering has political rewards also which go beyond pork barrel greed. It creates and sustains clout. Towns, which have new prisons constructed within their domain - or annex land, which includes a nearby prison-, can see their "population" triple or quadruple. Many federal grants are based on raw population figures, regardless of how many residents live in jail cells. Inmates become tokens utilized to obtain funds (embezzle?) for public housing, roads, infrastructure and social programs. Citizens in Lucerne Township, Pennsylvania celebrated when their area was chosen for a prison. It meant $4 million dollars worth of sewer improvements. Local governments collect federal windfalls because most inmates have low or no income, thus making the locales appear to be poverty zones. Florence, Arizona gets almost two thirds of its annual budget from federal grants keyed to the number of convicts within town limits. It's a cash crop.

The Wall Street Journal noted a few months ago that the prison phenomenon is also reshaping the political landscape. "Although inmates are not allowed to vote, they are counted for Legislative Appointment and redistricting. In states such as New York, the prison boom has helped shift political muscle from minority dominated inner-city neighborhoods to rural areas dominated by whites."

In the seventies, New York Governor Nelson Rockefeller, a Republican, launched the zero tolerance, mandatory minimum, lock'em up and throw away the key approach to drug offenders. It is not a coincidence that 40 of the 41 prisons built in New York since 1983 have been placed in Republican Senatorial districts. The city project reported in 2000 that 26 of the states 71 prisons enrich the districts of just 3 Republican Senators - the Chairman of the Senate Committee, the Chairman of the Crime Victims, Crime and Correctional Committee, and the Chairman of the Codes Committee. Prisons? Mo' money honey, mo' money!

Again they just don't work! I know it, you know it and they know it. It is now 3:16 a.m. as I write this. My keepers just came around (15 minutes late) to count. They were not so happy that my light is still on. I'm writing! My celly (Brandon) is above me in his bunk reading. We are treading on dangerous waters. Our keepers would rather we be drinking alcohol, fighting, playing cards, or smoking some of the weed that they smuggle in. To them we are a threat. The most dangerous prisoners in prison are readers and writers. Those people who keep us do not want the scales to fall off of our eyes. They'd rather us contrive to fight, stab, and kill each other. They purposely leak information from prisoner to prisoner "Hey that new guy is a chester (child molester) and if you kick his ass I'll turn my back." They don't want us to read, study the judicial system, or think. Because if I think I might decide that "Even if he really is a child molester, it's not my job to assault him. I'm not the judge. I may not like him but I will not risk my life and potential freedom by assaulting him." If I become a thinker I might realize that "he may be innocent. What if he just didn't do it." Prison authorities program inmates to react and not respond. They train you to become cynical, skeptical and pessimistic. They systematically make you believe that they (prison authorities) are your god.

They specialize in fomenting violence amongst inmates. As long as we are fighting each other we won't unite and as long as we never unite we can't attack them. There are more of us than them. They know this and their biggest fear is that inmates (regardless of color, sexuality, gang affiliation, etc.) will unite and assault them. I want to tell every law student, college student, high school teen, pastor, preacher, speaker, etc. to get this book to a prisoner.

Whoever it is that is reading my words right now I want you to get a copy of this book to a guy in juvenile hall, jail, and prison. I want to challenge every prisoner who is reading my words to stand up. Stand up, stand together, and fight; fight the power.

I want you to unite and assault the prison authorities! Fight them! Not with violence. Not with shanks (prison manufactured knives) or sticks or rocks. But I want you to assault them within the law and with the law. Assault them with your pens. The pen is mightier than the sword. Come together all over these prisons and assault those authorities by filing mass appeals, writing mass letters (to family, reporters, lawyers, and judges). You never need to assault them physically. Assault them legally. Organize and fight. You won't be able to get everybody to join the struggle but it if you get 30% or 40% of the prisoners in your joint (prison) to organize, you'll see a difference. It is time for prisoners to stop fighting and killing each other. Violence is not the way. Certainly violence against fellow convicts is foolish. Put down your physical weapons of devastation and pick up your mental weapons of elevation. Get off that dope and get on hope. Your keeper wants to keep you kept. You are his job security. As long as you can't think, won't study, won't pray, and won't read etc., he has got you by the balls. You are a boy, a slave, a fool, and a tool for the state.

You may as well tell your keeper "master - gimme that belt so I can whip my own ass." But I'm telling you to get off your ass and fight. Get your foot off of that brother's neck and put your pen to paper. Get up and fight. Prisoner! Inmate! Convict! It's time to fight back. It's time to dream instead of scheme. It's time for hope instead of dope. It's time to cope instead of choke.

I don't care what your circumstances are or how bad it looks you can make it. I don't care how long you have been down you can get back up again. You've got to believe in yourself again. You must pick yourself back up and get back in the game of life. You can beat the odds. You can change your life. You can change your circumstances. You can survive and thrive, but you must think you can. You must restore your souls and change your ways. It's dark right now but morning will come. You are still a man. You are still a human being. You matter and you can make a difference. You got to do the time and don't allow the time to do you. Get up! Get up. You have been sleeping too long. Nothing comes to a sleeper but a dream.

Get back in the fight. Pull yourself up by your own bootstraps. I don't care what the judge or prosecutor said. I don't care what your friends said. You gotta talk to yourself and believe that you can make it! I needed to put that out there for all of my brothers who feel like giving up. I want to tell prison guards, Administrators and even my keepers (C.D.C.) that you will lose. You prison guards need to straighten up! You need to get right with God. You need to straighten up your crooked ways. Most of the one's of you who are corrupted know better and you must turn from your wicked ways. One day, some way, the universe is going to pay you back. Call it Karma, reaping what you sow or whatever. But you're gonna pay. Some of these inmates are convicts and they are going to stick knives through your chests. They are going to catch you off guard and beat you so maliciously that you wish you were dead. I'm not being sanctimonious. It makes no difference whether it's you, me or whoever, you got to reap what you sow.

There is no escaping torture, conspiracy and abuse. You (guards) at Corcoran (State Prison), Pelican Bay, Reidsville in Georgia, Rikers Island, all those dark state prisons in Texas, you who are placing inmates in harms way. Setting us up to be raped, sodomized, tortured, and killed. You will pay. You will not get away. When your wife leaves you it's only payback. When your son ends up addicted to cocaine it's only payback. When your child is kidnapped, raped, and killed it's only payback. When you find yourself in a coma and wake up in hell it's only payback. (Again) I do not advocate violence. I am philosophically non-violent. I encourage inmates to sue prison authorities. I encourage reporters to do investigative stories, which expose the evils of the penal system. I encourage preachers to preach about it, teachers to teach about it, speakers to speak about it, and rappers to rap about it. Those are my suggested methods of warfare. I believe (and this tome shall prove) that the pen is mightier than the sword. But many guys agree with me in theory but not in strategy. I put my pen to paper and expose evils. Some guys put pens in eyeballs and blind evil. Some put pens and pencils in hearts and kill evil. Some of these convicts don't have the patience that I have. They are going to (sooner or later) get the upper hand and kill you. Prison guards beware!

I'm a pragmatist. I'm also realistic and more importantly I am a Christian. As a Christian I would be remiss not to recognize the difficulty, stress and dangers prison guards face. It is a difficult job. Yet the difficulties of the job do not excuse corruption. What I am advocating is a transformation of the prison system. If not for the sake of the prison inmate, for the safety of the public citizen it is time to change the way we hire and train prison guards. It is a tough assignment to work in a prison. Prison guards are human beings and anybody will be affected by working around killers, rapists, and child molesters eight hours per day.

To watch the arrest and trial. To hear the evidence. To read about the crime. Raping babies! Babies? Babies! To rape an innocent child. To molest a senior citizen. To kill your own kith and kin at point blank range. To sodomize the elderly and burn down churches. The tortures, the misery, the anger, hate, and racism, which goes into the commission of violent crimes. Who wouldn't have some anger and hostility in their hearts and minds? How many times have you and I watched a heinous crime unfold on TV. and said to ourselves, "I wish I could get my hands on that S.O.B. I'd beat the evil out of him."? It's almost a natural reaction. Yet, we tend to forget our own reactions to evil when we read in the paper about prison guards beating and killing inmates. This seems so hard for society to believe. We tend to think those inmates must be lying. We think why would a man risk his job by beating or setting up a convict to be raped, beat, or killed. What we must do is simply recall our own reactions to crime. Ask ourselves, "If I were a prison guard and I had the opportunity to beat or kill this pervert, this molester, this fratricidal miscreant would I do it?" If the answer is yes it does not make us bad people. It simply means we don't need to become prison guards! That sounds over simplified but it's the reality. We have too many people in prisons who don't have adequate training. A prison guard needs psychological training. We ought to require every prison guard to undergo extensive psychological testing. Extensive polygraph and criminal background testing. Presently any hillbilly with a G.E.D. who has never been convicted of a felony can emerge from the woods, farm, or field, and become a prison guard. One day at the all white high school in the rural country town. The next day at the prison with a badge, uniform and a high powered rifle keeping watch over mostly black and Latino inmates convicted of crimes. At the opposite end of the spectrum (but far less likely) one moment at the all black or brown high school and the next moment working in the prison. Your job demands that you keep the kept in prison and you must control, punish, and attend to convicts. Most prison guards have low self-esteem. Most prison guards grew up with little or no interactions with people who don't look like them and don't think like them.

I grew up being white, around whites and loving whites. I have no blacks or Latinos in my neighborhood, school or church. I get a job guarding blacks and Latinos? Their very lives are in my hands? I am the man! I know nothing about their life experience, I know nothing about their paradigms of the world, but I'm charged with the responsibility of housing, feeding, guarding, controlling their every movement. I'm charged with shooting the bullets that stop them from killing each other and stop them from killing me. Is it too difficult to imagine that bias, prejudice and racism will guide some of my actions? Is it a stretch to assume I'm gonna use 10 punches when five would have sufficed? Is it really a stretch to assume I might shoot in the head (to kill) men I had every opportunity to shoot in the leg and control?

Guards murder, torture and beat everyday. They do so under the color of authority and under the cover of their unions. The problem is not only that their actions are illegal and unethical, but the problem (also) is that some (we never know who) of these guys in prisons are actually and factually innocent! So the guy I'm beating or killing might be innocent! Never mind the fact that my abuse (as a prison guard), bias, and racism is illegal and unethical. The guy could be innocent, wrongly convicted and misplaced in prison.

Employment in the prisons is a difficult stressful and complex task, but none of this excuses misconduct, abuse and corruption. Society needs to take a serious look at who/how we hire to keep watch over these prisons. If not for the moral, ethical and humane implications etc. we must do so ever cognizant of the fact that most guys in prison today will be out of prison tomorrow. We've had to swallow our pill of reality (as a society) and admit the fact that we can't incarcerate ourselves into a crime free society. We are beyond admitting that prisons are not working and long sentences are not transforming lives and creating a more perfect society. We have got to look at prisons pragmatically and think outside of the box. Those (hundreds of thousands each year) guys in jails and prisons are going to get out one day and they will reside in your neighborhood. If we have allowed them to be mistreated, abused, raped, beaten, and tortured psychologically while they were in prison - how is that going to affect and effect our safety when they get out of prison?

If we continue to allow two bit prison captains -etc. to routinely place men in solitary confinement for months and years on end. If we continue to sanction torture via Ad/Seg (a disguised form of solitary confinement), the hole, SHU (Security Housing Units) etc., what/how is that going to affect that mans mind and actions when he walks through a park and sees your brother, sister, or child? I'm afraid we are (under the guise of punishment and corrections) creating rapists and killers and perverts. (Again I'm not bashing gays) we are even creating homosexuals. Prisons routinely lock down prison for long periods of time. Lets analyze a lock down and discover whether or not there are ramifications (physically, psychologically, and emotionally). Most prisons are set up with two inmates (men) per cell. The last face an inmate sees before he goes to sleep is his cell partner. The first face an inmate sees when he wakes up in the morning is his cell partner. These two men share a 6-foot by ten-foot cell. They sit on the same toilet, share the same sink, etc. etc. etc. Most heterosexual inmates are very selective when given a choice (however many prison officials such as California prison guards give inmates little or no choice in cell partners) about a cell partner. Ultimately you want someone who has a prison job. It is important that his work schedule is different from your work schedule. For instance, I work from 7:30 a.m. to 3:30 p.m., my cell partner should have a job working at night. Why? We call it cell time. Convicts are forced to have a cell partner. Keep in mind that you might have a two-year state prison sentence but your cell partner could be serving a sentence of life without parole. He will die here. That in and of itself is psychologically perplexing and intimidating. You find yourself having nightmares and fears that "this guy might snap and kill me to keep me from going home. This guy might rape me because he knows he'll never be with a woman again." It is outright haunting. But (as I was saying) you want as much time away from your cell partner as possible. There are a variety of things you'd prefer to do in the cell while your cell partner is at work or on the yard. There is one thing you are required to do while he's outside the cell (and vice versa), masturbation! Believe it or not inmates do that unless they are gay. All prisons allow pornographic materials in the prisons. It is mandatory respect to wait until your cell partner is outside the cell to break out your magazine and do your thing. But what do you do when prison authorities declare a six months "Emergency Lock Down". C.D.C. does it quite frequently. They lock two men in these small cages (so called cells) for five and six months straight. *No Time Outside* the cell. Every four days (on an emergency *lock-down*) both inmates receive a three minutes shower. And even if you tried to skip your shower and utilize your cell partner's absence to masturbate etc., how many of us can climax in *three* minutes (Speedy Gonzales???)? My point is simple; lock any two *men* in a small room for six months with no time apart, no opportunity to pray, think or meditate alone. No time to masturbate etc. alone. An unwritten rule against masturbating in the company of his cell partner and what happens? Two *horny* (non gay) men who have absolutely no opportunity to relieve themselves in six months? Tensions rise, fights, stabbings, *rapes* and even killings take place on these often unjustified, lengthy lock downs. Have correctional authorities noticed the propensity toward more prison (cell) violence, rapes and killings on these long "lock downs," of course they have.

"We invent reasons to lock you all down for 2 or 3 months at a time. It makes it interesting and it is good public relations," a Prison Sergeant told me.

"I've noticed more rapes, homicides and suicides during lock downs and in Ad Seg than at any other time. *Some* guys actually should never be placed into Ad Seg for mental reasons. All lock downs are dangerous", stated former C.D.C. Chief Mental Health Director, Doctor Sal Mennutti. I've told the Director we need to rethink Ad Seg, SHU and all of these routine emergency lock downs, but he don't listen to me," stated Doctor Mennutti.

I'm simply offering an inside view of how prisons work pro and con (no pun intended) from the inside out. And I hope to elucidate some of the prison subcultures in this brief section of this book so as to provide insight into why guys get out of prison and kill, rape and rob. There is no excusing these crimes, but we must fight the lawlessness *in prisons* if we are to fight lawlessness outside the prison.

If we really want Johnny to get out of prison in 3-5 years and have a chance at being reformed, transformed and rehabilitated, we damn sure need to keep him fed, protected, educated and *treated fairly while* we are punishing him. No one (not a good parent) beats their child maliciously and abuses them to *teach them a lesson*! Any Psychiatrist will tell you that if every time your child does wrong, you burn them with an iron, lock them in a dark closet for three days and/or sexually abuse them, you are raising a ticking time bomb. And we must also admit that when we punish adults by not only taking away their freedom, but teaching them to become helpless, sinister, racist and cynical. When we abuse, beat and rape them in prison, we are *creating monsters*. And these *monsters* (need I remind you) will (one day) *get out of prison*!!!

Los Angeles County Jail, LA County Jail is a reflection of the evils, which run through the ranks of the LAPD. I was (as you will read later) in LA County Jail. The prison mentality and jail subculture (at first glance) in LA County Jail is complex and quite difficult to comprehend. It is even more difficult to attempt to reduce to writing in any kind of comprehensive fashion. I dare not attempt to write any exhaustive examinations or explanations about the vicious, barbarisms and violence in LA County Jail in this tome.

Let me merely observe here that Latinos and Blacks (inmates) run the County Jail. It would appear that Blacks outnumber the Whites 3 or 4 to one. Therefore, White inmates make up perhaps only 20 to (roughly) 15% of the inmate population in the LA County Jail. And without embellishment, I found myself literally feeling sorry for each and every White boy who entered the LA County Jail. In prison (**State Prisons**, although the media mistakenly utilize the term **jail** and **prison** interchangeably) most Blacks and Latinos are at war with each other. It's a war (in California) over power, turf, and for the right to rule. In LA County Jail however, Blacks and Latinos work together to form a kind of Taliban against White folks. And the corrupted guards in LA County Jail routinely place 3 or 4 White inmates into cells with 40 or 50 Blacks and Mexicans. "What size shoes are those," states the Black inmate to the White inmate. "Size 10," comes the reply. "That's the size I wear, give them up," says the Black guy. "Then I won't have any shoes," states the White guy. Within a matter of seconds blood is everywhere. Three Black guys and two Mexicans are all over him. They beat him, they spit on him, they choke him, they take his shoes. They rip off his pants, "Don't get blood on his pants cause I want to wear them out of here when I make bail," yells one of the Latino inmates. They rip off his underwear. "White guy gotta fat ass," says one of the guys. They run what's called a train on him. A train is when they take turns sodomizing him anally. One of the guys says, "I want you to suck my_____." As the white boy begins to suck him, the inmate snatches his penis out of his throat and slaps him. "You got blood on my (expletive)," states the inmate. He beats the guy for getting blood on his private parts. Approximately fifteen minutes into the sadistic assault, rape and robbery, a guard comes by and pushes the alarm. Nine guards rush into the cellblock and merely remove the White guy and ask, "What happened?" Nobody says a word.

About two hours later, I watch five Black inmates and three Mexicans attempt to sodomize a young White inmate with a broom handle. They would have succeeded had I not stopped them. I would love to write here that I stopped them with force or power. I didn't. I used a little bit of psychology, a little manipulation, and a lot of prayer. "Call me a sellout, but this is sick. All of us got lil bothers and lil sisters. How would we feel if this happened to them." I yelled in disgust, fear and disdain. I distracted them. I was able to interrupt their excitement. They let him go, but they still took his shoes and watch. "White man runs the free world, Black man runs the chain gang," is the going theory running across the country. I can tell you that the LA County Jail is a deathtrap for any White person who dares get arrested. "I'd rather go to hell that go to LA County Jail," stated comedian Jamie Kennedy on "politically Incorrect."

What does all of this imply about society at large and does it matter? Jails and prisons are a microcosm of civilian society at large, and 95% of every inmate who was in LA County Jail with me in 1995 is now back on the streets.

I submit that each of those White guys who were beat, raped and robbed in LA County Jail is now a living time bomb. And each of the inmates who perpetrated the crimes upon those Whites are also a threat to Public safety. Your child, your momma and your daddy are walking the streets with the ex-cons, ex-victims and ex-perpetrators. Small wonder children and senior citizens are being molested and killed. Small wonder a *Judge* in Santa Rosa is on house arrest for receiving kiddy porn. Small wonder a Sacramento County *District Attorney* (Peter Harned) was caught with child porn in his computer. On March 18, 2002, the Federal Authorities did a special child porn sweep and arrested 40 people nationwide. Among the arrestees were a Police Officer, Prison Guards, a Judge, and (you knew it) 2 Catholic Priests, none of whom were ex-cons. I have never understood how/why any adult could rape (or in any way be intimate with) a child. Nor have I been capable of comprehending how those who rape children receive such short prison terms and get no treatment while in prison. But my point earlier was simple: The guys who enter LA County Jail (and most State Prisons) *will get out*. The things they did, had to endure, saw, will effect their behavior (by and large) when they get out. So (an understatement) it would behoove us to clean up the jails and prisons. And I'm not talking about any ladder (you'll read about a proposal for a ladder program by another author in another book later this year. This program is being rubber stamped by Prison Inspector General Steve White) programs which give guards here substantive power over inmates lives. The power to limit an inmates personal property allowances and canteen etc.. In the present climate with corrupted, racist, mostly white keepers, they don't need to be given any more power over the kept. The ladder program will cause more problems than it will solve.

We need to look at the direction of prisons. We must scrutinize every prison guard and every prison employee. We need to fire 50% of the people presently working in prisons and jails. They are incorrigible racists and thugs. We can't reform them. We need to eliminate them. Just the other day I saw on the news where Governor Gray Davis wants to close down 5 prisons in mid April. There are five *private* prisons, which are not owned by the *State*. Ipso Facto, the guards in those prisons are not affiliated with the CCPOA. (You do recall the California Prison Thugs Union I mentioned earlier do you not). The word from the inside is that it is politics and kickbacks. Apparently (according to rumor) Governor Davis promised the union he would (quid pro quo) shut down these prisons in order to help *State Prison* Guards. (And to pay them back for their large campaign contributions). The News Reporter stated, "Although many guards criticized the union, we were unable to find *anyone* to criticize the guards union *on camera*!" Union Power? That's too much power! That sounds like monopoly, Mafia, mob and manipulation. Facts such as these add credence to rumors of prison guards having their cars bombed, vandalized and being beaten by other guards because they snitch and report staff corruption, staff brutality and staff drug smuggling. The California prison guards union has created the myth that it is untouchable. But I still believe that the right *Lawyer* with the right evidence can bring them (the guards union) down. I believe James "RaceHorse" Haynes, Donald Watkins, Barry Tarlow, Johnnie Cochran, Dennis Riordan or a Gerry Spence can bring them down. A tough, courageous, arrogant and fearless Gerry Spence type can topple the *thugs* union. I know that *if* the California Attorney's for criminal justice would put out a call to assemble a dream team of defense lawyers and combine civil litigators as well as criminal lawyers; If they get Peter Eliasberg at the A.C.L.U., Mr. Kendall at the NAACP, Charles Ogletree out at Harvard, get the ADL and the NACDL to join forces and seal the deal with an attorney such as Willie Gary, David Cole, or Gerry Spence to do the oral arguments, we could defeat the thugs union and simultaneously clean up C.D.C..

Until this happens, the cover-ups, murders, rapes, and drug running in prisons shall continue. I've seen too much bloodshed, too many (set up by staff) stabbings, riots, and corruption in prison. I've watched too many prison guards lie, cheat, steal, kill and get away with it. I know that on *any* day of the week that I can wake up and be told to , "Pack it up, you're transferring to Mule Creek," or Lancaster or

Corcoran or Pelican Bay. I'm cognizant of the fact that they would love to justify placing me on lockdown, in some SHU program and to pretend it's for my safety. I'm well cognizant of the fact that they want me dead. I will repeat, the **Prison Thugs Union** wants **me dead**! And killing me at New Folsom Prison in general population (although **not** impossible) is difficult. I'm fairly safe on this yard and they **know it**. They could send sleepers (persons who don't have **sensitive** needs and don't belong on the yard). They would simply pretend he or they had slipped through the cracks. Case in point: Inmate **Dave Brown**. They allowed a White inmate to s**lip through the cracks** and he came out and viciously **stabbed** inmate **Dave Brown**. Dave almost died! Of course (C.D.C. foolishness) Dave was placed in Ad Seg while they **investigated** the C.D.C. set-up stabbing. The perpetrator was transferred and Dave Brown was released from Ad Seg for **one day**. In the wee hours of the morning, somebody **decided** that Dave Brown could no longer reside safely at New Folsom Prison on A-Facility so they snatched him up and transferred him also. So of course they **can** set me up by allowing a sleeper to come and **stab me**. And **if** I don't die, they will **transfer me** after the stabbing. Any Lawyer reading needs to find Dave Brown and help him to sue the hell out of the C.D.C.. I'm almost certain they transferred him to the so-called **Protective Housing Unit** at Corcoran State Prison (SATF),) is difficult. This is a fairly safe yard. So the game they play is to refuse to document my enemies at Mule Creek, Lancaster, Corcoran, etc., and they will capriciously, arbitrarily and retaliatingly transfer me. And upon my arrival, I will turn up dead. They will invent any excuse and justify my murder! But I want to reiterate that when and if I ever die in State custody, I want my family, friends, politicians, lawyers, CALJ, Spence, Haynes, Uelmen, Yagman, Tarlow, Johnnie Cochran, the NAACP, ACLU and all of **you** to sue! Sue them until they are bankrupt. If they kill me, I want my family to have the Director's oven, the Warden's shoes, the Captain's socks (at whatever prison I'm at when it happens). I want my family to take them to the cleaners. And I have established a voluminous record of their criminal misconduct. There are awesome lawyers in various locations around the State and around the country who have the data. They have records, notes from inmates, signed letters from professionals etc. etc.. The evidence of a conspiracy to transfer me to prisons where I have enemies………

# Introduction

My stomach turns, my throat becomes dry, my chest tightens and my head aches with pain when I think about these guys. Many of them are cloaked in (Black) Robes of (jurisprudence) Righteousness. Many of them wear expensive suits and have lavish offices in the Senate, Congress, State Capitols and even at the White House. They talk a good game and present a decent image. Yet, **You Shall Know Them By The Fruit They Bear.** Underneath these robes and inside these suits and ties they are ravening wolves. Congressman John Lewis, Maxine Waters, and even Joseph Biden should know of whom I speak. I love John and Maxine and have some respect for Joseph Biden and Ted Kennedy and a few others not named **herein.** But a large portion of these ravening wolves, vicious predators, shameless bigots and magnets of evil of whom I speak are **Judges, Prosecutors,** and **Politicians.** They stink in the very nostrils of almighty God. Have you heard about them. Gerry Spence speaks about them quite eloquently in his books, "Injustice For All" and "From Freedom To Slavery." Edward Humes (winner of a Pulitzer Prize) writes about them in "Mean Justice," and Johnnie Cochran gives an inkling of their evils in "Journey To Justice."

This book is an indictment against the corruption, deceit and fraudulent practices of corrupted judges and prosecutors. It is an indictment against rogue and renegade police officers. It is also an expose' on the perjured souls of some of our so called leaders in America: This book is **not** bestseller material, nor is it an Oprah pick; although I love Oprah and have the-highest respect for her integrity, care and concern. Bestsellers today must be **fiction.** And even much of the non-fiction we read is fiction at its core. I'll get no help from ABC, NBC, or CBS in publicizing and promoting this tome. But if you've ever heard of Harriet Tubman and the **Underground Railroad,** you are cognizant of the fact that any book can spread like wildfire in the **down low.** I consider this book as a **Chain Letter.** This is a **Chain Book** for defense lawyers, civil rights leaders, activists, pastors, and the real newspapers and newsletters across the country. This book is for Gerry Armsby to pass on to Monica Moorehead. It's for Mary Ratcliff to send to the L.A. Sentinel. It's for Katherine Garry to pass on to Michael Novick. This book is for the student activists at Harvard, Brown University and U.C. Davis to pass on to young activists all over America.

This book calls on the true warriors at A.C.L.U., ADL., S.C.L.C., NAACP, and the I.A.C. to take to action. We can not allow this writing to go unread. We also can not preach to the choir. So you (The Reader) are called upon to get this book into Law Schools, Colleges, jails, juvenile facilities, and prisons across the country. Talk about this book in chat rooms on the Internet, and more about it in school newspapers. Get the word out on the streets. You won't find any theories of relativity or discoveries of electricity within these pages. What you will find are factual cases of prosecutorial misconduct, police brutality, judicial recklessness and wrongful convictions within these pages. And you shall read about the lawyers who defend innocent men and women within these pages. You shall read about the investigators who leave no stone unturned in their pursuit for justice for their clients.

You'll read quotes from Doctor Martin Luther King Jr. as well as quotes from *Boy George W. Bush.* You'll read about injustice, spiritual wickedness and corruption in *high places* in America. You'll find hypocrisy, bias, bigotry, and classism which transpires in court rooms across the country on a daily basis *in this book.* I hope this book energizes the activist, transforms the prisoner, shames judges and fortifies pastors. I hope Michael Snedeker, Alan Dershowitz, F. Lee Bailey, Barry Tarlow, Gerald Uelmen, and Roy Black stumble upon copies of this book. I need readers out at Harvard to finish the book and then lend it to Charles Ogletree and Doctor Cornel West. I need my readers to send it to Patt Dunn, Mumia Abu Jamal, Brandon G. Martinez, and to prisoners all across this nation. I need my activist friends in New York to get this book to the students at Cardoza law School and New York University. I need my fellow fighters at the I.A.C. to get this one to Aaron Bentley, Doug Banks, Tony Brown, *Pat Robertson,* Jesse and Kweisi. I even want this one to go to Brother Al Sharpton and Minister Louis Farakan. I do not agree with his wholesale demonization of white people per se. Nor would I ever consider white people as blue eyed devils. Yet I don't want the data contained within these pages to *Remain A Secret Any Longer.* I want it exposed. If *Hitler* were alive, I'd ask you to send him a copy also. Perhaps he'd learn something and transform his racist ways in the process of reading. In *If It Doesn't Fit You Must Acquit* Book One, I began the book with a word to our youth and to teens in schools. I spent a lot of time trying to inspire our precious children to stop the violence, killings, shootings, and hatred. And if you (too) want to inspire and transform our youth, I suggest you get a copy of book one and get it to students. But in this book (part 2), I must confess that I open up hitting hard and throwing punches at the injustice that is running rampant throughout our nation. Reader discretion is advised. I have no doubt that great lawyers such as

Murray, J. Janus, Gerry Spence, Michael Morchower, F. Lee Bailey, Roy Black, Davis Boies and Barry Scheck will relate to this book. I know that if you (*The Reader*) will help me to get it in the prisons, it will inspire, educate, and elevate prisoners across our land. I know that the underground media will be enthralled and mesmerized. But the *Power Structure* and the Big Boys on the bench, in the courtrooms, and in the positions of power will hope like hell that you *don't read this book.* And if you read it, that you don't heed it, and they hope you don't take *actions* on what you read. To them I say, *Go To Hell!* To *you* I say, *Let's do this.* I want you to put this book *in their face and in their ear.* Let's go to work now and expose, inspire, inform and embarrass. Use your telephones, ink, internet, microphone, mailbox, and any other tool you can think up to put the data contained *hereafter in their face.*

**Sherman Manning**

# Dedications: Attorney Barry Scheck, Cardoza Law School and Betty Ann Waters

I am always amazed by Barry Scheck. This brilliant, energetic and high profile lawyer has a heart of gold. Barry Scheck is to innocent people in prison what Mother Teresa was to poor people. Barry Scheck is a man on a mission to leave no *innocent* person in prison. I want to dedicate this book to Barry and his students at Cardoza Law School in New York City. You will read a lot in this book about the Barry Scheck's, Gerry Spence, Johnnie Cochran, Professor David Protess, Professor Robert Cling and James McCloskey in this book. I want to also give applause to Betty Ann Waters. You will read her story in this book. Also, people like David Protess, Robert Cling, Peter Neufield and Barry Scheck have not forgotten the left out, locked in, and the forgotten about. When I think of politicians who pay no attention to the abuse, violence, rapes and racism transpiring in prisons across this country, it is heartbreaking. So many of our political leaders have sold us out. Moral leaders of substance don't follow opinion polls, they mold opinions. Not with their guns, or dollars, or positions, but with the power of their souls. Our politicians are a lost generation looking for the next poll to determine their next opinion. But Barry Scheck (in some sense) reminds me of Doctor Martin Luther King Jr.. Dr. King gave a voice to the voiceless and hope to the hopeless. Against the advice of all of his staff and confidantes, Dr. King was assassinated at Lorraine Motel while in town standing up for garbage workers. The media so often eviscerates the fabric of what Martin really was and what he stood for. Dr. King never forgot the least of these, our brothers.

Barry Scheck, Cardoza students and Betty Ann Waters have not forgotten either. I commend, salute, and congratulate them for their service, their dedication and their willingness to fight the power of a corrupted judicial system. Amen.

*Sherman Manning*

# Dedication: International Action Center

I want to salute the dedicated soldiers for justice who work through the International Action Center in New York City. To Monica Moorehead, Gloria La Riva, Larry Holmes, and the thousands of volunteers out at I.A.C.. I say keep up the great work. No group of people have worked more tirelessly, travelled more miles, put more effort and dedication into the challenge to free *Mumia Abu Jamal* than I.A.C.

This is one of the few organizations courageous, bold and strong enough to stand up to challenge the power structure. And one of the things that touches me the most is the fact that volunteers at I.A.C. respond to prisoners. So many men in prison write to various organizations and never get a reply. Not so with the I.A.C..

I can recall a letter I received from an I.A.C. volunteer by the name of Gery Armsby. Mr. Armsby had never met me but decided to answer my letter just because I was human. His reply reads in part: "Thank you for writing. I received your letter...... We have a special fund here at *Worker's World* to subsidize subscriptions for people in your situation. I have taken the liberty of making sure that You get the newspaper weekly....... I hope to see your book someday. As you may know, we cover the U.S. "In-Justice" system very heavily in our newspaper, so it is a subject I have great interest in.... Let me know if there are any political books you would like me to get for you. Stay strong and keep *hungering for justice.* We will win some day. Don't forget there are so many fighters with you in spirit.." Gery Armsby.

Again this was from a man who had never met me. This is true brotherly love. This is the kind of spirit which runs through the hearts of members of I.A.C. all over America and throughout the world. You'll read quite a bit about I.A.C. in this book. I.A.C. members have broken the voice of silence. They speak out and are not intimidated into silence by politics. They question wrong without hesitation. They tell the truth at the risk of losing social prestige, friends and even life. I salute them.

*Sherman Manning*

# Dedication: Bishop T.D. Jakes

False prophets! Phonies! Crooks! Money hungry wolves in sheeps clothing etc. I talk about them in my books. Nobody knows a Doctor like another Doctor. And I talk about preachers, not out of hate, but love. I love preachers because I was called to preach at the age of six. By the time I was 18 years old, I had preached for Reverend Jasper Williams, Rev. Joseph Wells, A. Lincoln, James Leroy Elliott, etc. etc. I lived to preach and I preached for my life. My calling was in my blood, my body and in my soul. The more I travelled, the more corruption, hypocrisy and gamesmanship I saw. And now that I am (Literally) in Joseph's predicament, I can see things that even then I couldn't see. I worked with Ambassador Andrew Young, Rev. Hosea Williams, marched with Jesse Jackson and John Lewis. And now I am in prison - seems like everybody has forgotten who I am. Preachers know better. "I was hungry and you fed me not... In prison and you visited me not... In as much as you've done unto the, least of these my breathen, you've done it also unto me..." Henry B. Lyons was President of the National Baptist Convention, all preachers took his calls. Now he is the least of these - nobody wants to talk to him. How soon we forget. I want to tell the world that Bishop T. D. Jakes is a tall timber in the forest of Christian Preachers. Bishop Jakes is a man on a mission for God. And he unlike many Big Shot Preachers, is a man not too big to preach in prisons. Recently he shook up San Quentin with "Prison Shaking Truths!" Bishop Jakes is a man who has an anointing on his ministry unlike anything I have ever witnessed. His ministry is reaching our people who really need it.      He's not just preaching to the choir. I *Thank God* for the work he is doing through Bishop Jakes and *The Potter's House* in Dallas Texas. You'll read numerous quotes from Bishop Jakes in this book. To Bishop Jakes, I say *keep on walking and keep on preaching.*

*Sherman Manning, February 2004*

114

# The Trial Lawyer of the Century

Johnnie Cochran filed a 2 Billion Dollar lawsuit. He sought one of the largest verdicts ever rendered in an American courtroom.

"Attorney Murray Janus please," Mr. Cochran spoke into the receiver. About three seconds later, Murray was on the telephone. "I need your help." Johnnie told Murray, "You are according to Bobby Lee Cook, the: Clarence Darrow of Richmond Virginia. I'm putting together a Superstar team of lawyers to help me file a $2 Billion Dollar lawsuit. Barry Scheck, Gerry Spence, F. Lee Bailey, Michael Snedeker, Gerald Uelmen, Charles Ogletree, and David Cole are on the team. Willie Gary has loaned us ten of his investigators. Ron Sanders of the NAACP is with us, and we're also consulting with Leon Friedman and David Boies out of New York. I don't want to talk over the phone, can you fly to the West Coast tomorrow?"....

"What the hell have I gotten into" Murray mumbled to himself as he cruised down Broad Street in Richmond Virginia. "I'm flying to L.A. and I have absolutely no idea what kind of case this is."......

## 9 MONTHS LATER

It was D-Day. Scheck, Spence, Lee Bailey, Snedeker, Uelmen, Olgetree, Cole, Janus and Cochran were all in court. The *Supreme Court* of the State of California. Willie Gary flew in. "Johnnie, I had to come when I heard that you and Janus flipped a coin to decide who would make the oral argument. I know *you must* have had a double headed coin." Johnnie smiled, "Murray is excellent, but I'm the best. This will be the defining moment of my entire career. I don't really expect to win, but just the media attention alone over the past nine months is a victory for our people. And the fact that some of the most pre-eminent Black, White, and Jewish Lawyers are working Pro Bono *with us* is a dream come true.

## ONE HOUR LATER

"Hear ye, Hear Ye, the Supreme Court of the State of California is now in session."

*Here's* Johnnie. "Thank you so kindly. We have brought this class action law suit against the State of California. We have named Governor Gray Davis as a defendant. Yet really, the defendant is really the entire State of California. We should have named George W. Bush and John Ashcroft as defendants also. The plaintiffs are all in prison. We are suing on behalf of every innocent prisoner trapped in the bowels of the California Prison System. Not just the Black and Hispanic prisoners, but also the poor White prisoners. They too have had their rights viciously trampled upon by the State system of justice in California. This law suit is about more than two billion dollars, it is about retraining every Police Officer out on the beat. It involves a desire to see every California Prison Guard undergoing sensitivity and diversity training. It is about every Renegade and Rogue Cop and Sheriff in Sacramento being fired and sent to jail. It is a far reaching and widespread system of unequal. unfair, biased, racist and bigoted judicial system that we seek to transform. Is there anybody on the court today who knows what it is like to be Black or Brown or White and poor in America; and to encounter the criminal justice system? The bottom line today is that there is *no equal justice* for poor folks in this country. This law suit is about the poor and down trodden, the left out, the locked in and the forgotten about. Blacks, Hispanic, and poor Whites, Asians, Jews and Gentiles being warehoused, abused and beaten in prisons all across America. Most especially here in California. This is about the dirtiness, the racism, and the classism of the L.A.P.D., the Police and State Troopers across California. The Sacramento Police Department and Sheriff s Department. This is about crime and punishment. As Justice Hugo Black wrote more than forty years ago: "There can be no equal justice where the kind of trial a man gets depends on the amount of money he has."

The majority of those in prison are poor; Black, White, Brown and Asians. Forty two percent of prisoners can not *read,* and sixty nine percent of prisoners did not have jobs when they were locked up. The per capita incarceration numbers amongst Blacks is seven times more than amongst Whites. Blacks make up thirteen percent of the general population, but more than half of the jail and prison population. Blacks serve longer prison sentences, have higher conviction and arrest rates.

Blacks (and Hispanics) have higher bail amounts, and are more often the helpless victims of police killings than Whites are. In 1995, one in three Black men were in prison or on parole. If incarceration trends continue, one in four Black males born today will serve time in prison during their life span. For every one Black man who goes to college in America, *100 go to jail!*

Seventy six percent of illicit drug abusers are White, twelve percent are Black, and seven percent are Hispanic. Yet, Blacks make up thirty percent of all drug arrests, fifty eight percent of all drug related convictions, and an astounding seventy seven percent of all prison sentences for drugs. In Baltimore, Blacks are six times more likely to be arrested than Whites for drug related offenses. In Columbus Ohio, Black men are less than ten percent of the population, but account for more than ninety one percent of drug arrests. In Jacksonville Florida, Black men are eleven percent of the population, but eighty nine percent of drug arrests. In Minneapolis, Black men are arrested at twenty one times the rate for Whites."

U.S. Attorney General, John Ashcroft stood up to apparently object. "Sit down John, this is my time," stated Johnnie Cochran. One of the Justices stated, "Mr. Ashcroft, we appreciate your presence as well at that of the *Christian Coalition*, Pat Robertson, Rush Limbaugh and our State Attorney General. But you'll get a chance to rebut. For now, please be seated."

Johnnie was sweating, I looked at Murray Janus, Barry Scheck, Michael Snedeker and the other members of the Dream Team and they all looked stoic. Rush Limbaugh whispered to someone sitting next to him, "These bastards did their homework."

"Continuing on," Johnnie said, "Not very long ago when we heard `Three strikes and you're out' we thought about baseball games. Now it poses under the guise of a Correctional Philosophy. The law is draconian, deceptive, misleading, bigoted and racist. It was sold to Californian's as a way to rid our streets of *violent* rapists and killers. But lets look at it. Jerry Dewayne Williams received a twenty five year to life sentence for stealing a slice of pizza in L.A.. Another young man received 25 to Life for stealing five bottles of liquor in a grocery store. Alan Stark got 25 to Life for stealing 4 cartons of cigarettes. In its first two years, California law resulted in Life sentences for twice as many weed smokers as murderers, kidnappers, and rapists combined. A CDC study reports that **88** percent of men sentenced under the three strikes law were convicted most recently of a non-violent crime. Robert Washington received 25 to Life for a minor drug possession charge; his prior offenses were two 8 year old burglaries and an intervening possession of contraband. *What's going on?* The California prison and jail population has increased by 195.6 percent and as Barry Scheck can tell you, many of these men are innocent. Most are Black and Hispanic. All are poor. And the California prison system is a monster factory. There is absolutely no rehabilitation in those warehouses. These are some of the most violent, abusive and vicious prisons on the planet. Men go here and get abused, assaulted and even raped by staff and inmates alike. Once men go to prison in California, they get schooled in racism, abuse, how to commit more crime."

"In Governor Davis' prison system, they get depressed, demoralized, sicker, slicker, and when they get out they return quicker.. Governor Davis' prisons are *producing* rapists, killers, and predators.

"For racial profiling, criminal profiling, false arrests, police abuse, unfair trials, railroading and scape goating; the allure of the entire criminal justice system of the State of California."

"No poor man (and this includes poor Whites, Blacks, Hispanics, and Asians) can get a fair trial in California. And the State provides them with overworked, under qualified, and under educated Public Defenders for trial. The State provides them with overworked, under qualified, and under educated Public Defenders only through the first level of appeals. But the rich have hired lawyers to appeal their convictions through *nine levels* of review. Poor Mexicans, Blacks, and Whites are abandoned and left to die in prison; often for crimes they did not commit. Because they can't afford a lawyer. *What is going on?*

"This is wrong! Therefore, on *this day* - October 25, 2004, on behalf of the poor, on behalf of every poor prisoner, especially those who are trapped in jails and prisons for crimes they did not commit; we seek punitive and compensatory damages in the amount of $2 Billion Dollars. Not only that; we want all 33 California prisons to be seized by Federal Marshals. We want education, workshops, and seminars in the prisons. We want every inmate who is serving more than a 20 year sentence to come under review by a Task Force headed by Judge Barry Loncke. We also want a *truth* and *innocence* Blue Ribbon Committee established immediately. The committee is to be headed by Professor David Cole, Professor Robert Cling and Attorney Van Jones. The committee will review the transcripts of every prisoner in the prisons who claim to be innocent to determine whether or not a reduction in his sentence, a new trial, or an overturning of his sentence is warranted.... One Billion Dollars of the Two Billion Dollars we seek will go directly to poor communities and barrios. This money will be utilized to mentor, tutor, and educate poor Whites, Hispanics, and Blacks in the hoods, to keep them from joining the prison ranks. We demand that every Police Officer, Sheriff and Correctional Officer in this State undergo retraining, sensitivity and diversity training beginning next month."

"We demand," Johnnie Cochran had tears in his eyes. I looked at Willie Gary, Barry Scheck, Murray Janus, Mr. Snedeker etc., etc., and the stoicism had vanished. they were all crying. Believe it or not, Rush Limbaugh had removed the smart ass smirk from his face. Even Rush appeared shaken.

"Entire communities have been robbed of men because we are sending them to jails and prisons. It costs more to send a man to jail that it does to send him to Yale. Every Black man, every Hispanic man, every poor White man in this State is now considered an *endangered species*. They are in *danger* of being stuck up, beat up and set up by Police Officers. They are endangered by the price of justice in this State. They are threatened by the *political ambitions* of a government and judiciary system that would rather incarcerate them in their twenties than educate them in their teens. They are *victims* of a government and a system which would rather place handcuffs on their wrists, and shackles on their ankles than to put books in their hands and shoes on their feet. They are the victims of the bigotry and the hypocrisy of ambitious politicians who are willing to spend more on incarceration than higher education. Victims of politicians who pass Draconian laws which disproportionately oppress and affect only the poor; but will pardon a rich White man in a heartbeat. Victims of a system which kept an innocent Geronimo Pratt warehoused for 27 years in prison for a crime he did not commit. Victims of the abuse, vindictiveness and cold bloodedness of politicians who shape public policy based on the results of private polls. Dr. Martin Luther King Jr. said that, 'Injustice anywhere is a threat to justice everywhere.' Dr. King dreamed of equality in a nation where all men are created equal. Yet his dream of a *beloved* community has been catapulted into a nightmare of a prison state. It has been transformed into a nightmare where *unequal* justice is the norm and innocence is stolen at birth if your Black, Brown or poor. Just look around at the poverty, the crime, the hurt, the sorrow, and the shameful conditions of the inner and urban communities. How can any man pull himself up by his own boot straps when he has no boots? These poor men who are forced to work for slave wages in these prisons *never had a chance.* They didn't just make a mistake, they were born into a mistake. I want every Justice sitting on the court today to look at the Blacks, Browns, and poor Whites in our jails and prisons and say, 'There but for the grace of God go I.' We demand that you open all the jail cells and set the innocent free. We demand that justice roll down like waters and righteousness like a mighty stream. WE demand equal justice, equal protection under the law. We........" Cochran neared his climax. "We are tired now. As a matter of law, we want protection. And when we come to a point and time when Black and Brown men are *afraid* of the very people who are sworn to serve and protect; we are not *one nation,* indivisible under God. When we have come to a point where we readily send 16, 17, & 18 year old babies to adult jails and prisons and we allow them to be beat and forcibly sodomized by men serving Life sentences; we are worse than Hitler. Governor Davis' 33 prisons are laboratories of hatred, racism, violence and sodomy. Every single day of the week; we send children off to prison and leave them there to die. When they complain, when they write politicians, etc., they are ignored because nobody gives a damn. And many of them, in fact, most of them will get out one day. In fact, 614,000 of them are going to be released *This Year* and I am afraid of them. And you should fear them also. But the *fact* of the *fear* is our fault. Because we are responsible for allowing the prison subculture to become subhuman. It does not take a Rocket Scientist to figure out that if you send a man to prison at age 17 or 18 for a minor crime, and that man goes to a place where there are true murderers, true rapists, and predators, and that young man lives in fear of being stabbed, killed and raped every day. And that young man is offered the option of joining a prison gang or becoming a prison faggot, that man will exit prison a worse man than when he entered prison.

The man who killed Jimmie Lee Byrd in Texas by chaining him to his truck and dragging him to death; that man was not a racist until he went to prison. In prison he was taught hatred, racism, anger, violence, and rage. He was taught by the inmates and he was also taught by staff... This law suit is about equal protection and justice for all of God's children. On behalf of these men who are in fear of being beat, raped, and stabbed as I speak to you, we seek justice for all. On behalf of every person in Governor Davis' prisons who entered prison with a few years sentence and was forced by gangs to commit another crime or die; and now has more time in prison.... We seek justice, no longer shall we allow their cries to go unheard. No longer shall we allow these letters to go unanswered. No longer shall we allow these prisons to be like the days of slavery or a modern day holocaust. Our babies, boys and girls, are crying. They can't understand why we treat them so bad. It just can't go on like this. Where is our compassion? When will we temper justice with mercy? When will we remember that the *least of these* are still human beings. I accuse the criminal justice system and all 33 of Mr. Davis' prisons of being an accessory to rapes, assaults and murders. This is wrong. Some of the cruelest and unfairest rulings ever rendered in criminal courts are transpiring right here in California. We demand justice, demand equality, we demand a change. This is wrong. the California Department of *Corrections* is *so wicked* that we should change the name to the California Department of *Corruption.* I won't stand by and let it happen any longer. Every time we take a man's life, we wreak havoc on the entire family and the entire community. Black men, Hispanic men, Asian men, and even poor White men have been wronged, cheated, mistreated, and devastated by the severe injustice and inequality of the system of so-called justice in California. We demand..."

Johnnie Cochran before the Supreme Court of the State of California. Wouldn't that be awesome? Spike Lee, John Singleton, Steven Spielberg??? Denzel Washington? You've just read the only fiction in this tome. The following pages are non-fiction, real life, true and authentic. Hopefully, art imitates life. Now read the real deal.

*Sherman Manning, February 2004*

# P.S.A.

Lots of you criticized Book *One* for two major reasons. I had suspected I'd be criticized for tautology and repetitiveness. I was wrong. The two reason you criticized me were for (A) *Failing* to send copies of the tome to movers and shakers. And, (B) Failing to write more words of encouragement to wrongly convicted guys in prison. I've taken my medicine and corrected those errors. Bill Cosby, Chris Gardner, Magic Johnson, Sean "P. Diddy" Combs, Queen Latifah, F. Lee Bailey, Donald K. Wilson Jr., Dion-Cherie Raymond, Billy Martin, and many others are receiving copies of the tome. Doug Banks, Tommy Goss, Van Jones, activist and grass roots groups are getting this book. Yet, I need *your* (the readers) help in getting this to our youth, churches and college professors across the country. Please put the word out!! If you are interested in an easy read or a politically *correct* type book, I must warn you now. *YOU GOT THE WRONG BOOK BABY!!* This book does not flow. It breaks writer's rules etc., etc., because it is written for folks like Chris Gardner, Spike Lee, Murray J. Janus, Gerry Spence, Van Jones, 3 Em, Youth Making A Change and law students etc.. It is written for folks who *care* about our America, the judicial system, the prisons, the courts, corruption in high places and how you can make a difference. I have absolutely no desire to win any awards for this book. I'm not attempting to soothe anyone's conscience or make any new friends. I am writing to (and for) Susan Taylor, Earl Graves, Bill Gates, Jeff Bezos, Ted Kennedy and Mr. George W. Bush. I intend to *embarrass* Robert Altman, Mary Hanlon Stone, Debbie Glynn, and corrupted prosecutors across America. I aim to motivate or inspire Mike Snedeker, F. Lee Bailey, Gerald Uelmen, Bobby Lee Cook, Barry Tarlow, Julian Bond, law professors and students across this country. I am sick and tired of rhetoric, arm-chair revolutionaries, slick politicians, and lazy public defenders. People are hurting, angry, depressed and dismayed and they need help! One way to help yourself is by *activity.* I shall endeavor to expand on that word *activity* in coming pages. If you are angry with the F.B.I. for losing your guns (which have been used in crimes) and the bungling of investigations. If you're angry about police brutality in New York, Cincinnati, and L.A.. If you are tired of predators getting out of prison and killing, raping, robbing and molesting children. If you want guilty men to be punished, but *innocent* and falsely convicted men to be released; you are holding the right book in your hands. I definitely need you to help me get my tome to the Stephen Brights, Charles Ogletree's, Rubin "Hurricane" Carter's, and Alan Dershowitz's of our society. And I am very interested in this book being disseminated to organizations which specialize in helping our youth. I'm fed up with people who see a problem and throw a word, a sound bite or a prayer at the problem. I want to reach out to people who will rise up and do something. Great trial lawyers such as Willie Gary, Morris Dees, and Barry Scheck Are the guys whose lives (dedication, brilliance, and perseverance) inspired me to write *this* book. Also my former close association with Ambassador Andrew Young and Martin Luther King (Chief Field General) aide, Rev. Hosea Williams has impacted this writing. I can remember viewing Craig Kielburger on *Sixty Minutes.* Later I also watched Craig as he was interviewed on Oprah. Craig is only 18 years old now, but he has been *fighting* to free the children, stop the exploitation of children and to *change the world* since he was only 12 years old. Craig was a normal middle class White kid from the suburbs. But this suburban White kid was transformed into an activist who fights against child labor on the world wide stage of *International Human Rights.* Craig read a story of stolen innocence in the newspaper when he was in the seventh grade. The very next day Craig asked his grade school teacher if he could have a few minutes to speak to the class. Craig strolled to the front of the classroom to speak to the 30 students. "I was wondering if anyone read the article on the front page of the *Toronto Star,*" he asked the class. He had made photocopies of it and passed it around the classroom. "So here is the issue, I don't know a lot about it, but I want to learn more. Maybe some of us could start a group to look at it together. Who wants to join?" Eighteen hands went up and Craig said, "We can all meet at my house tonight." And over soda pops and potato chips, those kids founded "Free The Children," six years ago. It is now one of the largest most powerful youth groups in the world. Craig *took action.* His business card says, "Kids can free the children" and "Today's youth, today's leaders." In a recent missive to me, Craig writes, "Thanks for your wonderful letter.... I am truly touched by your words and extremely happy that you enjoyed the book, "Free The Children",.... I would be thrilled if you are interested in becoming involved in our efforts. It would be a wonderful idea to organize American prisoners to become involved in such a worthy cause. I never realized that there were *two million* people in prison in the United States! Through writing letters, signing petitions, and fundraising, incredible change can come....."

This *young man* is a leader and it is my goal in this book to not only highlight the work of brilliant trial lawyers, expose the evils of the prison system and lambaste the asinine system of *Justice in America.* But one of my strongest intentions is to inspire, stir up, motivate and touch the youth of our world. I want to inspire all the **youth** who are already using their voices to make America better; to keep on keeping on. I want to inspire troubled youth to *find a cause* and get active. I want to reach out and touch our young people who are in gangs, using drugs, and in jails, to *turn around now.* And I also want Lil White Boys in middle class suburbia to hook up with Lil Black, Mexican, and other boys in the Hoods and to *Raise The Roof* with their energy and their enthusiasm. So we must not preach to the choir. Wherever you are (today) *reading my words*; I want you to get a copy of this book to a young person. Get it to college students. Let us work through this book to get our young people involved in social change. Let us tell them about Craig, Farrah Gray, 3 Em, Youth Making a Change and *Revolution.* Drug dealers bombard our kids with drugs and guns every day. So it is time we bombard our kids with books, Bibles, newsletters and tools for self improvement everyday. Even if we need to give them incentives to *read,* write and study; we must become innovative in our approaches to reaching our youth.

If we are truly going to leave *no child behind,* we need to wake up before it's too late. If *we* the celebrities, we the preachers, we the taxpayers, we the Christians, or we the Jews don't begin now to reach our children., I can assure you that politicians and police have a place for them. That place is a cold jail cell. That place is a monster factory, that place is evil, dangerous, and full of predators.

So now I reach out here and now to every High School, College and young person who is reading this book. I reach out to the Law Students, Journalism Students, and medical Students alike. To you I say, *Use Your Life.* I also reach out to teens trapped in gangs and hooked on drugs. To you who are hurting and you who feel helpless, I want you to know that you can make it. I know that life can be difficult and *your* spirit has been broken. But don't give up. I want you to *know* that your human mind has enormous capacity to adjust to trying and depressing circumstances. You can bear the unbearable if you can keep your spirit strong even in the midst of confusion. Your spirit can be full even when your stomach is empty. You can rise above any circumstance if you just reach inside yourself and tap the power of your spirit force. Don't give up. Being on drugs is bad, but not hopeless. Being in Juvenile or dropping out of school is not hopeless. Being a middle class kid with a void or emptiness in your life is not a time or a reason to give up . Struggling through college or law school is not the time to give up. As you sit there reading these words, I believe you will be inspired, motivated, propelled encouraged to *Go To Your Destiny.* I want young folks to help get this book to Michael Holt (middle school teacher in Sacramento California), Jonathan Peck and Joseph Shalaby (U.C. Barbara Students), to Michael Taketa (Sacramento California), Farrah Gray, Steven Cozza (Peteluma California), Eric Dane (Actor), Coolio, Seth Gray (Folsom California), youth in the suburbs, youth in jails and to the youth in the hoods. Tell everybody you know about this book. Lets get *busy* here an now. If you never ever read another book in your lifetime ~ read *this one.* It is important that you read this and every lawyer needs to read this. I am often accused of being an *incurable* optimist. Pessimism is not a companion of mine. Yet, in a more contradictory fashion and manner, I must admit that I have very little faith in politicians and so-called leaders. Perhaps I'm merely burnt out on sound bite, knee jerk, hypocritical reactionaries. So if any of the older *leaders,* movers and (so-called) shakers take *action* after reading this book I shall consider it a miracle. But you who are young, energetic and ready to rumble. You who want to rebuild America and build the beloved community. You who want to see *Justice Roll Down Like Waters AND Righteousness Like A Mighty Stream.* I challenge you to kick off your shoes and read on. You will find names, telephone numbers and addresses to organizations, lawyers, youth groups etc. in this book which are ready and willing to revolutionize America, the media, the courts, and the communities as we know them. Let me tell you that if you never *write* me a letter, it's all good. I can live with that.

But I want you to write, call, and support youth making a change, Jews For Justice, Justact, 3 EM, The Innocence Project, and many other organizations which are mentioned in this book. I want you to Fax, E-Mail, and call Governors, Senators and Congressmen and to demand action on the issues which are discussed in this tome. If you do nothing for me, it is (quite frankly) all right. But please *do something for somebody* else. Jesse Jackson said that, "We may not have come over on the same ships, but we are all in the same boat." Martin Luther King Junior said, "We are all caught in an inescapable bond of mutuality. Whatever affects one directly, affects all indirectly." Craig Kielburger says, "I am from a Canadian organization called *Free The Children.* It was formed by kids, it's led by kids and kids run it. You don't necessarily *have to wait* for your principal. You could start your own group and begin taking action......." So I say to Murray J. Janus, Attorney Van Jones, Barry Tarlow, F. Lee Bailey, and all of you legal thespians whom I feature in this book to *share your book* with a law student. You law students *share your book* with high school students and I guarantee you we will see people in high and low places begin to come together. I know what can happen when people pass a book around, discuss it in groups, write about it and take action on it. So to each of you who is reading right now; *share your book.* It is oozing full and running over with shocking, surprising, and unique information. I wrote it with my *heart* and not with my *head.* There are no ghostwriters here, it's just me. These are my words. Are you ready? **Read on............**

"As long as the world shall last, there will be wrongs, and if no man objected and no man rebelled, those wrongs would last forever."
*- Clarence Darrow*
(I think Clarence Darrow had great men such as Barry Scheck, Johnnie Cochran, and Roy Black in mind. He *knew them* before their time.)

"I've never been one for *inaction.* Everything I've ever felt strongly about, I've *done something* about. I guess that's why, unable to do anything else, I soon began writing........."
*- Malcolm X (1924-1965)*

"As an Attorney, I could be rather Flamboyant in court. I did not act as though I were a Black man in a White man's court, but as if everyone else - White and Black - was a guest in my court."
*- Attorney (President) Nelson Mandela*

**"...The three judges rose above their prejudices, their education, and their background. There is a streak of goodness in men that can be buried or hidden and then emerge unexpectedly."**
*- President Nelson Mandela*

"There is a little bit of the spirit of God running through the veins of every human being."
*- AmbassadorAndrew Young*

# My Personal Search

Today is May 28, 2003 and I wish to provide a kind of update on some of the issues pertaining to questions which hundreds of you write to me and call my office inquiring about.

Allow me to confirm that approximately 48 pages are *missing* from the book you are reading right now! We were challenged and met a multiplicity of stumbling blocks and pitfalls on the road to putting this book into your hands. Candidly, I almost didn't put this book in your hands. CDC has stolen about 48 pages of my book. The book will appear incomplete. I can't proofread it, correct errors, etc. and can't even see the galleys before it is printed and published. I can't organize it chronologically and structure it in its proper fashion because CDC literally stole it and I don't even know which pages they stole.

Did they steal the pages about Rocky (Gilbert Salazar) being murdered by his celly (Frank Christian) and CDC covering it up as a suicide? Are they livid because I revealed that Frank Christian should never have had a cell partner due to the fact that he had already murdered one celly before Rocky? (This happened in latter 2002 and CDC kept it out of the media). What's missing? I can't put this book out! I wrote to Attorney Murray J. Janus.

"Reverend, breathe easy. They want you to give up. Martin Luther King, Jr. published his letter from a Birmingham jail cell by any means necessary. He wrote it on the ledges of newspapers because he had no writing tablets. But the missive changed the country and mobilized ministers. Mr. President Nelson Mandela buried his manuscript in a prison garden and hid it for a year, etc., etc. But it was published six years later and changed the world as he described his 'long walk to freedom'. Reverend, you absolutely must allow *American Dream/A Search to Justice* to be published. Whether pages are missing or not, you will give us lawyers, judges, prosecutors, and students an inside look at America's penological system. Publish it! Get it on Amazon.com and Barnes & Noble and sooner or later it will become a runaway bestseller. With just the 126 pages you asked me to read, I know this *is your best* book ever!"

"I can *feel* your writing this time. I am willing to bet you that my friends Gerry Spence, Alan Dershowitz, Ephraim, Barry Tarlow and Blair Berk *will read this book* and they'll talk about it."

"Pastors will preach about it, professors will teach about it and singers will sing about it. You put that damned book out or *I'll* publish it," Attorney Janus wrote to me.

Ipso facto, you're holding this in your hands now... In "If It Doesn't Fit, You Must Acquit", the revised edition, I wrote about the *meanness* of a counselor (who is now a CCII) and her husband. Well, her husband temporarily acted as facility captain on our yard. He clearly retaliated against me for the exercising of my constitutional right to free speech and artistic expression in *that* book.

On April 3, 2003 I saw a Black inmate being escorted by two cops. "I hope that Officer Donald Deane (pseudonym) was not involved because he likes to beat up on Brothers," I stated. "What did you say Manning?" C.O.D. Deane asked. I repeated my words. A few minutes later the acting captain (who is really a lieutenant who was the prison spokesman and who failed the captain's test) ordered them to "lock Manning up"! The officer who reported my words stated, "I only wanted to write Manning a 128 (warning) but Captain *Billy* Brooks (pseudonym) ordered me to write a *serious* 115." And the lieutenant stated, "Manning, I was not gonna lock you up but Captain *Billy* Brooks (pseudonym) ordered me to lock you up." On April 11, 2003 I had an I.C.C. hearing. I looked out and saw A. W. (Associate Warden) Jimmy Walkerton (pseudonym), CCII Jannene Brooks (captain's wife) and Captain *Billy* Brooks.

This committee is an illegal committee. There is a conflict of interest (for all the various reasons) and no way Mr. and Mrs. Brooks should sit (simultaneously) on my committee. A. W. Walkerton stated that my objection was noted and denied and we're gonna retain you in ad-seg pending adjudication of the 115 for inciting inmates. Chief Deputy Warden Harry P. Rosario (pseudonym) is on the Board and backing the Brooks in this decision".... I spent twenty days on suicide watch sleeping on a floor in the infirmary. I was psychologically depressed, "duressed" and stressed by this clear free speech violation and retaliation by the Brooks. It angered, hurt and perturbed me. In ad-seg, the 115 was adjudicated and ("sweet justice") I was blessed, fortunate and lucky enough to get a fair hearing officer. "Not guilty... Why would they put you in the hole for this?" stated the lieutenant. Lt. Billy Hemron (pseudonym) said, "Sherm, you know me! I've found your ass guilty before and have no problem finding you guilty again. But *not this one*! I don't know all of the other things at play here, but there is *no way* anybody can find you guilty on this one." (I heard A.W. Sharon Stylistica (pseudonym) and Captain Brooks raised hell and asked him why he found me not guilty. But when I asked him about it he said, "Sherm, you know I'm not going to discuss any staff issues or comments with you. You're an inmate! But I stand by my decision and I sleep good at night."

There is a God! I am certain that as Pastor Elmore, Floyd Abrams, Mr. Spence and Attorney John Burris are reading this book; you (lawyers at large including Willie Gary and Willie Brown) are thinking of a number of ways in which I should be suing them for retaliation. You have my permission to come on board and help me sue!

Keep in mind that CDC specializes in thwarting justice by getting us to withdraw appeals so we can't take them to court. "Why are so many appeals being withdrawn in these prisons?" is what Steve White ought to be asking. Answer: Because inmates are punished for filing appeals. "Withdraw this or I'll transfer your ass," they say. And "withdraw this or I'll invent a reason to put you in ad-seg and send you to P.H.U. Whatever it takes. I can say I have confidential reasons, you're over-familiar with staff, safety issues, etc., etc. I have total control over your life," Captain Brooks likes to say.

And so I was uprooted and sent to ad-seg for more than forty days for nothing. "Oops, sorry. I guess we made a mistake. You can go back to A- G.P.," they say.      C.T.Q.?    Confined To Quarters. They could have allowed me to remain on A-Mainline in my cell while we waited on the 115 to be heard. But they routinely throw people into ad-seg. Captain Brooks' wife was moved to another facility to cure the conflict of interest issue on May 11, 2003 and if anyone believes the staff were pleased with the fact that I exposed the conflict, you're dreaming. They are livid, some of them. But as long as the public continues to monitor closely my well-being within CDC, they won't sic the dogs on me.

"Sometimes people get caught up in the emotions of things. The power and control issues kick in and they get vindictive! When anger controls your actions it often leads to trouble. Even you do it sometimes Mr. Manning. **Billy** (Brooks) clearly blew this! If this case is ever looked at by anybody outside CDC, I know trouble is coming. It's clear retaliation open and shut. And when they transfer you, it will be retaliation! And if (when) you get hurt at Salinas Valley, Mule Creek or some of the other so-called P.C. yards, your family must sue," a CDC (retired) staff member told me. (More on this fiasco in the next tome).

It has been a challenging and difficult month.... I missed calling home on Mother's Day. I love my momma. I want T. D. Jakes, Eddie Long and Attorney Janus to call my mother in Atlanta and tell her "God loves you and Sherman does too!!"

I had a dream in ad-seg about the ceiling caving in on my mother's house! The ceiling sort of blew off in a hurricane. I was on my knees praying and crying. After the hurricane, I saw momma (Cat) and daddy (James) and they were okay. I woke up. As soon as I got out of ad-seg, I called home and Cat (Dollie Manning) told me a bad storm had caused parts of the roof (ceiling) to crumble and cave in. "We're building a new room on the house and the guy doing it... a storm came and where he was working on the house began caving in... etc. Gerald was out repairing it in the middle of the night. The next night it happened again with the bathroom ceiling right next to the master bedroom. If it would have been our bedroom ceiling..."

I cried! God was telling me in the dream that a storm had come to my momma's house. But the Blood (of Jesus Christ) was on our house and I heard the Holy Spirit saying, "any room but not that bedroom". My Lord.

I want to tell the Brothers at Manpower with T. D. Jakes in Atlanta at the Dome Stadium... I need to tell the Brothers and Sisters at "The Potters House" in Dallas, Texas! I feel I got to tell somebody right now who is going through a storm in your life that you can't give up. If the Blood is on your house!! God won't let the devil kill you. "Touch me not". You better call 1 800 Bishop 2 and get "God's Weapons of Mass Destruction" by T. D. Jakes and learn how to put the Blood over your house! Put it over your family, car, airplane or train.

I still believe in the Blood. I can't see any way out right now! The situation looks mighty dark right now! I have seen my grapes of hope crushed into the raisins of despair. I'm way up here in California and I don't know how or when I can get Blair, Tarlow, Uelmen or a Gary to get me out of here.

I can't see my way out. But if I press my way forward and get the folks to pray for me. If I just get Bishop Jakes and Manpower to pray for me! My Lord!

If I get Eddie, Creflo, Rod, Noel and T. D. to pray for me, I know that I'll get out of here. I need prayer. I don't need a sympathetic missive nor do I need, "It's gonna be all right". But I need a prayer warrior to help me pray. If you help me pray for my freedom, I'll get out of this. I'll get out of this! My God is still able to do exceedingly and abundantly above and beyond anything we ask Him to do. There is something about God's power! It transforms lives. I can't die here. Already, I have to keep my mind right. There is nothing like an incarcerated spirit and a locked up mind. I got to dream freedom! I need to talk to somebody right now. I want to tell you that God's word has power! It has wonder-working power!!

I have a Brother here in prison with me who says he doesn't believe in God! He curses if you bring up the name of God! But I manipulated, I tricked and I conned Tu Tu into listening to a tape of Jakes at Manpower "A Prince of Egypt" and my God! I feel like shouting right now! I said I want to shout right now! I need somebody to call, write, e-mail and inform "The Potters House" in Dallas that whatever they do, they keep that big old bald-headed, Black Joker T. D. Jakes on TV. Did you hear me? A man who hates God listened to Jakes and God started working on Tu Tu! Amen! Praise the Lord!! The next day I saw tears in his eyes!! He said, "This Brother is deep! I listened to him twice! I wanna hear some more of his tapes!!!"

Somebody shout Hallelujah! God is still in the saving business! The heart of the king is in God's hand. I need to tell somebody right now!!! Don't give up! Don't quit the fight! Stay on your knees and keep the Blood over your house.

I..........

# American Dream, A Search for Justice

With what you have already read in this book is it still so difficult to understand how/why the prison system in California is in such a shameful condition when we have a guard's union, which will adamantly defend any guard accused of any crime, no matter how much evidence the authorities have against them?

Whenever (if ever) the Federal Authorities take a close, undercover look and examination of prisons such as Mule Creek, Lancaster, Calapatria, Corcoran SATF, etc. they will find Civil Rights violations, KKK member prison guards, promotions, scams and racism at the highest levels of C.D.C. And they will also encounter some of the most violent, deadly, treacherous and vicious predators whom they have ever encountered, not the kept but rather the keepers.

C.D.C. prison authorities routinely, vindictively, capriciously and arbitrarily transfer in/out any inmate(s) whom they get angry with.

"If Manning keeps on writing books and bringing heat on us, transfer him. Doctor (fraudulently) the paperwork to show he has no enemies at whatever prison we send him to. Just get rid of him, as we did Marvin Johnson, Berry and all the other litigators," one staff member said... Mail update? As of September 18, 2002, we are now receiving mail, which is twenty-nine and thirty days old when we get it. This is a threat to safety and security. Inmates borrow from each other and promise to pay back at canteen (store call). And when the check or money order their family members sent them arrives thirty days late - they miss store call, can't pay their bills and are often attacked, stabbed and even killed for their outstanding bills. Our present mailroom supervisor makes it clear, "I can't be fired. I'm untouchable." And he continues to run one of the slowest and most inefficient mailrooms in the state.

Smoking: Although all tobacco has been taken from inmates at New Folsom, staff continues to puff away in our face everyday. And the inmates who are addicted to nicotine, receive absolutely no assistance at all. C.D.C. created another avenue for corruption, extortion and violence by taking away tobacco.

One cigarette now sells for $4.00 on the yard. Where do inmates get them from? Prison staff. It is a fact that "cigarettes are given and sold to inmates *by staff* everyday" one source revealed.

For the life of me I cannot understand how/why we allow C.D.C. to get away with this. To allow staff to routinely smoke cigarettes in our presence (mental torture, cruel and unusual, second hand smoke, etc.) Yet stop inmates from being allowed to smoke; cold turkey...

Why do they do it? Because *they can* and because they feel that nobody gives a damn about "those people" in prison.

Yet, I believe that (thanks to Officer Neal Leash and the likes of him) the people are waking up to the reality that the violence and corruption we see *in prisoners* is a microcosm or a reflection of the violent and vicious nature of the *keepers* of the *kept.*

Prisons are dark, cold and lonely places. But men such as Harvey Silvergate and Andrew Good are the forces for justice which cause the wrongfully convicted to keep hope alive. The firm of Silvergate and Good spent many hours per week working pro bono on the case of Dr. Jeffrey R. MacDonald who is the so-called "Green Beret" or "Fatal Vision" killer. (More on this case in my next book - I'm waiting on Josh Gewolb in Mr. Good's law firm to rush me more data). Mr. Good and Mr. Silvergate are shining examples of what true and authentic lawyers are all about. They will fight until justice rolls down like waters and righteousness like a mighty stream. They work with Barry Scheck's innocence project. I encourage each reader to E-mail Mr. Silvergate and Mr. Good and to tell them to keep up the great work. You may E-mail them at agood@world.std.com. Every now and then I look around and lawyers similar to Mr. Good and Mr. Silvergate mail me a few hundred and sometimes a few thousand dollars and say, "Mr. Manning keep on writing great books about injustice, prisons and the judicial system." Many of them support me (via money) anonymously. And I appreciate each and every check and money order from the lawyers, politicians, advocates and law students who help me.

I salute Mr. Andrew Good, Mr. Silvergate, Gerry Spence, Edwin Spencer Matthews, Jr. and even the underpaid public defenders who fight for justice all over America.

Lord knows there are actually *some* public defenders such as Quin Denvir, Daniel Brodderick and Mr. Clinkenbeard who really do *fight* the good *fight* and secure justice for their clients. Public defenders catch hell because they are under funded and overworked. Many of them become jaded and quite frankly *sell out* their clients. But not all of them.

I think big law firms ought to take notice of the altruism and philanthropy of people such as Edwin Spencer Matthews, Jr., Andrew Good, Mr. Silvergate, Michael Snedeker and Barry Scheck. And they ought to step up to the plate and help public defenders. Take some of their caseloads and fight for the innocent.

Barry Scheck always can use help at Cardoza Law School. Brandon Gene Martinez, Adam Delgadillo, Mumia Abu Jamal and many indigent inmates sitting in concrete cages would be more than blessed if a Gerry Spence, Johnnie Cochran, Dennis Riordin, Donald Masuda or Clyde Blackman stepped in and said, "Brandon Gene Martinez, I'll take your appeal. *You* didn't kill him and you don't deserve to die in prison."

*Some* men in prison *deserve* to be punished but they don't deserve the lengthy sentences, which they are serving.

Guys like Pedro Armando Quant from Nicaragua who barely speak English and were coerced into pleading guilty by lawyers who barely speak Spanish - should not be in prison.

I've come across a lot of guilty men in prison. Many of them committed homicide and fratricide. Many killed their parents and siblings in cold-blooded murder! Many have come to prison and are arrogant, pompous and high-minded as if they did the nation a favor when they committed murder. Many of them have confused their *infamy* with *celebrity*.

But not all of us committed murder. *Not* every man accused of *rape* or child molestation is guilty. *We must* become sensitive to the rights of defendants to get fair trials and adequate representation. This is America!

"*You* should *not* be in prison," Peter wrote me the other day. "I wish Ephraim Margolin, Dennis Riordan, Gerald Uelmen or Andrew Good would take your case and get you *out of there*." Peter wrote. And I shall never, ever give up on my *fight* for justice. I still believe! But the fight for justice is not *limited* to my *personal* battle! It is about *all of us*. "Injustice anywhere is a threat to justice everywhere". I won't truly be free until Brandon G. Martinez is free. Brandon won't truly be free until Mumia Abu Jamal is free. And we can't be *selfish*. We must fight for Pedro Armando Quant! We gotta fight for *justice*! Liberty and justice (*should be*) for all!

I call on every lawyer and law student to get involved with fighting for the innocent. There are *some* evil, decadent and trifling people in prison (staff and inmate alike). And I've met many who should probably *never be free*!!

But I've also met men with psychological disorders and emotional problems, which led to their incarceration. They did not make a mistake they were born into a mistake. And society ought to balance punishment with treatment. We should temper *justice with mercy*.

I'm praying that brilliant men like William Bernhardt in Tulsa, Oklahoma will get back into the line of fire. Will Bernhardt is a masterful writer/author. But Bill is also a defense lawyer. I want readers to read all of Mr. Bernhardt's books and to also E-mail him at Willbern@mindspring.com. Tell Bill we love his books and will continue reading and buying them. But we want him to please join the fight to *free* the innocent! We need Bill to use his pen, which he so artfully utilizes to tell stories in tomes, to also write appellate briefs for the wrongfully convicted.

"What if Mr. Bernhardt wrote your appellate brief as skillfully as he wrote 'Dark Justice'?" Peter asked. I'd be exonerated and vindicated...

It is time for the talented and the powerful, the elite and the brilliant, the skilled and the scholarly to join the struggle to free the innocent.

Join with Rubin "Hurricane" Carter and help *free* the wrongly convicted. I hope each reader reads "The Miraculous Journey of Rubin 'Hurricane' Carter". And if you didn't see the movie "Mr. Hurricane" you must rent the video! Rubin is one of the few who got justice, got out and is now reaching back to help others who are trapped behind barbed wire fences! Rubin needs lawyers to align themselves with his organization and help him to free the innocent. Rubin needs volunteers, money, donations and media coverage. To help Rubin, you can call him in Toronto, Ontario, Canada at (416) 531-8019. Call him and help his association to free the innocent.

I've often reminded readers that I write more from my *heart* than from my head! And I am affected by what I see, hear, feel and read around me. It affects my writing, my tome and my style. I'm feeling another man's pain today. It is (right now) one o'clock in the morning here on the West Coast and I'm burning with anger, tingling with pain and absolutely frightened for another human being here. Robert Williams (a/k/a Wil) is dying! He lives a couple of doors away from me. I've known him more than three years. Robert discovered two months ago that he has lung cancer. What is so sinister is that C.D.C. doctors *knew four* years ago that he had cancer. They never told him! I'll repeat that C.D.C. doctors knew in 1998 that he had cancer and refused to tell him until a couple of months ago. It's too late now. He's dying. This is wrong. I trembled today when he told me he asked his family to come up and basically say goodbye to him... this is not an aberration for C.D.C. There are inmates here dying from hepatitis. We have discovered that C.D.C. *knew* years ago that some of them had contracted hepatitis but refused to tell them. This is a recipe for death. These are the ingredients of murder. I hope some of the trial lawyers reading this tome will call C.D.C. and demand an investigation into its failure to inform, disclose and treat diseased inmates. And be prepared to sue. C.D.C. specializes in covering up, disguising, false documentation and subterfuge. Russell Danser (T-55100) committed suicide on August 18, 2002. His mother came to visit him and died after the visit. It was his birthday. C.D.C. cops ignored his signs of depression and he killed himself. Gary Smith (J-59540) died in prison. He was only twenty-one years old (or twenty-two) and the nurse said he was faking. Twenty-five minutes after the nurse stated he was faking, he died foaming at the mouth. Gary died on August 7, 2002. This was willful, negligence. They threw him into the *hole* instead of putting him in the infirmary. "We don't have bed space for him and he's faking anyway," she said. "Put his ass back in the hole." Twenty-five minutes later Gary Smith (a young man) was no more. And hundreds of inmates die each year in prisons across this country because staff neglects them.

What staff banks on is public apathy toward and concerning *those* predators in prison. It is time for society to acknowledge the humanness of the people in prison. America is a great country. America is a compassionate country. In times of tragedy, pain and disaster - we come together. Well, the prisons are experiencing perilous, torturous and evil times. Lives are being cut short due to a lack of medical care. Men are being carried out in body bags with tags on their toes because prison guards are sleeping on the job, playing cards or watching footfall games on television. I see lieutenants, sergeants and doctors watching television and playing cards *on the job*. I've seen staff members *asleep* on the job. I've seen staff members drunk/intoxicated on the job. Is this what we pay prison guards sixty thousand dollars per year to do?

Today is January 12, 2003 and I'm angry! I am quite frankly livid. My blood is boiling and I am mad. I stopped writing this for weeks. There are perhaps spiritual reasons for the fact that I've not been writing lately, the details of which I won't divulge at this juncture, in this tome. But I will inform you, the reader, that I have been pulled out of my non-writing zone because of a shocking, tragic and catastrophic incident, which transpired Saturday night (January 10, 2003) at New Folsom State Prison. It was horrible, nightmarish and unsettling. Trying to describe it herein via the written word is complicated and quite complex. I don't consider myself a *master* of the *written* word. My critics complain about my rambling and ricocheting writing style. (Yet, of all the monuments and statues,

136

which have been erected, not one of them has been erected for a *critic*). My rambling comes with some benefits (I'm rambling now because you are still waiting to read what happened Saturday night!) such as truth, candor and the uncensored thought processes of an energetic mind. I probably *write* like I preach. I digress, stress, proclaim and prognosticate. And if all the things which my enemies and critics can say about me, being a boring or unenthusiastic speaker, is *not* one of them. The God of Abraham, Isaac and Jacob did bless me (indeed) with the gift of oratory. And when I speak, I try to *reach* people where they are. I try to move their minds, stir their emotions, stimulate, activate, enlighten, inspire, educate and empower. I can't do it without enthusiasm. When I see people hurting, bound mentally, trapped in poverty, full of pain, sorrow and hopelessness, my anointing is activated. And those people do not need three points and a poem. They don't need a quiet lecture, scholarly enunciation or theoretical proclamations. They need somebody who can read their mail and come where they are. They want help! They want hope and inspiration! And it is from my background as an orator, minister, leader and student of public speaking that I do my writing. Maybe (to appease my critics) as I continue to correspond with William Bernhardt (author extraordinaire) and other dramatic writers - I'll learn to structure better. But in the meantime, I shall remain one who writes from my *heart* and not from my *head*... and my heart is troubled tonight. In fact, my anger is simply disguised sorrow, hurt, pain and shock. Saturday night was awful. It was evil. It was criminal and it was preventable.

On Saturday evening, at about 8:00 p.m. numerous inmates heard an inmate yelling and cussing at his cell partner who is inmate Salazar. We call Mr. Salazar, Rocky. The inmates were accustomed to hearing this (Mr. F.C) guy whom I'll call Tommy (pseudonym) yell and raise hell about once per week whenever he was intoxicated. Yes, there is alcohol in every prison in the United States of America. Lots of it! Alcohol, heroin, marijuana, cocaine, speed, etc. are in every (and yes I do mean *every*) prison in the country. So Tommy got drunk once per week and yelled, cussed and fussed. He would do this and then get in bed and sleep it off. When you saw Tommy the next day after a drinking binge, he was an entirely different person.

So none of the inmates who overheard this yelling thought much of it. But most of them (us) did not have a clue as to what C.D.C. knew about Tommy (more on that later) and his past.

One of us decided to send a guy over to check on Tommy and Rocky to see if they were okay. Several guys went over and spoke to

Tommy. No bloodshed or weapons, etc. were visible. And it appeared Tommy was just ranting and raving as usual. By nine o'clock p.m. I was preparing to lock up. I showered and looked over at Tommy's cell. The light was off and it was quiet. I thought to myself "He's sleeping it off. No more noise." A few minutes after I got into my cell, I heard a loud yelling. The C.O. was coming through doing the 9:30 p.m. count. He yelled to the Control Officer (7 Block Control Officer, a facility at New Folsom. I'll use a pseudonym for all of the staff members' names that were involved in this horrific incident. I will note that the cop doing the count was *on his job*. He was professional, competent and quick) to hit the alarm. Hit the alarm. (Unfortunately the cop doing the

count had already turned in his body alarm. I'm not blaming *him* for anything as I've already noted, he did an excellent job. However, I wish he would wait in the future until after he counts to turn in his portable body alarm. The Control Officer was *slow* to respond. It took him at least thirty seconds to hit the alarm. He claims the alarm was malfunctioning. "I couldn't get the alarm to come on for shit," stated Officer Steve. Then the Counting Officer (we'll call him C.O. Gates) yelled, "Call for medical. Call an ambulance and bring some towels." C.O. Gates put on some gloves and (within a minute there were perhaps sixteen officers in the building. The *first* responders ran to A-section although the incident was in B-Section. C.O. Steve who was the Control Cop should have informed the first responders that the alarm was for B-Section). I saw Lieutenant Athens on the tier standing near C.O. Gates. "Cuff up Tommy," C.O. Gates yelled. C.O. Gates placed handcuffs on Tommy. (One must wonder, was this really necessary? Seven Block is not an ad-seg unit. Inmates are not required to have on handcuffs when leaving their cells in this unit, which is called mainline or general population. And when a man is bleeding profusely on the floor and his cell partner is standing there looking - you *might* not need to think about handcuffing an inmate. There was no fighting at that time. Rocky was on the floor bleeding pints of blood. And Tommy was watching. It's safe to assume that sixteen officers with high-powered rifles, pepper spray and batons could handle a drunk Tommy *without* handcuffs).

Nevertheless, once Tommy was handcuffed, C.O. Steve still would not open the cell door. "Steve open the door," C.O. Gates yelled with Lt. Athens standing nearby. One minute passed. Two minutes passed. I'm looking on and Gates is yelling to Steve for a gurney, towels, medical staff and to "Open the damn door." The gurney comes, but no towels. Finally, after four minutes and thirty two seconds, biohazard uniforms arrive. Gates and other officers put on the uniforms along with the gloves, which they've had on all along, and *then* C.O. Steve (Seven Block Control Cop) opens the door. They walk Tommy out and throw little Rocky (Rocky is his real a/k/a and Salazar is his authentic last name) is thrown onto a gurney. I see the MTA with no towels. A nurse just standing there. Nobody put a towel on his wound. They just threw him on the gurney and rushed him out. My celly and I are looking out the windows. I'm praying "God be with him in the name of Jesus Christ." Before they get Rocky out of the section, we see him raise up in a very jerky fashion and I mumble, "That's the last bit of life in him fighting." "He's breathing," C.O. Gates had yelled earlier. They take him out... my celly and I immediately began praying. We prayed separately and we prayed together. We prayed and prayed and prayed.

A while later, C.O. Gates finally came by to complete his count. "How bad is he," I asked. "He's bad," he told me. I saw alarm, fear and *care* in this man's eyes. At the eleven o'clock count, I asked another cop, "How is Salazar? Is he alive?" The cop said, "I don't know. He's at the hospital." And I asked, "Can you find out please?" My celly and I prayed some more. At 11:25 p.m. Saturday night, I saw the administrator of the day, S&I (Special Investigations Unit) and other higher ups coming in. "They called them at home?" Brandon asked. "Yes, anytime there is a violent incident, they call the A.O.D," I told him.

One cop came near my door and I said, "Hey C.O. , he didn't die did he?" And the cop said, "Yeah, we lost him." I banged on the door and let out a loud "My God!" When I turned around, Brandon was on his knees praying. I lost my composure and began to sob. I cried. Brandon was apparently also in tears.

After much prayer and some somber discussion, I tried to get some sleep at about 1:00 a.m. I tossed and turned. All I could see was Rocky rising up off that gurney fighting for life. I couldn't sleep. "I can't sleep," I told Brandon. "Give me the "Justice: Denied" magazine and let me read please." I read "Justice: Denied" (a magazine for the wrongly convicted. It is an awesome magazine also available via the Internet. Log on to www.justicedenied.org). I read for hours and prayed more. I couldn't watch Saturday Night Live when Rocky was dead.

I began to do what most people do when they're hurting. I blamed, I even wondered should I have gone to get the cops when I heard Tommy cussing at 8:00 p.m.! Let me state candidly that this question shall forever be in my mind on some level and in some sense.

I shall also admit that I wish I had gone and told a cop that Tommy was drunk, cussing and yelling. I fully admit this *here* and *now* beyond all doubt. Having said that I will also admit that had I or any of the guys who heard him gone to tell the cops, there is a ninety-nine percent chance that no action would have been taken (by the cops). They see drunks all the time. They don't (perhaps they should) move inmates or throw them in the hole for being drunk or yelling. I can truly write that more than likely the cops would have done absolutely nothing. But I would feel much (much) better if I had gone and told them anyway! The only reason I can sleep is because I *know me*. And I know that *if* I had thought anybody was going to get hurt, cut, stabbed or killed - I would have done everything I could (and some more) to prevent it. I detest violence. I abhor murder. I despise rape, molestation, homicide and fratricide. I could not knowingly and willingly kill anybody or allow anybody to die.

And perhaps you're wondering why I can criticize Officer Steve. I would reply that I don't necessarily blame him. He did not stab Rocky. C.O. Steve is not an inherently evil person. It's not his fault. But, he did not handle the situation correctly. He should have opened the damn door. The four and a half minutes perhaps could/would have saved Rocky's life. His left arm was nearly cut off at the elbow. Do you know how much blood he lost while Steve was refusing to open the door? And I must reiterate that no towels were brought to Gilbert Salazar's cell, although the initial responding cop asked for them. Now C.D.C. is claiming that their *policy* is to never open the door when there is blood unless and until they have these biohazard suits on. I'll assure you that if a C.D.C. Officer was trapped in a cell, beaten and bloody they would *not* wait on a suit. They would immediately open the door to try to save one of their own. But Gilbert "Rocky" Salazar was (to them) a poor, Mexican inmate. (Not all of them. I am a bit perturbed that the cop who counted did not have his body alarm on. Especially since it took the Control Cop a good while to respond to C.O. Gates yelling, "Hit the alarm." The Control Officer should have been at his control panel watching the officer do his count. Yet, I still know C.O. Gates reacted and responded like a hero. I'll never forget him almost begging Control to "Open the damn door.") But overall C.D.C. failed Rocky. A *policy* to never open the door if there is blood? A law is much stronger than a policy. And if their job as peace officers is to serve and protect, does this policy collide with their oath as sworn peace officers? If you are walking by a swimming pool at 6:15 p.m. and see a sign posted "State Law: Do not enter pool after 6:00 p.m." Yet, you see a baby drowning in the pool, will you obey the law or dive in and save the baby. My God this is sick! If they insist upon this murderous policy of never opening a cell door (when there is blood) without the bio uniforms on, then I suggest the public insist that C.D.C. officers wear biohazard uniforms during their entire shift at work. Why not? When officers enter any ad-seg building (in fact even visitors are *required* to wear them as protection…) they are required to wear a *vest* to protect them from being stabbed. When you work construction, you are required to wear a hard hat; why not require officers to wear these uniforms? These uniforms are not even kept in the housing building. They had to run from Seven Block to the Sally Port (four minutes to and from - probably six minutes considering the number of obese and out of shape cops working in C.D.C.) and get these uniforms and bring them to the block… The towels C.O. Gates called for? There were *none*. This is wrong. This is negligence and reckless disregard for life…

In schools, when a student is killed, you'll see grief counselors on campus monitoring, observing and counseling students. None of *us* were counseled. We had to grieve on our own and most guys in prisons cover grief with anger. We disguise hurt, pain and fear with violence and toughness. No wonder guys exit prisons (everyday) worse than they were when they came here. This place literally creates monsters and fosters anger and viciousness.

One inmate stated, "Well another one bites the dust," in reference to Rocky's murder. I told my wife this: "Baby, I fight and I write everyday about wrongful convictions and what happens when justice goes wrong. I write about the so-called *American Dream* (which should be) a search for justice. But I must confess that some people need to be here.

Some guys should never, ever get out of prison. They are cold, vicious, evil, malicious and degenerate…    I hope some of my fellow convicts *never* get out. If you, could see and hear how casually many guys reacted to Rocky's murder, you would break down and cry!

And I meant every word that I said. Bishop T. D. Jakes, Eddie Long, the T.B.N. family, Pastor Paula White, Pastor Juanita Bynum and pastors all over America need to pray and fast for the guys in prisons.

There are regional demons, generational curses and perverted energies running rampart in America's prisons. And one cannot depend upon the *keepers* of the *kept* to tell it like it is, i.e. Rocky's murder was not in the Sacramento Bee (I hope to change that because I called Attorney Paul Comiskey and told him all about it. I told him to find Rocky's family and tell them to sue) nor was it on the news.

C.D.C. swept it under the rug. I saw a story on the news concerning Mr. Davis increasing C.D.C.'s budget to almost 6 billion dollars (while cutting education's budget) but Rocky's murder was not reported. I saw a story about inmates being disallowed to smoke in a prison, but nothing about Rocky! They swept it under the rug. I thought about the movie "Boys In The Hood", when a guy was murdered. At the end of the movie, the murder victim's brother went over and told a friend, "I watched the news this morning and they showed all these stories about Ethiopia and other places. But they didn't say nothing about my brother being cut down by bullets. Either they don't *know*, don't *show* or just don't care about what's going on in the hood." It's a sad day when no smoking is more newsworthy than a man's life being taken. But we know C.D.C. hid it!

I'll make sure "Off Magazine" (Off Magazine in Binghamton, New York and "Turning The Tide" covers this murder. I'll be certain "Justice Watch" in Ohio covers it. But it will be difficult. The day after Rocky was killed C.D.C. confiscated all outgoing mail (U.S. Mail) and held it. They did so in order to prevent inmates from writing the public (Off Magazine, Sacramento Bee, Justice: Denied, Turning The Tide and Workers World newspapers) about the murder. Anytime people are given the power to withhold mail, I'm sending to a lawyer, judge or senator, etc. that's too much power. Power corrupts! *Absolute power corrupts absolutely*! Contact Senators' Richard Polanco, John Burton, Assembly Leader Herb Wesson, Critical Resistance (Rose Blaz), the prison law office, California Prison Focus, Prison Inspector General Steve White, and Governor Davis and demand an investigation. C.D.C. must train their officers better. When a warden (earning over one hundred thousand dollars per year) needs only a G.E.D. and a few hours of community college (even via correspondence) small wonder most officers are ignorant. (For more information on Rocky's murder and the C.D.C. cover up, log on to www.outlawsonline.com/Sherman Manning htm...)

Now allow me to (rambling? A trade mark for me. But if you didn't like it you would not be reading this... by the way, I must remind you I wanted to title this tome "If It Doesn't Fit, You Must Acquit, Part II" but Sabine insisted on "American Dream/A Search For Justice" and Peter concurred with her. So I was outvoted!) Shift gears a bit... I want to take a moment to *remind* you to read (tautology is another specialty of mine) "Justice Denied" magazine. I can't say enough good things about what Clara Boggs is doing through the powerful impact and scathing publication to help the wrongfully convicted. "Justice Denied" magazine is also on the Internet. Be certain to read, sponsor, support and buy this magazine.

I am also interested in saying a word about Attorney Isaac K. Byrd in Jackson, Mississippi. Attorney Byrd reminds me of Willie Gary. Mr. Byrd is brilliant, powerful and a rainmaker as one of the most preeminent civil lawyers in America. He's also altruistic and gives back to colleges, churches and programs for the less fortunate.

Lawyers such as Isaac Byrd, Roy Black, Donald Watkins and Michael Manning are the necessary ingredients for achieving a recipe for victory in our American Court System. Everywhere you go in the world people talk about the *American Dream*. The American Dream of which they speak involves money, power, influence and status. Yet life has taught me in no uncertain terms that (for many) the *authentic American Dream is a search for Justice*. The search is a meandering, curvaceous and mountainous search. It usually requires that one is born on the right side of the tracks. This search requires one to have the proper contacts and associates. And one must have money. At the risk of preaching to the choir and (writing) sounding like a broken record I must tell you that the guilty very (very, very) often go free and the innocent very (very, very, very) often are found guilty in their search for Justice in America. And the more people I meet and come in contact with, the more I discover that people (by and large) consider a search for justice in this country simply an American Dream; or more like a *fairy tale*. "You are *innocent* until *proven guilty* beyond a reasonable doubt is what the law says". "It's bullshit," is what famed Attorney G. Spence says. "Why do they lock you up in jail often with a high or no bail if you're presumed innocent?" asks a prisoner. It is more accurate to state that one is *presumed guilty* in America. And the sad, sad fact is that most of society turns a blind eye to the atrocities, evils and scandals which are perpetrated fraudulently in courtrooms across this country on a daily basis. We live in a society of the "haves" and the "have-nots". And we also live in a society dominated by extremisms. There are extremists everywhere we look in this great country. Zealots and extremists have even infected the church and religions across our world. I know Christians who say they love God, read the Bible and pray everyday, but they hate their brothers and sisters who don't share their denominational or doctrinal views. Some (certainly not all) Seventh Day Adventists think all Baptists are on route to hell. Some Presbyterians think members of the Church of God in Christ are going to hell. I know members of the Church of Christ who believe all churches that allow musical instruments in the church will bust hell wide open. I know many uppity Black folks who think only ignorant and uneducated people preach energetic sermons and have excited services. "I don't like all that whooping and hollering anymore. I used to like it but not since I got my *degree*." They tell me. Yet in this powerful country although so many of us are degreed down, we can't accept others who don't look like us or think as we do. And this same spirit of extremism has created a divide politically and socially in America. On the one hand, we have activist/advocates who think nobody should go to jail or prisons (I hope not to anger some of my close associates who are anarchists but I must write from my heart. If you want an easy read you'll have to get a fiction tome) and we should simply overthrow the government. On the other hand, we have a large portion of our society who simply believes in the government. They believe in police departments, prosecutors, judges and prison guards. "If he didn't do *something* he would not be in prison. I'm tired of these preposterous theories of conspiracy," they'll tell you. And when the dichotomy in our citizens' political beliefs is so wide, then change and improvement is rendered impossible. We must lessen the divide between Americans. I want to appeal to the radicals, militants and activists to come together with the scholars, conservatives and the wealthy and to carve out a plan to (at minimum) better the judicial system in America. We will never achieve success by merely blaming each other. We won't improve the system by yelling at one another or name-calling. One finger pointed at another person creates a powerless blame game. Five fingers joined together create unity, a fist and the power to fight for change. I believe most of us want a more perfect society. I believe most of us want safe streets for all people, safe schools for our children and safe homes for our elderly. I believe most of us don't want violence, starvation, murder and rape in our society. I believe almost all of us would love to be able to sleep with unlocked doors and to discontinue being prisoners in our own homes. Most Americans are good people. Most White folks do *not* hate Black folks and vice versa. Yet *many* Whites would never want their children to marry a person of color. Upon learning of a White's dislike of interracial marriage, we have options. We can immediately call him/her a racist! Or in the rational alternative, we can examine it. The only way to examine it is to discuss it. If we establish rapport and dialogue people's opinions do change. Biases, prejudices and even racism begin to change when people talk, listen and get to know one another. Our society however, promotes non-listening. Most of us tune out even family members who sleep under our own roof, so certainly we tune out people who wear cowboy boots, if we only wear snakeskin designers. If we see a hillbilly White guy in a pickup truck and we are in a Lexus, we automatically assume we have nothing in common, so we have no reason to talk. I like heavy metal and you like jazz. We are different. I like classical music, so I'm boring. You like rap music so you are a thug. Life is not that cut and dried. But many of us unconsciously live it that way. I want to also sound the alarm (as I'm well aware that many prison rights activists, lawyers, prison websites, etc. are sending copies of this book inside the prisons) behind the walls of prisons. I want to tell prisoners likewise to wake up and grow up. I get sick and tired of meeting men in prison who think like boys. You cannot watch cartoons all day, drink pruno (prison manufactured wine) all night and claim to want a revolution. I hear you talking Malcolm (X) talk but I don't see you walking the Malcolm walk. I hear all about George Jackson, Dr. Martin Luther King, Jr. Johnnie Cochran and Barry Scheck in the prisons. But I see very little positive action. You cannot live like gossiping women yet call yourself a man. By and large, I hear more rumors, innuendo, gossip and soap opera type conversations in prison amongst men than I ever heard from women in civilian life.

It is ignorant. We want society to believe in us. Believe in our humanity. Believe that we still have some worth, some right to life and a reason to one day be free. Yet, we can't figure out how to respect one another and get along in here. How in hell can I expect society to believe I deserve to be free if I am living like a vulture or an animal while in prison?

The minute I hear a guy is a child molester or a rapist, I am ready to kill him. But if he killed his own kid or his parents, he's a celebrity. That's ridiculous. Rape and molestation are sick perverted and terrible crimes. But let's stop fooling ourselves and take notice that the most horrendous and final crime one can commit is m-u-r-d-e-r. So if I murdered and you molested, we are both in the same hot water and I have no right to think my (final) crime of murder is more *honorable* than yours. Don't complain, gripe or moan to *me* about prison survival tactics, etc. I'm an expert on prisons and prisoners. (At the risk of sounding braggadocios, I must admit) I have spent a minimum of forty hours per week for the past seven years studying prisons, prisoner, prison guards and criminal *injustice*. I've read four hundred and ninety-six books on prisons and prisoners. I write at least two hours per day, each and everyday about the things I see, hear, say and experience in the belly of the beast. So to my fellow prisoners I must say *save the drag* (prison vernacular, i.e. drama) and keep it real. Lie to your family or your buddies on the outside. Scam your pen pals but come clean with me. I know the prison subculture inside and out.

And so I want to tell each and every prisoner who is holding this book in your hands right now, as you (the prisoner, that is) sit there or lay there on your bunk listening to your celly snore, or sitting on that hard stool which is attached to your prison desk, or as you sit in that poor excuse for a library in Reidsville Georgia, New Folsom, San Quentin, Rikers Island, Soledad or Y.A., etc. *you* are responsible for your actions. And we need to stop living like sissies and animals. How dare we call ourselves men if we are willing to get a life sentence by/for stabbing another inmate that we *heard* is a rapist or a child molester. That is stupid. Don't speak to him if you don't want. Stay away from him if you must. But don't you ever allow another *inmate* to manipulate you into stabbing, attacking or killing another inmate because we heard he was a "*chester* " (prison slang for child rapist). What if he was wrongly convicted? We are so narrow-minded and so ignorant that it turns my stomach. We want everybody to believe that we didn't do it. "They set me up. They lied. The judge was racist", etc and all too often those claims of innocence are authentic. And it hurts us when nobody believes us. Yet, *we* give not a second thought to the possibility that he may not have raped that baby, that woman or that man. We talk the talk, but don't walk the walk. Day and night, I hear the armchair prison revolutionaries who have not read a nonfiction book in twenty years talk about how we can't trust the media. The media will deceive you and "They lied on me", etc. But the moment we hear he molested or raped, we start sharpening knives and hoping he comes to our prison even before he has a trial.

We need to grow up. Society even manipulates us because we are so treacherous and foolish and I cannot count the times I've watched people *on the news* say, "We know when he goes to prison they will give him what he deserves." *They* meaning "you" and "me"... Translation? Those ignorant, low life, nothing to live for prisoners will (indeed) risk their chance at ever being free and going home to their families by assaulting and stabbing this guy when he gets to prison.

"We don't give a damn about *those* people in prison. We won't send them a *dime*. We would never consider writing, visiting or allowing them to call us collect. We would not even fathom getting them/him a lawyer. But we do trust that those prisoners are foolish, thuggish, senseless and animalistic enough to assault certain men who have been convicted of certain crimes even though they were convicted by the same system which they claim is racist and corrupt."

You fool! I'm not speaking up for molesters. I'm speaking sense to you. *You* are not a judge or jury. You need to concentrate on your demons, your secrets, your case and your life. I'll leave it at that. If you want to spend the rest of your life playing police/convict/tool/fool in prison going around stabbing people because you think the injustice, corrupt and evil court system must have gotten it right every time they send a man up the river for a sex crime, then you go ahead. You're just a fool… and I quite frankly am sick and tired of fools. Fools in prison, fools out of prison. Fools running prisons and fools run by the prison.

More then two million human beings are presently behind bars in America. Another four and a half million humans are on parole, probation, subject to reincarceration any moment. More than half of these people committed "non-violent" crimes. It cost tens of billions of taxpayer dollars to keep these people in prisons, billions more to get them there and to supervise them on parole, many more billions to build more prisons, and hundreds of billions to continue fighting the failed "war on drugs". Most states don't have the money to maintain their prisons. California spends more on jails and prisons/incarceration than it does on schooling, higher learning and education. We could/should spend this money more productively on rehabilitation and re-education, which could provide many thousands of creative jobs for teachers and trainees while "graduating" hundreds of thousands of prisoners able to handle productive jobs and contribute to a broader, stronger economy and democracy.

We need to elect legislators and change laws to end the death penalty. We ought to require college degrees for all prison guards. We must provide education, training and therapy and adequate library facilities for all inmates. We must outlaw the use of "maxi - maxi security" units and all other cruel and unusual punishment. We must end the war on the poor (drugs) and substitute effective social programs to prevent crime. We must build cooperatives and local community businesses and local infrastructures to save America. Clearly we must begin to undertake social transformation and local community empowerment (I suggest you log on to www. thejusticelobby.org. Send them an E-mail at justice lobby@es.com). A true *American Dream* would (indeed) be(come) a search for Justice - Justice for the tired and huddled masses. Justice for the downtrodden, the left out and forgotten about. "Justice too long delayed is Justice denied," stated Dr. King.

We need to bring together people from various religious and political backgrounds and teach respect for every human being and the obligation to care for the poor, the sick, the hurting and the imprisoned. We ought to be tired of being a voice crying in the wilderness about social and prison reforms in a great country which loudly boasts of spiritual and so-called religious roots, but has created and encouraged the world's most deliberately vicious prison systems. These vicious, shameful dark holes we call prisons crush and cripple minds. Prisons (as they exist) breed racism, anger, despondency, helplessness, crime, fear and generational poverty. We should call on each and every local pastor and call on Billy Graham, Juanita Bynum, Paula White, T. D. Jakes, Eddie Long, Gilbert Patterson, Paul Morton, etc. to do something (more) to transform prisons. Preaching sermons is wonderful. I love preaching. But we need *more* than preaching! Dr. Martin Luther King, Jr. didn't change the south and transform America by preaching *only*. He raised money, he gave money, he visited those in jails and prisons, he marched, he spoke up, spoke out and he fought corruption. And in this age of mega churches and mega ministries, etc., we have churches that take in millions upon millions of dollars yearly. There are pastors with salaries in the millions of dollars. I am not angry at churches which can afford to give their pastor a million dollars per year. But I am appalled when these ministries do nothing to help prisoners.

And I must state clearly that pastors and evangelists ought to visit men in prison. They ought to raise money to help the wrongly convicted in prison. They ought to do it. And we ought to get upset when and if they don't. It's right, it's biblical and it is Christ like.

The Civil Rights Movement grew out of the church. (Read Andy Young's book "An Easy Burden"). And the prison rights movement needs to grow out of the church. So call, write and E-mail Benny Hinn, Billy Graham, Kenneth Hagin, Creflo Dollar and every rich preacher you know and tell them we need their help in the *war on prisons*. Hell, if we are waiting on Gray Davis or George Bush to have mercy or do justice, we will be waiting until hell freezes over! How much do we need to read the Bible to understand that Jesus wanted us to visit those in prison? It is a sin and a shame to note that most big shot pastors have never seen the inside of a jail cell or a prison. When Juanita Bynum was raising money (a good and worthy cause, I feel) on a T.B.N. (Trinity Broadcasting Network) telethon she began to say "Do you realize that there are people in prison right now and the only word and church they get is on T.B.N. and if y'all don't support this station they won't get the gospel in those prisons. How dare you sit on your couch and not pick up the telephone and give to keep T.B.N. on. Can I call you a hypocrite to your face?" she said. (I hope somebody E-mails or calls Pastor Bynum in Waycross, Georgia and tell her I love her and I need her prayers). I don't understand how people can go to church

Sunday after Sunday and forget the least of these our brethren on Monday. Can I call you a hypocrite to your face? People are dying here in these prisons for lack of love. Many of them never get a letter a picture or a birthday card. Where is the church?

I believe "the hour cometh and now is" for the church to join with Critical Resistance, Rose Braz, California Prison Focus, Off Magazine and Amnesty International and fight the good fight. Yet, you won't do it if your church is too political. You won't take a stand if you're too busy trying to get a faith based grant from George Bush! God's church and God's people ought to assemble teams to look into inmate's claims of innocence, claims of prison abuse, brutality and racism. And these teams can raise money. (I am not singling out T. D. Jakes because it does not take a rocket scientist to figure out I love his ministry. This is merely an example). If Bishop Jakes and Bishop Noel Jones asked every man at man power to send ten dollars each to a fund for prisoner's rights, prisoners lawyers or a defense fund for the wrongfully convicted, etc. How much money would that be?

I.E. "I want every man here to send Roy Black, Murray Janus, Gerry Spence, Harold Levy, William Genego, Donald Horgan, Gerald Uelmen or Donald Marks ten or twenty dollars and earmark it for the appeal of inmate ___ ___". How many men would finally get the American Dream and achieve (successfully) their search for justice? I believe if enough of your reading will E-mail Paula White, Bynum, Jakes, Eddie Long, etc. and ask for help - they will.

And then we must call on Jesse Jackson, Al Sharpton, Gerry Spence, Earl Graves, John Johnson, Russell Simmons, Steve Harvey, Tom Joyner, Bob Johnson, Danny Glover, Arianna Huffington, Montel, Oprah, Keith T. Clinkscales, etc. to publicize this effort. Don't wait, you call them! You E-mail them. You can E-mail (i.e.) Savoy Magazine (Attn: K. Clinkscales) at Editors@ savoymag.com. and let's begin a revolution. You cannot convince me that Magic Johnson, Oprah, Bill Gates, P. Diddy. Johnnie Cochran, Willie Gary, Isaac K. Byrd, Roy Black, Anthony Brooklier, Quincy Jones, etc. won't help us… "I'm the type that if it's not enough, I'll write a check and make it enough," says Shaquille O'Neal! What are you waiting on? Call Shaq, Master P., Zay Z, etc. You will not convince me that *all* of them are selfish and self-centered. Oh no! Too many of them came from a poor environment themselves. Too many of them have been in prison or know somebody in prison themselves. Magic Johnson is a human being. But don't call them playing, conning or trying to scheme them. Come clean, come real and be authentic: "Mr. Johnson, my cousin says he didn't do it. He's rotting in prison. We need you. Dennis Riordin wants 100 grand to take his appeal. Can you please help us?" Don't call them with some game about "God told me to call you," etc. because many of these folks have the gift of discernment and they are savvy businessmen. They'll write a check if it is legitimate and worthy. But they want the facts, just the facts! One great thing is that most movers and shakers read voraciously. And when you send them this book they'll read it. When guys in jail write their public defender, family, lawyer, the media, etc. and tell them about this book, most of them will read it. Norman Mailer will read it. Pastors will preach about it and teachers will teach about it. And as the word goes out over the Internet, chat lines, Off Magazine, The Beat Within, Prison Legal News, Turning The Tide, Justice Watch and through your grapevine; we will transform the judicial system. This is why I've written this tome the way I did. Part sermon, part motivation, criticism, part inside view of the monster factory, part plea for concern and cry for help. I didn't want to do it any other way. I wanted you to read it raw, uncut, and hot off the press just as it is.

I think I've done my duty. Certainly we'll have more to say to you in book form by October of this year (2003). I'm not sure what we will title the next book, but I'm writing it now as you read these words. We live in (subject change; we ramble on but you love it) an age of a severe lack of integrity. Lies, lies, vicious lies. Some of us have sold our souls to the dollar bills. And it's almost the norm to lie. People look at you funny when you dare to tell the truth. And I will admit I was tempted to (at minimum) not tell the truth about the title of this tome. Initially I titled it "If It Doesn't Fit You Must Acquit, Part II". Once my staff convinced me to change the name, I was going to hire somebody to comb through the pages and delete every reference to that title and substitute it with the new title... but why not keep it real? So now you comprehend the name(s) of this book. Another confession: I'm not Toni Morrison! I ain't William Bernhardt, Scott Turow or John Grisham. I'm not that good! And my circumstances are perplexing, difficult and I face a myriad of inconveniences. Ask President Mandela how hard it is to write, retain (C.D.C. stole my manuscript three times) and publish in prison. Ask Rolling and Paul Wright. These people hate prisoners writing. And so I had difficulty getting this to you my friend. Ipso facto, these setbacks ended up working for me. Because C.D.C. tried to suppress, hamper, hinder and blockade the truth. We now have this book available on Amazon.com, Barnes and Noble, IUniverse.com, and in every major bookstore all over this country. "No weapon formed against us by the enemy shall prosper."

And I want to tell you today that wherever you are, don't give up. (I'm preaching now!) No matter how impossible, difficult or dark your situation may be, you can make it. Never give up! Never give in! Keep the faith. Hold on! Don't quit! Don't surrender. Somewhere down inside the fabric of your being you know you still believe. Every time I have come face to face with defeat or the inkling to quit, I have gotten suspicious. Suspicious that the force, which called the universe into order, had a better plan for my life. When I felt like giving up, I was still somehow suspicious deep down within that God would make a way for me.

When you've watched spiritual wickedness in high places all your life. When you've watched a plot of false accusations, lies, innuendos and scandal play out in your own life; it is easy to become cynical. You will think (silently), "Maybe I am the predator, the rapist, the killer or the monster they say I am. Maybe the profilers are correct." I'm telling you when you gain access to and peruse (meticulously) the files, the writings and the field reports which the F.B.I. and police have kept on you for years, it is possible to begin to question yourself. But I want to tell you (from experience) never judge the day by the weather. Never judge yourself by a file written by your enemy. Do you not know about co intel pro? Do you not know about files they kept on Malcolm X or Dr. Martin Luther King, Jr.? Can you fathom the fact that they (the officials, the feds, law enforcement) *profiled* Dr. King as a communist, evil, philanderer, homosexual and a crook. You'd better study. Do you know all the false reports kept on John F. Kennedy? Do you understand what an accusation is verses proof?

Do you know that any woman or man can walk into any police department today and say, "Joe raped me five days ago. I was afraid to report it." And without a shred of evidence the police will get a warrant and lock Joe up. If Joe gets lucky (fat chance) and the man or woman withdraws the accusation or refuses to show up for court, etc. and Joe gets the case dismissed, the rape charge is and will remain on Joe's criminal record forever! A year later Joe is dating and telling his new significant other the intimate details of his life and Joe confides, "I was arrested for rape a year ago"... this woman or man ends up arguing with Joe or trying to extort Joe, etc. Joe is a public figure. Joe is an evangelist, politician or entrepreneur. "I'll cry rape if you don't give me ten grand!"

The person goes and reports, "Joe raped me two weeks ago and he said he would kill me if I reported it. I was terrified. Joe says he was charged with rape a year ago, but got away with it because he says he's untouchable! Joe says he has friends on the police department." It's getting juicy now. Joe is going down! Public defender: "I know you claim you're innocent Joe, but there's a pattern here. If you go to trial and lose, you'll get twenty years. I can plead you out for five." Will Joe take this gamble? Probably, so now he's doing time. And when he gets out - if he gets out, I can assure you the beat goes on and the pattern will continue.

Who wants to hire a convicted sex offender? Who wants to tell the world he/she was down for rape?

I can assure you that profiles are worth no more than the pens that wrote them. Take the pro off and all you have is a file. Ask Chief Moose (a great cop) how *wrong* the profilers were in the sniper case in D.C. (Maryland and Virginia)?

They not only got it wrong, they blew it big time on national TV. The lone White (militia type) killer turned out to be as Black as an ace of spade! Double whammy; two Black guys! And we cannot trust the message if we cannot trust the messenger. If the messenger (Black, White, Latino or Asian) is racist, or a drug addict, or vindictive, or wants to win too badly, we cannot trust the messenger. (More on the results of mistrust or distrust of the messengers in a moment).

On February 14, 2003 I asked Sabine to conduct an Internet search for Peter Sussman. Mr. Sussman is a former editor for the San Francisco Chronicle and best-selling author. He is the President of the National Society of Journalism and a California Prison Researcher.

Sabine found him and gave me his address and telephone number. On February 15th, I spoke with Peter (Andrist) in Switzerland and Peter said, "Did you call Peter?" I explained how there was no way Peter (Sussman) would accept a collect call from me, etc. (cutting to the chase) I called Peter (Sussman) collect at 2:15 p.m. and he accepted. "Sherman, how are you? I went on to your Website yesterday and I'm glad you called." Unbelievable, but on another level, I always expect the unexpected.

My life has been the story of the unexpected showing up and materializing, like my chance meetings with the late, great Rev. Hosea Williams. My meeting with him developed into a close personal relationship. My chance meeting with former Ambassador (and mayor and congressman) Andrew Young and our relationship becoming close and personal. My chance meeting with my wife and Peter and Jasper and Leroy and...

The chances were not by accident, incident or coincidence. I didn't meet Jesse Jackson by accident or incident. It was divine providence. It was a sovereign God behind the scenes, opposite the curtains pulling my strings like a puppet master. It was the hidden hand of God orchestrating the events of my life. "It's a miracle that you would accept this call," I told Peter. He laughed. We ended up talking for fifteen minutes. Peter explained to me that he had lobbied for prisoners to be re-granted the right to correspond with the media confidentially and to have face-to-face interviews with the media again. "Believe it or not Sherman, I even had support from the CCPOA! Don Novey testified for me. I got the legislature to approve it three times. Governor Wilson vetoed it once and Davis twice." I said, "Davis has been a tremendous let down." Peter went on to tell me about one of his latest ventures which is a book called "Invisible Punishments". He said that Marc Mauer wrote it and Peter wrote a chapter in it.

Peter indicated that (former prisoner and author) Danny Martin would be in town the following week and Peter said, "I'll tell Danny about your new book and put him on your Website." I told Peter that Peter (Andrist) and I want to send gratis copies of the new (this) book to movers and shakers and people who care about wrongful convictions and prisoner rights." Peter shared some information I won't mention here. "What do you think about Barry Scheck?" I asked him. "Wonderful, he's awesome. I just love what he and those students out at Cardoza are doing to set the innocent free. And David Protess and those journalism students, they're unbelievable. I spoke for David Protess and the center on wrongful convictions last year," Peter stated.

I then asked the question of the day "tell me what you think of Governor George Ryan and what he did last month," I asked.

I could hear excitement, jubilation and enthusiasm coming out of his voice. Peter was almost screaming his reply. "Amazing! I was there when he gave the speech at Northwestern. Sherman"... he went on and on.

(As a matter of fact, we have an entire site set up in honor of Governor George Ryan. Visit www.outlaws online.com/Sherman Manning2htm).

Let the drums (in your mind) roll. Take a deep breath and think (really think) about what George Ryan did. He emptied death row. Scott Turrow had written "Reversible Errors" and Mr. Ryan read it. Mayor Jerry Brown's sister in LA had also sent Mr. Ryan a book her father (Fmr. CA Governor) had written about the death penalty.

People (especially death penalty supporters) would have us believe that Mr. Ryan made this critical, crucial decision easily. But this man did not.

Mr. Ryan analyzed, scrutinized and studied the issues thoroughly. Mr. Ryan did what any real leader must and should do. He formulated a task force to include defense lawyers, prosecutors, writers, law professors, etc. to study the cases, details and specifics of death row in Illinois. And I pause to re-state that this is what every Governor should do. Not only to study death row cases or the death penalty per se, but also to study the cases of men and women who claim to be innocent. Men who cannot afford Ben Brafman, Ephraim Margolin, Roy Black or Blair Bernholtz (Berk). We need to bring together (in every state) a task force on prisons (in general) and a task force on wrongful convictions. What Governor (Mr. Davis??) or Senator (Lott?) would not want a wrongly convicted man or woman to be set free from prison?

(They all practice acting, lying and the art of being politically correct, so we know the first reply) "A jury of his peers found him guilty so I'm not going to undermine or tamper with the judicial process," Mr. Davis will say.

But not so easy. As you will see in this book the appeals process is stacked against the poor and the price of justice is high...

With one stroke of a pen, George Ryan emptied death row. My God. (I must ramble a few minutes...). Do you have any idea what it must feel like to be on death row? Neither do I! What about being on death row for a crime you did not commit? Neither do I! But I do know what it feels like to be in prison (in general) for crimes you did not commit. T. D. Jakes is doing a series now called "The Breaking Point" (I'm not working for Jakes. I don't know what Jakes does at home or on his own time etc., but I do know he's telling it like it is!). And I suggest every man and woman in prison get a copy of the tapes "The Breaking Point".

I know exactly what it is like to sit by your window and look out into the darkness and wonder what happened. Who am I? Why am I here? How did I get into this mess? Where is God when the hurting, the trauma, the pain won't stop? Where are you God? I can't see you! I can't feel you! Lord help me. Is there a God? Yes, I know my Bible thumping buddies don't want to admit you've even questioned God! I also know my hardcore prisoners (reading) who think you're as tough as nails and nothing can break you etc. You don't want to admit that life can kick your butt sometimes.

I know the tough defense lawyer (i.e. Murray J. Janus, Johnnie Cochran, Gerry Spence, call Douglas, Isaac Byrd, Georgia Van Zanten) don't want to admit to fear, anxiety, pain and hurt.

But there are times in life (and especially if you're trapped in a concrete cage for crimes you know you did not commit and the authorities have profiled you and sized you up to a predator, manipulator, dangerous, violent, etc.) when you wonder, am I going to make it? Lord I don't know if I can take it anymore. I'm down to my last dime, last ounce of hope, faith and belief. You feel like a piece of gum wrapper on a trash truck headed for the city dump. You feel like, am I ever going to get out of this? I'm three thousand miles away from home. I'm from Atlanta. I have nobody in California. I don't know if I can bounce back this time. I don't know... Yes, I can remember when Ambassador Andrew Young lost his mother and stated at the press conference that "In a Christian family such as ours we give thanks for eighty-seven years of a wonderful mother." Andy broke down.

I also remember when Uncle Andy (Ambassador Young) lost Jean Young and Peter and I went over to his house (unannounced) at 10:00 p.m. one night "Come on in Rev. Manning," Andy said. "And tell Peter to get out of that car and come in too." I saw hurt, fear, pain, doubt and sorrow in Andy's eyes. " I was in the back on the telephone with Coretta (Scott King)," Andy told me. "I'm doing all I can to just keep my head above the waters," he told me. I prayed with and for him. He felt like he was drowning. Can I get a witness? If you ain't never been terrified, hurt and victimized, I'm not even writing to you. Put this book down and mail it to a real person with real issues. But baby if you have ever been in pain and didn't feel like getting up out of the bed in the morning, if you have ever had lonely days, troubling, painful and fearful nights, etc., then you might be able to (somewhat) imagine what it feels like to reside on death row... Governor George Ryan embraced Larry Marshall of Northwestern University Law School's Center for wrongful convictions the day he announced his historic, unheard of, incredible and awe inspiring decision to commute all the state's death sentences. This was the largest emptying of death row in U.S. history. With the stroke of an ink pen, Governor Ryan spared the lives of one hundred and sixty-four men and three women who served a combined two thousand years in prison.

Brother Ryan is not a liberal. He's not a democrat. He is a conservative republican. This bodacious move is being seen as the most significant action questioning capital punishment since the U.S. Supreme Court struck down states old death penalty laws, and it is certain to secure his legacy as our nation's leading proponent of changing capital punishment. "The facts that I have seen in reviewing each and every one of these cases raised questions not only about the innocence of people on death row, but about the fairness of the death penalty system as a whole. Our capital system is haunted by the demon or error, error in determining guilt, and error in determining who among the guilty deserves to die," Governor Ryan stated. Mr. Ryan acted forty-eight hours before the end of his term and one day after taking the extraordinary steps of pardoning outright four men on death row. In this historic speech (attended by my *new* friend Peter Sussman) Mr. Ryan quoted CA. Gov. Edmund G. "Pat" Brown, Bishop Desmond Tutu, Abraham Lincoln, Mahatma Gandhi and Supreme Court Justices Potter Stewart and Harry A. Blackman. Governor Ryan (visit a site completely dedicated to Governor George Ryan at www. outlaws online. com/Sherman Manning 2 html) told two stories about murders which transpired in his hometown Kankakee, Illinois in which he knew the gunmen and their victims, and stated that his wife, Lura Lynn, was "angry and disappointed" at his decision. What a man! What a man! But after meticulous consideration Ryan said he was left with Blackman's famous declaration in a 1994 dissent: "No longer shall I tinker with the machinery of death."

He said, "The legislature couldn't reform it. Lawmakers won't repeal it. But I will not stand for it - I must act because our three-year study has found only more questions about the fairness of the sentencing, because of the spectacular failure to reform the system because we have seen justice delayed for countless death row inmates with potentially meritorious claims, because the Illinois death penalty system is arbitrary and capricious - and therefore immoral."

In this speech, Ryan pointed out the unlikelihood of his crusade. Ryan is a pharmacist by training and he voted (as a legislator) in 1977 to resume the death penalty. But then he found himself at the helm of a state where thirteen condemned humans had been exonerated while (simultaneously) only twelve had been executed, a statistic he could not let stand.

His decision says, "You have to start all over again if you want the death penalty," stated Richard Dieter, Director of the Death Penalty Information Center, comparing it to the 1972 Supreme Court decision.

"I don't know how many times we're going to go through a revolution like this before we conclude that there's no way for humans to make these irrevocable and infallible decisions," Dieter added.

On the four men he pardoned, Governor Ryan stated, "Here we have four men who were wrongfully convicted and sentenced to die by the state for crimes the courts should have seen they (Madison Hobley, Aaron Patterson, Leroy Orange and Stanley Howard) did not commit. We have evidence from four men who do not know each other, all getting beaten and tortured and convicted on the basis of the confessions they allegedly made. They are perfect examples of what is so terribly broken about our system."

Hobley, who had spent fifteen years in prison said hours after being released, "It is a dream come true - finally. Thank God that this day has finally come." Now even though these four men were factually innocent and wrongly convicted, what do you think the D.A. had to say? "To grant these convicted murderers a pardon is outrageous and unconscionable."

As the 52-year-old Orange walked to freedom, he spoke of missing the birth of grandchildren, deaths in the family and graduations while he was in prison. "You name it, I missed it," he stated. To the Governor, "Thank you with all my heart and please *do something for the remaining group* on death row." This sentiment was echoed by Patterson. "It's very important, that you all look into other guys' cases on death row and in the prison population - *there are more innocent people locked up*," Patterson stated.

Ryan called the judicial system "inaccurate, unjust and unable to separate the innocent from the guilty, and at times very racist." He blamed "rogue cops, overzealous prosecutors, incompetent defense lawyers and judges who rule on technicalities rather than what is right". Ryan said at least thirty-three people convicted of murder and not sentenced to death have been wrongfully convicted. He pardoned one: Miguel Castillo, who spent eleven years in prison for a murder he could not have committed *because he was in jail at the time of the crime*.

My fellow Americans are you reading this? This man was definitely, really, factually and actually in jail at the time of the crime. What judge(s), prosecutors, etc. allowed this man to sit in prison for eleven years? Why did it take a Governor to pardon him? Why did America let him sit there? True answer? Many Americans did not give a damn. We are too busy living the so-called *American Dream* that we don't have time for a search for justice. But I want the thought to stick with you. I hope it haunts us. How dare lawyers, prosecutors, judges, senators, and our American Government let him sit there. What's going on? If this case alone does not tell you something, you are lost! My God! Ryan also pardoned Gary Dotson, who served several years in prison for rape, before his accuser and D.N.A. evidence proved him innocent.

Governor Ryan discovered men had been beaten maliciously by detectives during interrogation sessions. He found numerous instances in which several men had been suffocated by typewriter bags (covers) and one instance in which a guy carved into a wooden bench (in the interrogation room), "I was forced to make this confession". And these men would appear in court before a judge and prosecutor (an officer of the court) bloody, swollen and beaten stating "Yes, I raped her" or "Yes I did commit these murders." Why would the judge and prosecutor accept these pleas and not question why these people were beaten, swollen, bruised? Three of the men on death row had police mug shots taken of them immediately after leaving court and confessing and they looked worse than Emmett Till. They looked horrible. Why didn't a prosecutor or His Honor ask, "What happened to this man?"

Shortly after emptying death row Governor Ryan appeared on Oprah for two days consecutively. I must state that many have accused Oprah of being anti-prisoner and anti-convict, etc. but after these shows I *no longer* feel the criticisms have merit. Oprah went to death row and talked one on one with the inmates themselves. "I must admit that I was changed by talking to the inmates on death row. A lot of them said, "I'm guilty. I did my crimes. But I know some guys here are innocent. They shouldn't be here." Those interviews changed me and changed the way I look at the justice system," Oprah said. I love myself some Oprah Winfrey. Last year she gave Morehouse (ain't but four houses - my house, your house, the Whitehouse and mo house) College in Atlanta 2 million dollars. Last week she gave Morehouse 5 million dollars. A few weeks ago, she built a school in South Africa and broke the ground with President Mandela.

And perhaps soon she will be led to contribute to Innocence Projects, Centers on Wrongful Convictions or secretly pay for the appeals of some wrongful convicted inmates, who knows? But I must reiterate that God can tear up heaven to get His child out of prison. God still does the Almighty (emptying death row) through the least likely (a conservative republican). God is still sovereign.

In this book, I will show you (if I ain't already done so) the injustice, the horror, the senselessness. The brutality and the senseless waste of taxpayer's money, the ineffectiveness and the miserable failure of the correctional and judicial system - for all prisoners and especially for those suffering from mental illness. I will show you how the system as it is remains a cesspool of sin, hatred and racism. This system is a time bomb waiting to explode. I will show you the preposterous and ludicrous notion that proposes keepers (prison guards) with only G.E.D.'s being sergeants in C.D.C. One month flipping hamburgers at McDonald's never ever finishing high school, the next month earning seven thousand dollars monthly and being a Sergeant in the Department of Corrections. Do you understand you only need a G.E.D. to work in C.D.C.? You can climb to the rank of sergeant and earn up to one hundred thousand dollars per year (including overtime) in C.D.C. with your G.E.D. Small wonder many keepers across the country are corrupted and vicious.

I watched an ad seg (A-facility/New Folsom Prison) captain (I'll call him Captain Martel. Not his real name) a few weeks ago blatantly, rudely, deliberately and capriciously fire a Puerto Rican, mentally ill inmate from his job for a minor infraction. The lieutenant (a minority) stated, "He didn't do anything to get fired." And the sergeant stated, "He's not fired." And he called him back to work on February 12, 2003. He worked all day on February 13, 2003. Captain Martel (Partel, Lartel or any similar name you want to call A-facility's ad seg Captain) walked in and told the inmate "I fired your ass. Get out of here. Go work for Jimbo (a pseudonym for the acting Associate Warden). "But Earl Wilson (an inmate) was also fired by an arrogant racist in 1994. Earl Wilson sued C.D.C. and won! Attorney Georgia Van Zanten stated after the victory, "I've been involved with cases involving multimillions of dollars. But I'm more proud of this victory because all Earl wanted was his job back. Now C.D.C. must pay him thousands."

Well C.D.C. will eventually pay this inmate also. But the sad fact is captains think they're untouchable - Big cheese, etc. and many times they win. People are afraid of them. But the saddest part is that when C.D.C. defends these arrogant, egotistical and racist thugs and then loses, guess who pays? Taxpayers! It's your money.

One lawyer indicates, "C.D.C. paid more than thirty million dollars last year settling brutality rape, racial and discrimination lawsuits. And they paid nearly ten million dollars on attorney fees alone." Who pays? The taxpayers. After reading this it might become apparent to you that you (should) have a vested interest in cleaning up C.D.C.

And you should want to know what's going on inside because ninety percent of the folks in the "Big House" will be paroled. So when authors (such as this writer) piss them off they retaliate by any means necessary (i.e. arbitrary transfers, ad-seg placement, short terms, or pretending "we're concerned for your safety so we must transfer you to PHU for you own protection" etc.). Time and again an inmate alleges officer misconduct and their reaction is to place the inmate in ad-seg for the "safety and security of the institution". If the officers are clean, professional and law abiders why must the inmate be punished (ripped out of his cell, stripped of his property, etc.) and put in the hole while they "investigate". A law-abiding officer is not (is he?) going to assault the inmate. And if somebody must be moved why not reassign the officer instead of placing an inmate's mental health at risk by putting him in the hole? And do you think they're angry with me? Yes they hate me. And the only hope I have (because since this book is on Amazon.com/Barnes & Nobel and allover the Internet) is that you (Michael Irving, Jr., Craig Scott, T. D. Jakes, Andy Young, CA. Prison Focus, Roy Black, Jesse Jackson, President Mandela, Bill Clinton, John Samuel, Peter Sussman, Danny Martin, etc.) readers will inundate them by fax (916/322-3842 or 916/985-8610) or by email (at RPMB@ executive.corr.ca.gov) and check up on me. "Is Sherman Manning alive? Is he still working? If not, why not? Did you transfer him? Why? Is he in the hole?" And when they doctor up paperwork to justify (they do it all the time. They're experts at false documentation - masters of deception. The better they lie the more they get promoted) transferring me or putting me in ad-seg, etc., interrogate them. Call the Sacramento Observe, CA Prison Focus, T. D. Jakes, Al Sharpton, Tom Joyner, Doug Banks, Peter Susman, Rose Braz, Dr. Terry Kupers and senators. Call the radio talk shows, E-mail the U.S. Senate, contact Betty Jean Allen at the FBI in Washington, DC and tell them to look into it.

In spite of the dangers of C.D.C. potentially retaliating against me by locking me down and punishing me, this book is a profile on C.D.C. corruption. It is a profile on wrongful convictions. It is a profile on Innocence Lost to the tune of multiple thousands of humans who are trapped behind prison walls because they could not *afford justice*.

An editor read one hundred & twenty pages of this book a while ago and stated, "Awesome, scathing, vivid and maddening. This book will be a *must read for America*. But Sherman do you think anybody gives a damn? Do you believe that after they read the book they're going to do something? To change the justice system and prisons?" She then went on to say, "You can make this a bestseller but since you're not available to do book signings etc. and to traditionally market the book yourself I think the keys to your success are going to be Internet, media and church. If you persuade church members to get their pastors to announce your book, you'll win. If your everyday readers will go online and tell others (i.e. David Protess, Cornel West, Barry Scheck, prison rights groups and Just Friends in general) about your book, you will win. And if a Tom Joyner, Doug Banks, Tommy Goss, Steve Harvey, Martin Sheen or Larry King will tell their listeners about your book, you'll win."

So it is in your (the reader) hands now. It is in the hands of Peter Ninemire, Christopher Ferguson, Brian Oxman, Daniel Garcia, David Replogle, Kbut, Nate Berkus, Dan Rather, Peter Jennings, Michael Grimstead, Craig Scott, Paula White and every reader reading. It is in your hands now. I have nursed this baby (book). I have put myself on the line. I have burned the midnight oil. I have written thousands of letters, read hundreds of replies. I have studied books, newspapers, scholars' journals and magazines. I have prayed and fasted and lay awake in the midnight hour saying "Lord, please, please help me to get this book into the right hands. God I know it's too long, rambles and shifts etc. but that's me. It's raw, real and authentic. God even if I never get my justice and freedom, my God, if I don't ever make it out alive will you please make a way for this book to be read by Oprah, Tom Joyner, Dianne Sawyer, Montel, The Honorable Nelson Mandela, Bishop Jakes and Deion Sanders. Lord, I know you can do all things. I need you to help me. This is not just *my* book. But it is a *voice* for the *voiceless*. It is for the Jacobs and Josephs in prison that I know you want to raise up and out of prisons. My Lord and my God will you let one life be saved by this book. Let one young man in juvenile read it and decide to stop selling drugs or get out the gang and not graduate to the adult prison system. If they come here they'll be raped, ruined and rotten for life. Let just one prison guard read it and decide to stop beating prisoners. Let Willie Gary, Isaac Byrd, Jonnie Cochran, Roy Black, Tom Messereau and Gerry Spence read it and decide to go get a wrongly convicted man out of prison. Let the American Bar Association, NACDL, ACLU, Mr. Shaw, NAACP, SCLC, District Attorney's, judges and Supreme Court Justices read this book and decide to be a little bit more fair in court. Lord, I ask you to please touch Bishop Desmond Tutu and get him to read this book. I know you can. If you will orchestrate it I know it will be so. And this book will help make a difference. Lord I want freedom so badly I can taste it. I long, yearn and hope to see my grandmother's face again. I want to see my momma so bad. I want to smell her scent, taste her biscuits, hug her and cry on her shoulders. I'm tired of the coldness, meanness, and viciousness of the prison. I'm tired of looking over my shoulder, crying myself to sleep and dreaming of freedom. I want to go home. But Lord, as stupid as this sounds, I'd be willing to

die here if you'll just promise me to cause at least a half million people to read my book. I don't want to die yet, but if it takes that to get Danny Glover, Dick Gregory and Jesse to read every page; here am I. God, I need you! I can't orchestrate it. I can't manipulate it. I can't make it happen. I need you! You don't know how many nights I've prayed like that to God. Why? There is medicine in this book. Medicine, healing and solutions. We need it. America is heading to Iraq in our search (as I told you) for justice. America spends billions searching for Osama Ben Laden. Our President (God bless him) has an American Dream to bring Osama to justice. But I must tell our
                president, our senate, congress, governors, pastors, teachers and students that these beautiful journalism students such as Greg Johnsson at Northwestern University, David Protess, Andrea Lyons, Larry Marshall, Katherine Zellner, etc. got it right; the search for justice starts at home here in America. "I'll sleep well tonight," Governor Ryan stated after he shut down death row and set those captives free. God Bless Mr. Ryan and as great a man as he is, he ought to sleep wonderfully.
                But I'm not sleeping so well. I'm awakened at the slightest sound. I am living in a horrendous place where it seems nobody cares and everybody thinks you're guilty until proven innocent. It's awful. It will make a grown man weep.
                I'll sleep better when some of you write to me and say, I'm praying for you. When you write to me and tell me you gave this book to a young man in juvenile, jail or prison. When you write and tell me you sent this book to Oprah, Rubin Hurricane, Magic Johnson or your local newspaper. When you write me and tell me your pastor read this book and said a prayer for all prisoners; I'll sleep better. When I know that you're writing the president, the government and the senate and telling them that the American Dream is a search for justice and one need not look beyond the county jail, the courthouse and the prisons to begin a (real) *search for justice*. You tell them to go get our babies and boys out of jails and prisons. You tell them to go study the prison rosters and on a case-by-case basis; set the innocent and wrongfully convicted free. Demonstrations and protests are fine. But if you want to make a real change, we need money, media and mega lawyers. Those are the 3M's of change for the judicial system and the prisons. Let's cut to the chase. We can talk, argue, yell, cuss and fuss all day long. But if we want C.D.C. and prisons across the country to stop killing and beating prisoners, we must utilize the 3M's. If we want to get the wrongfully convicted out of prisons, we must employ the 3M's. If we want to rid police departments of rogue cops, we must call on the

(3M's), media, raise money and get mega lawyers on our side. That's just the bottom line. Write to me at Sherman Manning J98796, Mule Creek, FA2-240, P.O. Box 409099, Ione. Ca. 95640-9099 USA. Visit me online at www.outlaws online.com/ Sherman Manning htm. or www.outlawsonline.com /Sherman Manning 2 htm or http:// www.ThePamperedPrisoner.com /SManningCA.htm or at http www.Inmate-connections.com /CA /Manning-Sherman/Manning.htm.

And lets talk about it all. Let's talk about spiritual wickedness in high places. But let's also talk about the incredible, splendiferous and monumental actions taken by that great man Governor Ryan. We cannot fail to note that a tome, President Mandela and Bishop Desmond Tutu affects Mr. Ryan's decision. As I told you, Kathleen Brown (Fmr. CA. State Treasurer) sent Mr. Ryan a book "Public Justice, Private Mercy: A Governor's Education on Death Row" by (her late father) Edmund G. "Pat" Brown. And Kathy thought perhaps Mr. Ryan didn't even read the book because (and as many of you in record numbers buy this book and give it to your pastor mayor, senator or a prisoner, etc. know that it will impact them in ways you may never know...) for a long time she never even got a thank you note or acknowledgement that the Governor received it. But on Oprah, Governor Ryan stated, "I was profoundly affected by that book." And he talked about the influence of President Mandela and Bishop Tutu on his decision. You just never know. Information, action and prayer is powerful... On February 21, 2003, I spoke to Michael Jackson's lawyer. Yes, I spoke to Attorney Brian Oxman. The contents of our chat can't be fully disclosed here (remember prison guards are reading this book) and now. But I made it clear that I was struggling with what I might, should or could write about Sir Michael Jackson in this book. Is he a sick, evil child molester? Is he a "wanna be" White boy? Does he really lure children in with toys and joy rides at Neverland just to destroy their innocence? Perhaps the verdict is still out and I'm tempted to submit to public opinions and go with the flow of Michael haters. I can't defend him. The brother is, at minimum, eccentric. But I must also remember how easy, how simple, how convenient it is to label people without knowing all the details.

Michael Jackson is probably one of the most misunderstood people on the planet. There is a strong chance that the man is absolutely not a molester and not a pervert. I mean, can't we imagine what it feels like to be Mike? The man cannot be normal. Society demands that he adjust and readjust his lifestyle. Most of *us* can't even fathom what it must be like to be one of the most recognizable persons on this planet. We think he'd enjoy this fame and acclaim, etc. but let's look closer. For more than thirty-five years of his life he has not been able to exhale, relax and be normal. What must it feel like to never be able to go to a grocery store, a mall, a restaurant, and a cinema? To never, ever be able to go to a high school graduation of a friend's kids, not go to church etc. Can you imagine? It's fun for a while, but forever? My Lord! I wish I could paint a picture for you. But no privacy and no security. Nobody you can trust. To think "How many people really like *me* because of *me*? My personality, my charm, my personhood? How many of them would like me if I could not dance, moonwalk, sing and perform! They *think* they love me; but they don't even know me. They don't know the me that makes me, me. If they knew me they would leave me alone *sometimes*. They would let me live a life. I love people. I love my fans. They are so beautiful! They are wonderful! They are magnificent! But I need some time, privacy and serenity. I..." I can hear Michael Jackson saying and thinking that. And I want to tell the world he is a human being. He has done many, many great things. He (too) is innocent until proven guilty. I would never let eleven and twelve-year-old boys (or girls) sleep in my bed. But I don't eat lobster, many do. Different strokes for different folks.

Finally (on Michael Jackson) let me write what (perhaps) Michael can't say... "Why would you settle a lawsuit and/or pay a boy's family if you didn't do it." I'll answer that one, because he can afford it!! Period! Here I sit in prison for a crime I know that I did not commit! Yet (can we be real) if I thought I could legally and legitimately pay my adversary (i.e. accuser and make my criminal case go away, I would and so would most of you reading! Save all that gibberish about if you were innocent you wouldn't do this or that! If you know anything about the American judicial system, you would know guilty men often go free and innocent men often go to jail.

So why would any rich man take that kind of gamble when freedom is at stake? Yes, even an innocent man. And perhaps the real question should be, "If Michael really raped or molested that child, what decent family member would sell their child's innocence"? I would not! No way! There is not enough money in Bill Gate's bank account that would cause me to sell out if you raped my child.

I would want you punished, in *prison* and treated while in prison. And after your criminal conviction - then I would (being real) sue you civilly for money. O. J. Simpson was found innocent in criminal court and then sued and found guilty in civil court. Do you understand (clearly) that the family of this child could have and (in my opinion) should have pursued the criminal case and put Michael (where a true molester should be) in prison. And then sue him for money?

But they agreed to drop all claims for money! That's a sell out. And *they* should be criticized for this - not Michael. And if you dislike me because it seems like I'm speaking up for Michael - so be it! I'll tell you like Mike that you ought to start with the man (or woman) in the mirror. Look at yourself! Look at you... D.N.A. freed Eddie Joe Lloyd from a Michigan prison after seventeen years for a rape and murder he did not commit... Greg Wilhoit was on death row wrongly convicted, but he proved his innocence. He now goes around the country speaking out for the wrongly convicted. Thank God for columnist Diana Griego for telling the nation about his wrongful conviction. And thank God for Attorney Ellen Eggers in Sacramento, CA. for fighting for Greg! The American Bar Association has now recommended overhauling fourteen-year-old standards for capital defense lawyers in the face of criticism from Supreme Court Justices and others about the quality of legal representation... Praise God!

I must salute (and one thing which we must/can change is the fact that bad news travels so fast and good news so slowly. A lie will travel all over the world before the *truth* even gets out of the bed in the morning. I get tired of hearing "Sherman I read your name in a book three years ago and..." So I can't let that happen here. I want *you* to *call* these people today and tell them you read about them in this book) a group of great lawyers who fight for prisoner's. Let me salute the following: Terry Smerling, Richard Goff, Michael Satris, Don Specter, Allyson Hardy, Millard Murphy, Steve Berlin, Michael Bien, Sandy Rosen, Warren George, Luther Orton, Jordan Budd, Dan Lipmanson, Charlene Snow, Jamie Fellner, Dani Williams, Chris Daley, Dean Johansson, Leo Terrell, John Burris and James Chanin. All of who give a darn about prisoners. God Bless them and help them.

Seven jurors who convicted a prominent medical marijuana activist demanded a new trial in February. They're rebelling against what they say was a misleading case and an intimidating atmosphere.

At a strange rally outside the Federal Court in Sacramento, CA, February 4, 2003, the jurors were defiant and shaken, and expressed solidarity with defendant Edward Rosenthal four days after convicting him of running a massive pot-growing operation in West Oakland, CA.

"Both the jury and I were victims of vicious persecution," Rosenthal stated. The jurors said they had misgivings as soon as the trial was over. They learned Rosenthal had been *deputized* by Oakland to supply the city's pot program and they said had they known, they would have acquitted him.

"It was a nightmare for us once we realized what we had done here," stated Juror Marney Craig. "I really don't care if there are legal reprisals against us for rallying... I feel we were sheep. We were manipulated and controlled," she said. Charles Sackert (jury foreman) read an apology to Rosenthal and stated, "I truly don't know if writing you this letter is a contempt of court... If it is, perhaps *we can share a cell*." What a jury. This jury is sending shockwaves throughout California. Jurors often try to do the right thing and they "want to do the right thing," stated Paul Comiskey, but they're denied the information they need in order to make a fair decision. Ipso facto there are "thousands of innocent men trapped in hellholes across this country simply because the jury was mislead by the prosecution with the court's blessing," Comiskey says...

And then they end up here (in prison) with twenty-five-year-old (boys) prison guards who barely have a high school diploma telling them, "I control your life. My daddy is a big shot downtown. He got power! I can get you transferred or put in the hole any day of the week. Yes..." Such as a cop told me on February 21, 2003.

Same officer who many inmates say, "He is responsible for Gilbert Salazar dying. He was too slow. Probably playing dominoes or asleep. He took too long to hit the alarm. And refused to open the cell door. He let that man die. Any why did the other officer not have on his alarm?" That is what they are saying. If some of my lawyers (reading) want to know the cops name I'll simply tell you to *write me* and I'll be glad to tell you his name.

I have so much more to write. "Write your Black ass off," says Andy Young. But I gotta quit here. Here's the book thousands of you have been waiting on. God Bless you... Check up on me. Write me. Pray for me. And on the following page, let the book begin....

# Newly Revised: American Dream, A Search for Justice

Is there anything that could be worse than being arrested, tried and convicted of a crime that you did not commit? How would it feel in your soul and what would it do to your belief in the American Judicial System if you knew you were innocent yet convicted? How could you go to bed every night and then get up every morning knowing that you might be in prison for crimes you did *not* commit? How should the Black man feel knowing that only twelve percent of the drug crimes in America are committed by Blacks; yet, seventy-two percent of the drug arrests are indeed the arrests of Black men? How should the Indians and Latinos feel knowing that less than five percent of the judges and prosecutors in America are Indian or Latino?

What would you do if you wrote over sixty thousand letters to the media proclaiming your innocence and nobody wrote back? What can you do when it seems *like all hope is gone*?

There is no crime in being a coward. But a coward just should not be cloaked in a black robe! Every day of the week so-called judges *rape* the sixth amendment of our constitution. Everyday judges send innocent men to prisons. Every day of the week prosecutors suborn perjury, withhold exculpatory evidence and violate their oaths of office. They do so under the color and cover of authority. They do so in the name of public service. They lie, they cheat, they deceive and they wrongfully convict men and women in courtrooms everyday.

In *The Room*, in the courtrooms, in every major city and in rural towns across the USA, unlawful, illegal and corrupted proceedings march on to the beat of their own drummer. It is scary and frightening to see that the checks and balances system is leaning more and more in the direction of prosecutors everyday.

Gerry Spence, F. Lee Bailey, Barry Scheck, Murray Janus, Bobby Lee Cook and Attorney Barry Tarlow tried to warn America that the Government and its officers were getting too much power. And along with this unchecked power came shabby investigations, lying witnesses, prosecutorial misconduct, juror tampering by detectives and judicial terror.

One needs not look very far to see how many times corruption has been exposed even at the highest levels of government. Even the FBI has been proven to be untrustworthy and in some instances corrupted.

Go ask Richard Jewell in Atlanta, Georgia. Richard was trailed, surveilled and badgered by the FBI. The media camped outside his house and watched his every movement because the FBI targeted him as a *prime suspect* in the Olympic Bombing in Atlanta, Georgia.

Richard, like many other poor Whites, was *presumed guilty* by the FBI. Ipso facto; he was presumed a murderer by the media. Ipso facto, he was presumed guilty by the American citizens.

The FBI began to leak information to the press. FBI psychologists began to put together this psychological profile of the Olympic Bomber that allegedly *fit* the *profile* of *Richard Jewell*. Their need for a *conviction* caused them to look an innocent man square in the eyes and see *guilt* written all over his pupils. Profiles, profiles, patterns and profiles. Richard Jewell *fit* the *profile*. Yet, in the end, it didn't fit and they had *no choice* except to acquit.

And the taxpayers paid millions of dollars to cover for the FBI's mishandling of the Olympic stadium's bombing case. Now Terry (I won't give Terry the glory of using his last name in this book) has had his execution delayed because of FBI misconduct and a botched investigation, once again. The FBI withheld evidence in Terry's case and this again demonstrates how little confidence we can put in the FBI. I do not support the death penalty. It is *rage* and state sponsored vengeance. It is not a deterrent to crime. And it is racist.

*We* created Terry. We drafted him into our military and brainwashed him. We taught him to shoot, kill and destroy. We taught him to hate Saddam and that all Iraqi's are evil. We built a *monster* and failed to adequately *debrief* and *deprogram* him. And now we solve a murder with a murder. I am sick and tired of the hypocrisy. I am sick and tired of the deception. We know darn well that Terry did *not* act alone. He had help, lots of help. But in our rush to judgment and in our rush for a conviction, we are willing to allow other killers to *walk free* as long as we can claim a victory in the death sentence of *one man*.

And *if* the FBI will bungle evidence, withhold documents and lie in a case that they know the *world* is *watching* through the all-seeing, all-knowing *eyes* of the media; what misconduct is taking place in cases that the American public never hears about?

"I am totally convinced that at least one indigent defendant goes to prison for a crime he or she didn't commit everyday in America," stated Attorney Murray J. Janus.

"Justice has a price tag in this country. I have bribed district attorneys, police officers and even judges. No judge will turn down fifty thousand dollars in cash to dismiss a case unless he does not *trust* the lawyer," stated a well-known defense attorney in the New York area. And this is a high profile lawyer who's on TV all the time. He's also a former federal prosecutor. I promised to withhold his name. "Your word is as good, if not better than some judges," stated the lawyer. I was *not* amazed.

"I could walk you through every prison in this country and show you at least ten people in each prison who was wrongfully convicted," stated Atlanta Attorney Michael Bergin. "The reason I fight so hard is because I am quite cognizant of the fact that although it's you today, it could be my child or friend tomorrow. There but for the Grace of God go I," Attorney Janus said.

"Judges set themselves up as high priests. But many of them are evil devils," the New York lawyer added. It takes Gerry Spence of Jackson, Wyoming to really talk about the evils of the judiciary. The high bench of our courthouses has become the low mark of the scum of the earth.

It is quite difficult to comprehend how some prosecutors and judges can sleep at night.

The death penalty? Again, it is ludicrous, hypocritical and preposterous. A life for a life. A death for a death. "Let's fry him," say the judges. What would I look like if I advocated the killing of Mary Hanlon Stone, Judge Robert Altman or Debbie Glynn? How would it sound for me to advocate that somebody should go assassinate Mary and Altman for what they did to me in Santa Monica Superior Court? OK, someone should kill Debbie Glynn in Sacramento for her efforts to work in collusion with Mary and Robert and to attempt to secure a seventy-five years to life sentence in prison for two pieces of paper?

I have not, cannot and will not advocate murder to avenge evils perpetrated against me. I don't want to see anybody hurt or kill Mary, Robert or Debbie, just get them *out of office*. Just hurt them (non physically) in the media, at the church or in the ballot box. I don't ever advocate violence to right a wrong. But John Ashcroft and George W. Bush both support, state sanctioned murder. And these two men say they are born again Christians and full of Christ's "compassionativity" (Mr. Bush's word). But just as ole Boy George W. misuses the English language and mispronounces certain words; he misuses the Bible and misunderstands certain scriptures. Jesus Christ *never* supported the death penalty! Never! When the Jews wanted to stone the woman caught in adultery in accordance with Jewish traditions etc. Jesus commutted the death sentence. Jesus gave her a compassionate reprieve. He did *not* obey, enforce or adhere to customs and traditions.

So George and John can go to hell with that rhetoric about an eye for an eye and a tooth for a tooth. This is wrong!

But everyday the government's *power* to trample on citizen's rights are being increased and inflated. In some sense, it would appear that the American Judiciary and Penological Systems are filled with undercover militia-minded employees who hide their racism and biases under their uniforms

The mere thought that Mark Fuhrman once wore a uniform and a badge and the fact that a militia minded, racist, violent predator carried a gun and arrested people is frightening. Mark was/is a racist, vindictive, evil, biased madman who was exposed for all the world to see on TV who also happened to be a police officer. Can you imagine being Black or Brown and being stopped on a lonely highway at 11:00 p.m. by detective/racist/evil/mean spirited/corrupted Mark Fuhrman? It is absolutely terrifying! And yes it happens everyday of the week.

The Mark Fuhrman type, Gestapos, vigilantes, racist, kick ass and take names later type cops make arrests all across America; every day and night of the week.

And if you were a Black man and your White girlfriend accused you of abuse and detective Fuhrman responded to the call - what would he do when he got there? *If* I am Black and I *hate* Whites, if I am an undercover racist Black cop and I respond to a call by a Black woman claiming her white boyfriend attacked her, is it hard to imagine how I'd treat the White suspect? And the truth of the matter is there are more White police officers in this country than there are Black men in college. And many of the White officers, FBI agents, district attorneys and judges are biased at minimum and racist at moderate and thus far society has refused to demand that racist cops be weeded out of our police departments.

We have allowed racist, alcoholic, drunken, cowboy and hick type judges to continue to fart through our courthouses all across this country. *We* have allowed this to continue!!!

"We cannot sweep under the rug the shame and the pain of what our government does to innocent people," says Barry Scheck.

What is the profile of a killer? What's the profile of a terrorist or a rapist? Can we trust the paperwork of the police or the paperwork of prosecutors? How can we when the FBI stated unequivocally that Richard Jewell *fit* the *profile* of the Olympic Bomber? Didn't they claim Rolanda Cruz fit the profile of a child-molesting murderer? Didn't they claim Rubon "Hurricane" Carter fit the profile of an anti-White, violent, racist triple murderer? Don't they say Sherman

170

Manning fits a profile? And about Richard, Rolando, Rubin and Sherman, they were wrong, wrong, wrong, wrong!!

How much power do prosecutors have? *Most* of it! How much power do prosecutors seek and want? *All of it*!

Ask Attorney John Keker, Johnnie Cochran, Gerry Spence or Bob Smith how much power the government and its prosecutors have. Ask them how they've screwed up voir dire. Go talk to Attorney Willie Gary about how money buys courtroom justice and big corporate donors control the judicial process.

Recently the U.S. Supreme Court refused (hard to believe with Clarence Thomas sitting on the Court) to allow California prosecutors to present anonymous testimony by jailhouse informants in a murder trial. Prosecutors sought to keep the names of key witnesses *secret* from defense lawyers claiming their safety would be jeopardized. Los Angeles Deputy D.A. (a friend of Mary Hanlon Stone's and Judge Robert Altman) Brentford Ferreira asked the U.S. Supreme Court not to allow defense lawyers to know who was testifying against the defendants. San Francisco Prosecutor Alfred Giannini chimed in that he tries to remove jurors who live in the same neighborhood as the defendant because they may be afraid to vote for a guilty verdict.

Yet, defense lawyers such as Murray Janus have (for years) argued persuasively that they need to learn witnesses' names to *investigate* their backgrounds and *motives* for testifying. "Otherwise, you are depriving the defendant of any real ability to meet and challenge the prosecution case. And when the prosecution depends on *jailhouse informants* (especially) you want to know what gang these people had belonged to. Might they have a reason to commit murder themselves? Might they have some vendetta against the defendants?" stated Attorney Robert Gerstein, the L.A. Defense Lawyer who argued the case. And finally, the defense lawyers won one.

In mid May, Inmates Charles Sheppard and Anthony Faison were released from prison after serving fourteen years for a murder they did not commit. No DNA freed them. Anthony, however, wrote over sixty thousand letters from prison proclaiming his innocence. Finally, a retired N.Y.P.D. cop who is now a private investigator, took on their case; pro bono. Mr. Mike Race took their case and found the eyewitness who testified against them. "She was on her death bed, dying from aids. She admitted she lied on them to collect a one thousand dollar reward," stated Mike Race. And Mike Race and Attorney Ron Kuby got Anthony and Charles out of prison. Fourteen years of innocence stolen by the prosecutor, judge and jury. This is scary. And I'm certain that Anthony wrote Oprah, Montel and all the other media. But none of them gave a damn. Who gives a damn about the least of these our brethren?

It's mostly about politics. We have so many spineless, worthless and corrupted politicians in office that it is pathetic. They support these rushes to judgment, overzealous prosecutors and rogue cops in an effort to get *re-elected*. Re-election is all that matters to them. That's why they support the death penalty.

The death penalty by and large is for Blacks, Browns and poor Whites that can't afford a good lawyer. Show me *one* of Murray Janus', Michael Morchower's, Stanley Greenberg's, Ephraim Margolin's or Barry Tarlow's clients who received the death penalty! Even U.S. Supreme Court Justice Ruth Bader Ginsburg stated in May of this year that she would support a *moratorium* on the Death Penalty.

"I have yet to see a death case among the dozens coming to the Supreme Court on the eve-of-execution stay applications in which the defendant was well represented at trial," stated Ginsburg during a lecture. "People who are well represented at trial do *not* get the death penalty," this justice stated. How much more do we need to know it is unfair, racist, biased and classist? What if Anthony and Charles had received the death penalty? Two more innocent people would have been dead now.

What if Robert Gerstein had lost before the Supreme Court? What if Anthony and Charles had been disallowed to know the identity of their accuser? Mike Race would have had no way of getting that deathbed confession. The thought is absolutely breathtaking.

I can tell you from experience with probity and veracity that when an *innocent* man hears a judge pronounce his sentence, it feels as if someone has sucked all of the oxygen out of the room. And if our citizens sit back and allow prosecutors to gain more power, America and her citizens are in *trouble*. Serious trouble!

And we need Bishop T. D. Jakes, Jesse Jackson, athletes, celebrities and everyday citizens to *Rise up and take the power back*. We must take our power back.

I see a lot of these televangelists trying to praise Bush because Bush says he believes in faith-based programs etc. What most of these preachers are really doing is hoping George will hear about their program and give them some money for their church. *Shame on you*!

Have these preachers forgotten about spiritual wickedness in *high places*? I'm sick and tired of weak, timid, lying and con artist preachers who refuse to see it for what it is and tell it like it is.

Preachers should be spear heading the cause for the least of these.  We should demand a *weed* and *seed* program for every police force and FBI Agency in America.  Weed out the bad cops and plant seeds for good cops.  We need to set up task forces which will better train our cops and teach them sensitivity, diversity and tolerance.  One need only look at the vicious killing of a nineteen-year-old Black kid by a White cop to see that something more than mere rhetoric must be done.  Cincinnati's out of control police officers are not an aberration.  They are merely a microcosm of society at large.  We have racist and corrupted Black officers in these big cities also.  The only comfort for the White man is that there are not that many Black officers in most cities.  And usually, if the Black street cop is racist, his sergeant or lieutenant or his captain is White.  So this sometimes keeps the racist Black cop in check.

I saw Kenneth Starr join forces with Johnnie Cochran a few months ago to defend clients.  Ken and Johnnie are the legal odd couple.  No one would have ever guessed this conservative, republican hit man attorney would join this brother from the hood on anything.  But they did.  They are defending the Civil Rights of Rev. Walter Fauntroy, one other Black and a conservative White man who protested outside the Sudan Embassy in D.C.  Johnnie (believe it or not) is representing the conservative White defendant.  And Ken is representing the two Blacks.  I love that and I will hope that more legal odd couples will come together and defend the innocent.  What would happen if Johnnie and Ken decided to take on an appeal for Brandon Martinez?  What would happen if Gerry Uelmen and Johnnie Cochran took my appeal?  What would happen if Johnnie Cochran called a summit meeting for lawyers?  What if he asked Murray Janus, Barry Tarlow, Bobby Lee Cook, Michael Morchowse, Ira Landon, Roy Black, F. Lee Bailey, and Stanley Greenberg etc. to join with him and Barry Scheck and take on the appeal of one innocent, imprisoned person per month?  What if Johnnie called Willie Gary and asked Willie to take one criminal appeal per year?  Willie Gary is a brilliant, articulate, Christian, rich and powerful lawyer.  Willie Gary is known for winning before all White juries.  We need more legal odd couples.

When one thinks about Anthony Faison and Charles Sheppard, one must be moved to take action.  Upon being exonerated, Mr. Faison stated that *"we cannot forget* the thousands of innocent here in prisons across this country - we cannot forget them."  And I would say its time for Anthony Raison, Anthony Porter, Ken Maters, David Quindt, Jeff Pierce and the others who have gotten their miracles to get involved in *helping* others. Words alone won't get us out. We need action.

We need these guys to go on radio, TV and write letters to the editors of newspapers across this country and get the ball to rolling. If I offered you (the person reading this book right now) *ten thousand dollars* in cash for every single person you convinced to *read this book*; how many people would you get to read it? If I offered you ten thousand dollars for every telephone call you make to a radio talk show about this book - how many talk shows would you call? If I offered you five thousand dollars for each letter to an editor you write about this book - how many letters will you write? Cash money! Can I get your help? Well hold the phone; if I still had access to that kind of money do you think I'd still be in prison? Don't you think I could motivate Gerry Spence, F. Lee Bailey, Stanley Greenberg, Ephraim Margolin, Barry Tarlow or Johnnie Cochran to *get me out of here* if I still had a million bucks? Alan Dershowitz would bail me out of here for perhaps a hundred thousand dollars.

And it is not all about *me*. There are so many others here who don't need to be here. Lawbreakers should be arrested. If you do the crime, you should do the time. Yes, we do need to be tough on crime. But we must re-think crime and punishment.

Rape is a senseless, shameful and a horrible crime and it is also senseless, shameful and horrible to be *falsely accused of rape*. Murder is a tragic, evil and inexcusable crime and it is also a tragic, evil and inexcusable crime to be falsely convicted of *murder*. How much dehumanization can people take and not *fight back*? How many more Anthony Faizons, Charles Shepards, David Quindts, Jeff Pierces and Kenny Waters must we see before we re-think how easy it is to send a man to prison for a crime he did not commit?

I'm telling you that cases such as that of Richard Jewells are exemplifications of the fact that we can't trust profiles and we cannot trust the profilers. The public confidence in police departments and FBI Agencies has been severely undermined. And I've stated before that every time we arrest, try and convict the wrong guy for murder; not only do we snatch an innocent man's life away from him; we also allow a murderer to remain free. This is dangerous.

Geronimo Pratt is free today after the tireless and dogged efforts of Stuart Hanlon and Johnnie Cochran. Somebody murdered that woman and has not been brought to justice. Geronimo was innocent. It took twenty-seven years for him to prove it. Twenty-seven years in a racist prison system for a crime he clearly did not commit. The FBI coin tel pro and a vicious prosecutor was involved in that. And taxpayers paid to the tune of 4.5 million dollars for Geronimo's suffering. But who killed that woman?

And let me remind America that it is quite frankly next to impossible to languish in the bowels of prison for a crime you did not commit and not become bitter.

Prison is a hate filled place. Prison (especially the California prison system) is a racist place for example: The best little prison job you can get is the job of a *clerk*. I call them male secretaries. And lots of them are the biggest rats (snitches) in the prison system. Here at New Folsom, we have about sixteen prison clerks on this facility. Out of sixteen, guess how many are Black? Do you think it's eight? How about seven, six, five? The answer is we have Uno! *One* Black clerk. One! One Black inmate with the job of clerk.

How about staff? Out of ten *captains*, *none* are Black. None! Zero! All are White. But that is the story of C. D.C. I call it the California Department of *Corruption* and the inmates are pitted against each other. Black on White. White on Black. Then you have tribalism within the races. Northern Mexicans against southern Mexicans and vice versa. White skinheads against White nazi low riders. Black crips against Black bloods.

Some of the most senseless, foolish, childish and *dangerous* stupidity I have every heard of. And C.D.C. allows and facilitates this racial discord. I wish Johnnie Cochran, The A.C.L.U. Gerry Spence or Barry Scheck would sue the hell out of C.D.C. These are some of the most evil people I have ever seen in my life. And they are ignorant! We have sergeants, lieutenants and captains who can't even read and write at the seventh grade level and they are charged with the serious task of supervising prisoners. If I were not here seeing it with my own eyes and hearing it with my own ears, I would not believe it either. And we now have an *Inspector General* who supposedly reports to the Governor. His last name is White and yes, *he is* (also) white. And yes he rubber stamps C.D.C. misconduct in a consistent fashion. Oh, by the way, he used to be a district attorney.

I want to warn the American public that most prisoners will *get out* one day and yes, they will return. But the life they take and the child they rape before they return may be you and yours. Y'all better demand that those prisons clean up their acts. This is only a word to the wise. The *prisoner*s of *today* are *your neighbors* of *tomorrow*. And if you wanna know who smuggles in the drugs and weapons, etc. you need look no farther than the almighty prison guards. And if they remove (transfer) me from this relatively safe yard and if I'm killed in C.D.C., I want Johnnie Cochran, Murray Janus, Jesse Jackson and my family to look no farther than prison guards. They (prison authorities) will have set me up. They do it every day. They have a lieutenant (B. M.) reading this book right now, using red flags and reporting every word I write to a thug task force called S&I. Yes - some of the staff on our FBI (S&I) task force are also corrupted and racist. And they specialize in twisting the facts to fit and support any outcome they desire. To lieutenant B.M.'s credit, however, at least he can *read*. Yes, I'm giving them *hell* because most of them are going to hell when they die.

So, I want America to read my words and ***demand*** that overzealous, corrupted police officers stop locking up innocent people. We must demand that prosecutor's stop suborning perjury and covering up police misconduct. Demand that judges stop excusing prosecutorial misconduct. We need more honest, fair and unbiased prosecutors like David Hicks in Richmond, Virginia and Aubrey Davis in Chesterfield. We need fair judges like Barry Loncke in Sacramento, CA and we need lawyers, law students and law professors to stand up against wrongful convictions here and *now*! -Once and for all.

And more guys like Murray Janus make a telephone call they get an answer! I can recall a rich White kid who was twenty-one years old in Richmond Virginia. I think it was in the latter part of 1994 when this kid whom I'll call Joseph threw a big party at his condo. There were about sixty people in and out of the party that night. And somebody placed a prank telephone call, which was deemed as harassment. The callee had Caller ID and also recorded the harassing telephone call. The next day a sergeant with the Richmond Police Department called Joseph and asked him to turn himself in on this misdemeanor complaint. The sergeant also informed Joseph that his probation would be violated etc. Joseph had been placed on probation for several DUI's - so he was actually facing about four years in prison. Joseph's girlfriend was a good friend of my fiancée. My fiancée called me at my suite at the Jefferson Sheraton Hotel. "Joseph is going to prison!" she yelled into my ear. That was a helluva wake up call. When I got to the bottom of the ordeal, I called Magic Michael Morchower. I figured Mike could handle the case. But Mike was in New York in a federal trial. So I then placed a call to my friend Mr. Murray J. Janus. "Reverend, bring the kid to my office in one hour and I'll take care of it." I had my driver to pick Joseph up and I walked the few blocks from the Jefferson Sheraton to Murray's office.

When I got there, Mr. Janus' pretty little receptionist (Jackie) said, "Mr. Janus is on a conference call with a judge in Washington. He'll be finished soon. Would you like some coffee?" A few minutes later, Joseph walked in looking as if he was about to attend a funeral. Finally, Mr. Janus came out. "Good morning Reverend. Is this the kid who's on his way to prison?" He asked. This really drove Joseph into a panic. We exchanged handshakes and Mr. Janus lead us into a large conference room similar to the one on "The Practice". It took Janus ten minutes to get Joseph's story. Mr. Janus said, "Who was the sergeant that called you again son?" After Joseph repeated his name, Murray said, "I know him. Give me five minutes and I'll be back."

Within sixty seconds, Murray had the sergeant on the telephone. He was down the hall in his private office with the door closed, but I could *hear him yelling*. Joseph looked at me and said, "Can you yell at the police like that?" I said, "I can't. You would be wise not to, but - Murray can." Joseph said, "I've seen him on television and in the newspapers, but I didn't know he yelled like that." I chuckled.

Few minutes later, Mr. Janus returned and stated, "son that call will cost you three thousand dollars. You won't be going to jail or prison. You're probation won't be violated. You won't even be going to court and you'll never hear from the Richmond Police Department again. Now how and when are you going to pay me?" His dad paid the bill. Great lawyers who are known for winning can often keep a case from ever going to court. But it comes with a large price tag. Who knows what Murray was yelling about. He never told me. I guess it was on a *need* to *know* basis.

In *If It Doesn't Fit, You Must Acquit Book One*, I promised to reveal the outcome of Beverly Ann Monroe's murder trial. She was convicted. Murray J. Janus and (then) Defense Lawyer David Hicks tried one helluva case. But this one (very, very unusual for Murray J. Janus) they lost. How or why I don't know. I cannot truly tell you that Beverly didn't commit the crime. Maybe she did. And *if* she did, she deserves to remain in prison. But the case I saw as I sat through the trial was way short of the reasonable doubt standards. *If* she did it they didn't prove it to me. In fact, I know a television reporter who lost a one thousand dollar bet on the case. Shameful, I know, to *bet* on a person's life. But all of the reporters were making bets on the outcome of the trial. This particular veteran reporter stated, "I know Murray Janus inside out. He can't lose. He doesn't lose." And I'll fess up and admit that I too placed a bet. I bet on a hung jury. I lost.

In a surprising move (over the miraculous power of Murray Janus again) the judge temporarily granted Beverly Monroe *bail* even *after* her conviction on first-degree murder. *Money* and *Murray* (the

M&M factor) moves judges. Mr. Janus, of course, filed an appeal but at the time of this writing I do not know where the appeals are.

A lot of people think that lawyers, such as Murray Janus, Bobby Lee Cook, Jonnie Cochran, Barry Tarlow, Michael Snedeker or Gerry Spence, are just *lucky*.

But I think Willie Gary's wife said it best, "If you go to bed as late as Willie does and wake up as early. If you work as hard and study as much as Willie does then you'll be lucky too." Amen.

The weak, timid, tired, scared and shabby lawyers who often represent the poor and indigent are usually ill-prepared and under-trained. And quite frankly, they just don't give a damn about their clients. Many of these lawyers have been known to come to court drunk and to even sleep through trials. In the case that I know about, a guy received the death penalty and his lawyer slept through most of the trial. Why didn't the judge stop the trial and give the man a new lawyer? One answer may be that the judge was drunk too. But a better answer is that the judge didn't give a damn. This is wrong. And that man, this day, is sitting on death row partly because of an incompetent, ill-prepared and sleepy lawyer.

In defense of the public defender, I must say that many of them really do care. And some of them fight. But they have caseloads that are out of this world. And they are underpaid. They fight an unsinkable fight with the little pennies our states and countries are willing to pay them. And you won't see anybody out fishing for more money for public defenders. No mayoral, gubernatorial or senatorial candidate will make better pay for the poor people's lawyers an issue of debate. They'll promise you more police officers. They'll give the DA's office all the money they need. But the supposedly innocent until proven guilty will continue to remain innocent until proven indigent partly because their (poor folks) lawyers barely earn enough money to pay their own bills.

I wish the NAACP, ACLU, Operation Push and all these other groups who fight for poor people would demand *more pay* and resources for poor people's lawyers.

We must equip public defenders with the resources they need to give the poor a fighting chance. Public apathy about people in prison and folks accused of crimes is largely due to the media. It is also due to politicians. To a large degree, before I was personally a victim of a wrongful conviction, I was quite skeptical because my experience as an evangelist and entrepreneur had taught me that claims of innocence from convicted criminals are often made, rarely proved and usually untrue. An entire nations' fear of crime and longing to feel safe has made the conviction of innocent people startlingly common.

"The function of the prosecutor under the Federal Constitution is not to tack as many skins of victims as possible to the wall. His function is to vindicate the rights of the people as expressed in the laws and give those accused of crime a fair trial," stated Justice William O. Douglas. Somebody ought to remind Mary Hanlon Stone, Robert Clancy and Debbie Glynn of that statement.

As I stated earlier, I used to believe that all "those" people in prison should be right where they are. And my only job was to pray that God would save their souls. But their bodies should remain behind the barbed wire fences. Oh what a change has come over my life as a result of this firsthand experience of a modern day lynching by Judge Robert Altman, Dave Winkler and Mary Hanlon Stone. I still believe to this day that if investigator Tom Owens could have sat down with Ricardo Calvarrio as did Mike Race with Anthony Faison's (and Charles Shepard's) accuser. Tom Owens would have gotten Ricardo to admit he was lying. Plain and simple. But Mary Hanlon and Dave Winkler threatened Ricardo with extradition to Mexico and they threatened him with a jail sentence for perjury if he talked to Tom Owens. Tom told me, "Mary Hanlon and Dave Winkler committed prosecutorial misconduct and both Judge Kamins and Altman know they did."

In 1990 Clarence Brandley was exonerated and released from Texas' death row after more than a decade. Every level of his case was infected by misconduct. From the threatening of exculpatory witnesses who wanted to testify for Clarence (they were threatened by police officers in George W. Bush's state) to the prosecutor and the trial judge holding *secret meetings* to rehearse rulings and objections. Evidence planting, evidence tampering etc. You name it if it's illegal; the prosecutor and judge did it in this case. It reminds me of the fact that Mary Hanlon and Robert Altman had secret meetings during my trial. Someone even told me that Mary Hanlon and Robert Altman had an affair. Yes, a love affair. Russell Camosky went back to Richmond, Virginia and boasted (see Book One) that Mary Hanlon came to his hotel and screwed him to death. This is what Clay Hollifield told one of my investigators. In Clarence's case the detective who arrested him told him "since you're the nigger, you're elected." Clarence came within days of being executed before a last ditch appeal spared him. Subsequently, all charges were dropped. An appellate judge who examined the court later wrote: "In the thirty years this court has presided over matters in the judicial system, no case has presented a more shocking scenario of the effects of racial prejudice, perjured testimony, witness intimidation, an investigation the outcome of which was predetermined, and public officials who, for whatever motives, lost sight of what is right and just". This case was not in 1950 or 1960. It was in 1990! Go pull the records and transcripts. I'm *not* making this up. This is *real*. I challenge any reporter to prove me wrong.

Yet you can't ever gauge the prosecutorial misconduct and police corruption by the sheer (large) number of cases that are being overturned everyday now. Why not? Because by and large the Appeals Courts rubber stamp wrongful convictions everyday. The justice system is reluctant to overturn any conviction even when it is clear the conviction was obtained by tainted evidence. They consistently uphold wrongful convictions because they don't want to disturb a jury decision. This is absolutely ridiculous. And so the Mary Hanlons and Robert Altmans march on. I challenge any reporter to ask Mary or Robert to take polygraph tests. They would refuse! Mary may not have had sex with Judge Altman. That's only rumor. She may not have had sex with Russell Comosky; rumor again. Pure rumors. But I affirm here and now that it is a *fact* that Mary Hanlon Stone knew I was innocent of this crime. She and Judge Altman knew the testimony was false. I wish Mike Race would come to L.A. or perhaps Tom Owens would ask Mary to let him hear the 911 call placed by Ricardo Calvario. Ask them to let you hear the taped interview that Ricardo gave that night at 3:00 a.m. She'll *swear* the 911 call is gone and the tape was lost or was never made. Corrupted people utilize corrupted tactics and they cover their tracks well.

I still know that Barry Tarlow, Barry Levin, Barry Scheck or Stanley Greenberg could get at the truth. I know this in my soul, in my spirit, in my heart and in the very fabric of my being.

I'm gonna move on through and to some other cases of wrongful convictions in a moment. Let me state again that California prison guards make the L.A. Rampart Division look like Sterling Characters. A lot of prison guards across this state are just thugs. Right now they are calling people asking them not to read my book and they are (again) attempting to invent a reason to transfer me. They don't want me at New Folsom. Our warden (C.K.P.) is a good woman. But they intercept my complaints to her. She is not corrupted in my opinion and she seems to be very fair. But as with all CA prisons we have our share of corrupted and rotten staff members. Even more frustrating is the fact that many inmates are simply programmed robots. Some don't deserve to ever be free. I understand more clearly now why so much of the public doesn't give a damn about prisons and prisoners. Many prisoners don't give a damn about themselves. A few months ago a show aired called ***D.N.A. Judgment Day***. It showed men wrongfully convicted who got justice. At the time this show aired we were having dayroom. There were about thirty inmates out in a large room where there are tables and a television. I put the TV on the television show. I just knew my fellow prisoners would gather around as they do when the Lakers and the Sacramento Kings are playing on TV. I could not believe my eyes. Not one single inmate was watching the show. Some were gambling; some playing scrabble and one guy asked me to put the TV on Smack Down. This is sick and shameful. A group of grown men, some of whom have ***no way out*** and don't have a lawyer, would rather watch grown men pretend to be wrestling than to watch Barry Scheck exonerate innocent men. I don't understand this. It's sick and shameful.

I want to tell America that we need to come together and rethink the whole issue of crime, punishment, police and convictions. Juno Durden and Ray Perez should have taught us. Officer Rafael Perez was a police officer at L.A.P.D. - a "star" officer. And two years ago he was found out. Evidence tampering, false testimony, wrongful shooting, stealing cocaine and false arrests are just some of the crimes he confessed to. He implicated a wagon full of other officers. Many of them went to jail and many innocent inmates got released. Gil Garcetti pursued and arrested all the Black officers whom Ray Perez implicated. But when he started naming White cops - Gil Garcetti lost interest.

Frontline on PBS aired a program a while back about the LAPD. The featured Chief Bernard Parks. Bernard is Black and to my utter surprise they showed a White investigator who works for the Chief referring to Blacks as "a person with Negro features". In 2001, this White cop still calls Blacks "Negro" and he works for a Black Chief. Damn.

Ever heard of Margarette Kelly Michaels? I'm sure Barry Scheck, Lisa Short, Michael Snedeker and Anthony J. Serra have. What do you think about child molesters? I think they are sick, evil, perverted and shameful. We must get a handle on child predators. This is just sick, very sick. And it is also very, very, sick when police officers ***frame up*** a person and send him away when they are innocent. Margarette spent over five years in prison, labeled a ***child predator*** and yet she was innocent. This case occurred in New Jersey. The Appeals Court found out that the detectives coerced kids to lie on her. Do you still believe in the police?

What about Christopher Ochoa and Richard Dansinger? They were convicted of rape and murder. They spent twelve years in prison convicted of a heinous, brutal and sickening crime. The kind of rape murder case that just makes my blood boil. The kind of case, which brings tears to your eyes. It was a rape and murder so sadistic that even veteran homicide detectives were shaken. So shaken that they had to solve it and they convinced the victim's family that they had their men. The presses rolled the cameras flashed. The headlines convinced all of us that Chris and Richard should never see the light of day again. Just lock these predators up and throw away the key. Who gives a damn about what happens to them in prison. In fact, Richard got what was coming to him. A fellow prisoner beat him so viciously that he suffered brain damage. Richard can barely wipe his own butt now. I'm sure Chris and Richard wrote letters to all the talk shows and newspapers. But nobody wrote back. These were violent sexual predators and sadistic murderers. Who cared about them? Well Barry Scheck and his Innocence Project at the Cardoza Law School cared. And they exonerated and vindicated both Richard and Chris. They were totally innocent. Innocent the day they were arrested! Innocent, the day they went to trial. Innocent, the day they were convicted and innocent, when they begged Governor George W. Bush to look into the conspiracy totally, one hundred percent *innocent*. Yet, nobody believed them. But thank *God* for Barry Scheck. He administered the Scheck-Effect and got them out after twelve long years. The murder victim's mother now says of the Police Department and District Attorney, "They lied to me all that time." Barry Scheck had tears in his eyes when the judge released them. Christopher stated, "To all those innocent men in prison; never give up hope. Never, never, never!"

Chris was talking to *me*. Ralph Armstrong was a twenty-one-year-old White guy out in Wisconsin. There was a vicious rape and a cold-blooded murder. And the Madison Police Department knew Ralph was their man. He had to be. He knew the victim. He had a *history*. Hell, Ralph was on *parole for rape*. A sexual predator! He fit the profile. Come on, the guy was on parole for rape. The famed Madison Police Department turned up a witness. The witness was a transvestite (Ricardo Calvario?) The police brought the transvestite in and hypnotized him/her. Under hypnosis they showed him four photos of this convicted rapist Mr. Ralph Armstrong. The transvestite identified him as the killer. After serving ten years, Ralph had D.N.A. taken on his semen. D.N.A. proved that the semen on the victim was not his. It didn't fit, but they did not acquit. The Appeals Court refused to give this violent predator a new trial. Come on, the guy was on parole for rape. He had to be guilty. Somebody (anybody? Or the right person) has to *pay* for this crime. Well a few months ago now after twenty-one years in prison Ralph had more D.N.A. testing done. Guess what? The D.N.A. on the blood conclusively proved that Ralph Armstrong has sat in prison for twenty-one years for a crime he did not commit. The rush to judgment, the overzealous prosecution and illegal tactics by the police department has stolen twenty-one years of an innocent man's life.

The police department just knew that "He's on parole for rape, he knew the victim so he's got to be guilty". This is why they invented evidence via the hypnotized transvestite. Twenty-one years stolen. I'm sure Ralph wrote all the newspapers, television shows and celebrities. Their reply? "They all say they are innocent. Gimme a break, the guy was, on parole for rape. He's got to be guilty". But they were all wrong. Again thank God for the Barry Schecks, Gerson Horns, Peter Neufields, Lisa Shorts, Gerry Spences and Barry Tarlows of our society. Mr. Armstrong is labeled for life for a crime he clearly did not commit. "I essentially lived on the streets mentally and emotionally, but physically I was trapped in a cage for a crime I did not do," stated Mr. Armstrong.

Ronald Keith Williamson spent nine years of his life on Death Row. Do you know how cold, scary and evil Death Row is? What does Death Row do to a man's mind? I'm sure Ronald Keith Williamson wrote to Johnnie Cochran and many other big shot lawyers. But most inmate mail is rejected and sent back. Nine years on Death Row and guess what? He (too) was innocent. Absolutely and completely innocent. When he finally got justice and proved it didn't fit and they did acquit; he got fifty dollars and one suit of clothing. Fifty dollars when nine years of his life has been stolen! Stolen innocence! Deprived of freedom and almost murdered by the state for a vicious crime you did not commit and the way they say sorry is with fifty bucks. That is absolutely a sin and a shame. It's a disgrace to America. And we need more lawyers to join forces and fight. Again, Barry Scheck *cannot do it alone*. We need the brilliance, status and assistance of the Johnnie Cochrans and even Jesse Jacksons of our society to come together and do God's work. It's just as humbling and redemptive as the work that Mother Teresa did.

Martin Luther King, Jr. will smile down on any lawyer, preacher or celebrity who will help the least of these thy brethren. And there are thousands of us all over the country who needs help. For every innocent man in prison, I make the plea to help. Help! Help! We need your help.

Let me tell you about another case. It is a strange and fascinating case. It's another case that will make your blood boil and send chills down your spine. It is a case that will bring tears to your eyes. It is a tragedy and an embarrassment to our great country. This kind of case is not supposed to happen in America. Not the land of the *Free* and the home of the *Brave*. Not a country whose president brags about leaving *no child behind*. Not a country that says that racial profiling is wrong. Not a country with a checks and balances system. *Not* a country that boasts about *Due Process* and a fine, fair and unbiased judicial system. *Not* in our America with all these lawyers, reporters and investigators. No way; not in America. Are you crazy? Are you living in a dream world or do you just not give a damn? *Give me a break*! There are thousands; multiple thousands of innocent men sitting in prison right this minute as *you read this book*.

Do you think Barry Scheck is a fool? This is a brilliant, rich, powerful D.N.A. expert. Why would he waste his time building *Innocence Projects* across America if wrongful convictions were just an every now and then occurrence? He does it because he know how often police officers lie. He knows how often district attorney's don't play by the rules. He knows many judges are racist, corrupted and a dishonor to the courtrooms they sit in. Barry Alda knows many lawyers won't answer a prisoner's mail. Barry knows some lawyers are greedy and if you have no *dime* they have no *time*. Barry Scheck knows! He cares! He is real and authentic.

*This* case really moved Barry Scheck. And it will move you too. "Ray Charles and Stevie Wonder could have seen through my case," stated Herman Atkins. And Herman was absolutely correct. Any blind man could have seen that Herman was railroaded. The most difficult thing for an incarcerated person to do however is get somebody to *look* at your case. "Somebody please help me," you pray to God. Bishop Noel Jones, Bishop Jakes, Bishop Gilbert Patterson, Jesse Jackson, Al Sharpton, NAACP, ACLU, *anybody* just *look* at my case. The world is passing me by and I'm sitting here for something I did not do. These are the mumblings and grumblings of an innocent man in prison. You write Oprah, Montel, Queen Latifah and nobody seems to care. Preachers send you a copy of a form letter asking you to join their church. We are literally dead men trapped in a steel cage and we write, cry, hope and pray that somebody will come to our tomb and cry "Lazarus, come forth."

But the real Barry Schecks come far and few between. Herman Atkins received a forty-seven year sentence in prison. Conviction? Another one of those rapes and murders. Some victim's true killer and rapist is walking the streets free and Herman sat in a California prison paying a fine and doing time yet he didn't do the crime. One day a fellow inmate gave him Barry Scheck's address. It took seven years for the Scheck effect to pop off. After serving fourteen years being abused by prison guards and prison inmates, Herman finally got justice. Real justice. Herman stated that child molesters and rapists are treated like the scum of the earth in prison. Abused, vilified and mistreated. In fact, the more I think about it, I believe I met Herman years ago at this prison. I really believe he was here and tried to give me advice on my case. Barry got him out and proved that in spite of profiles, reputations as a predator etc., Herman was completely innocent. Herman got out and is now attending Lais Southwest College.

"I was robbed of fourteen years of my mother and my mother was robbed of fourteen years of me," Herman stated as the tears began to pore out of his eyes. "And now my mother is dying of cancer." He cried. "And now I must stick by her just like she stuck by me. I just hate I must stand by and watch her die."

That is sad. It's very sad. Willie Gary, Gerry, Bobby Lee, Murray; y'all gotta help us. Barry Scheck cannot do it *alone*.

We all know that if we are waiting on George W. or John Ashcroft or the FBI to help us we'll be waiting 'til hell freezes over. It's professor, David Protess and his journalism students, and Professor Robert Cling and his students in Chicago who give the innocent a fighting chance. And all y'all on TV and in magazines claiming you want to help to heal the world. You want to make the world a better place in which to live. You love what Martin Luther King, Jr. and Mother Teresa stood for. Well, why are you waiting? Why won't you write back? Why won't you send a hundred dollars, a thousand or a hundred thousand dollars? Why have *you* done nothing for the *least of these thy brethren*? I see you in Ebony Magazine, on 60 Minutes and all over the place talking about *unto whom much is given, much is required*. But I still don't see *you* doing anything about, "I was in prison and you visited me not". You know we can do better than this. This is America. We defeated Jim Crow, Bull Connor and the colored-only fountains. We defeated segregation and fought for the right to vote. We sing "Keep Hope Alive" and we can survive and thrive. We defeated *slavery*. Can we not also defeat wrongful convictions? Jesse, Al, and Kweisi - we need *you*. We must do something differently.

Look at *pedophiles* and child molesters. To rape an innocent child is sick, senseless, shameful and dastardly. Yet child molesters get *probation* everyday! And prisons are full of real thieves with priors. You can rape a *child* and get probation or a two or three-year sentence in prison and walk out free. Yet you can steal a loaf of bread and serve twenty-five years to life in prison. This is ridiculous and absolutely preposterous.

And as I have stated, we must stop pretending to trust the police and prosecutors to be fair, wise and truthful. Let's look at the headline grabbing prosecution and conviction of San Diego Mayor Hedgecock, which was thrown out when it was discovered that the bailiff in the 1985 trial had tampered with the jury. He coached and coerced the jury. This bailiff also supplied the jurors with liquor, and talked about the mayor's guilt during and throughout these deliberations. The prosecutor kept his information secret for five years! Finally the California Supreme Court compelled the prosecution to divulge this information, Hedgecock was exonerated. He is now a radio talk show host.

What about Dale Johnson! He was sentenced to death for the vicious and sadistic murders of his stepdaughter and her fiancée in Ohio. Yet, Dale was freed after six years because prosecutors hid evidence that showed his innocence. Once he was released the state chose not to re-file the case. Stolen innocence!!!

In 1991, Jeffrey Jenkins prison sentence and conviction for possessing an illegal sawed off shotgun who overturned because prosecutors knowingly used a confession against him, which had been obtained by *death threats* and *beatings* by the police. Do you still think the Rodney King beating was an aberration? What about Jimmy Lee Horton? Lee was sentenced to death for a murder. Yet he has a new trial because a Georgia prosecutor had systematically kept Blacks off the jury and had issued a memo to the court clerks on how to keep women and Blacks off the jury without getting caught.

Gary Nelson was exonerated and vindicated after nearly twelve years on death row for the 1978 rape and murder of a six-year-old in Chatham County, Georgia. What went wrong? Just a harmless technicality? Hell no! It was brought to light that his conviction was based on official lies, knowing use of false testimony, the suppression of exculpatory evidence and the hiding of evidence, which implicated another man. This is evil and this is wrong.

What about Titus Lee Brown? He was exonerated from his 1984 murder conviction with a life sentence when it was revealed that in Los Angeles (Mary Hanlon Stone?) Assistant D.A. on this case knowingly presented false evidence linking this to a murder robbery. This case clearly showed how difficult it could be to win a new trial, even when prosecutorial misconduct is proven. The California Court of Appeal upheld (rubberstamped) the conviction, while condemning the D.A.'s actions; the State Supreme Court refused to take Brown's side and also ordered a lower court's opinion "de-published", so as not to embarrass the prosecutor. The case had to go all the way up to the U.S. Ninth Circuit Court of Appeals - one level below the Supreme Court - before the man got a new trial. The court wrote: "The prosecutor's actions in this case are *intolerable* possessed of knowledge that destroyed her theory of the case, the prosecutor had a duty not to mislead the jury. Instead, she kept the facts secret . . . And then presented testimony in such a way as to suggest the opposite of what she alone knew to be true . . . Such conduct perverts the adversarial system and endangers it's ability to produce just results." Is it still so difficult to believe Mumia Abu Jamal is innocent?

In 1992, Kerry Kotler was freed after eleven years in prison for rape, burglary and robbery in Suffolk County, New York. Years before his release he had proved he was the victim of prosecutorial misconduct and police errors. Yet he lost all appeals because the court system called all the misconduct "Harmless Errors". Yet DNA finally proved he was completely *innocent*. This is tyranny. This is absolutely wrong, yet judges overlook wrongful convictions everyday of the week mostly because our fine-suit wearing politicians say nothing and the public seems not to give a darn.

Where are our leaders? Where is my congressman, Mr. John Lewis, who had the courage to be *beat* savagely in the 60's in the Civil Rights Movement? Where are Joseph Biden, Maxine Waters, the NAACP and the ACLU? Where is the courage and the love? This is America! This is supposedly the greatest nation on the face of the planet. How can we sit idly by and know that poor, indigent men and women are trapped in mean, cold prison cells for crimes they did not commit?

I am asking (again) the San Francisco Bayview Newspaper, the LA Sentinel, the Atlanta Voice, the Atlanta Daily World, the Afro-American newspapers today to begin to expose this consistently. We must put innocent prisoners right to be free before the public's eyes on a daily basis. We cannot afford to continue to allow this to happen in *our* America.

I want you reading my words right now to call your leaders, call your pastors, call your congressman: E-mail them, write to them and tell them we want a change in this dirty, classicist, racist and bigoted system of injustice. We want Judge Robert Altman derobed. We want Mary Hanlon Stone dethroned. We want action.

To those of you who have sent me letters expressing sympathy. Thank you. Your concern is admirable. But concern alone won't exonerate me. *Money*, a lawyer and action will. Concern won't free Mumia Abu Jamal. Sit down and write a check for ten, twenty, fifty, one hundred or a few thousand dollars and send it to me with your letter. And call F. Lee Bailey, Gerry Spence, Barry Tarlow and Gerry Uelmen about my case. Call the newspapers and radio shows. Take action!

It is me today and it could be you, your son, your husband or your brother tomorrow. You can be falsely accused of a crime any day of the week in any city or town in North America. And you may find yourself in the awful bowels of the California prison system looking around at racist segregation and spiritual wickedness in *high places*.

You could find yourself trapped in a system (like California's prison system), which foments racial violence and promotes gang and racial violence. You could see (as I have seen) a man who tried to commit suicide; an officer, who sexually assaulted a female officer in this prison, got promoted to the rank of sergeant instead of demoted and fired. Yes, an officer tried to kill himself; he sexually fondled a female employee. He has severe mental problems and he just got promoted to supervisor. He knows somebody downtown. There are promotion scams going on within C.D.C. all the time. And those good ole hicks are in charge of prisoners.

Small wonder that men leave these prisons worse than they were when they came.

The guards feel untouchable even after the feds took over Corcoran State Prison. And they feel the public doesn't give a darn. John Lewis? Maxine Waters? Ted Kennedy? Joseph Biden? Richard Polanco? Diane Feinstein? Barbara Boxer? Back media? Where are you? Where are the lawsuits and accountability? If I'm arbitrarily transferred tomorrow, the media must react. Somebody must hold C.D.C.'s feet to the fire if Brandon Martinez is transferred from a safe prison tomorrow or next week. With the witch hunt C.D.C conducted on me by calling almost every institution (Lancaster, SATIF, Mule Creek, Corcoran) in the state interrogating any ex-cellies and saying inflammatory things about me etc. I'm not safe anywhere else but *here*. My rights were violated in a very demeaning, dehumanizing and a selective manner. This is wrong. There is a C.O. working in ad-seg who is a racist, bitter, evil, lying and violent officer. C.O. (W.) scares even fellow officers. But this guy is still working for C.D.C. Mr. W.

is worse than Bull Conner and everybody knows it. But they won't fire him. In fact, he'll probably make sergeant within the next year or so. This is the story of C.D.C.

But allow me to digress a moment and express to you that there are many working in law enforcement who are really dedicated to serving and protecting all citizens. I want to make it absolutely clear that we should support the good police officers that are out on the streets day and night trying to make our cities safe. They risk their lives for us for so little pay. And I believe all good police officers should get a pay raise. We do not train and screen our police officers adequately and we do not pay them well enough. It's a sin and a shame that many good policemen and policewomen can't feed their families. And although this is no excuse for corruption, I must say this is why so many of them become corrupt. To work day and night for a few thousand dollars per month and to lay your body and life on the line trying to catch the bad boys. It is mighty tempting when a drug lord offers you ten thousand dollars per month just to keep him posted on major investigations. We need to pay them more money plain and simple. Tell George W. Bush I said that. No more talk! Pay them more money! Every one of us wants a response when we dial 911. So all of us should pay for it. Pay teachers more and pay police officers more.

I think Sheriff Mike Hennessy in San Francisco, CA has the right idea when it comes to crime prevention. Inmates in Sheriff Hennessy's jail are called *clients*. They get acupuncture. They do yoga. They receive intense rehabilitation and deal with the roots of their rage, anger and violence. Sheriff Hennessy says most inmates will get out one day. And if all we do is cage them like animals and abuse them while they are incarcerated; what kind of neighbor, citizen, employee, etc. will they become when they get out? One of Mike's inmates stated that "most prisons have at least four fights per week. We have had only four fights in the past five years. All of us, Black, White and Mexicans live together and we get along". I think this guy must have been reading my books. I wish Sheriff Hennessy would talk to the powers that be of C.D.C. This place absolutely refuses to become proactive, innovative or creative. These people absolutely have a vested interest in violence, drugs and racism. But until society, until you who are reading at this moment do something to *change* it - it shall continue. We will continue to lock up men, warehouse them, cage them, abuse them and send them home worse than they were when they entered prison.

189

As long as you, who are reading this book, continue to read and do **nothing**. As long as Murray J. Janus reads it and says, "That's a pretty good book" and puts it down. As long as mayors, governors and housewives read it and put it down. Nothing will happen. But when you begin to **do something**, we can transform America. The issues of crime and punishment are bigger than Jesse Jackson, Al Sharpton, Jerry Falwell or Pat Robertson. These issues are about the people, all the people of our America. Didn't you see the riots in Cincinnati a few months ago? The people are raging with anger, hurt and frustration. And a lot of this anger is due to the fact that a very large portion of young Black men, Latino men and poor White men have at some point been in these vicious jails, juveniles and prisons. They've been here and they were **raped**. Raped by prison guards and fellow inmates. Physically and sexually raped. And they were abused, scared and humiliated by vicious prison officials. And some of those who went to prison and got raped, stabbed or humiliated should not have been in prison to begin with. There are no rapes, stabbings or inmate rivalries at San Francisco County Jail #8. Sheriff Mike Hennessy won't allow it. "Most prison systems overlook therapy and only harden criminals," said the Sheriff. Urban Poole is now a program facilitator at the jail. Inmates are anxious to get out and return as program facilitators. They participate in programs such as (R.S.V.P.) Reform to Stop the Violence Programs. And the recidivism rate for those who get out is down to fourteen percent! That's effective and I hope every inmate in Mike's jail get a copy of this book. I commend them.

I also salute guys like Bobby "B.J." Davis. Bobby Davis is an ex-con who changed his life. Five years ago he was in prison. Two months ago he graduated from American River College Magna Cum Laude. You can do it too.

Programs work and we can't argue with success. Why wouldn't any warden of a prison want to model Mike Hennessy - Jail number 8? These prison wardens who claim they are tired of the stickings, stabbings and killings in prison - why won't they model Mike's program! Hell, I'm no fool. I know that the warden of Pelican Bay will not allow prisoners there to get acupuncture, massages and yoga. But why not bring in facilitators to help inmates deal with the roots of their rage? I challenge the governor **here** and **now** to call Sheriff Mike Hennessy and then model his program here at New Folsom Prison. I challenge the Honorable Mayor Willie Brown, Jesse Jackson, Monica Moorehead, Al Sharpton, the NAACP, ACLU, Johnnie Cochran and others to **demand** that prisons get back to rehabilitation and move away from warehousing criminals. John

Lewis, Maxine Waters, Ted Kennedy and others need to demand that we transform these prisons. If we are waiting on C.D.C. downtown to do it we will be waiting 'til Hell freezes over. And let's weed and seed prison guards. Guys like (C.O.) Mr. W. who works here in Ad Seg, Sgt. B. who just got promoted and is a threat to the safety and security of any prison. C.O.'s like Sgt. R. S. and C.O. B. Mudy be weeded out. These are Rank Racists. These are thugs with badges. These are tyrannical minded renegades who have no place in law enforcement. And we must seed in programs to transform lives because the guys getting out of here *tomorrow* are moving to your neighborhoods. They will walk the streets with your kids and your family. Get it in your mind today that most prisoners will get out. And we need to reach them while they are here.

America must make a shift in our mentality. We must change the way we think about justice, trials, crimes and the treatment of offenders. What will you do? Mr. Janus, Willie Gary, Gerry Spence, F. Lee Bailey, Stanley Greenberg, Barry Tarlow; all of you reading my words right now: What the Hell are you gonna do? Which one of you lawyers have the balls, the courage and the tenacity to take on C. D. C.?

Paul Hoffman, Roy Black, Ephraim Margolin, law students, law professors - who will take on this system? Who has the courage? I darn sure hope and pray that you reading will call Tommy Goss, Doug Banks, the Black media, the Worker's World newspaper and all the grassroots people and tell them two things: 1. *Read This Book*. 2. Let's take on the penological system. I challenge you right now. I'll work with you. I'll work day and night. Bishop T. D. Jakes. I have so much love and respect for Bishop Jakes. Bishop Jakes understands men and man talk. T. D. Jakes could transform these prisons. I challenge Bishop Jakes to help us. NAACP, ACLU, IAC, Shape Center, California Prison Focus, San Francisco Bay View News and Southern Poverty Law Center lets come together here and now. Lets start *Operation Hope* behind these walls. And don't you dare ask George W. for a dime. We cannot ride to freedom on a grant from King Pharaoh. We got the money. We got Shaquille O'Neal, Sean Puffy Combs, Oprah, Bill Cosby, Jeff Bezos, Don King, and Mike Tyson. We got the money. We got Spike Lee and T. D. Jakes. We got the money. We can use this book to help raise money. As a matter of fact, I want Bishop Jakes, Tommy Goss, Doug Banks, every preacher and radio host to know here and now that you can sell this (my) book. Sell it and keep almost half the money. Yes, announce that anyone who wants this book can send you twenty-four dollars.

You send me sixteen dollars and the address where the book needs to go and keep eight dollars for yourself. Let's do this.

I believe in America. I mainly believe in our youth. The youth are our future. And I'm tired of seeing seventeen and eighteen-year-old boys come into this place and leave out in critical (mental) condition. I'm ready to go to war. I'll join with the California Prison Focus, the ACLU, the NAACP and anybody else who wants to change the system. I'm ready to go to war. So CA Prison Focus, ACLU Prison Law Office, Prisoner's Focus Organizations, etc., you who are constantly corresponding with prisoners, you have my permission to tell inmates about this book. Sell it anytime you want. And we need preachers and churches to buy five, ten, twenty or a hundred copies of this book and send it to jails. Send Mike Hennessy fifty copies of this book for his inmates. Send it to law schools and lawyers. Send it to colleges. And I want every inmate reading this book to stop the violence. Forget the gang mentality. You are stuck in prison for a while. And some are stuck forever. You need to build your life. Pump up your mind and your spirit just like you pump up your body. Stop sitting around gambling, drinking and doping your life away. If you say you're a man, then act like one. Grow up and get some self-control. Find out who you are and how you got that way. And work to improve yourself. It's time to transform the inner you. Get some education in your life. Get God in your life. Find some inner peace. Find a little bit of love and hope. And all hope is never gone. If we would quit stabbing each other with knives and start stabbing the system with lawsuits, we would transform prisons. If we would pool our money and quit wasting it on dope, we could fund some true reform programs. We could make our voices heard in the courts, in the Congress and even in the Senate. We could help the ACLU, NAACP and CA Prison Focus to fight for us. These organizations need money. The public won't support them. There are over a million of us in prison. If each of us hustled up one dollar and sent it to CA Prison Focus in San Francisco, or the I.A.C. in New York, they could hire brilliant lawyers to overturn these three strikes laws. If California Prison Focus carried a million dollars to Johnnie Cochran, Willie Gary, Gerry Spence, Gerald Uelmen or Barry Tarlow, they would take on C. D. C. They would take on the fight against three strikes and the Prison Industrial Complex. But prisoners must get *serious*. We are too busy stabbing suspected child molesters. What if they had killed Rolando Cruz? Rolando was innocent. And we know how corrupted some police officers, prosecutors and judges are. We know cops have planted dope on people, etc. So we can't trust the system well enough to go stab a man who's convicted of molestation. He may be innocent. And if he is guilty, the court gave him his sentence. Let the fool do his time. It he's guilty, he is sick, perverted and severely disturbed. God will judge baby rapers! God will reward their evil and vicious deeds. But you and me cannot resort to violence.

Let us concentrate on dealing with why we are here. Those of us who are here for crimes we did not commit; let's fight like hell to get our freedom back. And let's transform ourselves in the process. Those of you who did the crime need to get some skills, knowledge, God, and restoration in your lives. Read, study, think and pray. Read autobiographies, get in the library and write letters to Congress and the Senate. Do something constructive with your life. Gang those books and bang the court system. Transform yourself then transform the prison system. Gray Davis won't do it for you. The prison wardens won't do it for you. You must do it. And we need lawyers to come to our rescue. I want those journalism students with David Protess, the students with Robert Cling, the students working with Susan Christian of U. C. Davis, and all lawyers to fight for your clients. You must beat the hell out of a corrupted system of justice. Take on those cowardly judges like Robert Altman. Take on those corrupted, fictitious prosecutors like Mary Hanlon Stone. Take them on in the courtrooms all across this country and fight like hell to free the innocent.

Lawyers you know the system. You know that guilty men go free and the innocent get convicted every day of the week. What the hell are you gonna do about it? Help Barry Scheck. Help David Protess. Help Robert Cling. Get involved in some way today and help the innocent to get our freedom back.

I got to digress here. Gladys Knight, Chaka Khan and Jennifer Holiday broke my train of thought. These sisters were just singing on the Essence Awards. They made me weep. I wept for Ennis Cosby and Bill and Camille Cosby. I wept for mothers. All the mothers of murdered children. I wept. I wept. I wept. I wept. I wept for the children crying out from cold graves whose lives were cut down by violence and guns. We have yet to *save* the *children*. We must cherish, honor and protect the precious gift that's called life. It's going to take *all* of us prisoners and pastors, others, fathers, brothers, lawyers, doctors, the rich, the poor, the saint and sinners. Can't we all love the children? Is there anyone so cold, so evil, so vicious that you, me, we don't give a darn about precious children? I can't imagine that kind of coldness. I can't fathom anyone unwilling to play a part in the salvation of the youth of America and youth of the world. I want every lawyer reading my words right now to *help save the children*. I want you to get involved by way of lectures, workshops, mentoring etc. in protecting the innocence of our babies. White babies, Black babies, Brown babies, etc. - *all children*. I want you prisoners to pray for our youths and when you get back out, try to help somebody else to never come where you've been. I want to honor my strong, faithful, praying mother, Dollie Manning. Without her prayers, I'd be dead. I honor Clara Jackson (belatedly), Brenda Smith and all the mothers of the world. The streets of our cities are covered in blood. The blood of our children. And all of that blood is Red Blood. The blood is Red and we want to mop it up and turn our heads. This is wrong. God will judge America for our failure to save the children. Susan Taylor - keep on doing what you are doing. Bill Cosby, Camille, Willie Gary, Randall Robinson and Naim Akbar - y'all keep on doing what you are doing. And each of you reading my words ought to do something to join on the fight to save the children. Do something.

Alright, I'll get back to this book now. I know I write in a very all over the place way. But these are my words. And I write with my heart and not just my head. I always know that just one page, one paragraph and one sentence in a book can change, save or enhance a life. I gotta digress again. Let me tell my fellow prisoners that we fall down but we can get back up again. Donny McClurkin can tell you that. For a saint is just a sinner who fell down but got back up again. I know that there are many reading this and you are not innocent. You actually committed the crime and you are doing the time. You're dealing with guilt, anger, hurt, pain and loneliness. I want you to know that you can get back up again. You need not wallow in despair, corruption or deceit. You can live again. Pick yourself up, dust yourself off and move on. You cannot change the past, but you can change the here and now. You need to get back up again. Open up your mind, your hearts and your souls. Read books by Les Brown, Anthony Robbins, Zig Zigler, Randall Robinson and Iyanla Vanzant. Read the Bible. Change your life. Malcolm turned a jail cell into a classroom. You can do it too. You can't help your keepers keep you in prison. Free your mind, my brother, and your heart will follow. What grows in your mind will grow in time. Be real. Don't try to con yourself. Don't play a game. You must be real. The warden sees you as a slave. Look at all these for profit, private prisons being built. Well they are all for profit. And they pay you subhuman wages to do their paperwork. Build your own prison for them, cook the food and clean the master's shoes. Prisons are the new plantations. And the slaves come in all shades. You need to rise up and fight back. Fight the system by disciplining your mind. Don't fight with knives and sticks or shanks. Use the power of your brain to free your body and your soul. Use your life. It ain't over 'til you quit. And to the men and women in prison who are innocent, I especially know your pain. It is excruciatingly painful and a nightmare to go to bed at night and get up in the morning knowing you shouldn't be here.

You cry out and it seems like nobody will hear you. I am exactly where you are. You pray, you write and nobody answers. Looks like the media politicians and over family members don't give a darn. Don't you quit and don't give up. Rise above the prison subculture. Rise above your pain and hurt and never quit. We can fight back. We need to unite in prisons across this country. Unite in prayer. Unite in writing the press. Unite in seeking redress and due process. The answer and strength is in unity. And there is power in numbers. Let's put our heads, hearts and minds together and figure out a way out of here. A legal way out. And when get out, let's unite and help others who are trapped. Let's join with Rubin carter, Anthony Porter, David Quindt, Rolando Cruz and lawyers and let's launch an all out war against wrongful convictions. Let's demand that politicians, organizations and churches fight with us. Let's tell our families not to attend any church that won't help free the innocent. Let's tell our families not to vote for any politician that won't fight for innocent prisoners. Let's join with Monica Moorehead, Barry Scheck, CA Prison Focus, the Southern Poverty Law Center, the Southern Human Rights Center and the Wrongful Conviction Center in Illinois. Let's raise money and get lawyers. Let's use our lives to help somebody else. You can do something here and now. You can send this book to your family and ask them to take it to the church pastor. Ask the pastor to read it and take it to the city council, the mayor and the governor.

Use that money you just won in the football or basketball pool and buy another copy of this book. Mail a copy to Jesse Jackson, Al Sharpton, the NAACP, the ACLU, and the local newspaper, etc. You got nothing better to do so why not be a part of mobilizing and publicizing this book. When you get this book into the right hands, Queen Latifah, Sean Puffy Combs, Johnnie Cochran, Barry Scheck, Maxine Waters, Randall Robinson, Shaquille O'Neal, Kobe Bryant, John Johnson, Susan Taylor, Magic Johnson, Denzel Washington, Bill Gates and Jeff Bezos will eventually get it. And when they read this book they will get involved. This book just might change the way they view the **system**. You get it to them. You can send this book to the publishers of "The Source" magazine. Send it to Low Rider and all these other magazines you subscribe to and tell the Editor "I want you to read this book." You have the power to affect society from your jail cell as long as you're willing to fight. Just imagine what would happen if twenty thousand prisoners across this country individually mailed a copy of this book to: a law professor in your state. Imagine five thousand prisoners sending a copy of this book to a Congress member or a Senator. What's holding you back?

And all you great defense lawyers for whom I have so much respect; you can help. You can buy a few copies of this book and send them to a few of your clients who are trapped in prison. Lawyers - what's holding you back?

I am aware of the fact that there are many greedy lawyers out there who dump their clients and sell them out. Shame on them. But as I've said, it is the Barry Schecks, Gerry Spences, Peter Neufields and John Kekers that give me so much hope. These are bare-knuckled warriors who will fight for justice. They won't back down. I encourage you to read every book Gerry Spence has ever written. Read "Trial by Fire" and "Injustice for All" by Mr. Spence. Gerry is a man. He tells it like it is and he is not afraid to stand up to corrupted judges. Gerry Spence knows courts, judges and juries inside out. I would hope that all of you law students who are aspiring to practice law will study the success of Gerry Spence, Barry Scheck, Alan Dershowitz. Find out how they got where they are. If you find out Mr. Spence, Mr. Tarlow, Gerson Horn, Elisabeth Semel, Stephen Bright, Morris Dees or Willie Gary is giving a lecture somewhere, you need to be there.

When Johnnie Cochran speaks you need to listen. If you want to learn how to prepare for trial, defend your client relentlessly, and fight for liberty and justice for all, you need to read Johnnie Cochran's book "Journey to Justice". Read F. Lee Bailey's "The Defense Never Rests". You cannot and will not become a successful warrior for the people unless you are willing to sharpen the tools of your mind by learning from those who have been where you are trying to go.

Think about David Boies in New York. I saw David Boies argue before the United States Supreme Court with no notes, no pad and no pen. That kind of attention to detail, memory and recall must be developed and honed.

On May 24, 2001 Rosie O'Donnell had a New York University student named Dan on her show. Dan wants to go to law school. I want Dan to write me a letter. I want Dan to read this book. I want Dan to read everything he can by Johnnie Cochran, F. Lee Bailey and Gerry Spence. Guys like Deveren Farley out at San Juan High School need to buy Gerry Spence's Books - "How to Argue and

Win Every Case" and "From Freedom To Slavery". These kinds of non-fiction books help to broaden your mental horizons.

I applaud Oprah for having a Book Club. I agree that we need to get our country back to reading. And most especially those who are contemplating the possibility of becoming an attorney or entering politics *need to read*.

I know for a fact that great lawyers like Murray Janus stay on top of their games by reading. The Willie Garys, Bruce Harveys, Steve Sadows and Roy Blacks are readers.

And these guys know about the fact that in many cases it didn't fit but the jury didn't acquit. I just wish more of them would rise up and fight for the innocent and indigents who desperately need lawyers. We must get more lawyers, law professors and law students to join Barry Scheck, David Protess, Charles Olgetree and Robert Cling in helping to set the captives free pro bono. And I assure you I am gonna deal with a few more specific cases of wrongful convictions and the lawyers who defend the innocent in the next few pages. But I want to try to stir the fire of love, activism and care that's in your bellies before I get back to these various injustices. I want to connect with the left out, locked out and forgotten about. The people who deserve to be heard and have so much to say. But few people seem to care. Think about it; old folks in senior citizens homes who never get a visit. Out parents and grandparents who have reared us, educated us and sacrificed so that we can have what we have. And now we push them aside and never go to see about them. These older people feel the same pain that the prisoner who never gets a visit feels. These older people feel like they don't matter to us anymore. We have forgotten them. I want you who are reading to not only save our children, but I want you to go take care of our elders. Give them some love, time and affection.

Like many of you who are reading this book, I have worked the eighteen-hour days. I've been so busy that I thought I was important. But I am a witness that you can often get too busy to remember how to *live*. What is *life*? Who are *you* and why were you sent to the planet? What is your purpose? I am not anti-wealth. I'm not anti-success. I believe we should live life to the fullest. But I also know we must share our wealth, share our time and share our lives. Some of us feel that as long as we take care of our kids and our family, then nothing else really matters. I remember being moved tremendously by something I read in one of Gerry Spence's books. He was talking about representing criminals in court and how tough it can be for the lawyer. And Gerry basically said that when a lawyer looks into the eyes of a killer - the lawyer must see the baby in the man. Imagine the person as a little innocent baby. Imagine what that person was like *before* he became what he is today - that little innocent sweet baby - that bundle of potential joy and love. Think of what that person was like before he even used a drug, saw a gun or committed any crime and when you allow your mind to go there you'll recognize that there is a little bit of the spirit of God running through the blood of every human being. Perhaps if we, as humans, begin to recognize the spirit of God and the leftover baby in every man and woman then we'll be more willing to serve, love and fight for the least of these our brethren. But a lot of us are confused. We have convinced ourselves that we are so important, so brilliant, so busy and so infallible. We have tuned out the voices of death all around us. We have turned our heads away from the homeless, helpless and the defenseless. We have begun to live as robots. We are doctors, lawyers, pastors, housewives, students and entrepreneurs. We are trapped in the rut of everyday life. We will do the exact same type things today that we did on yesterday. We have totally forgotten how to stimulate the life force. Any neuro scientist or brain surgeon will tell you that we utilize very little of our true brainpower. Many of the neural pathways of our brain are almost dead. Not only because we kill them off with hate, prejudice, alcohol and drugs but also because we don't use them. The child stimulates brain nerve growth or activity by utilizing all of the senses. Look at the eight-month-old baby who picks up a new toy off of the floor. The baby ... Murray Janus before he came the noted Defense Attorney. The baby ... David Hicks before he became the District Attorney. The baby ... Johnnie Cochran before he became the Trial Attorney of the century. The baby looks at the toy (visual). The baby touches and feels the toy (kinesthetic). The baby smells the toy (olfactory). The baby tries to eat the toy (gustatory). The baby shakes the toy and listens to it's sound. The child engages every sense, nerve and lights up the electric circuitry of his mental screen. But we grown, boring, ritualistic adults, we don't smell our food. It's uncool and not adult like. We don't feel or touch rocks on the ground anymore. We find no splendor in the beauty of the universe. We are no longer amazed by the rain, rainbows or the snow. We don't meet new people or try new things. And that's why we are unhappy, stressed and we die early. When you get out of your routine, out of your norm and out of your habits you use brain cells that are lying dormant. I'm telling you today that if and when you decide to help somebody else, do a new kind of volunteering, adopt a prisoner, mentor a child or take a senior citizen to the shopping mall or movie theater. It does something in the neurons of your brain that helps prevent senility or old age. We are around here looking and searching for the Fountain of Youth. The Fountain of Youth is not in a pill, not at the gym, not at the plastic surgeons and not in a face-lift. The Fountain of Youth is in a *life lift*. I'm being very serious and authentic. A lot of you great trial lawyers who are reading my words right now need to try this. Ask Murray Janus how he felt when his beautiful daughter (who is also an attorney) gave him his first grandbaby. Ask Murray how he felt the first time he held his grandbaby in his arms. To see, touch, feel and hold his grandchild. That's awesome! Ask Barry Scheck, David Protess, Robert Cling and Peter Neufield how they feel when they watch an innocent indigent man who's been in prison for something he didn't do; walk out free. Awesome. Ask T. D. Jakes and Bishop Noel Jones how they feel when they watch a man who was addicted to crack cocaine clean himself up dust himself off and transform his life because he heard the gospel preached. Awesome. And we can also get these long lasting feelings of joy, worth, usefulness and somebody (ness) when we take two hours out of one busy week to help lift the life of a child, a prisoner, a senior citizen or any of the least of these our brethren. It's time to revolutionize your life and you can do so by helping somebody else. Oprah has not replied to me. Maybe she just thinks I'm just another one of those prisoners who write everybody on the planet. It's okay, but I'm still going to speak my mind and my heart. And when I think Oprah is right, I'm gonna echo it and Oprah is one hundred percent right when she says one of the best ways to heal your heart is to help somebody else to heal theirs.

Use your life for good. You will absolutely and definitely transform and revolutionize your life when you begin to give a damn about others. All you can do is all you can do, and all you can do is enough. But most of us are not doing all we can do for others. We are so selfish, self centered and vain. We gotta get out of this trap and quit finding fault and criticizing so much. We spend, utilize and exert so much of our energy and valuable time speaking ill of others that it is pathetic. I am not condoning sin or impropriety. I dare not put Jesse Jackson on a pedestal. Jesse is another one who has not even dropped me a single letter (unless the prison is stealing his letters. And prison guards do steal inmates' mail, stamps and photos). But give me a break. I don't care about Jesse's adultery! David in the Bible was an adulterer. And he was a man after God's own heart. Jesse's sin is between him, God and Jackie. It's not my business so spare me the details. But we are programmed by the media to love the gory details of people's private lives. And we will forget the good a person did

199

yesterday, but remember the bad they did fifty years ago. Get a life! Do something. Help make the world a better place in which to live. You wanna help somebody? Bombard Oprah, Rosie, John Johnson, Earl Graves and Susan Taylor with E-mails about this book. Don't you have a computer? Go buy a subscription to a newspaper and send it to a prisoner. Go take a senior citizen out to lunch. Adopt a child. Help some poor kid go to college. Go back to your law school and inspire those students. Use your life! Use your life for good because you are gonna die one day and life can change in the splitting of a second like all those young, happy and energetic people in Israel who were at a wedding having fun. They were having a good time. They were dancing and enjoying life. But the floor fell from right beneath their feet. Over thirty of those dear people died. They were crushed to death at a wedding. They never thought life would end that way. Three hundred people were injured. For those who died, it didn't matter in what law firm they were a partner. It did not matter what type car or mansion they owned. They are dead. Anyone of them would have traded their cars, homes and money for just another day of life, another opportunity to see the sun rise again. Just to smell another flower! My God, I hope you can see my point. I am praying for those families in Israel. Life is fragile. Life is unpredictable. And we never know when the death angel will come knocking at our door. It can be over in a heartbeat. It can be all over.

Sean Puffy Combs, Bill Cosby, Susan Taylor, Spike Lee, Bill Gates, Donald Trump, Don King, Jeff Bezos please, please say, do and pay something to help men trapped in prisons. These are human beings. These are sons, daughters, mothers, fathers, sisters and brothers. And y'all know damn well a lot of them did not commit the crime. But they are doing the time. Their crime (in many instances) is the color of their skin. There crime is poverty or a lack of celebrity. I'm not criticizing Sean "P. Diddy" Combs. I believe he was innocent. I'm excited that he's free. But if Sean didn't have 300 million dollars worth of C-notes, chances are slim to none that he would have gotten justice. Sean said it was a life *altering* experience and yet he got off. How much more life altering would it have been had Sean been convicted and gotten fifteen years in prison? You can go from joy to horror without a moment's notice. I'm crying out here and now for every prisoner in America, even those who are guilty. They are being abused, mistreated, beat and killed by vicious prison guards because the prison wardens know most citizens don't care. If Sean, Bill, Don, Donald, Jesse, the NAACP and the ACLU began raising hell about cruel and unusual treatment and the prison industrial complex we'd see a change come. And now I'm writing exclusively about wrongfully convicted prisoners. If Oprah, Bill, Sean and Susan got involved they'd start setting the captives free. But some people just don't get it. I challenge Bishop Jakes, Gilbert Patterson, Jesse Jackson, Jerry Falwell and all other high profile celebrities to remember that Paul and Silas were in prison. Joseph was in prison. And I challenge you to stand up for the fair treatment of prisoners. Do something! Ministry is about more than preaching and teaching. Ministry is about more than reading the Bible. Use your ministry, influence, wealth, status, power and positions to help the least of these thy **brethren**. The wedding in Israel ended with the floor crashing and the shouting, yelling, screaming and the dying. That tragedy in Israel (May 24, 2001) is a metaphor for life. They went from joy to horror, from laughter to sorrow without a moment's notice. One minute they were on the dance floor the next on their deathbed. So Mr. Janus (trust me, Murray is reading) are you really too busy to come to California? Mr. Dershowitz, Tarlow, Margolin, Spence, Bailey, Greenberg, Uelmen, Cochran are you really too busy to help Barry Scheck one month per year? I love you guys. Everybody knows the respect and admiration that I have for Murray J. Janus, Johnnie Cochran and Gerry Spence. They are warriors! And I think all of the aforementioned are good human beings. But I'm pleading with every successful attorney to rise up and fight to free the innocent. Give something back.        There is a guy by the name of Chris Gardner. Chris was homeless and poor. Chris slept in a shelter with his eighteen-month-old son. Rev. Cecil Williams and the Glide Memorial Church gave Chris shelter and food. And one day Chris decided to transform his life. Chris Gardner scratched and clawed his way from the slummy side to the sunny side, from shame to fame and from disgrace to amazing grace. He knocked on doors and pleaded for a job. He wanted a hand **up** not a hand **out**. And now Chris is having the American Dream. Chris is a multi, multi-millionaire. He's a stockbroker. And he's also African American. And he did not forget the bridge that brought him across. Chris has given thousands of dollars to the shelter at which he used to sleep. I applaud Chris Gardner for giving back and feeding the hungry. And I pray daily that some way, somehow I can get guys like Chris Gardner to **help to free the innocent**. So I again make the humble plea: Murray Janus, Gerry Spence (anybody reading) please send a copy of this book to Chris Gardner. Ask him to read it and give you his opinion. I know Chris will read this kind of book if only he gets it. All successful, driven and motivated movers and shakers - Read. Get this book to Chris! Get this book to Chris! Chris (in my opinion) looks so much like Bishop T. D. Jakes. They could be twins. Mentioning Chris Gardner and Bishop T. D. Jakes in the same vein - wouldn't that be a headline: Gardner and Jakes fighting the snakes of wrongful convictions. They say *art imitates life*. Well why can't life imitate art? Wouldn't that be a made for TV Hollywood-type story. If a former homeless man turned multi-millionaire (Chris Gardner) joined with Bishop T. D. Jakes and said "Bishop you pray, and I'll pay, were gonna get Rev. Sherman Manning out of prison." Now wouldn't that make the evening news? Let me tell you that a lot of my readers and the people who buy my books are Caucasian. Yes, more White folks than Black folks are reading my books. And I love all of God's children. And I'll accept help, prayer and support from *anybody*. I care less about color. I'm more concerned about character. And having said that, I still need to tell Black America we ought to be ashamed. We ought to be ashamed. We have more Black men in prison in America than we have in college. We have an entire generation that is about to be lost to the new prison plantation. Yet, with 500 billion dollars yearly in income, Black America has sat back and allowed this to happen. Black celebrities, actors, lawyers and politicians have sat back and allowed a generation to be lost to drugs, gangs, alcohol, violence and prisons. What would happen if Shaq dedicated his next basketball game to innocent men in prison? What if Bill Cosby called Governor Gray Davis and said, "I'm not going to let you keep killing Black men in prison?" Somebody - Monica Moorehead, Willie Ratcliff, Earl Graves, Susan Taylor, Bishop Jakes, Jesse, and Al - somebody needs to call a summit meeting and put together the money necessary to educate, rehabilitate and liberate Black (and Brown and poor White) men in prison. Somebody needs to call Kobe, Michael Jordan, Magic Johnson and Evander Holifield and tell them let's put together an innocence fund. Lets get to Sgt. Phil Harrison and Shaq will listen to his daddy. Tell Sgt. Phil Harrison to tell Shaq that we need help. What the hell's going on? Dick Gregory, Julian Bond, and Congressman John Lewis: Did Black people march, sit-in, pray-in, bleed-in, get beaten-in and jailed-in for the right to vote, only to have an entire generation of Black male voters locked out because of criminal convictions? How in the hell have the John Singletons, the Bill Cosbys, the Spike Lees allowed this to happen to us? This is wrong.

Let me tell you something; I remember one of the first times I was stopped by a police officer. I was outside Atlanta, Georgia in Dekalb County. Dekalb County police officers hated Rev. Hosea (unbought and unbossed) Williams. They had a vendetta against

Hosea.  And I had been on television and in the news working with Rev. Williams.  A White cop by the name of Weaver stopped me for speeding.  I was guilty.  I was speeding.  Officer Weaver said, "Are you that young nigger preacher out here protesting against the police with Hosea drunken Williams?"  Those were his exact words.  I won't (in all integrity) repeat my reply.  Nevertheless, Officer Weaver saw three Percodan pills on my dashboard.  These pills were in plain sight.  He inquired.  I explained that I had been in a car accident a week earlier.  Hospitalized at the Clayton County Hospital.  The Percodan was prescription medication.  It was prescribed to me at Morehouse Medical Associates.  I gave the officer the doctor's name, etc.  He said that he didn't care whether they were prescribed pills or not.  He cited an antiquated, rarely enforced Georgia Law that stated the prescription must be *on your person* at all times.  He threatened me. He spit on me and I took off.  A chase ensued.  He caught me.  He beat me.  He arrested me.  Concisely - in court, Judge Arnold Schulman indicated, "There is no question as to the legitimacy of this valid prescription. No one is accusing you of being an illicit drug user.  You had a prescription.  But it was not on your person.  I'm sentencing you to seven years in prison for a violation of the Georgia Controlled Substance Act."  District Attorney Mike McDonald high-fived his assistant, "Yes - that's for Hosea!!"  Don't take *my word* for it.  Check the courthouse archives and transcripts.  This judge gave me a *seven-year sentence* in *prison* because I had three of my prescription pills in my car without the prescription on my person.  They verified they were my pills.  I took a blood test to prove there were no drugs and no alcohol of any kind in my system.  I served very little of the sentence in prison because of the intervention of former Mayor Andrew Young and Chief Eldrin Bell of Atlanta.  But the fact remains that I was sentenced to *prison* for a prescription drug.  Attorney Mike Bergen told me, "Reverend, they *never* prosecute those kinds of cases.  This type of human error case is always dismissed.  Your Hosea connection sent you to prison period."  And guess what?  They had successfully eliminated me as a voting citizen.  And what would happen the next time I got stopped by a police officer on a lonely highway in the wee hours of the morning for a traffic violation?  (Me, a young Black man driving a luxurious automobile wearing a $1,750 suit and a Rolex). When a cop stops me and ran my name through his computer.  When he sees "arrested viol. GA. cont. subs.".  What do you think would go through his mind?  "This Black guy must be a drug dealer."  And with this kind of suspicion, how do you think he will begin to treat me on this traffic stop?  Wake up America and smell the coffee.  This stuff happens everyday! Ask Mike Bergin, Michael Morchower or Gerry Spence. Ask Johnnie Cochran. Before Johnnie became a celebrity, he was a Deputy District Attorney. Johnnie Cochran had a Rolls Royce (a Black man driving a Rolls Royce in the 70's and 80's). When the White cops saw him they slammed Johnnie Cochran on the hood of his car and called him *nigger*. They did this in front of his *children*. And finally one of the cops stumbled upon his I.D. He saw Deputy District Attorney on a badge. They began apologizing and calling him *Mr. Cochran* when they discovered he was a D.A. and Johnnie has never forgotten it.

And I want to remind all Black celebrities, sports starts and politicians. I need to remind you that if you ever get stopped in your Jaguar, Rolls or Mercedes by some hick cop, you better hope he recognizes your face from television. If not, you can become another Rodney King. And/or you can have bullets pumped in your belly because of driving while Black or Brown. You brothers ought to do something about this. What the hell's going on? Just a generation ago you couldn't find ten Black people in a straight row that could *read* or *write*. But look at you now. You can read and write and then translate what you read. Just a generation ago in Georgia if you were Black and you read, you died or went to jail. How soon we (Clarence Thomas and Ward Connerly) forget. And now that we are marching to the tune of earning 500 billion dollars per year what's wrong with us? Why won't we come together and feed our hungry children, raise our fatherless sons and educate our illiterate youth? Why won't we put computers in our schools and libraries in our communities? Where is our pride? Where is our dignity? Where is the love? What have you done for the hood lately? We cannot ride to freedom on a grant from King Pharaoh. We owe it to our people to each one - reach one. How soon we forget? Where is the love? Where is the care? What the hell is wrong with us? It's Black folks who are being arrested and filling the jails and we are allowing this. Why won't we collectively save our people? How foolish, how stupid, how crazy can we be? It should not have taken almost twenty years for Anthony Porter or Rubin "Hurricane" Carter to get free. Mumia Abu Jamal should not be on Death Row. What if Bill Cosby had put up his money to get Anthony Porter a dream team defense when he was on trial? Anthony would not have spent decades waiting on Professor David Profess and his journalism students to free him. David Protess is White. Barry Scheck is not a Muslim. He's not a Baptist preacher. He's not a Civil Rights Leader. He's not a Supreme Court Justice. Barry is not a Black politician. He didn't march with Dr. King. He is a White man who sees red blood and is moved by *injustice*. How many of you Black lawyers, doctors, multi-millionaire sports stars have called Barry to say thank you? What the hell have *you* done to help this White man free your people. You fool! You poor excuse for a human being. You sorry, low down, whitewashed piece of trash. What's going on? Marvin Gaye asked that question. With all the brothers dying, with their childless mothers crying, with the sisters with tears in their eyes and you are riding around town in your limo, in your "beamer" pretending that it's not going on. You whitewashed, Uncle Tom politician sitting up in your corner suite, in the ivory towers trying to forget that you are Black. Trying to forget where you came from. Trying to pretend not to see the poverty, the hurt, the pain, the genocide, and the new plantation. You ought to be ashamed. You ought to remind yourself that just a generation ago you went to jail, or were castrated or lynched for even looking at a White woman. And now while you date and marry White women you want to pretend not to see the plan. I am not against interracial dating. I am not against White people. I know there are millions of non-racists, caring, loving and sharing White people in the world. Many of them are my close personal friends and loved ones. But I am as angry as hell with anybody who tries to pretend not to see the plight of Black men in this country. I'm sick and tired of us coming together for the Essence Awards and the NAACP Award and giving our two bit, sound bite speeches about Black activism and then driving off into the sunset. I'm sick and tired of keeping *hope alive* while *dope* is killing us. I'm absolutely tired of watching this tragedy, conspiracy, travesty and new plantation grow before my very eyes and Michael Jackson won't give a dime to help heal this world. Take your speeches, take your rhetoric and shove it up your butt. Take your talk and ram it as far up your rectum as you can get it. And then after you are feeling the pain of your hemorrhoids why don't you hobble back to the hood and save our people. Why don't you hobble back to the hood and give Morehouse College some money. Why don't you fight racism, hate, wrongful convictions, and the prison industrial complex and police brutality? Why don't you save the drama, forget the cameras and get off your butts and keep the dream of Dr. Martin Luther King, Jr. alive. Why don't you use your life, your talents, your gifts, and your wealth to help somebody else? You ought to be ashamed. The blood of the youngsters who are dying on the streets is on your hands. The cries of the mothers who have lost their children to gang gunfire is in your ears. The hurt, void, trauma and tragedies of the homeless and illiterate is in your belly. You have been deceived. *You* can change this. *You* can save a life. You can transform lives. We need Ice Cube, Sean, Queen, Oprah and Bill to come together and use their remarkable wealth to change the course of humanity. God has been good to Black folks. God has shed his love, his grace, his wealth, his wisdom and his mercy on thee. There but for the grace of God go you. Are you really that crazy? Have you really forgotten that your mother, father and grandparents shed their blood in the streets so you could be where you are today? Don't you know that a way was made for you? You have been bought with a price and paid for. There would have never been a Michael Jordan or a Magic Johnson had there been no Hosea Williams, Julian Bond, Martin Luther King, Jr. or Malcolm X. I don't care how much talent Kobe Bryant had if he were born in 1948 instead of 1978, he wouldn't be a millionaire basketball player. People died so Kobe could play. People took bite marks from dogs in their butts so Uncle Tom Clarence Thomas could sit on the bench. People went to jail so Bernard Parks could be a police chief. People swam in the waters from water hoses in the streets so Colin Powell could become a General in the U.S. Army and the Secretary of State. Martin Luther King, Jr. paid the ultimate price so you could have the job you have. You wouldn't be on television, radio and in filmmaking if some big butt, uneducated, dedicated, rusty feet Black folks hadn't put marching feet in those street for you to have the chance to get in those doors. And now that you've made it through those doors, you not only want to shut them behind you. You put a padlock, chain and a deadbolt on the doors and have the audacity to forget about the least of these thy brethren. You fool! You are being used as a tool of racist White people. They are building, empowering and funding entire neighborhoods and cities on the backs of poor White boys and uneducated Black boys in prisons across this country. And you sit there with your sheepskin on your walls, a N.B.A. Ring or your finger, an Oscar nomination to your credit and you won't do a damn thing to empower, to educate, emancipate and liberate poor people. You distance yourself from Louis Farrakhan, you won't support Al Sharpton, and you criticize Jesse. You are above everybody and connected to nobody. You are a little bit of this and a little bit of that. You are conflicted and inflicted with hypocrisy. You write and E-mail Dr. Phil but you won't attend a lecture by Dr. Naim Akbar. You watch Montel but you won't watch Tony Brown. You are uppity, sophisticated while your people are devastated. You allow the media to select, elect and anoint your leaders, your doctors, your lawyers and even your politicians. If the media don't praise them, you won't praise them. You've heard of Dr. Phil, but you know nothing about Cheikh Anta Diop, Cornel West, Randall Robinson or Naim

Akbar. You know about Shakespeare, but you don't know Maya Angelou, James Baldwin, Langston Hughes, Toni Morrison or Frederick Douglas. You are a fool! You are a sell out. You are a disgrace to the human race. You are sick. You have forgotten about reconstruction and the gains Black folks made prior to that error. You won't build your communities! You won't lift up lives. You are . . .

I'll stop there and move on back to wrongful convictions and America's system of *in*justice. Injustice for all people. All races, colors and creeds. The White, the Black, the Mexican, the Indian, the dark and light men who are sitting in prisons for crimes we did not commit need help. And we need it now. What would happen if I could get that brilliant entrepreneur Chris Gardner of Gardner, Rich & Co. to put three thousand copies of this book in homeless shelters, schools, juveniles and prisons across the country? What would happen if we started the homeless people to reading? Everybody talking about getting the country back to reading. Well what about those who can't read. We need them too. We can't ever forget the value of human life. And although I would love to have the help and intervention of Chris Gardner, I must give him credit because it is due. Chris Gardner feeds the hungry and he helps house the homeless. Chris is a bright and shining example of a true rags to riches story. He's an example of what it means to use your life to help somebody else. And to never feel that you are above those people. Those people? The homeless, prisoners, senior citizens, working class people and the mentally retarded. Let me take a minute again to salute all mothers. Black mothers, White mothers, Mexican, Korean, Swiss, Japanese, etc. All mothers. Mothers give so much for so little in return. Mothers are the queens of the universe. The *mothers* of our world. Where would we be without them? I just needed to write that because I miss my mother(s) so much. Dollie Manning and Brenda Smith. It's been six long and lonely years. Wow.

I saw a movie the other day that can be a metaphor for what I've been trying to inspire, coerce and shame people into doing. Bare with me for a few minutes. Basically there was a young (eighteen years old) rich White guy. He grew up on the right side of the tracks of life. His parents sent him to all the right schools. He had a nanny, housekeeper and a butler. He was about to graduate high school. He was almost a womanizer. He had the young, rich girlfriend that his parents seemed to adore. Both he and this girlfriend were about to graduate high school and had been accepted to an Ivy League College. But this young boy (Greg) also had another girlfriend. Her name was Emily. Emily was poor. Emily's mother waited tables in a restaurant.

Emily had been dating Greg for two years, but has never once been taken to his house or met his family. Emily was Greg's secret. She loved Greg and Greg loved sex. He always took her to an abandoned warehouse owned by his father to have sex. Emily got pregnant. Wow! When she told Greg he went crazy. Greg looked into the futuristic galaxy beyond. He saw his future going up in flames. He saw his girlfriend, Nicole, leaving him. He also imagined his family's reaction when they found out he had some poor girl pregnant. College, business, football and his future seemed all to be going up in flames right before his very eyes. No way! Greg told Emily to have an abortion. She refused. She was not about to murder her child. Greg took her home from the warehouse after getting this news. He distanced himself from her. He no longer called her or returned her calls. "Hold all my calls" was his new motto. And one night Greg's family threw him a birthday party at their mansion. Greg's friends, family and his *right* girlfriend (Nicole) were at the party. Greg's dad bought him a new SUV for his birthday. But wait, while Greg was inside the mansion blowing out candles, while Greg was drinking champagne, receiving his high fives and enjoying the life, Emily was sitting outside hiding in her car. Emily was sitting outside wondering how the father of her baby could be inside partying. He was totally oblivious to her pain, her suffering, her plight and their baby in her belly. To make a long story short, Greg killed Emily to prevent her from exposing this secret to his family after she refused to let him buy her off. He killed her and an innocent man (temporarily) who fit the profile of a killer went to jail for her murder.

Art imitates life. I see Greg as being like some Black (and White or Mexican) people. While we are partying, drinking the champagne, blowing out the candles, celebrating the victories of our successful ball games, business deals and political victories, our secret (Emily) is sitting outside our office (Greg's father's house), sitting outside our bank, sitting outside our suite, church or mansion. Sitting outside locked out. Sitting in prison, locked in. Sitting out in the cold hungry, homeless, illiterate and indigent. And like Greg, we want those people to go away. We want to pay them off. Throw a dollar in their face and tell them to vanish. The poor, the innocent in prison, the elderly in convalescent homes, etc., they are our Emily. We are connected by the child in her belly. We are connected by our bloodlines, history, heritage (often) skin color, etc. We belong to them and they belong to us. But we'd rather kill those people than raise them up, dust them off, educate, emancipate and liberate them. Five hundred billion dollars we earned last year. Five hundred billion dollars in the pockets of Armani suits, silk dresses of Black men and women last year. Yet we consider our Black brothers and sisters trapped in poverty and prisons across America somebody else's problem. Damn!

We have entrusted the judicial systems across the country with the educations, rearing and care of our people. And so we allow them to be raised and schooled by killers, murderers and rapists in the jails and prisons all across America. There is no excuse for violence, rioting, looting and shooting. But I must confess that now I have come to realize why so many kids and teens across America are lashing out and rioting. I am more cognizant of the fact of the divide between the rich and the poor in this country than I was when I was riding in the back of limousines. Our poor and even the prisoners of this country are sitting at the gate outside your investment company, outside your law office, outside your church house doors and your Mercedes. They are begging for bread for their hungry bellies and water for their dry and thirsty mouths. They are in Lazarus predicament and like the rich man in the Bible you will give them not. Not even the crumbs that fall from your table. You sic the dogs on them and send them off to prison. You're too busy! You're too proud. You have no time for *those people*. You've made it to the NBA, NFL and to your career in the movie industry on the backs of your slave forefathers. The blood in the streets and the calluses on the feet of the Medger Evers, Ralph David Abernathy's and Harriett Tubmans of yesterday have brought you to a new day. Your front row seat on the bus was made possible by the jailing of Rosa Parks. Your accommodations at the Waldorf Astoria were bought with the blood, sacrifice and assassination of Dr. King on the balcony of the Lorraine Motel. Dr. King went to his grave marching for *those people*. He was in town at the Lorraine standing up for *those people,* the garbage workers. He did so that some of the least of these our brethren would be where you are today. And you've made it to the top and gotten comfortable. Now you have snatched the ladder down which you climbed up to get there. You are sick. I thank God for Gerry Spence, Johnnie Cochran, Barry Scheck and Peter Neufield. I am so glad that some men are willing to stand up to the system and say, "he is innocent 'til proven guilty". I am glad that some lawyers and investigators have seen how often the police, prosecutors, judges and juries get it wrong. Barry Scheck is quite cognizant of the fact that courthouses all over America are death houses and guilt projects. So Barry has responded by building *innocent projects* to fight the *guilt projects*. Mother Teresa responded to poverty, aids and homelessness by building shelters to combat these problems. She didn't turn her head but instead she opened her heart. On some levels Barry Scheck has done for innocent, convicted offenders what Mother Teresa did for the sick and the oppressed. She never threw words or a speech at the problems. She used her life and love. And Barry uses his mind, his brilliance, his status, his time and his life to set the captives free. Barry has been able to look into the eyes of men convicted of rape, molestation and murder and developed compassion and concern. Some way, some how Barry has developed a burden and a care for innocent prisoners unlike I've ever seen in another lawyer in this country. And I'm quite cognizant of the fact that there are many other lawyers who also care and fight. I know about Michael Snedeker, Barry Tarlow and Gerson Horn. I'm aware of men like Gerry Spence and Roy Black. I would hope that (by the thousands) other lawyers, law professors and private investigators will show up and say, "Barry, I'm ready to help you to set the innocent free." I'm aware of our public perception that everybody in prison claims they are innocent. I know that most of us feel that our judicial system is imperfect. But that it is the best we can hope for. That's a lie and the truth is not in it. We can and must do better than this. We need to collectively over haul the system. We need to collectively and consistently expose the prosecutors misconduct, judicial bias, jury tampering and police misconduct that is infesting and infecting cases all over North America. Politicians need to come out of the ivory towers and talk to former police officers; some of who are willing to admit the racism, classism and false convictions which transpired on their watch. Let's talk to private investigators that see miscarriages of justice everyday in cases they work on. Laura Lawhon in Los Angeles will talk to the media and to politicians. Laura is one of the best private investigators on the west coast. She cares about her clients. She cares about justice. She cares about what is right, fair and unbiased.

I wish I had Laura Lawhorn on my case before the trial. I have a feeling that I would not be in prison today. And even now if I could get a brilliant investigator like Laura to ask the right people the right questions, I could get out of here. Mine is not a complicated case. It's an open and shut case of lies and injustice. Mary Hanlon Stone, Detective Dave Winkler and Judge Robert Altman fixed the verdict. Hanlon and Winkler pressured Ricardo Calvario to maintain the lie because they wanted me in prison. They knew for a fact that Ricardo Calvario was (indeed) a street prostitute and yet Altman claimed, "If I get any credible evidence that Calvario is a prostitute, I will dismiss this case." Having said that the dishonorable Robert Altman proceeded to call witnesses from his chambers, outside my presence and convince them not to testify for me. I think Laura Lawhorn could have and still can get to the bottom of these lies. Laura would have interviewed Richard Martz. Laura would have found Brett Nelson again. Laura, Laura, Laura; I need Laura to help me accomplish the Scheck-effect in my wrongful conviction. It can still happen today.

So for great, brilliant and powerful lawyers who have been sitting there in your comfortable homes in Richmond, Virginia, Chicago, New York, Atlanta and Los Angeles; reading on and saying, "Yeah give rich Black people hell, Sherman. Keep on!" How dare you sit there and do nothing. Barry Scheck, Peter Neufield, Professor David Protess, Professor Robert Cling and Attorney Stephen Bright need your help. They need you to skip golfing one Saturday a month and abandon the yacht one Sunday per month and donate that time to helping them to right the wrongs of a judicial system that is out of control. If you are a *lawyer* then you're in a much better position than the average citizen to know when an injustice has transpired. Lawyers *know* the law and you know the rules. You're not fooled by so called profiles of rapists, murderers, robbers and molesters. You are quite cognizant of the fact that police officers and prosecutors can twist facts to support any theory they desire. You (lawyers) are much more informed of the intimate affairs, goings on and happening behind closed doors at courthouses and police departments all across North America. You (lawyers) know the real deal. Let's be authentic, sincere and candid about this thing called justice. You have used loopholes, technicalities and statues of limitations to set guilty men free. You have argued before judges and juries for clients who did the crime but didn't do any time. And by the same token, you've seen with your own eyes police set up an innocent person. You have witnessed the tramping and stripping of the rights of innocent persons. You've seen vendetta and vindictiveness in courtrooms. You've watched prosecutors get more and more power. You've seen drunken, bribe accepting judges similar to Judge Robert Altman. You've seen judges who are drunk with power and corrupted by politics. You lawyers have seen this. You not only watch "The Practice" on ABC on TV, you live "The Practice" in Richmond, Virginia, Atlanta, GA, Boston, New York, Los Angeles, Sacramento and in Jackson, Wyoming. You are not hoodwinked by the trickery and deceit of politicians. You are not fooled like much of the public is by the media. You know that wrongful convictions are not an aberration. Murray Janus knows there are many Mary Hanlon Stones in prosecutor's offices in Virginia. Gerry Spence knows many Judge Robert Altman types in Wyoming. Johnnie Cochran has seen many Mark Fuhrmans, Davie Winkler and Rafael Perez types in LA, New York City and in Atlanta, GA. Roy Black, Steve Sadow, Bobby Lee Cook, Mike Snedeker, Blair Bernholtz, Barry Tarlow, Stanley Greenberg, John Keker, Bruce Harvey and Charles Ogletree, etc. You know what's really going on. And the challenge is for you to do something about these injustices. You can make a difference. You can fight, change and rebuild this broken system of injustice. You know that when an innocent man goes to prison he'll never be the same again. You can convince Richard Polanco, Joseph Biden, John Lewis, Maxine Waters, senators, governors and Congress that something must change. Just a few months ago (May 24, 2001) I saw officers in #2 Block at this prison, push a Black inmate one hundred yards outside, freedom, butt naked on a gurney. They stripped him of his dignity and robbed him of his humanity by exposing the backside of his body for all inmates to see. You lawyers know that we have prison guards at New Folsom, all over the State of California and across North America who are members of militias, hate groups and the mafia. You've seen the corruption. And you need to fight for the victims of the system. Victims! Victims! Victims! Brandon Gene Martinez is a victim. Sherman Manning is a victim. Patt Dunn is a victim and we are yearning to breathe free. And on a whim, they will arbitrarily and capriciously transfer us to other prisons where we may be stabbed, assaulted or killed and they get away with it everyday of the week. But when Mayor Willie Brown, Al Sharpton, Jesse, the NAACP or the media starts asking questions they'll stand up, clean up and take notice. If Shaquille O'Neal, Kobe Bryant, Magic Johnson, Mike Tyson, Bill Cosby, Oprah, Sean P. Diddy, or Spike Lee sent lawyers to check on C.D.C., C.D.C. would get in check. And it's not gonna get better until Murray, Barry, Gerry, Johnnie and F. Lee start calling Willie Ratcliff, John Johnson, Earl Graves, Susan Taylor and Tony Brown and ask them to expose these evils. Somebody ought to say something about out of control, abusive and corrupted prison officials. Somebody ought to say something about the absolute power of prison wardens to extend the prison sentences of inmates trapped in these prisons at taxpayers' expense everyday. We need preachers to preach about it, teachers to teach about it, mothers to pray about it, reporters to write about it and lawyers to litigate about it. Once a Willie Gary, a Gerry Spence, a Gerald Uelmen or a Johnnie Cochran files a class action lawsuit against C.D.C. (in California) G.D.C. (in Georgia) and a jury renders an eight-figure verdict against these prisons - the prisons will get better. Prisons will stop race baiting and segregation. Klansmen like

Sgt. (pseudonyms) Saunders at this prison, Sgt. Blackwell, Captain Shivellyn, Officer Woffrey and Lieutenant Triello will stop beating and abusing inmates. The corruption at Mule Creek, Lancaster, Corcoran, High Desert, etc. will stop. It will reach a screeching halt. Women prisoners will stop being raped and men prisoners will stop being killed. Non-violent prisoners will stop being assaulted and prisons will get back in the business of rehabilitation. As it stands now, prisons are full of exploitation. California pays prisoners less than thirty dollars per month to work jobs that pay more than thirty dollars per hour. It's slave labor in the prison plantation, and yet inmates are denied the right to an education. C.D.C. is like a black hole, a cesspool of violence, anger, hatred, racism and abuse. C.D.C. is absolutely corrupted, destructive, abusive and racist. C.D.C. is absolutely under the oversight of racist, vindictive, abusive and undereducated captains and wardens. Rodney King-like beatings absolute take place in the administrative segregation units of New Folsom, Mule Creek, Corcoran, Lancaster, High Deserts and all prisons across the great State of California everyday of the week. Drugs are absolutely smuggled into prisons across the states of America by prison guards everyday. Weapons and alcohol, etc. absolutely smuggled in by prison guards across California, New York, Florida, Arizona, etc. everyday of the week. And the politicians, media, lawyers and the public let it happen. I want Johnnie Cochran, Willie Gary, Gerry Spence, Gerry Uelman, Barry Tarlow or Peter Neufield to expose this and bankrupt the system. Sue the hell out of California. Sue them until they mind somebody and obey the rules of the law. Get these racist, abusive, cruel and evil murders, captains and lieutenants out of their guard towers and put them in jail where they belong. They are breeding, exacerbating and schooling prisoners on how to become more violent, evil and vicious everyday. And these humiliated, devastated and violent offenders will rejoin society tomorrow. These guys who have come to prison and had to join gangs and become racist in order to survive in prison because C.D.C. refused to protect them. These men will get out of prison tomorrow, next week, next month and next year. And since prison guards taught them how to be cold, callous, racist and violent, they will return to society and rape your children, kill your brothers and rob your sisters tomorrow. They will go out and shoot senators, congressmen, legislators and citizens tomorrow. They will shoot up day care centers, rob banks and abuse children tomorrow using the strategic techniques that they were taught in prison. These vicious, evil and cold-blooded people who learned their skills from power hungry and sadistic prison guards will be your neighbors tomorrow. And thousands of these men were sent to these vicious havens of hate, violence and despair for crimes they did not commit. We are here because Mary Hanlon Stone, Ed Jagels, Robert Altman, Mark Fuhrman, Rafael Perez, Dave Winkler sent us here. Ask Rubin "Hurricane" Carter, Kenny Waters, David Quindt, Anthony Porter or Rolando Cruz how easy it is to be sent here for crimes you did not commit. Ask them how it feels and what it does to your heart and mind when you write letters and get no answer. When you call people and they won't accept your collect call. Ask them how unfair, biased and racist many judges, prosecutors and police officers can be. Ask them about the set ups, police brutality, planted evidence, judicial misconduct, prosecutorial bias and jury tampering that takes place each and every day of the week. You know the truth! Lawyers know and the public needs to know that a Federal Appeals Court in San Diego threw out the convictions of four Mexicans and three Bolivians who were supposed to have run a large cocaine importation ring called the "Corporation". The court threw out the convictions because federal prosecutors hid a memo from the defense that cited the many lies of their chief witness, his lack of credibility and the numerous false accusations he had made in the past. The feds also kept another *big secret*. They withheld the fact that this living informant (snitch) was given full access to government offices, telephones, luxurious undercover sports cars, penthouses and numerous other perks in exchange for testimony for the prosecution. By keeping all of these *big secrets* the prosecutors were able to convince the jury that this snitch was credible and had no incentive to lie.

The public has a right to know about the case of the "prime time rapist" in Tucson, Arizona, in which an innocent man was wrongfully arrested, held incommunicado, interrogated relentlessly, then publicly named even as police knew they had the *wrong man*. In a surprise ruling the U.S. Ninth Circuit Court of Appeals decided that the normal immunity from liability, which shields law enforcement authorities, did not apply. The court decided that Michael Cooper, falsely accused of being the culprit, would be allowed to sue officials for their misconduct, as the violations of Mike's constitutional rights were simply too premeditated, systematic and egregious. Tucson had been terrorized by a serial rapist from late 1984 to 1986. Mike was the victim of a frame up because of a rush to judgment. This rush to judgment was the result of overzealous police officers needing to solve the case because of public outrage, fear and anxiety in the city. The Appeals Court was so disgusted that it began its opinion! "It is an abiding truth that nothing can destroy a government more quickly than it's failure to observe it's own laws, or worse, it's disregard for the charter of its' own existence."

The public needs to know that in Lancaster County, Pennsylvania, a young woman named Lisa Michelle Lambert, sentenced to life in prison in 1992 for murdering a romantic rival, was set free in April of 1997, after a federal judge declared her innocent, and wrote a riveting opinion. The judge said prosecutors had knowingly obstructed justice, knowingly put in perjured testimony, suppressed exculpatory evidence and manufactured evidence against her. After Judge Dalzell's ruling, he (the judge) became a target of the long prosecutorial reach of the prosecutor's anger. A drive to impeach him was launched. Prosecutors across the country filed "Friends of the Court" Appeals briefs demanding the decision be overturned, on the grounds that it suggested judges held too much power over prosecutors. And I wish defense lawyers: Barry Scheck, Willie Gary, Johnnie Cochran, Murray Janus, Gerald Uelmen, Alan Dershowitz, Ephraim Margolis, Barry Tarlow and Gerald Uelmen would get together and file "Friends of the Court" briefs to free Mumia Abu Jamal, Sherman Manning, Brandon G. Martinez, Patt Dunn and others. I wish the Gerry Spences of America would organize defense lawyers and get them to team up against injustice, wrongful convictions and false accusations the same way prosecutors across America teamed up against Judge Dalzell. Legislation was immediately proposed on the U.S. Senate to limit the power of Federal Judges to proclaim a prisoner's innocence because prosecutors felt shamed by Paizell's ruling. A conservative lobbying organization, the free Congress Foundation, condemned Dalzell in a fundraising video as yet another liberal judicial activist appointed by Bill Clinton's administration. When in fact, Judge Dalzell was known as a conservative, law and order jurist and he was appointed to the bench by Boy George Bush!! And guess what? I said - guess what? Because of the prosecutorial strength of district attorneys across this country seven months later the U.S. Court of Appeals for the Third Circuit in Philadelphia overturned his ruling and returned Michelle Lambert to prison where she remains. The reversal did *not* occur. Because the Appellate Justices disagreed with Dalzell's factual findings, but rather because of a procedural technicality cited by the almighty prosecutors. The courts ruled that Michelle Lambert, who had filed her own handwritten appeal to Judge Dalzell after she had been *raped* by a *prison guard*, had not completely exhausted the state process before going federal. In the face of the law, innocent was irrelevant. I repeat - innocence was irrelevant. Back in Lancaster County, before the same judge who had sentenced her to live in prison, Michelle's appeals and Judge Dalzell's findings were dismissed out of hand. All the prosecutorial misconduct, police errors and Lambert's rape in prison were "harmless errors", and I can't understand what the hell Murray Janus, Michael Morchower, Bruce Harvey, Steve Sadon, John Keker, F. Lee Bailey and the great (dedicated and high profile) lawyers are waiting on. Defendants' rights are being usurped and the police and prosecutors are gaining more power. And defense lawyers won't come together and fight. When Shaq and Kobe were unorganized and not unified the Lakers lost. When that brilliant coach Phil Jackson got them to play together, they won. Shaq began to praise Kobe and Kobe praised Shaq and the Lakers swept the Sacramento Queens (or was it Kings) and the San Antonio Spurs. Togetherness is what we need from Gerry Spence, Gerry Uelmen, Barry Tarlow and Roy Black - unity and togetherness. If Sgt. Phil Harrison got arrested for a crime, he did not commit tomorrow, I'll bet you my life that Shaquille O'Neal would bring together a dream team to defend his father. I know Shaq (read Shaq's book called "Shaq Talks Back") loves his daddy. And we need to get mothers, fathers, daughters and sons all over America who love these people who are trapped behind these walls to assemble dream teams to free the innocent. And one of the ways to raise the money to pay for this will be by suing these state-run prisons. I'm telling you there is more violence in prison than there is in Palestine. There are more weapons in prison than in any ghetto in Los Angeles. There is more racism amongst staffs of prisons (especially in California) than there were in the Jim Crow South. Tons of cocaine, heroine, marijuana, acid and speed are in prison. Smuggled in by the guards. And inmates are scared for their lives. Prison guards order more hits on prisoners than John Gotti ever ordered. If Richard Polanco wants to know what's going on in prisons, he needs to give inmates what's called "queen for a day" status. Bring trustworthy investigators into New Folsom, CMC East, Corcoran Pelican Bay, Lancaster, High Desert, Solano, San Quentin, etc. and promise not to allow prison authorities to retaliate, etc. and you'll find out about the rapes, murders, drugs, racism, guard fomented stabbings, etc. in California prisons and at prisons across the nation. But if we tell it openly, we will be punished by the worst punishment any prisoner can get; *solitary* confinement in ad-seg. And we will be stigmatized, brutalized, transferred and perhaps even killed. Prison guards are *deadly*!!! And these wardens and prison (wanna be) cops know that prosecutors rarely prosecute prison guards. They know most high profile lawyers rarely sue prison guards. They feel invincible.

The public needs to know that in United States vs. Yizar, the U.S. Court of Appeals for the Eleventh Circuit in Atlanta overturned an arson conviction because the prosecutors had failed to reveal evidence that an accomplice in the case said the defendant was innocent. Muneer Deeb, David Wayne Spence, Sidney Williams, Kerry Max Cook, Andrew L. Golden and Mark Bravo, etc. - what about them? All wrongfully convicted (in separate cases in various trials across the country) and all eventually exonerated. All sent away to lonely prison cells while prosecutors drank champagne and police officers continued their frame-ups!

Edward Honaker? Released after serving ten years in prison for a rape in Nelson County, Virginia that he could not have committed. Why? Prosecutorial misconduct, perjured testimony, secret, hidden and withheld evidence. The public needs to know. This is wrong! Did I mention Ronnie Bullock who was convicted of the 1985 rape of a nine-year-old girl? He was released after DNA proved he could not have committed this rape. He was attacked and humiliated in prison by guards and inmates (just like they do in California) and labeled a child molester. But he was innocent.

John Spencer was released from a fifty years to life sentence when state police in New York had to admit they planted his fingerprints at the scene of a double murder. Three state police troopers later were convicted of falsifying fingerprints in a massive, far reaching scandal that affected more than one hundred and fifty cases. Damn!

Adolph Munson, Richard Aldape Guerra, Joseph Burrows, etc. - what about them? Oh, they all happened to be released from death row in various prisons across North America because of wrongful, shameful and unjust convictions.

Bruce Turner was freed and exonerated from his 1991 conviction and decade long prison sentence for assault and battery because a Middlesex County, Massachusetts, prosecutor (Mary Hanlon Stone? Debbie Glynn?) threatened two defense witnesses who were going to testify of Turner's *innocence*. The public needs to know. We need the Workers World Newspaper, Atlanta Daily World, Atlanta Voice, Afro-American newspapers, Black Voice in Riverside, CA, the LA Sentinel, the San Francisco Bayview Newspaper, Tony Brown, Jesse, Al, the NAACP, the ACLU, the ADL and lawyers to help us inform the public. I challenge Murray Janus, Mike Morchower, David Hicks, Gerry Spence, F. Lee Bailey and Roy Black to help me tell the public through this book about these blatant abuses of power which you're up against everyday of the week. The public needs to know and they deserve to know. And defense lawyers need to start (collectively) gunning for justice for the rights of the people of this great country. I have absolutely no desire to see guilty defendants walk free. I do not want the streets terrorized by child molesters, murderers and drug dealers. But when we allow the prisons to overflow with innocent people, we are allowing killers to stay free. When we send even the guilty to prison and abuse them by allowing prison guards to beat, mistreat, neglect, disrespect and abuse them, we create predators and racists and rapists *in* the prison systems. We allow our politicians to react to crime in the streets by passing new laws in the suites. And these new laws make it harder and harder for the innocent to get justice. There are a record number of cases wherein judges will admit a man is innocent but because of new laws even a good judge can't set them free. The public needs to know.

Here is a case that sort of exemplifies the effect of foolish new laws and the power of the government in America to incarcerate. This case demonstrates just how difficult winning freedom for innocents can be. An Oregon judge refused to set aside the murder convictions of a woman and a man although even the prosecutors who convicted them said they were not guilty and despite the fact that another man confessed to the murder and provided detailed, specific evidence that police said no one but the killer could know about. Sixty-two-year-old Laverne Pavlinac had falsely confessed to the killing of a young female in Portland and had implicated her forty-one-year-old live in boyfriend, John Sosnovske, in order to get out of their abusive relationship. She recanted later but they were both convicted anyway and were sentenced to life in prison. Keith Hunter Jesperson, who was a serial murderer known as the "Happy Face Killer", later confessed and convinced prosecutors that they had gotten it wrong. Prosecutors petitioned the court for a belated acquittal. Yet, tough new Oregon laws limit the time for presenting new evidence to *five days* after sentencing, which is a rule intended to preserve the integrity and finality for a jury verdict, but which implicitly assumes that all new evidence of innocence is bogus and false. In these cases, there was virtually no legal route of appeal, and Pavlinac and Sosnovske languished in cold prison cells for another three months after everybody in the case agreed that they were innocent. Finally, the judge decided that the solution was to proclaim that Sosnovske's Civil Rights had been violated by Pavlinac's false allegations, thereby erasing his convictions on constitutional grounds. Livid by Pavlinac's lies, the judge refused to erase her conviction but ordered her released on the grounds that it would be *cruel* and *unusual* punishment for her to serve any prison term for a crime she clearly did not commit. Whether or not this ruling met the letter of law was irrelevant, because the prosecutor made it clear they would never appeal their release. This is a clear example of achieving justice in spite of tough new laws and not because of them. This is why we need brilliant men like Murray, Barry, Tarlow, Ira London, Mr. Uelmen, Mr. Spence, Dershowitz and Margolin to fight. Nobody can convince me that Mr. Janus, Margolin, Dershowitz, Uelmen or Neufield couldn't get me free of my wrongful conviction. You can't convince me that Scheck or Neufield or Protess can't find a way to get Brandon G. Martinez free from prison.

But this is why we need desperately to get strong men like Bishop T. D. Jakes to preach about it. We need Dean Sanders and Michael Irvin to talk about it. We need to employ the influence of Denzel Washington, Spike Lee, John Singleton, Ice Cube, Queen Latifah and Oprah. We need Bill Cosby, Earl Graves, Susan Taylor and Robert Johnson to raise hell about it. Bishop T. D. Jakes once stated that "When the church doesn't talk, people die." No truer words were even spoken. And when preachers don't visit, comfort, care and fight for innocents in prison people die. I am a preacher of the gospel. I've preached for and with Jasper Williams, Joseph Wells, Clay Evans, Leroy Elliott, C. Howard Nevette, etc. I love to preach, I love God and I love the church. I am a preacher's preacher.

But I must tell it like it is. While preachers are sitting back eating fried chicken, catfish and thumping Bibles, a whole generation of Black, Brown and poor White men who are innocent in prison are dying. They are dying while the church remains silent and does nothing. I love Bishop T. D. Jakes and I've said clearly that I hope people will support his television ministry en masse because he is *reaching* and *inspiring* men in prison. But I want to see preachers help the innocent. Barry Scheck and his innocence projects ought to have large donations coming in from pastors, churches and civil rights leaders all over America. How much money has Jerry Falwell, Pat Robertson or the Christian Coalition sent to Barry Scheck, CA Prison Focus, the ACLU and the NAACP lately? How many churches are standing up for the least of these our brethren? I'm all for rhythm, rhyme, cadence, shouting, dancing and praising God! I love to praise the King of Kings. He is worthy to be praised. But what are we gonna do when we finish shouting? Will we do the work of Jesus or will we send out a letter asking for another donation? Bishop Jakes preached in San Quentin Prison a few months ago. When was the last time Jesse preached in prison? Has Robert Schuller preached or sent any of this ministerial delegates to preach in prison. Churches have drives to raise money for building funds, new vans, choir robes, etc. What churches are raising money to help Deacon James McCloskey's centurion ministry in Princeton, New Jersey, which frees innocent prisoners. There is more to ministry (preachers) than preaching. Jesus took two fish and five loaves of bread and fed over five thousand people. He believed in *feeding* the *hungry*. How many of you would welcome Chris Gardner to your church today and allow him to speak to your congregation? Most of you would today because Chris Gardner is now a multi-millionaire (tithes and offerings?) stockbroker. But *when he was homeless* would you have taken Chris in your fine ten thousand member church? Preachers we must do better. I wrote a preacher in Chicago, Illinois three months ago. This pastor on the west side of Chicago was my friend, my buddy, and my comrade. I only asked him to send me a tape of one of his sermons. He never replied. "I was in prison and you visited me not". When Rev. Henry B. Lyons was president of the National Baptist Convention every preacher would take his call. Leroy Elliott would be glad to talk to him. Dr. E. V. Hill, Jasper Williams, Clay Evans, and A. Lincoln James would all take his call. But how many preachers will accept a collect call from Rev. Henry B. Lyons today while he's in prison? Preachers? Aren't we the guys who remind our congregations that Saul was a murderer before he became Paul? Don't we remind them of King David's adultery and conspiracy to commit murder? Don't we recall the false imprisonment of Joseph in prison for attempted *rape*? Preachers? It's time to get real! *God is not pleased. God is not pleased! God is not pleased! God is not pleased!*

And you can change this. You who are reading this book right now can make a commitment. You can say *today* that, "I'm gonna take this book to my pastor and ask him to read it." You can say today that, "I'm gonna write Sherman a letter and get a book to send to Jesse, Al Sharpton, my local newspaper, etc." And when your preacher reads this book in its entirety, if he is sincere (and many preachers like Bishop T. D. Jakes and Bishop Noel Jones are sincere (anointed men) he'll take action. He may not visit *me*. He may not write to *me*. He may not help Sherman Manning, but he will write, visit and *help somebody else*. And God is my witness that that's all I'm asking. Hell yes, I need somebody to help me. Hell yes, I need a sharp, relentless investigator. Yes, I need a brilliant lawyer. That's for sure because I'm innocent of this crime. But this book is not all about Sherman Manning. I'm just a tool. This book is for prisoners, lawyers, preachers and sinners. This book is to awaken the sleeping giant amongst lawyers and inspire them to rise up and fight for all innocent people. This book is to inspire men in prison to get up, clean themselves off, stop gambling and smoking dope and start reaching for hope. This book is to spark a flame in the pit of the bellies of activists and cause them to stand up against wrongful convictions. This book is a wake up call to politicians. It's a plea to the Black media and to all media. This book is *anointed*. I'm very serious. It's anointed in such a way as to *haunt you* until you do something to stop police brutality, wrongful convictions and cruel, unusual punishment. This book is strategically, spiritually, and factually written so as to cause you to close the book; forget about typos and the breaking of writer's rules and think: "What would I do if my son, daughter, my brother, sister, my wife, husband or anyone I know (including me) was arrested, tried and convicted of a crime they did not commit?" What would I do? How can I use my life today to help the least of these my brethren? How bad, epidemic, widespread and systematic must it be if David Protess and journalism students out at Northwestern have to free innocent men from prison? How bad must it be if Professor Robert Cling and his students at Chicago Law School have to use their time to free innocent people? This book will cause you to ask those questions. But the ultimate test will be what you do after you ask the questions. Will you continue to believe the foolish adage that, "All of them claim they are innocent"? Will you wait on Barry Scheck to free another one? Will you wait on Robert Cling, David Protess and Deacon James McCloskey to take on the thousands of cases of wrongful convictions? Or will you use your law firm, use your church, use your newspaper, radio and television show, and use your money and life to help somebody else?

This book is not a fiction. It is not a novel. It is real. I have blood running through my veins right now. I am human. I am a person and while you sit in your easy chair in the comfort of your home, I am sitting in the discomfort of my concrete prison cell. If the people don't speak out, I will die here.

On May 27, 2001 at 9:00 pm I received a memo from prison staff indicating that we were being *locked down* due to the "violent incident, which occurred on May 25, 2001". Ever heard of Monday morning quarter backing or a day late and a dollar short? Usually in prison, after a stabbing or a killing, inmates are locked down immediately after the incident. This is usually to protect the integrity of the investigation, prevent any further victims or victimization, etc. I am in facility "A", which is a protective custody yard. This yard is for *high profile cases* such as mine, which includes snitches, informants,

221

child molesters, and inmates who have dropped out of gangs, etc. Quite frankly this is/this has been *one* of the (very few) safest facilities in C.D.C. because there is rarely a serious incident of major violence. But within the past year (slowly but steadily) staff (either purposely or inadvertently) have been releasing a few *racist* and violent inmates who have no real need to be in this facility. And the climate seems to be getting a bit more violent. But my point is this, why would any sane official declare a lockdown two days after the "violent incident"? Did some sergeant, lieutenant or AOD drop the ball? Were we at risk during the two days staff forgot to lock us down? Or was the lockdown necessary at all? Here's your answer; we have many insane, uneducated supervisors in C.D.C. Captains are earning eighty thousand dollars per year, but didn't graduate from high school. No college education, no sensitivity, racial diversity or people skills at all. Yet they are *running* the prisons. And C.D.C. very rarely promotes a Black or Mexican to the rank of captain. And the few who make it are tokens. House Negroes. The public, Joseph Biden, John Lewis, Maxine Waters, Ted Kennedy, Jesse, Al Sharpton, the NAACP, ACLU and the ADL needs to know that prison authorities are racist, unfair, law breakers and out of control. I can't believe Richard Polanco has any idea about what's really going on *behind these walls*. Consider Robert King Wilkerson. After thirty-one years, twenty-nine of which were spent in solitary confinement, Roger was set free in February of this year. But his long, strong battle for justice is not yet over. He's now fighting to free the other members of the Angola 3. "When I was released I made a commitment that was whatever time I had left, I would try to free my two comrades," Roger stated.

Roger along with Albert Woodfox and Herman Wallace, strived to end the rape and torture of prisoners and establish unity between Black and White inmates at Louisiana's Angola State Prison. Wallace and Woodfox founded a prison chapter of the Black Panther Party in 1971, which Roger joined in 1972. Prison officials retaliated (just as they do in California prisons) and framed Wallace and Woodfox in 1972 for murdering a prison guard and in 1973 charged Roger with killing another inmate.

A short while after Roger was thrown into the hole; a prisoner on his tier was murdered in a shank (knife) fight. Prison officials initially issued a blanket indictment against all the prisoners on that tier. Shortly thereafter, however, they forced two other prisoners (CA authorities do it all the time) to implicate Roger and another man in the murder. During their trial they were shackled, handcuffed, and their mouths were covered with duct tape. They couldn't present any defense and they were found guilty. Subsequently the State Supreme Court overturned this conviction stating Roger should not have been gagged because he demonstrated no signs that he would be disruptive. He was tried again. Based on one prisoner's incredible testimony, he was convicted and given a life term again. A breakthrough came in 1987 when the two jailhouse-snitches that testified against him recanted. One of the inmates stated the guard had threatened to pin the murder on him if he didn't implicate Roger. In spite of credible evidence of Roger's innocence, the courts would not exonerate him. In 1991, a three judge panel offered him a new trial - not based on innocence but because no female had been on the grand jury which indicted him. The full Appeals Court later overturned that decision. His case went before the Appeals Court again in 2000 as a result of a ruling by the U.S. Supreme Court. A two-judge panel found that his constitutional rights had been violated. This ultimately led to his release. But Roger says it was the support of people who filled the courtroom during his last trial that won his freedom. As a result of people pressure, the court considered evidence that it had previously ignored. The International Action Center helped Roger. "They (IAC) threw the first pebble into the pond and the ripple spread," stated Wilkerson. Richard Becker, Co-Director of the IAC's East Coast Branch, said, "I don't know how many people could have endured what they did for three decades and held to their beliefs. They were persecuted barbarically by the prison system for fighting against the most corrupt and inhumane conditions." "Eighty-five percent of those who go into Angola die there," stated Marina Drummer. Luis Talamantez with the IAC and California Prison Focus in San Francisco also praised Roger Wilkerson. So did Corey Weinglass of CA Prison Focus. "I am committed to the struggle against the prison industrial complex and the exposure of it," stated Roger. The public needs to know and the people need to take action. We need to get the involvement of activist students like the "PSU Village" out at Penn State University. We need to find Lakeisha Wolf out at Penn State, the Southwestern College Rainbow Alliance, the Native American Rights Network, Workers World Party, The Wall - Las Memorias Project, Joe Delaplaine, Tim Helsley, and Monica Moorehead. We need to bring together Steve Millies, Julian Bond, Leslie Feinberg, Howard Zinn and Gery Armsby. We need John Sweeney and Linda Chavez Thompson. We need Roona Ray, Pacho Valdez, Jane Martin, Al Cho, Aaron Bentley, Ashwini, Sukthankar, Fuerza Latina, and all those students out at Harvard to help us spread this book around and stir up the issues in the hood. We can't do it without Monica Moorehead and Larry

Holmes. We can't do it without *you*. Get this book to the inmates trapped in jails and prisons and juveniles. Call up Doug Banks, Tony Brown, Al Sharpton and Jesse Jackson. Call the Workers World Party at (212) 627-2994 or fax them at (212) 675-7869. Call Deirdre Griswold, John Johnson, Earl Graves and Susan Taylor. Find out if they have this book. If not, get them a copy. Call Rebecca Toledo, the Bar Association in your city, Tommy Goss at KBMB in Sacramento and tell them to put the word out about this book. Let's come together for Mumia Abu Jamal, the Angola 3 and all political prisoners. Let's get this book to Forrest Schmidt, Adiya Hines and Carlos Pedilla from students for justice. Get the word to the Brown/Student/Labor Alliance out at Brown University. Find Michael Shaw and get this book to him. Ask IAC, CA Prison Focus the Southern Human Rights Center in Atlanta, GA how you can help. Ask them to give you the name and address of a prisoner who might want to read this book. Ask them to give you the name and address of a student at Brown University, Harvard, Johns Hopkins or Moorehouse College who you can send this book to. Ask the IAC and/or CA Prison Focus what you can do to help free Mumia Abu Jamal. Call Mary Ratcliff at the San Francisco Bayview Newspaper and the LA Sentinel newspaper. Many of whom I can't reach because I'm in prison. You can get the word out. Find Rubin "Hurricane" Carter's address in Toronto, Canada and get this book to him. I am telling you here and now that if you will make sure five people other than yourself read this book, we will come together. We will stop police brutality, prosecutorial misconduct, judicial corruption and prison abuse. If you decide that you are unwilling to fight the system yourself. If you are honestly not going to join in then at least help those who will fight. Give IAC, The Innocence Project, Centurion Ministries, the Workers World, CA Prison Focus, etc. a donation. They can use your money to help them in the struggle even if it's only one or two dollars. You can do something today. Get the word out. Tell every doctor, professor, lawyer, politician and preacher you know about, "*If it doesn't fit, you must acquit*". Joe Willhite writes for the "Stag" somewhere in California and he is also in ACLU activist. Find him and get him this book. A woman wrote me four months ago to tell me she loved the book, would like to help etc. She said "How can I send a copy to somebody like Shaquille O'Neal?" I said, "Easy just call information in LA and get the address to the LA Lakers and mail it to him." Use the telephone, Internet and word of mouth. If I could get one hundred people to do what this woman is doing we could shake up the nation. I need your help. By all means you can write to me and send a contribution of at least twenty-one dollars and we'll get another copy of this book to you. I do not want you to read this book like a novel. Don't close the book and be impressed. Close the book and be inspired to take action. Start by writing me a letter. Then call the Doug Banks Show. Call Tommy Goss at KBMB in Sacramento. Call PBS, the NAACP, ACLU. Call people who will expose this book to their readers, listeners, callers and sponsors. Doggonit, I need help!!

Thousands that are innocent, men and women sitting in prisons all across the country, also need help. They (the innocent) come in all colors - Indians, Blacks, White, Latinos, young, old, gay, straight, etc. They need help. They need books, tapes, newspapers, prayer, visits, money, lawyers, etc. They need you. You can reach them and help them. Call organizations and say "I want to write a prisoner" or "how can I send a book to a prisoner". And when you guys in prison begin to correspond with people on the street *don't try to con them*. Keep it real and genuine. People don't have time for crooked prisoners. Very few people out there give a damn about us. So when we are blessed enough to contact someone who cares, we don't need to try to misuse on manipulate them.

And I need the great organizations across this country such as the IAC, WWP, students against racism, CA Prison Focus and FAMM to call and E-mail your congressmen and senators and tell them about this book. Raise hell with them about innocent men in prison. Raise hell about the conditions are these prisons. Raise hell about the lack of education, rehabilitation, etc. and also about the *rapes* and *beatings* of prisoners by guards. Tell them you don't want prisoners pampered but you do want prisoners treated with basic human respect. Tell them about the slave labor, racism and violence in prison. Tell them you don't want men returning to society in worse condition than they entered prison. Tell them you are sick and tired of the rhetoric and gamesmanship. Tell them we need action. Talk to them about Sheriff Mike Hennessy in San Francisco and ask them to model and duplicate his programs across America. Talk to your pastors, city council members, mayors, high school coaches and principals. Let's *do something*. I am telling you if you continue to leave the fate of this great country in the hands of politicians, America will collapse. Big money buys politicians. Big money buys the White House. Big money buys the passing of new laws. You need to write or call in, march in and hunger strike in until we begin the process of transformation in this country. Read Gerry Spence's book "Injustice for All" and you'll get verification on what I've written here. I need you (the reader) to get active. Dr. Martin Luther King, Jr. use to say,

"If you can't run, walk. If you can't walk, crawl. If you can't crawl, roll. But keep moving". And I say help. Help get this book to lawyers, students, politicians, doctors, mothers, and prisoners. Help! Help the I.A.C. the ACLU, the Innocence Project, I-May, the NAACP and WWP. Send each organization some money. If you can't send a hundred thousand dollars, send fifty thousand. If you can't send thousands of dollars, send hundreds of dollars. If you can only send one dollar, they can use it to help people. I can use any help you send me. You can feed the hungry, clothe the naked and take care of the least of these our brethren. I'm sorry, whether you believe in socialism, capitalism, communism or Marxism, I don't give a darn.

Whether you think all poor people are lazy or not. I don't care. I spent so much time feeding the hungry and homeless to believe such foolishness. We are the richest nation on the planet. And we can feed our hungry people. I know we can. You don't have to give away your mansion or your limousine. You can keep a few billion or million dollars for yourself and your family. But how much wealth does one man need? A hundred billion dollars! Come on give me a break. That much wealth is sin. Let's create jobs in the inner and urban cities. Let's build schools and libraries for our youth. Let's build their minds, hearts and their spirits. If you are against social programs and welfare, so what. Go mentor a child in Perry Homes, Nickerson Gardens, Watts, Fair Street Bottoms and the slumlord of New York. They can't pull themselves up by their own bootstraps if they have no boots. If you refuse to give them a handout give them a *hand up*. These are human beings. You can't wait on George W. to feed, clothe and house them. There are homeless people sleeping right outside the White House in America. George W. doesn't give a damn about those people. He could care less. They don't matter. They can't vote because they don't have an address. They can't vote because they have no identification. But they do have names, hearts and feelings. They're human too. And we pastors, doctors, lawyers, and Christians can and must care for them. We can sponsor workshops for them. We can teach them how Chris Gardner pulled himself out of the streets and became a millionaire. But it's difficult to believe rhetoric about the American Dream being possible when you have hunger pangs clamping your belly. Y'all know that we can do better. Yes we can. If we don't take care of them now, we'll take care of them later. Because corrupted prosecutors who need to reach some quota, renegade police who need to meet their felony arrest quota will pin a rape, robbery or a murder on him. And when they go to jail, who pays to feed them? You do! When they go to prison, who pays to secure and house them? You do! Who pays the officers, prison doctors, prison dentists and prison wardens? You do! So you'll either pay now with a chance at creating a decent, self sufficient, productive member of society or you'll pay later after the person commits a robbery to try to feed themselves and their children. Or after an overzealous prosecutor sends them to prison for a crime they did not commit. And once they go to prison - they'll never be the same again. Prison is a horrible place. And we must stop losing our children and teens to jails and prisons. Young people you don't want to come here. It is a disastrous way to live. I want somebody to find Christian Acosta and send him this book. Please get it to him. Christian is a student (freshman) at U.C. Davis. Find Erik Else in Susanville, CA and get this book to him. I need strong-minded activists such as those as the I.A.C. or Workers World or CA Prison Focus to use the telephone or Internet and help me locate Christian and Erik. Just call information and get the addresses to me and I'll send them a book. If this tome inspires our teens to stay in school and off drugs then my work won't be in vain. We must save our children. *Destiny's Child* gave their church a half million dollars donation the other month! Amen! Use some of that money to help our youth.

Here's a real tearjerker. In a high school outside of St. Louis, Missouri, a mostly White student body chose a Black janitor to give their graduation speech. George Smith, the custodian who cleaned and prepared the same auditorium he gave the keynote speech in was chosen because those students said he was a *real man*. Amen. This is why I hope and pray that you will help me get this book to students. High school, college and law students are open-minded and energetic. They won't just read the book and put it down. Those activists out at Harvard who stood up for a living worker's wage, students at Penn State, Brown University, Moorehouse, Howard, Spellman College and Stanford University will take action. And that's what we need. Students will bombard radio stations, PBS, National Public Radio, the Congress, legislators and the Senate and say, "What's being done to free innocent prisoners." They'll send this book to Joe Biden, John Lewis, Maxine Waters, Richard Polanco and say, "What are you gonna do about racism and violence in prisons." The students will call Monica Moorehead, Millions for Mumia and the I.A.C. and say, "How can we help Mumia?" Students will protest, demonstrate, organize, galvanize and strategize. So I challenge Murray Janus, Willie Gary, F. Lee Bailey, Barry Tarlow and Mr. Fieger, etc. Even if you don't help Sherman Manning, order twenty or thirty copies of this book and send it to colleges. Send it to law prosecutors, law students, etc. make sure that every one of those journalism students at Northwestern, all the kids at Cardoza Law School, U.C. Davis, Harvard activists, etc. get a copy of this book. I love the Lord! I know I'm digressing without a warning but I can do that. I love God so much. I was just praying and I began to think about how God has **kept me** in spite of all my sins, wrongdoing, game playing, etc. God has spared my life and had mercy on me. I praise Him today. As a kid I wanted to be just like Jasper Williams, Leroy Elliott and the late Leo Daniels. And God gifted me so that I could preach just as powerful as those guys can. But in addition to being able to say it, God had another plan for me. I was not to pastor. I wasn't called to be an inside guy. God wanted me to serve the least of these our brethren. What better way to teach me compassion, love and care than to allow me to be wrongly convicted and falsely imprisoned, to be vilified and humiliated. What better way to make Joseph never forget to feed the hungry than to allow him to go to prison accused of attempted rape. God wanted the life of Joseph to come alive in my life. And I am a living witness today that if you don't need the calling of God, He will allow you to be broken so badly that only He can mend you. He allows situations so that He can get glory, He can get revealed and He can use us. We are so arrogant, puffed up and pompous that God has to purify us through pain and suffering.

But if he calls you out He can bring you in. Jesus waited four days so Lazarus could die. Somebody had to die and He chose Lazarus to die. He did it to reveal His power. He passed them up from the grave. In my case, somebody had to go to jail. And He chose me. And now I believe He is teaching lawyers, law professors and students and He's gonna use them to bring me out. I better stop before I start preaching. God is awesome! God is all knowing and Almighty. I Bless His holy name. He called Moses and Moses didn't want to go. Why did He harden the heart of Pharaoh? God had a plan. He had a Red Sea. Paul had a thorn in the flesh and the thorns serve as a reminder to keep us humble. A thorn in the flesh reminds you that God knows **who you are** underneath. All the cologne, facelifts, suits, dresses and ties. "I know who you are," says God. I believe Joseph's prison sentence was a reminder. No matter how much power he had he was still an ex-con who did time for a crime of moral turpitude. And he never forgot about it. Paul was a Chief Apostle and he was still an ex-con. He was still an ex-murderer but wanted me to know why my friend Rev. Hosea Williams never forgot to feed those homeless people. Hosea owned a Bingo Hall, a Chemical Company; he had a degree in chemistry and a few fine cars. But he never sold out or forgot his people. You could call him at one o'clock in the morning and he'd tell you "I'm out here fighting for those poor people. And Hosea went back and forth to jail, sometimes for the Civil Rights, sometimes for DUI. He took beatings on the media but he kept on walking and he kept on feeding those hungry people. When I get at out of here I'll have this thorn in my flesh. I'll never get rid of the fact that I was in prison. I'll never outlive my ex-con status. Some preachers will never invite me to preach again. I may not get silver and gold again. But I'll be able to truly say "Silver and gold have I none *but such as I have give I unto Thee*". I can serve now. I don't have to imagine it. I've been broken down to life's lowest denominator. I've been counted out and written off. But "Your situation is not too bad that God can't raise it up," says Bishop Noel Jones. And God will tear up heaven to get you out of this," says Bishop T. D. Jakes. In the natural, I can't see a way out of here. I'm going back to trial soon with no lawyer and no money facing seventy-five years to life in prison. In the flesh it looks bad. Prosecutor Mary Hanlon Stone is behind the new charges. I can't see my way out of here. But in the supernatural, I know that all things are possible. Barry, Gerry Spence, Johnnie, Stanley Greenberg and even Willie Gary can be used by God to get me out of here. I'll never let it happen to somebody else. I've surrendered my ego, pride and defects and I've had to give it to God. "Who will go and who shall I send?" I'll go Lord; please send me.

A major study of the so-called quality of government-appointed defense lawyers revealed that most minimum wage workers at McDonald's earn more money per hour than some states pay defense lawyers for the indigent in murder cases. According to the Southern Center for Human Rights in my hometown (Atlanta) the maximum indigent defense fee in Virginia, for instance, is $265.00 for investigating, litigating and defending a felony charge that carries a punishment of twenty years in prison. The fee rises to a maximum of $575.00 if the case carries a life sentence. By comparison, top defense lawyers earn more than five hundred dollars per hour in murder cases. The average court appointed lawyer in Alabama who spends two hours preparing for a death penalty trial would earn four dollars per hour. Is it still so hard to understand why innocent people routinely go to jail?

Go to Wenatchee, Washington and ask Mark and Carol Doggett how easy it is to go to prison for crimes you didn't commit. (I want somebody to find Carol and Mark Doggett in Wenatchee, Washington and send them this book). V. James Landano in Newark can tell you how often prosecutors lie, cheat and hide evidence.

Don't take my word for it. Anthony Porter, Shareef Cousin, Steven Smith and David Quindt can attest to the fact that paper trails, false arrests, plea bargains, etc. will cause prosecutors to sell a lie to a jury and convince them that you are a predator, rapist, child molester or a murderer. Prosecutors consistently fail to observe ethical and legal restraints. Ask John Thompson in New Orleans about DA Harry Connick. Ask John Duval in New York, Dennis Fritz or Ronald Williamson how often the police and courts get it wrong. Prosecutors possess sweeping power in contemporary America, which is often the answer to no authority except their own biased and racist consciences. They manipulate grand juries as their tools rather than as a checks and balances system.

They lie, they cheat, they steal and they kill. And we can't let it continue. We must rise up in schools, churches, colleges, law schools, law firms and prisons across this country and say "No more". We won't take it any longer. A government should be one of the people, by the people and for the people. No police officer, prosecutor or judge can be *above the people* they serve.

I challenge defense lawyers, honest judges, the IAC, CA Prison Focus, pastors and students across the country to rise up and make a change. Rise up and fight the power fight with your money. Fight with your student newspapers. Fight with your protests, sit-ins, demonstrations, letters to the editors, get out to vote campaigns, etc. Fight on the Internet, with your telephones and fax machines. Fight! Fight the power. Fight until justice *rolls down like waters and righteousness like a mighty stream.* Call the judge in Pennsylvania and tell him to free Mumia Abu Jamal. Call Mary Hanlon Stone and Judge Robert Altman and tell them it *doesn't fit, you must acquit.* Free Sherman Manning. Go to the courts and protest. Fill up the courtrooms and sit in. Find out where they live and protest in the streets in front of their homes. Don't be violent! Never use violence. But use the tools of non-violent demonstration, prayer vigils and the voting booth to *fight for* the *least* of these thy brethren. All *power to the people*!

Power to the people not the prosecutors. I want to tell all the gang members in the streets as well as in the prisons. Especially young gang members, unite! Unite! Unite and fight for peace. Your enemy is not each other. Your enemy is a corrupted judicial system that will send you away for an eternity. Police officers in Cincinnati, Ohio, Los Angeles and New York will kill you in a hot second and plant a weapon on you after your body is riddled with bullets. Rev. Luis Barrios, Hector Torres, Sara Catalinotto and Malik. John Parker and

Gery; I want you all to bring the gangs together for a summit meeting organize them in the struggle to fight police brutality, racism, sexism, prison abuse and the P.I.C. Leave no gang member, no worker, no janitor, no gay, no straight, no Black, White, Mexican or Asian behind. Bring the people together. Put the word out that we are putting down the weapons of violence and division. And we are picking up the militant weapons of protest sit-ins, demonstrations, campaigns, voting, Internet and telephone campaigns. We demand to be heard and respected. Shirley Bushnell, Monica Moorehead and Gloria La Riva need help. Let's come together. We cannot leave the fate of our children and loved ones in the hands of the police, prosecutors, judges or even the FBI. They are demonizing our youth and incarcerating them. This is not a Black problem. It is a White, Mexican, Asian and a human problem. Gang members are not flying any drugs into this country. Gang members are not shipping planeloads and shiploads of cocaine and heroin to America. Gang members are not manufacturing any guns, bombs or nuclear weapons. Who is the real enemy? I do not support any racist militias. But I am beginning (somewhat) to understand their paranoia. I want you young people to stop smoking their dope. Stop drinking their alcohol. Stop killing each other with their guns. Stop destroying your own neighborhoods. Organize and fight the power. Use your mind, use your charisma, use your spirit and use your soul force. Bring the power structure to their knees. How much dehumanization and discrimination can we take and not fight back? We can't trust the process to keep itself in check. Lawyers like Barry Scheck, Gerry Spence and Johnnie Cochran protect the integrity of the process of the system. They are well cognizant of the fact that the system cannot be trusted. Ask Gerry Spence.

The recent headlines are replete with stories of the FBI, which is the highest law enforcement agency in the land being corrupted. Look at all of the PD 302 Forms, which were withheld, lost and hidden from defense lawyers in Tim's case. FBI Agent Rick Ojeda told Dan Rather that he uncovered exculpatory evidence that was withheld from Tim's lawyers. FBI Agent Jeff Jenkins who received a commendation from FBI Director Lovih Frieh said he was the victim of racism within the department and when Special Agent Jenkin's White supervisor tried to get an agent to apologize to Jeff, he (the White supervisor) was fired from the department. Numerous FBI whistle blowers were told about cultural problems and racism within the department. No wonder the Justice Department routinely clears racist police officers accused of murdering innocent victims of any wrongdoing. Who polices the police? Who polices the FBI? The people must do it. And when gang members stop killing each other on the streets and organize with the IAC and WWP and sue the hell out of the FBI in class action lawsuits - they'll clean up. We must come together and love one another. Love is a powerful weapon. Love is the most powerful force on the face of the planet. I was watching Kobe Bryant on TV a few months ago. Why is this twenty-two-year-old kid so awesome on the court? He loves basketball. He said, "I love the sound of the basketball, the smell of the basketball, the feel of the basketball, the sound of the sneakers on the floor." And he's a *practice-a-holic*. Guys like Murray Janus, Gerry Spence and Willie Gary love the law. They just love it! And when you and I start loving one another again we can move mountains together. We can feed the hungry, clothe the naked and set the captives free. Part of the reason C.D.C. and prison systems across the country abuse inmates so terribly is because nobody seems to love prisoners. When we organize, pool our resources and make our voices heard, we can put jails and prisons in check. We must come together. As long as we are *divided* they will *conquer* us. But start raising money and sending it to the Innocence Project. Do fundraisers, car washes, book sales, basketball exhibition games, telethons for the IAC, CA Prison Focus, the NAACP, etc. and put some money behind the muscle. Expose this corruption and politicians will take notice. Send some money to Steve Bright and the Southern Human Rights Center in Atlanta. Help get this book to prisoners, youth, churches, barbershops, politicians, sports starts and celebrities and we'll transform the nation. And again, y'all need to call C.D.C. in Sacramento and check up on me. If they transfer me, you wanna know when and where to and why. If I'm (again) in solitary confinement, you want to know why. Call the department. Fax Governor Gray Davis. Contact the NAACP, ACLU, and People Against Racist Terror and tell them to check up on me.

And I want you to get active today in helping to end prosecutorial misconduct and immunity in this country. Again, we must become pragmatic and view the struggle from an angle of unity. It can't be a Black struggle or a Mexican struggle. It must be a people struggle. As long as we are divided they will kill us and get away with it. What would have happened if Martin and Malcolm had gotten *together*? What would happen now if Jesse, Farrakhan, Al Sharpton, Monica Moorehead, Gloria La Riva, Gery, the ACLU, NAACP, the ADL got *together*? They could not kill us! If the Mexican Mafia, Northern Mexicans, Southern Mexicans, Nazi Low Riders, Aryan Brotherhood, Bloods and Crips called a *truce* behind these walls and organized for prisoners rights, what would happen? We can't forget the fundamental adages that together we stand and divided we fall.

Stand for what? Liberty and Justice for all. All people! We must lift our fists and no longer cry Black or White power. Lift them and cry people power. Get a plan and roll with the plan. We can't trust politicians to stop the school massacres. We create these young killers and then lock them up for emulating us. I am telling you we are responsible for the school shootings. But if the F.O.I. were in the schools there would be no shootings. If the guardian angels, Millions for Mumia were in the schools, there would be no killings. And these massacres by and large are transpiring in White suburbs not in inner cities. They are not about poverty they are about powerlessness, anger, void and a lack of understanding. We can stop the massacres! Alienation, melancholy and rage leads to explosive violence. We must reach our teens. Bryan Mabe went to Thurston High School in Oregon. Some of my friends at the IAC need to find Bryan and get this book to him. He can help us stop the school killings. He knows what to look for. I need you to help me reach out and touch Bryan in Springfield, Oregon. Help me reach the Doggcats in Wenatchee. Let's reach out and touch the pulse of the suburbs, hoods and churches of our nation and network against violence, rage and killings. The students at Harvard and Penn State can help us reach these teens and dig under the shells, shields and the layers of loneliness. IAC, SCLU, ACLU, students against racism, *let's go to work*. Ted Koppell surprised me a few months ago. He blew Corpus Christi Superior Court Judge Manuel Banales out of the water. Judge Banales requires sex offenders who are given probation to place a sign on front of their residence stating they are a sex offender. He also required him to place this sign on their cars. This is unconstitutional. *First* of all, I do not think sex offenders should ever get probation. Never! Send them to prison. And while they are there, we should treat them for their perverted sickness. No probation! Ted asked the judge wasn't it double jeopardy, etc. Wouldn't it cause vigilantism, etc? There are cases where people have burned down the houses of sex offenders. The judge said the *signs* are to *protect* the *children* not punish the offender. Ted pointed out that the law should be consistent. On the one hand, we want special laws to protect the children because they are so vulnerable, etc. Yet, on the other hand we routinely try the children as adults when they are accused of committing a crime. Where is the conspiracy? As victims let's treat them with kid gloves. But as victimizers, let's try twelve-year-old boys as adults and give them life in adult prisons. We cannot have it both ways. And why in the hell will we give a *child molester probation* and send the alleged rapist of an adult to prison for life. This is inconsistent, foolish, stupid and asinine!

We must begin to conduct psychological autopsies on any pervert who dares harm or abuse our children. We can't give a child predator probation and let him walk free. By the same token we cannot continue to allow prosecutors to scam and con children into false allegations. And when we find evidence of this kind of prosecutorial misconduct, judges must uniformly strip them of their cloaks of immunity. False evidence, evidence tampering and willful police misconduct must have no place in the criminal court system. In my case, I watched Mr. Calvario give testimony, which was riddled with inconsistencies and falsehoods, raising reasonable doubts as to the fundamental credibility of his testimony per se. Prosecutor Hanlon was negligent, reckless and careless in bringing my case to trial. The bias, prejudice and sleaze factor reached epidemic proportions during my trial. There was not a shred of credible, legitimate evidence to support the prosecutor's erroneous accusations. I unequivocally, unambiguously and categorically denied all charges. But within the compressed corridors of power (such as the courthouse) a lot of racism, profiling and stereotyping transpires. I could not believe that this all White jury convicted me on Mr. Calvario's lies. But the more I think about it the more I see that the trickery of Mary Hanlon Stone and the unfair rulings by the judge are the chief reasons that I'm in prison. Judge Robert Altman is a cancer that should be excised from the body of jurisprudence. And Mary Hanlon Stone is evil, wicked and biased at the very core of her being. She reminds me of the Philly DA that lawyer's call the "Queen of Death". Chief of Police Bull Connor used vicious dogs against civil rights troops in Birmingham, Alabama. Mark Fuhrman planted evidence to try to convict O.J. Simpson. But they have nothing on Philadelphia DA Lynne Abraham or Mary Hanlon Stone.

Since Lynne Abraham's appointment as District Attorney in 1991, she has put over one hundred and five African-Americans on death row; more than almost any other district attorney. The New York Times labeled her America's "deadliest D.A.".

When White racists attacked Black students at George Washington High School in January, Lynne pressed charges only against the African American victims, until public outcry forced her to back off. She held a Black mentally retarded child in an adult jail, yet refused to try White teenagers accused of raping a Black child as adults. She routinely goes out of her way to protect the police against victims of their abuse and brutality. Her office has failed to convict any cops for the killings of Kenneth Griffin, Jamel Nichols, Phillip McCall, Moses DeJesus, Jahlil Thomas, Erin Forbes or Robert Jones.

Even in the brutal beating of Tom Jones last summer, which was captured on live television, not a single police officer was convicted.

Prosecutor Abraham's office was also tainted by the 39th Police District scandal. Over two hundred and fifty convictions were overturned and dozens of innocent prisoners released after police frame-ups and manufactured evidence by cops and DA's against the Black community were exposed.

The key word being *exposed*. So many innocent, poor, indigent men are sitting in prison today merely because ABC, NBC and CBS have not chosen to expose these cases, which sometimes involve no DNA and no high profile client, etc. The innocent sit trapped behind concrete walls and nobody seems to care. That is why I challenge every defense lawyer who is reading my words today to help expose the criminal corruption in the judicial system of America. I challenge lawyers to rise up en masse and work with Barry Scheck and law students across the country to free innocent prisoners. I want Travis Cully, (young author) Seth Gray (Folsom CA) Gery, Monica, Gloria and Richard Becker to pump up the troops in the streets and let's come together and fight the power. We can't do it if you read this book like a novel. You must take action on what you read. Do something! If Murray Janus was told by God, "you must take one wrongful conviction case pro bona or you'll be dead within a week." What case would he take? What about F. Lee Bailey? Roy Black? Gerry? Johnnie? I love lawyers! I'm proud they can command $500.00 - $750.00 per hour. David Boies, Willie Gary, Gerry Murray, Stanley, Alan, etc. are all brilliant, rich and powerful. They earn their money. I salute them! But someway some how we've got to get lawyers to feel the sense of injustice that Barry Scheck feels. That feeling has got to compel them to give something back! Damn! None of them would go bankrupt if they (each) just took on two pro bono cases per year. Brandon Gene Martinez needs them. Patt Dunn needs them. There are a lot of us who need help. We must come together as human! We can't wait for the media to tell us what to do. We've got to initiate change and fight for justice. We must rise up and make a change in the justice system. Justice must be *blind*. And right now, she has vision. Her eyes see prejudice, bigotry and bias. This is not the America our forefathers had in mind, a bunch of greedy, lying, cold, manipulative and power hungry politicians. We must find a way to get them out of office. We've got to be innovative, creative and strategic in our efforts. We need high school students like Ashley Greer (Wood Creek High School) to use her newspaper (WolfPack Press) to write articles about judicial corruption. We need teens across the nation to come together against political, judicial and prosecutorial corruption. We need to use our brains, our bodies and our money to make our voices heard. We got to stop school violence, hatred, racism and bias. And stop trusting an American media. They whitewash issues. They sensationalize issues. They are reactionary and quite selective.

They don't ever give us a true picture of Dr. Martin Luther King, Jr. They never told us how he really was. We need to read Dr. James H. Cone's book "Martin and Malcolm and America". Dr. King was moved by injustice! "The slum is little more than a domestic colony which leaves it's inhabitants dominated politically, exploited economically, segregated and humiliated at every turn." Malcolm's words? No! *Dr. King's* words! "We've got to ask questions about the whole society. We are called upon to help the discouraged beggars in life's market place but one day we must come to see that an edifice, which produces beggars, needs restructuring. It means that questions must be raised. "Who owns this oil? Who owns the iron ore? Why is it that people have to pay water bills in a world that is two-thirds water?" King stated shortly before his death. You won't hear George W. or John Ashcroft quoting him on those words. But they'll quote "I have a dream".

"The vast majority of White Americans are racist whether consciously or unconsciously." King told a group in Louisville. And in the '60's that was definitely true. It was not innate. It was learned behavior and I am not demonizing White America. I still believe there are multi-millions of good non-racist and caring White people in America. Unfortunately most of them are not judges, DA's or politicians. They are just everyday careers going about their lives. They raise their children, feed their families and pay their bills. These are the people we must reach. The time to reach them is now. Before the militia rescues them. Before the government rescues them. If we are to become one nation, *indivisible* under God, the people must rise up and take charge now. We must organize our youth nationally and internationally. We must get the students at Harvard, to work with those at Cardoza Law School. Bring the students at Spellman, Moorehouse, Penn State, U. C Davis, Brown University and New York University together and take the country back. I hope this book is a clarion call to lawyers, law students, professors, activists, teens, pastors, prisoners and all people of goodwill to come together right now. May I remind you *once more* to (please, please) pass this book on to somebody else. Share this book with a lawyer, doctor, professor, student, pastor, etc. Send me a letter and request more copies of this book today. I'm waiting on your letter, your action and your commitment. We must establish an underground railroad type group of grassroots people who network to get this book out to the people. I know for a fact that if y'all get this book to Spike Lee, John Singleton, Susan Taylor or Doug Banks in the morning they will tell our (grassroots people: Black, White, Mexican and others) people about his book. I want youngsters to read it and I want them to heed my warning; stay off drugs! Stay off alcohol! Leave the guns alone! Take it from me you don't want that kind of life. Use your youth, energy, drive and determination to run the world and to change the world! And to you shallow politicians talking about getting tough on crime, etc. I say *go to hell* and get a *life*! I'm sick and tired of police officers going into these ghettos in the inner and urban cities under the guise of getting guns and drugs off the streets. They lock up these small time dealers and pretend they've made a difference. There are no Black, Mexican or even poor White people shipping planeloads of cocaine and heroin into this country. No Blacks, Browns or poor Whites manufacturing any guns, rifles or bombs anywhere in the world. If they truly wanted to stop drug trafficking in America they would protect our borders and man these airports, etc. They know how to stop it. But instead they nab the poor off of street corners and make it all look good. They're game players, so I want my young readers to stop falling for these hideous ploys and traps. Don't buy *their* alcohol, drugs and weapons. Don't destroy your minds and bodies. Stay away from their traps and *do the right thing*. Because once you find yourself entwined with police and prosecutors and judges, you'll find that so-called justice in America is *mean*. It's mean justice and unjust. You don't have to fall for their traps. The American police officer is under trained, undereducated, underpaid and should be unemployed. The less crime in the street, the fewer police officers on the street. And I wish these bribe-taking pimps that we call politicians would demand that we train our police officers better. These guys don't even kick butt and take names later. We could tolerate that but they shoot, kill and take names later. They are ill-prepared to handle pressure and crisis. And this lack of training results in discrimination against the poor and disadvantaged.

What of the mentally ill and retarded? Let me paint a typical scenario for you. The police are called by a screaming woman, "My son is going crazy. He's acting like a madman. Throwing things all over the house and talking to himself. He's a mental outpatient and he's not taking his medication. Please send an officer. He needs help. I want him out of here!" Well now, it's ten minutes later and a Mark Fuhrman, or Dave Winkler type officer arises on the scene. He's so afraid of this Black neighborhood that he sits in his car awaiting back up. Then more cop cars pull up. All four officers get out. They approach the apartment and knock on the door. They yell, "Come out sir. Let us see your hands. Come out." They hear some yelling and banging near the door. Remember they're here to serve and to protect. They back off from the door. They're back now about six feet from the door. "Come out," they yell and the door abruptly opens. This mentally ill man stands in the door clearly unarmed. He has no shirt on and no trousers, only a pair of pocket less boxers and socks. No shoes. He jumps up and down yelling. The cops yell, "Put your hands in the air and step out of the door son and get down on your knees." Instead this guy yells, flails his arms and barks like a dog. Then he runs out of the door. All four police officers open fire on him. Sixteen shots total. And yes, he dies. An unarmed, mentally ill, half naked man gets killed. Murdered by the men who serve and protect because, they claim, felt their lives were in danger.

The aforementioned scenario is much like the killings that happen at the hands of or by the bullets of police officers everyday in ghettos across this country. And I must reluctantly and sadly admit that some of these officers actually don't intend to commit murders. They mean well. They just don't know any better. They are not trained adequately. They were not taught many (if any) alternative ways to deal with a mentally disabled, yelling, barking, clearly unarmed man. Just because he ran. Four police officers don't know any way to catch, control and restrain one man and they feed off of each other. One shoots and all shoot. Now a mother has to live with this hurt, paid and feelings of guilt for the rest of her life. She only wanted to get help for her son. The people she called to help him, hurt and killed him instead. She sees the blood on the ground. She smells death in the air. Her son is dead and what do the police say? "We had *no other option* - we felt *threatened*." What do their supervisors say? "We will be investigating this matter but it appears to be a justifiable homicide." What does the local media say, "A crazed Black man was shot and killed by officers. Last night when he attempted to attack the officer." What does Montel, Oprah, or Barbara Walters say? N-o-t-h-i-n-g! We allow them to get away with murder! We need to train our police officers better. They need help. They really need help. And as long as we sit back and take it they will continue getting away with murder. The only way we can change this is if we all get involved in fighting for what's right. And our way to fight is by bringing people together. We can do it. I need your help. If miscreants and pedophiles can network and sell child pornography on the Internet, you can't convince me that we can't put this book on the Internet. I don't believe it. We must come together. I need Murray Janus, Gerry Spence, Dr. Fred Allman, Jr., Chris Gardner and all of you to (you know what I'm gonna say so what are you waiting on?) Put this book in the hands of the people. Go back and remember how prosecutors came together all over America and flexed their muscles against Judge Dalzell and you (we) should be embarrassed. (I hate to say this because, I love these guys) where was Murray Janus, F. Lee Bailey, Roy Black, etc.? All that it takes for evil to rage is for good men to remain silent we must lift up our voices and be heard. "If it doesn't fit, you must acquit".

Just a few months ago six children holed themselves up in their house in Idaho. They were afraid of the government. They had attack dogs and rifles. The police had arrested their mother. The authorities claimed they were only paranoid and irrational because of parental brainwashing. A few years ago, I would have agreed wholeheartedly with the authorities. But I'm beginning to wonder. I'm still not a conspiracy theorist. I am sort of hesitant to always think in terms of genocide and paranoia. However, with what I have seen, read, heard and experienced these past few years, I am here to tell you that (at minimum) I better understand why many people do totally mistrust and distrust the government. Yes, I do understand their fears. WACO, Ruby Ridge, Counterplot and even now the Oklahoma Bombing FBI scandal. If we can't trust the feds to turn over evidence, follow procedures and abide by the laws of the land, how can we trust the local police? Can we even trust George W.? Does corporate America own him? Is he (too) in the hip pocket of big tobacco and other special interests groups? He is a Texas oilman isn't he? How much money does our vice president have? I don't want to just slam George W. but I want y'all to pray for this man. God can still change him. I know that a lot of preachers are praising George for his faith-based programs initiative etc and they are lining up to try to get a grant, etc. That's all good but we must pray for this man. I'm sorry to tell you but Mr. Bush has blood on his hands. Too many have been killed in Texas on death row under his watch. Christopher Ochoa? I told you about how he was exonerated from death row earlier in this book. But don't forget that Christopher wrote (then) Governor George W. The man who actually committed the crimes wrote Governor George W. and confessed. Did Mr. Bush free Chris and give him justice? No, he did not! Politicians (by and large) ignore prisoner's mail. Just as they ignore homeless and hungry people. The homeless can't vote. Neither can prisoners so they don't count. That's why I urge you to answer prisoners mail and to be careful how you treat the hungry and homeless. Your Bible readers should read Isaiah Chapter 58. Did George W. free Christopher Ochoa? Of course not! Can he free Mumia Abu Jamal? Yes! Will he? No way! Mumia is not White nor is he rich. George W. says he's *born again*. Born again of what? So I encourage you to pray for George W. and pray for his housemen such as Clarence Thomas and Ward Connerly. Few months ago a White gentleman named David (I'm very *unsure* of his last name so if I error forgive me) Carthcart was freed from a Mexican prison. He spent seven years in a Mexican prison accused of molesting four boys. David is American. Did our government help free David? The answer is *no*. He was clearly innocent. The boys (finally) confessed that they were forced to *lie* on David a week before his release. David will live with this scandal, stigma and pain of having been a convicted (formerly) child predator for the rest of his life. That is traumatizing and humiliating. They took seven years of this man's life before they admitted that *it didn't fit*. David has now, supposedly, cleared his name. But how do you ever clear your name of such (unearned and undeserved) shame? David spent seven years in a Mexican prison. Why the child predator and boy molesting charge? Turns out that the boys David was accused of molesting were in an orphanage and David had *audited* the orphanage. The owner of the orphanage was angry about the audit and convinced the boys to lie on David. That is absolutely unfair.

My mind goes back to a great private investigator that, as you know, I've written about before. Investigator Paul Ciollino. He's a mountain mover. He and Al Pharr specialize in moving mountains of false evidence to free innocent people from prison. Presently these two great men are working pro bono to try to exonerate Stella Nickells. Paul and Al are the exceptions and not the norm. We need more ex-cops, ex-FBI agents, etc. to work pro bono to free the innocent and I hope that Paul will send this tome to Stella and it will be an inspiration to her to keep hope alive. Prison can damage a person. Especially an innocent person. And often state prisons arbitrarily throw people into solitary confinement and Dr. Stuart Grassian (Harvard psychiatrist) says "psychosis results from prison isolation." He calls it insecurity-housing syndrome. Dr. Terry Kupers concurs. She tours isolation units for the Human Rights Watch. Ad-seg in prison causes "free floating anxiety, hallucination, self mutilations and delusions" they've found. But ask any prison warden (especially in C.D.C.) do they care? I've been there and I am well cognizant of what ad-seg does to a man's mind. But prison officials will throw a man into the hole in a heartbeat. And they get away with it because the public doesn't seem to care. And for the life of me, I still can't comprehend how/why we allow this in America. Why we allow people to be homeless and hungry. Why we allow cruel and unusual punishment in our prisons. With preachers on television and radio and churches on every street corner; how can we allow this? And the church remains silent. Jesus showed compassion in the gospels. One day he departed into the wilderness to pray. When the multitudes discovered where he was they followed him and brought all their sick. What did Jesus do? Read Matthew 14:14. That is compassion.

If Jesus had reacted the way the modern church does, he might have gathered his disciplines for a *committee* meeting. He would have analyzed the people and discussed the sin that had brought society to this place or like so many sanctimonious people "Look - I'm tired. I've worked hard ministering to you. But I'm exhausted and I need to talk to my father. *I feel your pain*. I'll call my disciples and will have an intercessory meeting. Go in peace." That's the modern church; everybody is willing to *pray*, but nobody is willing to *act*. Read Matthew 15.30. I told you earlier to read Isaiah 58. Christians are dry and have lost the joy and are bound up because we refuse to deal with Isaiah 58. Why aren't shepherds teaching these people to reach out to human needs, so that when the needy come to church they'll find a well-watered garden, a deep source springing up? God will provide for anybody willing to give of himself. "For I was hungered, and ye gave me no meat . . .." Read Matthew 25:42-46. Why won't the church deal with this? We all can quote John 3:16. But what about John 3:17? This is sad! I got some church people reading this book right now. I want you to pray for me. I need your prayers. But also I need action. Why can't a church member go on the Internet and find a prisoner who needs this book and send it to him? Find Paul Guigni of Fairfield High School in California and send him this book. Locate Trevor Loflin in Sonora County, CA and send Trevor this book. Will you do it or will you just pray for me? I need some pastor to decide, "I'm gonna call Spike Lee, Cornell West, the NAACP, etc. And tell them about this tome and we're gonna come together in our ministerial union or the National Baptist Convention and we're gonna help the least of these our brethren." How to help? (Again) Call Barry Scheck, CA Prison Focus, The ACLU and the IAC and ask them how can you help prisoners. And/or write me a letter.

Write to *me*. So many people read Book One and talked about what a unique book it was. They called around asking what they could do to help. Don't call around. Write directly to me today. My address is in this book several times. I need men who got out of prison and their families to help me. There is a *secret fraternity* amongst those whose commonality is *pain* and *suffering*. Pain transcends color, status, class and gender. We need to join forces. I don't need you counseling me if you haven't been through some struggles of your own. God has done more through my struggles than He's ever done through my successes. My successes are made of the ingredients of my struggles. I've had so-called friends to walk away from me while I was in the midst of my struggles. But even then I learned to lean, trust and depend on God and not man. Many of you are going through different types of struggles and you're crying about people who left you when you needed them most. I want to tell you that when people walk away from you let them go. If they can really leave you when you need them most *let them go*. Your *destiny* is not ever tied to anyone that left. Some people are gonna leave you no matter what you do anyhow. You can get *super glue* and you still can't make them stay. When they leave it simply means that their part in your story is over. That chapter or paragraph has ended. Let them go. But when God gives or sends somebody to help you they'll stay no matter what they say. People can cry Hosanna and they'll stay with you. When they cry crucify, they'll stay with you. The cops can claim you fit the profile of a serial rapist, pedophile or serial murderer but those whom God has sent will stay with you. Ruth stayed with Naomi. Consider David and Jonathan. Consider the fact that Elijah left his natural mother and father and clinged to Elisha to wait on him and clean his clothes. Timothy left home to hang outside a jail cell to hand books to a man that was about to be beheaded. But these are things, situations or people whom God joined together. Ruth and Naomi didn't have any *sexual* attractions and neither did David and Jonathan or Elijah and Elisha. But when critics see two women who proclaim that *as sure as there is a God I will never leave thee*. Critics assume it must have been a same sex type relationship. Yet, there are just some people whom God will send to help you and even they won't know why they came. We must realize that there are no coincidence in life. Nothing merely happens. You did not just stumble to where you are now. God is behind the curtains like a puppet master pulling your strings. God put you in your destiny. He reached down and grabbed the dust and formed you in His own image. He planted you in your mother's womb and caused her to extract you into this planet in this time and in this place. You and me are up under the banner of the *"will" of God*. Jonah was in a whale and still in His "will". He disobeyed and went the wrong way. But why was the big fish waiting by the boat? Because he was still in the "will". This backslidden, rebellious, disconnected, disobedient and reprobate preacher came up out of the whale, still in the "will" - in the third day. Jonah had to get up when he got up and he had to go down when he went down. All of your pain, tragedies, struggles, sorrows and mistakes are in His "will". So you may as well shout (now) *right where you are because nothing just happens*! God has (I believe) a divine will and a *permissive* will. So we need to learn how Paul learned to be content no matter where he was. God is not asleep. God is still on the throne. He orchestrates the affairs of your life. Even when we experience betrayal on the highest level in our lives, God is there. Still on the case. You had to go through what you went through in order to get where you are. You didn't fit in where you came from because you were dressed for where you're going. And you cannot allow your history to interfere (or inhibit) with your destiny. Keep on moving! God will help you. But you must help yourself also.

All right enough of that, I must remember I have atheists and agnostics reading this book also. How would it feel if you received a life sentence in prison for a crime you did not commit? How long could you take it? A year? Five years? Ten? Fifteen? Well Glen "Buddy" Nickerson was serving a life sentence in prison for a crime he says he did not commit. On June 11, 2001 Glenn saw his prison cell open wide and the stone of bondage was rolled away. Because of the tireless and brilliant efforts of Attorney Gerald Schwartzbach, Glenn is free today. Attorney Gerald Schwartzbach worked to exonerate Glenn for five years pro bono. Gerald has some Barry Scheck in him. He did it for free. This is the story of a true defense lawyer. One who is moved by injustice and propelled into action. Buddy literally picked Gerald up while hugging him when we got out of San Quentin Prison. "Everyday you hear I didn't do it. (From then in prison) well I did *not do it*," stated Buddy after his release. I got all misty eyed when I watched him walk *out of prison* gates. I thought about calling Gerald and begging him to please, please, please help me prove my innocence. But I did finally get a miracle just the other day. Remember the twenty something year old White guy I told you about in Book One? You've got to remember David Quindt. He was a convicted murderer. He'd receive a life sentence in prison. The Sacramento District Attorney's Office had what they called an airtight case. But David was factually innocent. And he got his freedom a year go. Thank God it only took David a little more than a year to get out of there. "Well what is the miracle Sherman?' All right, I'll tell you. David announced upon his exoneration that he wanted to help others innocent men in prison. David reached out to *me*. "What can I do to help you get out of here?" David asked me over the telephone. "I read your book Reverend and it really touched my heart. My wife read it also. I couldn't get you out of my mind. Especially because of all the encouragement you give to youths in that book. We must work together. Can I visit you? I *am going to get you out of there*. If I have to call every lawyer, senator, congressman, talk show host, investigator, etc." That is a miracle! I didn't let David hear me but I cried. Yes, I literally cried. God is still in the prayer answering business. David and I compared us to Rubin "Hurricane" Carter and Lesra Martin (see Book One or rent the video "Mr. Hurricane"). David is my Lesra Martin. He's my Godsend. If you only knew what it meant to have a man who has been through it to reach out to me. Our community is pain, suffering and injustice. I jokingly told David that in three years they would be making a movie about us. Hollywood will be calling. Let's contact Bill Cosby, Spike Lee and John Singleton. White innocent prisoner gets his conviction overturned. White guy reaches back to help somebody else. David Quindt uses his life to help Sherman D. Manning! David calls Gerald Uelmen, Gerald Schwartzbach, Alan Dershowitz, Barry Scheck, Gerry Spence, investigators, the Black pros, Queen Latifah, Montel Williams and Sean "Puffy" Combs and says help me free Sherman Manning." Yes! I can sense something very special again. This connection. By the time you're holding this book in your hands David and I will have met each other face to face. But even now we are planning to *free me* and to set up our task force to help others who are innocent. And David shares my passion for youth. Don't get me started but y'all know I go on and on when I start talking about saving our young people. And I hate to have to write this but I must. There are a few people calling around requesting money to help me. They are frauds. Anyone who is led to help me needs to write *me* and only *me*. Send checks, etc. to me and only me. Write me directly at the prison. So if anybody (anybody) sends you an E-mail, letter, etc. requesting money for me. *Do not reply*. Write me directly at the prison.

But (again) I believe David will definitely be a part of my freedom and a part of my life, business and I-may. I think God reached out and touched him and sent him my way. And I believe David will call, write and E-mail senators Richard Polanco, Ted Kennedy, John Burton, Maxine Waters, John Lewis and Cynthia McKinley. I think David will work tirelessly to see me get justice. "I feel that you are innocent. Don't give up Reverend. *Never lose hope*.

*I'm with you,*" he told me. And I pray everyday that God will send some other angels to help me see my family again. A Gerald Schwartzbach, Barry Scheck, Gerry Spence, Gerald Uelmen, Ephraim Margolin, Shawn Chapman or F. Lee Bailey to free me. An investigator like Paul Ciollini or Al Pharr could get the evidence to completely exonerate me in one month or less. The case is simple. And as I've stated (over and over) in a few weeks I'll be entering the Sacramento County Courthouse to face off with the lying Santa Monica prosecutor who sent me here on a lie. *Mary Hanlon Stone.* She and *Debbie Glenn* want to secure a seventy-five years to life in prison sentence for me for two pieces of paper. Why? It does not take a rocket scientist. Mary wants me to die here. Perhaps she thinks I may get out and try to harm her (in 2010) because she lied, cheated, paid a witness, set me up and put on perjured testimony. I *guess* if I did, to an innocent man, what Mary Hanlon did to me, I'd be worried too. But vengeance is God's not mine. She will reap what she has sown. I would not even think about doing anything to Mary Hanlon Stone. If I thought anybody was gonna try to hurt Mary, I would call the police myself. Violence does not solve anything. That's not the way. The *ballot* not the bullet. Bishop Jakes said last week on TV "God is getting ready to do something for you." Well voila; here comes my own little (Lesra Martin) David Quindt. I had to pinch myself to be sure it was not a dream. God is an awesome God. I look forward to David beginning to visit me every week. After we discuss all the sensitive case issues, etc. After a few months of one on one (man talk) visiting, perhaps he'll bring his wife to visit me also. She has also offered her support. I want David to write a book about what they did to him. He must write a book. David Quindt is a shining example that "If it can happen to me, it can happen to anybody". God I hope the lawyers, housewives, pastors and leaders reading my words will help me get my freedom back. And, at any rate, I hope you will help save our precious children. The children are our tomorrow. They are our only hope of a future. They are more precious than all the diamonds in Africa. Please mentor, tutor, teach and reach our children. It is a shame that we have homeless, hopeless and abandoned children in America. If God does not judge America for forgetting the children, God may have to apologize to *Sodom* and *Gomorra*h! As much as I need help, I'll have to tell you I'm pleading for me but begging for our children. You lawyers and doctors etc. need to follow Willie Gary into the schools and reach our youth. Please help save the American child. "Suffer the little children and let them come unto me". I want to say to every innocent person in prison in the words of David Quindt to

"Never give up". Help will come. Keep writing, reading, praying, fasting and keep hope alive. Your breakthrough is coming. Somebody will say, as did Wentley Phipps: "I had to do something about it . . ." Wentley reached out to the children of prisoners through his "Dream Academy". I've asked David to get me Wentley's address and I want to send him this book. I hope Wentley will share this book with his wife, kids and friends. To every man (even the guilty) in prison I say *Change Your Life*. Stop the violence! Stop the racism and tribalism. Use good books, prayer and knowledge to transform your life. There are too many followers in prison. Be a man. Be unique. Be your own man. Get some books by Dr. Na'im Akbar, Randall Robinson, Cornell West, Anthony Robbins, Les Brown, Bishop T. D. Jakes, etc. and *Change Your Life*.

To Coolio, Suge, Ice Cube, Susan Taylor, earl Graves and everybody, I say Please Help Me.

I don't want to die here for something *I did not do*. I need your help today. And y'all better rise up and do something about these prisons. All over the country people must rise up and change this system. The prisons are a national failure. The prison violence is a national tragedy. An epidemic. These are monster factories. When one takes a closer and a more analytical look at the California Department of Corrections it becomes clear that the public does not have a clue as to what an expensive failure this system is. What person in their right mind would pay to produce mad men? Who would pay to produce bank robbers, killers and rapists? Economically speaking would you invest in a company with a sixty-three percent failure rate? Would you voluntarily invest a thousand dollars when you knew you would lose six hundred and thirty dollars? If you knew that for every one thousand dollars you invested in me, I could not return the principle and could only give you three hundred and seventy dollars back? That is preposterous. Well California taxpayers pay more than 4.5 billion dollars into the CA Prison system each year and yet the recidivism rate is about sixty-three percent. More than sixty-three percent of the fellas released from prison tomorrow will return to prison within three years. And tomorrow they'll go to the streets to commit crimes. Why? Because they got no help.

While they were in prison, they were fed and bred on hatred, racism, sexism and violence in prison. "This place is built for destruction. It is designed to destroy and everything that comes into contact with it, for it is unnatural, it is anti-human, and it must destroy! It has no other choice. So being frightened is not being afraid; it is being smart! Being frightened means not helping your keepers keep you kept, and handling this place and its people as one would handle a poisonous rattlesnake. Always being completely respectful of it's nature and what it is designed to do, and making damn sure that you always stay away from the business end of it," stated Rubin "Hurricane" Carter. I concur fully.

The biggest kept secret in the nation is the fact that the largest gangs in the state of California are in CA's prisons. Recruitment into these gangs is **automatic**. The option is rape or death. I'm not exaggerating. Any White inmate, entering prison in California tomorrow will immediately be recruited into a gang. **Any** Black, Mexican or other inmate entering this prison system next week will be forced to join a gang. It is survival. If a White, Mexican, Black or other refuses to join, they will be gang raped or killed. Period! You must join a gang in the prisons in California if you want to live. You will not live in the same cell with a person who does not share your skin color even if you were friends in civilian life. Think about it; a nonviolent, blonde-haired, blue-eyed, fresh-faced eighteen-year-old White guy comes to prison tomorrow with a five-year sentence for auto theft, drugs or burglary. The White Nazi Low Riders, Aryan Brotherhood, Skinheads, etc. will tell him you belong to us. Now take this knife and go kill that child molester." What if he runs to prison staff? Staff will tell him "you're a man, handle it." And then staff will go tell the gang leaders that the guy is a "snitch". He will be assaulted, raped, cut and possibly killed. C.D.C. facilitates murder and foments rapes, violence and racism. Staff is behind the scenes pulling the strings to keep the gang violence rampant. The more violent prisoners there are the more staff are needed, compensated and the more overtime pay they get. This White guy who came in with a five-year sentence more than likely will acquire a life sentence for the stabbing he committed during his gang initiation. And/or he will acquire aids while being raped. It happens everyday in California. It happens every single day of the week. Governor Davis appointed Steve White as the new prison Inspector General. He's supposed to be cleaning up C.D.C. I have not seen a change. In fact, any candidate who wishes to defeat Mr. Davis at the next election needs only point to the thirty-three prisons, 4.5 billion dollar failure called C.D.C. It is a monster factory. It is awful, tragic and a shame before God. I have met more racist, vindictive, duplicitous and mean spirited people in the form of C.D.C. prison guards than I ever met in Alabama or rural Georgia. And they pay these wardens upward of forty thousand dollars per year to run these monster factories. Yet we can't pay teachers to educate our children. When will we learn? C.D.C. is a covert operation. It is like a militia. Its guards are devious criminals in uniform and they pit inmates against each other. It's a slave plantation and for the few staff members who are righteous and want to do the right thing, it is hell on earth. One former sergeant at Tchachapi got off work one day and went to the prison parking lot to find his car spray painted with the words "inmate lover" on the doors and windows of his car. One prison guard who was honest and fair had his *house* burned down by fellow (thugs) guards.

The California prison guard; he is egotistical, pompous, arrogant, deceptive, well paid, well insured and well fed. He brings no lunch to work because he eats prison food. He buys no toilet paper, trash bags or razors because he smuggles them out of prison. He smuggles weapons in (for the inmate gangs) and prison supplies out (for his family). Happens everyday and the lonely, helpless inmates are trapped here knowing there is no way out. Who can we call? Who can we write? Prison guards read all our mail. And if they don't like what we write or whom we are writing, they shred it. Confidential or legal mail. Opened in error, lost in mail or destroyed! My cases pending in Sacramento County Court are compromised because almost every letter I receive from my lawyers discussing defense strategy is opened and read by staff. It is copied and mailed to The District Attorney. I am not sitting here complaining about bad prison food or the fact that there is no rehabilitation in here. I take those facts as givens. I am talking about staff corruption, racism, murders, criminal misconduct and abusive treatment in the severest fashion. I am talking about prison guards getting promoted to sergeant who have been accused of sexual harassment and rape by other staff members. I am talking about inmates being beat maliciously by staff members simply because they wrote a letter to Richard Polanco or Andy Furillo. I am talking about federal crimes being committed by staff on a daily basis. David Quindt? I sent him one letter Sunday night, one Monday night, one Tuesday night and one each Wednesday and Thursday nights. Friday morning he had still not received a single letter yet he lives less than forty-five minutes away from this prison. Friday he called Steve White's office about my mail and lo and behold Saturday he received all five letters from me simultaneously. Had David not called the Inspector General, he would never have seen that mail. Can you imagine for one moment what it feels like to reside in a place where you will be stabbed if you choose to associate with people who are not your color? If you're White and you accept a cigarette from a Black guy; the Whites will beat, assault and stab you in any prison in California. This is not fiction. This is the reality of the California prison system. And the California authorities can argue all day long that it's not their fault but they are lying. Prisons are not this racist in Georgia, Florida and many other states. In Georgia, you will find White guys and Black guys living in the same cells. You won't find many race riots and race wars going on there. And C.D.C. only *reacts*. They will know a murder or a stabbing is about to take place. They'll watch it happen and turn their backs. Yet, the minute the press finds out about it or a prison guard gets hurt they simply lock down the entire institution for months. And inmates sitting locked down in their cells get angrier and angrier. And in those dark, dismal cells the inmates plan the next uprising or gang hit. Nobody tries to ameliorate, disband or prevent the gangs, drugs, weapons and violence. And the prison wardens *laugh all the way to the bank* to the tune of ninety thousand dollars per year. And you (the taxpayer) pay for it. You pay over 3.3 million dollars per year to CA prison *wardens alone*. Not including associate wardens (over 5.4 million) or prison captains (over ten million dollars). If we add up the salaries of lieutenants, sergeants and officers, we are talking hundreds of millions in salaries for people who often dropped out of high school. Your money pays to support prison gangs, violence and rapes. And most of the inmates here will be out someday and they are coming to your neighborhood. This is wrong! This is expensive and this is a failure. And when they return to the streets after living in a cesspool of sin and evil they'll be sicker, slicker and return to prison quicker. But while they are out they'll rob, steal, rape and kill. Who will hire them on a job? How will they pay rent? What kind of social skills will they bring to the table of civilian life? They got stabbed, mistreated, stuck up and beat up in prison. They were denied an education, paid fifteen and twenty cents an hour for slave labor and they were forced to assault and stab others, so what do you expect them to do when they get out? How can they love, trust, care and be civilized again? Go figure! You figure it out! How in the hell can we pay prison guards more money then we pay schoolteachers, paramedics and even college professors? They build entire communities around prisons across the nation. This is big business! Again, I want to remind you that any young non-violent or semi-violent offender who enters California's prison system will be forced to join a gang! He will be initiated into the monster factory. He will be raped, sodomized and beaten if he refuses to join the gang. Period! James Byrd was dragged to death in Texas. Children lost their father. A mother lost her son at the hands of a racist former prison inmate. An investigation into the killer's background proved he was forced to join a prison gang for protection while in prison. This White guy was not raised as a racist. He was not brought up to hate people merely based on skin pigmentation. Yet, while in prison, he was forced to stab, assault and attack anybody who didn't look like him. And when he got out of prison, he carried that prison learned hate, anger and racism with him into civilian life. Jimmy Lee Byrd's blood and life is on the hands of the prison authorities. Formerly Governor George W. Bush is an accessory to Byrd's murder because he failed to stop, curtail and prevent the gangs, violence, racism and rapes in his prison system. And Governor Gray Davis (to my knowledge) is following in Mr. Bush's footsteps. I can't see a (not yet anyway) damn thing the new Inspector General has done to stop the prison's notorious prison gangs, discrimination and staff led inmate segregation. I want to see the ACLU, CA prison Focus, the SCLC, NAACP, ADL, The FBI or Morris Dees, or Stephen Bright do a study on CA Prison gangs, racism and inmate sexual assaults. If we wait on C.D.C. to tell the truth, we will be waiting until hell freezes over. I have no confidence in the willingness of the police to police themselves. They specialize in sweeping their own criminal misconduct under the rug. So I want to (redundantly) reiterate my call to inmates to transform your own situations. Don't wait on prison officials to clean up. You clean up yourself. There is a death that removes you from productive chances and opportunities to operate in society. Ipso facto, the vast majority of the creative minds in America who are males are locked up in prisons during their most productive years. During the years when most White males are present in colleges and training institutes, obtaining the skills that are necessary to continue to *run the world*; our (Black, poor Whites, Mexicans and others) future learners, leaders, lawyers and advocates can be found in the jails and prisons. Locked up, locked in and locked out of society. Unable to think, under the daily watchful eye of sick minds that would rather see them dead then to see them learning. Those men who show the greatest promise of ability, self-motivation and direction are the least likely to ever obtain probation or parole. When they do get paroled they are stigmatized and ostracized in such a way that they can never obtain the effectiveness in this society to utilize what they know. They have been removed, not by physical death but by institutional death! They have been eliminated and wiped out as agents of productive ability and agents of change. I am confident that if those confined, imprisoned men want freedom they must free their brains and start not being "prisoners" and start redefining what their situation is. Let their protests be for books, for data and for programs that shall transmogrify them into real men. Let their protests be non-violent. Let their weapons not be weapons of violence but weapons of the mind. Incarcerated people should begin to utilize prison as an opportunity to develop "Think Tanks" rather than sitting around and getting high or drunk. Stop sitting around trying to get off on some type of substitute sexual gratification. Since we are trapped here with nothing to do; rather than slave for the masters and turn on each other; why not work for our own mental and spiritual development and turn toward each other. People on the outside ought to start sending in books and if prisoners read and apply those books they would start letting men out of prison wholesale. "Get the hell out of my prison. We don't want you here. Please go back out and find you a needle or a gun. Go commit a rape or a murder. Anything but get out of here. We want violent slaves and predators in here not mental giants and thinkers." We can defeat the prison industrial complex. But we must do so with our minds, prayers, spirits, lawsuits and political support. Not with riots, stabbings and prison killings. *I know I'm right!* David Quindt can attest to the fact that the authorities respond to telephone calls, letters and intervention from folks on the outside. David can tell you that as long as you read this book as if it were a novel or fiction and do nothing you get nothing. But David will tell you that when you close up the book and call the Governor's office, the Inspector General, New Folsom prison, the mail room, Richard Polanco, John Burton, Willie Brown and the media. When you call and say where is the mail Sherman, my son, my cousin . . . mailed to me a week ago." When you call and say, "Why is he in ad-seg, why has he not called me, why is he being transferred," etc. They will react and if that doesn't work you call the CA prison Focus, the ACLU, the NAACP, Al Sharpton, Farrakhan and the media. You tell the community, the city, the state and the nation what's going on in the prisons and they will respond. You write to judges, politicians and activists. You call them, fax them and tell them you don't like what is going on and they will reply. You organize, strategize and fight for the least of these and you will save the prisons and transform the prisoners.

You tell the politicians that you want a better return in you 4.5 billion dollar investment. You are tired of eighteen, nineteen and twenty-year-olds entering prisons as followers, naïve and exiting as racist leaders, predators and killers. You tell the Governors, you are tired of prisons being dark monster factories and institutes on how to commit more crimes. You make the difference!!! Again, their monster factories are also housing thousands of innocent, wrongfully convicted men and women in addition to young, naïve non-violent offenders.

Just the other day, Mr. Townsend who is a forty-six-year-old Black man with an IQ of an eight-year-old child was cleared by DNA of serial murders; murders for which he had pled guilty. A shame before God. A retired homicide detective said, "Townsend is retarded and will say anything you tell him to say." Mr. Townsend was depicted by the media as one of Florida's most notorious killers. He fit the profile (they say) of a serial murderer. Well after twenty-two years wrongfully imprisoned, Mr. Townsend was proven innocent. Mr. Frank Lee Smith was not so lucky. He was also convicted of murder. DNA proved him innocent but he died in prison of cancer while awaiting his execution. Damn! This is why I urge you to get involved in freeing the innocent now. We will die here if you don't help us now. Call Peter Neufeld, Barry Scheck, Professor David Protess, Robert Cling. Lawyers need to step up to the plate and fight for us. We need you! And I encourage you to also call Attorney Van Jones in San Francisco, call the IAC in New York, and call Choices for Youth and America's Promise. Support these groups that are mentoring and protecting our children. Do anything you can to keep young men and women from ever coming into the monster factories. Reach out and touch seventeen-year-old Andy Cooney in Boston. Reach D.J. in Conyers, Georgia. Reach eighteen-year-old Max Carlson, Andrew Heyman, Seth Grey (at Folsom High School), Travis Cully (young author) and reach Trevor Loflin (he has a Website) in Sonora, CA. Trevor will be attending Bob Jones University in two years. Reach out and touch the lives, hearts and minds of these teens before the drug dealers, hate groups and police officers reach out and touch them first. If the police and gangs reach them before you do they will end up trapped in the monster factory. And many will never make it out of here alive! I am very serious! I want you to call Van Jones, the IAC, Youth Groups and organizations that mentor our teens. I want you to use your life to help change the life of a student today! We must reach out to Brett Dewitt at Folsom High School, Attorney Bryce Powell in Idaho, Michelle Alexander at ACLU; Dixon Osborne, Judy Carnotte and Jason Flores in Tampa, Florida, Shawn Armbrust and investigator Paul Ciolino in Chicago. I need you to reach these people and get them this book. How hard can it be for you to look up Gladys Williams or the NAACP in Stanislaus County and send her a fax about this book? Is it too much to ask you to look up Rev. Tim Malone at U.C. Davis and tell him about this book? Is it impossible for you to locate Michael Smith at U.C. Davis (American Studies) or Ryan Hanson (football Player) at the University of Iowa and tell them about this book? David Quindt has proven to me that you can find anybody on the Internet. Can't some of you look up Trevor (as I asked you before) Loflin on his Website and send him this book or my address? Do something! And for my rich lawyer readers who received this tome free of charge how *dare you* not send me a check to help defer expenses etc. Write your check today and send it to me today. Don't go calling people asking how to reach me you write directly to me at New Folsom Prison in Represa, California, right outside of Sacramento, CA. I need help today. "*I want to get you out of prison and get you back home to your family. I want you out of there!*" is what David Quindt told me last night in our 22nd telephone call. What if Johnnie Cochran, F. Lee Bailey, Barry Tarlow, Peter Neufield, Gerry Spence or Paul Ciolino felt the same way? David has been here and he was innocent. He knows what it feels like to be trapped in the monster factory when you're innocent. I want David to make sure Richard Polanco, Maxine Waters, John Burton, Ted Kennedy, Jesse Jackson, Bishop T.D. Jakes, Rev. Al Sharpton, Minister Louis Farrakhan and WW publishers get a copy of this book. I want David to E-mail, fax and call all of the aforementioned to double check and see if they read this book. And to each of you reading who want to help David help me, just write me a letter. Write to me, directly, and I will put you in contact with David and others who are willing to help me. If one of you sent me a check for one hundred thousand dollars, I'd be free in less than twelve months. If everybody reading sent twenty, fifty, five hundred, five thousand dollars or anything, I would get my freedom soon. But you must help. You must get involved. This place is absolutely intolerable and I can't stay here much longer. I will die here if I don't get help soon. Gerson Horn, Barry Tarlow, Gerry Spence, Willie Gary, Shawn Chapman, Stuart Hanlon, Tony Serry, Gerald Uelmen, Alan Dershowitz, and Ephraim Margolin - somebody please help me. I am innocent. I *did not commit this crime* and I should not do this time. Somebody *please call* M. Gerald Schwartzbach in Mill Valley, CA and ask Gerald to help David to help me. Please help me get out of here! I need your help ASAP. I need help. But in spite of the fact that I need help personally I cannot allow you to forget the fact that thousands are in prisons across America and they are innocent. Never forget that when most men come to prison they will never get out. Not without a fight and not without being recruited into a racist, violent and vicious gang. Especially in the California prison systems. I do not give a damn what prison authorities tell you, they can *stop* this. They can stop little non-violent eighteen and nineteen-year-old White boys from being sodomized and victimized by fifty and sixty-year-old White men in prison. They can shut down the prison gangs.

But they are too busy fomenting violence, racism and inmate rivalries to try to stop them. Inmate Charlie Baddaker (or Badakkee) needs help. He's a nineteen-year-old White inmate. Charlie has been in prison since he was fifteen years old. I met him six months ago in ad-seg in B-facility at this prison. "Reverend I'm in prison for rape. I am guilty. I was drunk and I committed the crime. But I am scared. The Whites are trying to kill me because a prison guard told them why I'm in prison. And the inmates are gonna kill me. I want to go to protective custody on A-facility but the captain only wants to throw me in the hole. And the psychiatrists say I'll lose my sanity in the hole. I can get protection in the yard. But it would cost me my dignity and manhood!" I want y'all to call C.D.C. downtown and find out where Charlie is. He may be twenty years old by now. And do not call these corrupted counselors because they will lie to you. Call downtown C.D.C. and call the Inspector General. Call Senator Richard Polanco and Senator John Burton. The CA Prison guards think they are invincible but you are paying their salaries. *You* are paying them to smuggle drugs, weapons, alcohol and other contraband into prisons. You are paying them to abuse, discriminate and foment violence behind these walls. It happens every single day of the week. Don't take *my* word for it. Call Andy Furillo at the Sacramento Bee. Get Polanco, Burton, Waters and Willie Brown to visit the prisons *unannounced*. Get them to talk to inmates one on one. Don't allow the staff to select which inmates you interview. They have inmates whom they pay to lie and cover up their wrong doings. You select the inmates. It's time to transmogrify the prisons and get some real treatment and rehabilitation behind these walls. The guys who are guilty ought to be mentored and treated while in prison. They ought to have to *face their victims* and let the victims tell them what it did to their lives to be raped, robbed and assaulted. Men who molest our children must be cured before being released. And they ought to have to face the parents of their victims and hear what their crimes did to the family. Victims ought to be able to look the perpetrator in the eyes and tell them what the crime did to them. There is healing and closure in confrontation. We want to fight crime and take a bite out of crime? Take a bite out of the 4.5 billion dollar prison budget and give that money to programs to transform the lives of the guilty guys in prisons. The NAACP, ACLU and IAC ought to rise up and sue the hell out of C.D.C. They ought to bankrupt the prison system and clean up the corruption. Every C.D.C prison guard, sergeant, lieutenant, captain and warden ought to undergo psychological evaluations, drug tests and polygraph tests: "Are you a racist? Do you smuggle in weapons? How many prison stabbings have you set up? Do you know of any prison guards stealing the inmates' mail and money? Have you ever turned your back on a prison rape?" Oh yes, we can change the system. Citizens must unite against gangs and corruption in prison. Fight corruption in the system. Fight the racist death penalty. Fight poverty and illiteracy! Fight it! Fight it! Fight it! You can do it!

Ever heard of Ronald Cotton? Well let's start with a twenty-two-year-old White woman who was viciously raped for hours at knifepoint. During the hours of repeated rape she studied the rapist's face meticulously. She said to herself that if she lived through this she wanted to be able to identify the perpetrator so he could be caught and rot in *jail*. Who could blame her? I can't. She lived through it and went to the police station and gave a description. They drew up a sketch and ran it in the newspaper the next day. Someone called Ronald Cotton and told him the composite looked like him. He voluntarily went to the police station to clear up his name. Instead they nailed him for rape. In a line up, Jennifer picked Ronald out. Jennifer's compelling testimony sealed Ronald's fate. He received a life sentence plus forty-two years. Jennifer felt like justice had been served. For eleven years Jennifer's hate for Ronald consumed her being. But after eleven years in prison D.N.A. proved Jennifer had put the wrong man away. Ronald didn't do it. He spent 4200 days locked up for a rape he did not commit. My God, the pain Ronald felt. Convicted rapists are treated like the scum of the earth in prison. Especially in California. Often C.D.C. guards set them up to be assaulted. Staff mistreats inmates convicted of rape. And with Ronald, a Black man, in prison convicted of raping a White woman he was in trouble. It is a scary position to be in. Especially when staff are preoccupied with there own racism, corruption and are unwilling to protect inmates. If pushed, they will simply place you in the hole - Solitary Confinement. You are locked up in a tiny cell twenty-four hours per day, seven days per week. You get very little recreation, rarely shower or shave. You are not allowed to go to any chapel services. You get no telephone calls. Ad-seg is hell. Yet C.D.C. will throw you in the hole in a heartbeat. I have spent nearly three and a half years of my prison stay in the hole. I'm very sure Ronald Cotton was treated viciously by staff while wasting his life behind bars for crimes he did not commit. "I truly believed that he was the man who raped me, but I was wrong," stated the victim.

This is just another of the myriad examples of people, the judicial system, prosecutors, police and juries getting it wrong. Damn. Can you see? I hope to God that David Quindt will go testify before the House Judiciary Committee in D.C. about wrongful convictions. Joe Biden, Ted Kennedy and Maxine Waters need to hear from David Quindt. We need to find Ron Dipolla (Corona, California), Igor Stebakov and Ryan Hanson (University of Iowa student) and get them to help us fight! There is a sixteen-year-old Black millionaire by the name of Farrah Gray. Farrah Gray has an office on Wall Street and a World Wide Website. Farrah will help us. If any of you reading would simply send him this book, I know Farrah would get involved. This young man started a lemonade stand at eight years of age. He now has several businesses for youths. Farrah shares the passion that David and I have for youths. And it wouldn't take much to get Farrah on the crusade to free the innocent. But get him this book. Do it!

I'm tired now. I look all around me in this racist monster factory and all I see is stupidity, hatred, racism and a new form of slavery. I see it all around me. This is what Ronald Cotton, who was also innocent, saw all around him. Ronald should never have been here. David Quindt should never have been here. Anthony Porter, Rolando Cruz, Clyde Charles, etc. should never have been here. That's why Michael Snedeker, Barry Scheck, Johnnie Cochran and Lisa Short are so important to us. This is why we need Murray Janus, Mike Morchower, Gerry Spence, Roy Black and Barry Tarlow to fight with Barry Scheck to free the indigent innocent. This is why we need David Hicks and Aubrey Davis to keep on being fair and honest prosecutors. We need help. I need the IAC, the NAACP, the ACLU, the SCLC and pastors to help us. We need to hear from you. Today, I am trying to find the address to Steve Birdlebough who is a lobbyist for the Friends Committee on Legislation, which is a Quaker non-profit organization in Sacramento. I need the address for the national office for the Quakers. I want Steve Birdlebough to read this book. I need Ed Sluss who was in prison for a long time but got out and changed his life. Ed Sluss is now a supervising counselor at Ironwood Prison in Blythe, California. I want Ed to read this book. Steve Rigg was a prison guard at Corcoran state prison. Mr. Rigg blew the whistle on fellow guards for setting up fights and rapes in prison. He is now a prison consultant. We need to get him this book. Prison authorities just opened up forty new prison guard positions to the tune of eight million taxpayer dollars! They're opening a new program at New Folsom Prison, which proposes to stop violence by denying inmates telephone calls, yard, recreation and canteen. Isolation cells will be the norm. Yet, prison consultants, former inmates and even forensic psychiatrists say programs rescinding privileges or sending someone to isolation is unproductive. They say programs that work are ones emphasizing positive behavior. The carrot and stick method is unconstitutional and does not work. This foolish, preposterous and ludicrous idea of controlling violence by controlling privileges is flawed, agreed Steve Birdlebough. Steve says, "Helping inmates develop through other kinds of programs would be more effective. You can't tell someone they'll lose their canteen (store) privileges if they're violent. The dynamics of an eighth grade mentality will persist as long as we allow people to remain stunted in personal and spiritual growth." Steve is absolutely correct. In isolation as I stated - you are not allowed to go to the prison chapel. You sit in a tiny cell twenty-four hours per day getting angrier and angrier. You get depressed and stressed. The problem is the folks downtown running C.D.C. are operating with an eighth grade mentality. They (C.D.C.) basically tell all professionals who tell them how asinine their prison programs are "we don't want your opinion." A Black prison staff member told me that C.D.C. does not employ one single penologist not one! Zero! Successfully controlling violent behavior involves educational opportunities, psychotherapy, spiritual growth and immediate intervention from professionals who specifically know how to deal with violent behavior. Dr. Jim Gillian, a former psychology professor at Harvard Medical School and President of the International Association for forensic psychotherapy says its a *mistake* to emphasize *deprivation*. After opening psychiatric emergency rooms in Massachusetts's state prisons, homicides and suicides went down from several a month to none (zero) in a year according to Dr. Gilligan. "Inflicting pain on people is the quickest way to make them violent. This approach is only likely to increase the level of violence before and after they leave prison," states Dr. Gilligan. Ed Sluss of whom I wrote earlier spent almost twenty years in prison for crimes of violence. Now, as I said, he is a counselor at Ironwood Pison. "I would rather feel physical pain then emotional pain. A guy won't suppress violence for a telephone call. I didn't realize what I was doing. After addressing those issues and letting go those reservoirs of pain, I started getting a different sense of the world," he said.

Former prison guard Steve Rigg says we must train prison guards to interact more humanely with prisoners and supervise more thoroughly. This would curb violence. "We need to quit pretending that every inmate is an animal," stated Mr. Rigg.

"I am twenty-one years old. I'll get out of prison when I'm twenty-nine years old. C.D.C. got me raped, stabbed and labeled. I came here when I was eighteen. The Aryan Brotherhood told me I had to stab this guy. I was afraid. And I went to a captain and he laughed at me and sent me back to fend for myself. An older White dude serving life promised to take care of me if I became his sex slave. I'm not gay but it was my only way out. I became his boy and now I have aids. C.D.C. refused to protect me. There ain't *no way* around gangs for a youngster like me in prison. Getting P.C. (Protective Custody) is too hard to do. It's a war zone in these yards. It's a deathtrap for any youngster like me. I'd rather fight Saddam Hussein than try to fight C.D.C.," an inmate told me in the van the other day. I was being transported to court in Sacramento. I'll tell you again! For any politician, activist, leader, pastor or office reading this book. To Richard Polanco, John Burton, Joseph Biden, Steve White, Willie Brown, even Jesse Jackson and Al Sharpton: The California Department of Corruption (or is it Corrections?) is creating **monsters** on a daily basis. Any young man, White, Black or Mexican who enters any prison in California will be forced to join a prison gang. It is the only way to survive in this prison system. He will be forced not to live with anybody who does not share his skin pigmentation. If he refuses, he will be assaulted, stabbed, raped and maybe killed. C.D.C. allows and even promotes this kind of segregation and gang activity. Oregon prisons are not like this. Georgia prisons are not like this. There are only one or two prisons in this entire state (thirty-three prisons) where a Black and White inmate can live in the same cell without being killed. New Folsom's A-facility is one of the few. Even here it is slowly changing because C.D.C. is allowing more racist and violent inmates to come to this facility and these people are arbitrary, capricious and vindictive in their transferring policies. Again, where is Charlie Baddaker? When and where will they transfer Brandon G. Martinez? All Brandon Martinez needs to do is piss off a captain or a lieutenant and he will be in ad-Seg tomorrow. Then they will transfer this young twenty-four-year-old inmate to a prison not as safe as New Folsom - Facility A. The word will be out when he gets there that he **violated** the Code of California's (staff sanctioned) prison rules. Martinez celled with other inmates who are not Mexican. Brandon is a quiet, studious, Christian inmate who should not be in prison. The right lawyer could get him out of here. Yet, he is not racist. He is not a slave. But at the drop of a hat, they will put him on a bus to Corcoran, Lancaster, Mule Creek, etc. and tell him "You'll be safe. You have no enemies here. We are downsizing our facility." These are vindictive, racist and angry staff members who are militia minded, covert and evil at the core of their beings. They steal, hinder and sabotage mail. They are unprofessional and lack gumption. They are reactive and unstable. Don't take my word for it; just come take a look at C.D.C. for yourself. Come and watch how arbitrary and racist they are. Watch them pepper spray, beat and abuse inmates in Ad-seg. Watch captains get approval for cell extractions over the telephone when an associate warden is supposed to be present. Watch them manipulate and edit video recordings of their brutal cell extractions. Watch them threaten medical staff to pretend wounds, abrasions and swellings are self-inflicted. Watch them send litigious inmates to solitary confinement on a whim. It happens every single day of the week. Inmates overhear staff discussing sensitive case factor data. Inmates prepare sensitive case factor information. And nobody does anything about it. C.D.C. needs a catharsis. C.D.C. needs to be seized by the Federal Government. Those prisons are an abomination before God and taxpaying citizens are footing the bill to train criminals on how to commit more crimes. Simple warehousing buildings of concrete and barbed wire fences. And those uneducated and ignorant captains and wardens, who earn in excess of seventy thousand dollars per year, not including perks, laugh all the way to the bank. Morris Dees and Stephen Bright ought to investigate C.D.C. There are, indeed, criminals, thugs and racists running C.D.C. and innocent men such as myself are high profile victims of this system. Y'all gotta clean these prisons up. You need to help set the innocent free. We need help. We need it now. I don't believe Ida Sydnor of the Sacramento NAACP would allow this to continue if she really knew what was going on. Judge Barry Loncke wouldn't go for this - Kweisi Mfume, Al Sharpton and Louis Farrakhan would not go for this. The ACLU and the ADL would not go for this. Young, good-looking Jewish guys who come to prison don't stand a chance. They will be stabbed, raped and abused. And I'll stake my life on the fact that at the most, C.D.C. will sentence him to solitary confinement. They will not clean up the yards. They will not integrate the cells. They will not integrate their staff and demystify race in the prisons. They will not disband the gangs. Homosexuals in prisons? They are stomped on like roaches and passed around like hot dogs and staff does nothing to protect them. Did you see the movie "Boys in the Hood"? At the end of the movie I think it was Ice Cube who was talking about the fact that the news never mentioned his brother's murder. "Either they don't know, don't show or just don't care about what's going on in the hood." Likewise when I think of the powerful prison gangs running rampant, drugs, rapes, assaults and killings in these prisons. When I see the abuse of power and the cruel and unusual punishment. When I look at young prisoners being forced into gangs and forced to hate and I see the lack of public exposure, "Either they don't know, don't show or just don't care about what's going on in the prisons," I say. We need to do something because every batch of prisoners being released into your community tomorrow (especially in California) is a time bomb waiting to explode. The person they rob, rape, molest, shoot or kill could be *you*. It could be your child, your brother and your sister. Call C.D.C. and find out how many are being released tomorrow. And you can put bars on your doors, get bulletproof windows on your cars and send your kids to school wearing bulletproof vests. You can go buy you a machine gun and try to protect your life and limb against the violent C.D.C. produced predators who will get out tomorrow. Or you can insist on a better return on your 4.5 billion dollar investment. You can demand and insist upon the gangs being disbanded in prisons. Demand that the rapes, assaults, murders and drugs be eliminated from prisons. Bloods, Crips, Nazi Low Riders, the KKK sponge, the A.B., Mexican Mafia, Northern Structure, etc. These people who are arrested for gang hits in the streets, simply come to prison and set up shop in the prisons. They do so with the approval of C.D.C. It's a quiet, well-kept and hidden C.D.C. secret. And they recruit every inmate who walks through the prison gates. Everyday of the week. Everyday month of the year. We have got to clean up C.D.C.

Don't you ever forget that there are thousands of innocent men who are raped here in this cesspool of sin. We should not be here we need help. I need you to find (E-mail) Attorney Evan Wolfson, James Dale and Farrah Gray. Get this book to them or write me a letter and send me their addresses and I'll send them a book. I need Steven Cozza and Ann Cozza who founded "Scouting For All" in Petaluma. These are young activist who would join us in petitioning, faxing and E-mailing lawyers and politicians about wrongful convictions and judicial corruption. Steven and Ann Cozza are not judgmental, biased or racist. They will hear my humble plea if we get this tome in their hands. I know that great legal minds such as Murray J. Janus, Michael Snedeker, Lisa Short, David Hicks, Barry Tarlow, Gerry Spence and F. Lee Bailey are reading this book right now. Murray, Barry, David and Aubrey are holding this page between their rich fingers right now. Guys, I'm not writing a novel here. This is non-fiction. I need you to help me to vindicate my rights. Please don't allow me to *die* here for crimes I did not commit. C.D.C. will never willingly let me go! Pharaoh must be told through appeals, evidence and a fight to "loose that man and let him go." and "If it doesn't fit, you must acquit". I need help. I know Mary Ratcliff of the San Francisco Bayview newspaper is reading right now. Mary, I need help. I need you to write about it, call other Black papers, radio shows,

Tommy Goss, Doug Banks, Tony Brown, Susan Taylor and ask him to please help me. Write me a letter today in this prison and I'll answer any question you have. Mary, help me reach Spike Lee, Bill Cosby, John Singleton, Queen Latifah, Sean Combs, etc. I don't believe that they will allow me to die here. I am here, suffering and I am innocent. This vicious monster factory which is teaching young people how to commit more crimes when they get out is being funded by you, the taxpayers. This is *your money*. I refuse to believe that most of America is still racist. I don't buy that. Dr. Martin Luther King, Jr. died in the name of justice and racial harmony. There were tens of thousands of White people at the Mall in Washington, DC who stood with Dr. King. I refuse to believe that if Jason Williams and Chris Webber were sent to prison tomorrow, they wouldn't want to be cellies. They have a lot in common. Jason (White kid) Williams was at Chris (Black kid) Webber's house watching the playoff games after the Kings were eliminated from the playoffs. Jason drank from glasses in Chris' house. Jason sat on furniture in Chris' house. They are buddies. How would Jason's family feel if (God forbid) he and Chris were sent to prison tomorrow (Corcoran, Tchachapi, Mule Creek, San Quentin, etc. and Jason called his mom to tell her "I can't live in the cell with Chris because he is Black. I have to either join the Skinheads, Nazi Low Riders, or the A.B. because if I don't, I'll get killed or raped. That's the way it is in all CA Prisons. I went to the captain and told him I was not a racist and I get along with everybody. The captain told me, that's not the way it's done in C.D.C. What would Jason's mom think?? Again, I need to remind you that these guys who have been forced to live this way will return to civilian life. C.D.C. refuses to do anything about it. The Little Hoover Commission stated, "more importantly, the failure of parolees to reintegrate into society exacts another cost: more crimes and more victims, demonstrating that public safety is ill-served by a corrections strategy that only protects the public when the inmate is in custody and does not prepare the inmate to be a responsible citizen. The state cannot tolerate a system that results in two-thirds of parolees quickly being re-incarcerated. ."

"Most inmates do not have jobs in prison that develop skills transferable to the marketplace. Few inmates received needed education. Fewer still receive effective drug treatments. Substantial evidence including some developed in CA prisons - shows that certain programs can significantly reduce recidivism. Expanded and improved, these programs could be confidently expected to reduce crime and the demand for additional prisons. Approximately ninety percent of the inmates in state prison are eventually released back to the community. *More than half of the 154, 000 inmates in prison today will be released within the next two years*. It is known that within the next two years more than half of the release inmates will be *convicted of new crimes* California's recidivism rate is among the highest in the nation. So the state can proudly point to it's high incarceration rate and low escape rate as positively protecting public safety. *But to the degree that inmates released from California's prison system are more likely to commit another crime than their peers in other states, public safety is compromised.*" That's a part of the little Hoover Commission's Report on CA prisons. Not my words and make no mistake about it there are some good people working in C.D.C. But they can't change the bureaucracy. The bureaucracy is dangerous, powerful and vindictive. I am very serious. California runs a brutal and inhumane prison system in which prisoners are beaten, gang-raped, forced to segregate while their pleas for help and protection are met with deliberate indifference from guards and prison officials. Government sponsored torture in state prisons thrives. Victims are isolated in solitary confinement (Ad-seg) and abused by prison guards. These inmates will be released into your community soon. Inmates who file grievances and litigate are set up, locked down, harassed and transferred on a daily basis. Even at New Folsom State Prison, they are housed in 6x12 foot cement cages. Trapped/isolated and forgotten by staff. Inmates are discouraged from getting visits. There is a degradation ceremony, which consists of stripping the inmate so he is nude, in front of a group of officers, who then force him to bend over in an attitude of obedience and to spread his cheeks (buttocks) so that the anal orifice is completely exposed to the group. This occurs before and after every visit; even legal visits from an attorney. Blacks? In the U. S. Blacks go to prison more often than Blacks in South Africa. The U. S. Black imprisonment rate is the highest in the world. From 1990-1995 alone, a total of two hundred and thirteen prisons were built in America. And Mexicans or Latinos are not far behind. C.D.C. purposely keeps Blacks and Mexicans at odds, in war and rioting in an effort to control them. Are you getting the picture here? And again if some warden would rise up and try to change this his/her life would be in danger. Not in 2001 you say? Consider this: December 15, 2000 (not 1900 - but in 2000). Humanitarian, historian, writer, and community leader Derwin Brown was gunned down in front of his home just outside Atlanta, Georgia. This is my hometown. The town where Dr. Martin Luther King, Jr. was born. Derwin Brown was hit eleven times. Assassinated -

execution style. Derwin had a penchant for speaking and writing the truth and for exposing the racist ways of doing things in America. He had a firm commitment to change the corruption at the Dekalb County Jail, and the Sheriff's Department. Derwin was the first elected Black Sheriff of Dekalb County. He was a grassroots activist and once installed as Sheriff, was going to enact the massive measures of prison reform, which would have brought greater scrutiny with respect to the abusive conditions and profit making schemes within America's present prison system. Brown ran for Dekalb County Sheriff to cleanse the system and make it responsive to the taxpayer. He lost in 1996 and won in 2000. He would have been officially installed on December 18th, but on the 15th an assassin's bullets overrode the will of the people. After securing election, Derwin Brown had compiled a list of thirty-eight officers at the jail and in the Sheriff's office that he promised to fire as a first stop in converting these departments to the type of institution, which would serve the people instead of the system of corruption. Derwin's brother, Ron Brown of Roosevelt New York stated, "Derwin understood that the prison system was being used as a business, and he was going to stop that. Furthermore, he had written articles about prisons and how they were being used to warehouse his people. He had labeled the tough sentencing of youth offenders as 'just another war on Black males'." White one's too. In June of 2001 Kenny Webber was sentenced to twenty-five years to life in prison under the new three strikes law for stealing *four cookies*. What were his first two strikes? Rape? Murder? Hell no! His first two strikes were for burglary!!! He will serve a minimum of twenty-five years in the CA prison system to the tune of over seven hundred and fifty thousand dollars at taxpayers expense for stealing less than one dollar's worth of cookies.

Sheriff Elect Derwin Brown hosted a television show called "The Naked Truth 2000" on which he lambasted the criminal justice system for being a modern form of slavery. All the suspects in his execution style assassination are deputy sheriffs! So I assure you that any one C.D.C. staff member who vowed to clean up C.D.C.'s monster factory could be *risking his life*. Ask Steve Riggs. Again, I am risking my life by writing this out of retaliation. C.D.C. could transfer me tomorrow no matter how wrong it is and have me killed! They could harass any inmate or staff member whom they think is close to me just to get back at me for writing this book. They know I'm physically safe at New Folsom on A-facility. But they are vindictive and cold-blooded. It does not have to be this way. This is wrong. Inmate rehabilitation is making a strong comeback in the State of Oregon.

Oregon has implemented a new program to deal with the high and growing rates at which released inmates end back up in prison. Oregon and Missouri have each begun a comprehensive effort to remold offenders, requiring them to work, study or undergo drug and other treatments full time. "The bottom line is, we want inmates practicing on the inside what works on the outside to try to undo all the bad crime inducing habits they learned in the years. Before they got here," stated Steven J. Ickes, an Assistant director of the Oregon Department of Corrections. John Jay College of criminal justice (in Manhattan) professor Todd clearly stated, "With the huge expansion of prisons starting in the 1980's, most prisons gave up believing they had any responsibility for changing offender's or what happened after offenders were released. The objective became that prisons should be just for punishment; and politicians competed to see who could make prisons more unpleasant, by taking away things like television and recreation and education classes." Oregon prison officials called on business executives for advice about how to run prisons more productively. Inmates in Oregon are even given *bonuses* for good work, etc. A few years ago a guy walking out of prison in Oregon had nowhere to go and no job skills, so they often ended up coming right back to prison. At least in prison they had everything they needed: Food, clothing, a bed and their buddies. The percentage of inmates admitted to Oregon prisons in 2000 who were returning parolees was only twenty-five percent, down from forty-seven percent in 1995. Inmate behavior in Oregon's thirteen prisons has also improved, prison officials say. There has been a sixty percent reduction in prison fights and assaults. Michael Jacobson, a professor of criminology at John Jay College of criminal justice and a former Director of New York's Department of Corrections says that finding ways to ease the return to society and reduce recidivism "is the hot topic in the criminal justice system, because of huge costs and numbers involved". About 614,000 people will be released from state prisons this year, said Allen J. Beck of the Bureau of Justice statistics, the statistical arm of the Justice Department. Within three years, based on studies, sixty-two percent of them will be arrested again, and forty-one percent will be sent back to prison. In California alone, Professor Jacobson stated about 70,000 people seventy-five percent of the state's total number of parolees, are sent back to prison each year for parole violations. Oregon should be a model for California. Even some people in the *tough on crime camp* say they like the state's new approach. Steve Doel, the president of Crime Victim's United in Oregon, whose twelve-year-old daughter was killed walking home said, "The thing people need to know is that most of these folks *will come out of prison again*. So we think it's a smart policy to try to *change them while they're locked up*, so that when they return to society there *will be fewer victims on the street*." California could transform its prison system. They could to it. There are dedicated people such as the Quakers who would help them. Steve Birdlebough, Shirley Price, Vickie Valine, Kenneth Larsen, Peter Crysdale and all those at Friends Committee on Legislation in Sacramento are willing to help C.D.C. Abel Maldonado, Carole Migden, Tony Cardenas, Richard Polanco, John Vasconcellos, and Darrel Steinberg would be willing to help Governor Davis transform these prisons. That's why I urge you, the reader, to support and fund organizations such as the Quakers and the Friends Committee on Legislation in Sacramento. They are trying to save the taxpayer's money. They are not *soft on crime*. They are *smart on crime*. They make Isaiah Chapter 58 come alive. Again, if y'all help me get this tome to Bishop T. D. Jakes, Steven and Ann Cozza (Petaluma, CA) Attorney Evan Wolfson, James Dale, Wentley Phipps. Chuck Colson, Greg Jonsson, Prof. David Protess, Actor Eric Dane, Judge Gary Ransom, Attorney Jerry Singer, Paul Ciollino, Farrah Gray, James Shelby, Mike Schneider (San Francisco State University) and Michael Taketa. (Go back and read each name. E-mail them and tell them about this book. Get their mailing address and send it to me at this prison and I'll send them the book). If we get this book to Edward James Olmos, Spike Lee, Chris Gardner and the NAACP. If we get it to the NAACP's Julian Bond, Ted Kennedy, Joseph Biden and John Lewis, I believe something will happen. I do not believe a youngster like Ann or Steven Cozzo, Michael Taketa, Farrah Grey, Michael Schneider, Ron Dipolla (in Corona, CA) Jonathon Lewandowski (cable TV host in Atlanta, GA) etc. will read this book and not take action. How hard can it be for you to find Lewandowski on the Internet or in the telephone book in Atlanta?

I need help. I want you to help me get this book to somebody else. I want the world to know what the DA did to David Quindt in Sacramento, CA. I want the world to know what they did to Anthony Porter, Rolando Cruz and Jeff Pierce. I want the world to know what Mary Hanlon Stone and Robert Altman did to me. And what Mary and DA Debbie Glynn are doing to me now. I want young people to know that the CA prison system is a *monster factory* in which they will be raped, assaulted and killed if they ever come here. I want taxpayers to examine the facts for themselves and to decide what needs to be done about warehousing criminals.

I want America to know the ***naked truth*** about crime, punishment, wrongful convictions and corrupted prisons. I want lawyers like Mike Snedeker, Murray J. Janus, Willie Gary, Gerry Spence, Barry Tarlow, Johnnie Cochran and Gerald Uelmen to get this book. I want my readers (you) to save our children. I want you to help Barry Scheck! I want you to help the Quakers, ACLU and anybody else who is trying to change America. I want students in colleges to get this book. I want students who are activists to inundate Governor Gray Davis and C.D.C. with faxes, E-mails and letters about this book. I want you to do something about what you have read in this book. Read Isaiah Chapter 58. Then pick up you pen and write me a letter today. I am an innocent man trapped in prison. "It's never, ever too late to care about the truth as it relates to innocence or guilt," stated Dan Rather. "If we are to maintain integrity and confidence in our honorable and often admirable, although imperfect judicial system, we must always leave room to re-look at a case especially when someone's life is at stake," he went on to say. On June 21, 2001, I had a long conversation with the chief deputy warden at this prison. I complained to him about the biased, unfair and illegal witch-hunt, which I'd just undergone. I.S.U. (Investigative Services Unit) had just completed the process of (literally) calling every single cell partner that I have ever had in five years of prison via the telephone and asking , "Did Manning ever try to rape you"? What bothered me most was not only was I being racially and sexually profiled by C.D.C. But also the fact that inmates report being raped everyday in C.D.C. and staff routinely dismiss their claims out of hand. Yet, my investigation was capricious and arbitrary. Not a single inmate (praise God) has ever accused me of rape. Yet, a counselor took it upon herself to launch an investigation for the simple reason that she thought I might potentially fit a profile. After interviewing more than twenty-six inmates they came up empty. "No, Manning never tried to rape me" was what each inmate told them. However, C.D.C. has boxed me in with this asinine type investigation. They have (even if inadvertently) poisoned my name throughout the prisons. Inmates talk, embellish, dream and exaggerate. Although (by God's grace) none of them claimed I ever tried to rape them; just what do you think Brian Thomas Cruz told all the fellas on the yard (at Corcoran SATIF) when he got off the telephone with I.S.U.? "Damn, I wonder what's up with Manning? Is he a pervert or child molester? Did he try to rape somebody or what? Hell, I.S.U. just called me on the telephone and asked me did Manning ever try to rape me when we were cellies? I wonder where that idea came from?"

In fact, a buddy of mine who is at Corcoran SATIF wrote me a letter after the investigation and stated, "Whatever you do don't come to SATIF. They got all kinds of rumors whirling around about you. They will kill you at this prison. That interracial celling stuff does not go down here. And the *fact* that you do it is already on the yard. Please don't come to Corcoran SATIF".

Even more - two days ago I was told, "they don't want David Quindt visiting you. They are gonna try to transfer you as soon as you are finished with court. Watch your back. Guys at Lancaster, Satif and Mule Creek all know who you are. You need to stop at New Folsom." I don't put it past these people to try to send me to another prison. If and when it happens it is total retaliation for this tome. I plan to write our warden about this. Cheryl is usually fair and I know she does not want to lose her retirement or house or pension. And if those people send me anywhere after their witch hunt, I will be hurt if not killed. This is a death trap! That is why I hope, I pray, I wish and desire to get this book to young men, men in juveniles and high schools to try to let this vivid picture of what prison is really like, to cause them not to come here. I'm sending the alarm and telling any young White, Black, Hispanic or other young man you don't want to come here. This is a sick place. Whatever does not work, C.D.C. does more of it (More on that in a moment). In that lengthy conversation with the C.D.W. there was one bright moment! "Sherman, I read every word of the DA's reports on your crime. It's not my place to judge you! I'm neither the judge or the jury. I just gotta keep you here 'til they tell us to let you go. I'm no lawyer, but I must say I don't believe from the facts of your case that you committed this crime. From what I read this seemed to be a prostitution deal gone sour. I do not believe everything you or any other inmate tells me. So I don't know if you are lying or not. But the case doesn't make sense. I could not get past the fact that the alleged victim (Ricardo Calvario) claims he was walking around Santa Monica Blvd. at 2:40 a.m. but was not a prostitute. He admits he voluntarily got in the car with an unknown man (me) just to get a ride. Then you pull a gun on him and after you pull the gun on him, he decides to voluntarily put on his seatbelt. How did that jury convict you? Were there any Blacks on the jury?" I replied, "No Terry, not a single one." He said, "Then it was not a jury of your peers. But anyway, I'm finished discussing your case. I don't usually read all data in inmates files but in your case I read every word."

I tried to get Terry to understand how unfair, abusive and racist some officers are. "How many Blacks are on I.S.U.? How many

Black or Hispanic captains do we have here? How did C.O. Blackwell (pseudonym) get promoted to sergeant? Where is C.O. Acosta? Where is the C.O. who stole my mail to Rev. Jesse Jackson? Why is C.O. Woffrey (pseudonym) still working in seven block? This stuff may not be your fault, but you're at the top and you need to clean this place up!" These people specialize in screwing up. They are vindictive, racist and evil. Anything they can do to destroy peace and tranquility, they do. "You and Brandon Martinez get along too well. You both read. You're both Christians. You're quiet and you stay out of trouble. That works too well. If they don't transfer you soon, I guarantee you Martinez will either be put in the hole or transferred," a Black sergeant told me last week. This is a fact. They do it all the time. If they think you're getting along too well and you're too peaceful etc. They stir up the post. Ipso facto "Let's get rid of Manning or Martinez. Doctor up the paperwork to justify it so that the C.S.R. will go for it."

C.O. Acosta? He was on the elite I.S.U. team. Guess what he did? He was bringing in hit lists and contract assault plans to gang members. He allegedly smuggled weapons and drugs in to prisoners. They (C.D.C.) turned their heads for quite a while. If an inmate snitched on Acosta they simply put the inmate in the hole or transferred the inmate. Yet, word got out that the media was about to delve into Acosta's past and so they fired him. How many more Acosta's are left?? On a positive note, the plan to reform violent state inmates by withholding privileges, was denied in budget negotiations in the legislature last week. As I stated, it would have cost 8 million dollars and required forty new prison guards. A joint committee of assembly and senate members agreed to not pay for this asinine experiment this year. Money for a fund to pay off lawsuits for C.D.C. was also denied. "The idea of a violence control needs a lot more thought," stated Attorney Robert Navarro, who is an attorney who handles prison civil rights cases.

"They have to stop treating them like they are some sort of object that can be changed by sheer force to go through some maze." Mr. Navarro advocates C.D.C. consulting with inmates who are in maximum security. He says the Department should get a multi-racial perspective on what would work. "It would behoove them to work and consult with prisoners on how to make them less violent. Believe me, most prisoners want to be safe", stated Attorney Navarro.

A twenty-six-year-old inmate who has been in and out of C.D.C. since he was eighteen years old stated, "I got busted when I was seventeen the first time. I came to prison when I was eighteen. I was scared out of my pants. They put me in the cell with a lifer. I didn't sleep the first three months, I was so scared. I had to ride with the northerners for protection. They made me slice (stab) Chester (child molester). I didn't want to do it. I felt bad. But I learned how to just do it and let my mind go blank." He learned *how to do it* and let his *mind go blank*! That's deep! Quite thought provoking. Yet when you're in a scary place and you have nowhere to run to, when you are not given food for thought, spiritual or educational nourishment, when you have the option of either joining a prison gang or going to solitary confinement, etc., you will either die, kill or survive. You will get killed or kill. To kill or not to be killed. You give up your soul to the prison subculture or you give up your anus to the prison predator. And ninety-seven percent of the captains presently working in California's prisons are from the old guard. They came up through the ranks in the 60's and 70's when you earned rank by kicking butt and taking names later. They believe that when you come to prison whether you are seventeen or seventy-seven years old. You must "Fend for yourself. Stab, be stabbed or get locked up in the hole." If C.D.C. wants to allege that they protect would-be victims, etc., the proof against this is in the pudding. "We have thirty-three prisons in this state. Only four protective custody yards. And three of the four are not really P.C. Satif, Mule Creek and Lancaster are rocking and rolling like mainlines," stated a C.D.C. captain.

Again, I refuse to believe that the good citizens of this state have a clear picture of the inner happenings of California's prisons. I dare not believe that if the people knew the truth, they would support this system. Even the people from the tough on crime camp agree that the system is a complete, miserable failure. "I want guys to leave prison better than they were when they went in. And if there is an innocent man in there, I want him out of there," stated Nelson Wilson. " The alternative conception of punishment that I have proposed is one informed by communitarian rather than liberal ideas. I have asserted punishment is a process of communication between the community and offenders . . . communicative punishment with a restorative process is specified by the four aims of repentance, self reform, reparation and reconciliation," states Tim Newell. Mr. Newell has been a prison governor in England for over thirty years. Based on his expertise and Quaker beliefs, he explains how victims and offenders are unnecessarily damaged today and explores possibilities for change in the culture of crime control. I suggest every C.D.C. warden read Tim Newell's book entitled "Forgiving Justice: A Quaker Vision for Criminal Justice".

269

Abel Maldonado, R., San Luis Obispo sought to bring restorative justice into the state's juvenile courts and local juvenile justice programs. Law enforcement and victim's groups supported it and not a single legislators voted against it. Governor Gray Davis vetoed the bill. It is an alarming fact that if we don't intervene in our teens lives during their formative years, they will ultimately and inevitably end up in the big house (monster factory). And once here they will be schooled in how to commit more rapes, robberies and murders. With everything in my soul and heart I can tell you I want to cry sometimes when I see all of these young men coming into this deathtrap on a daily basis. Every one of them is one we failed to teach, to reach and to save. We need to save our children. We need to develop turnaround programs and reach them while they are young and then we won't have to incarcerate them when they are old. The juvenile systems all over America are failing. Richard Polanco (D. Los Angeles), John Vasconcellas (D. Silicon Valley) and Tony Cardenas (D. Panorama City) all tried to implement bills to better fight crime and reform prisoners. Senate Bills 127, 1348, 2885 were each vetoed by Governor Davis. So with this monster factory, that I'm telling you about it should be of no surprise that Assembly Bill 2101 which was proposed by Carole Migden (D. San Francisco) was vetoed by the Governor. This Bill proposed to authorize news reporters to conduct interviews with state prisoners, a right which was lost due to regulations that were promulgated during Peter Wilson's administration. Why did Mr. Davis veto the Bill? Many allege that the Governor does not want taxpayers to become cognizant of the events, which I've painstakingly described in this book. They indicate that if taxpayers knew that the biggest and most powerful gangs in this nation were organized behind the walls of C.D.C.'s prisons and that prison officials condoned and in many instances fomented their violence, stabbings and murders the taxpayers would demand a change. They contend that if the public really knew that nine out of every ten prisoners in C.D.C.'s thirty-three prisons was forced to join a gang or be raped the public would rise up and protest on the State Capitol. Governor Davis obviously does not want young, brilliant men such as Greg Johnsson who was trained in investigative journalism by professor David Protess to come inside these walls. If any one of David Protess students could get in these walls, I believe that brick by brick these walls would fall. No sane mind could see the way these prisons are run and not conclude that something's wrong. And that what we are doing is definitely not working. My desire is to see Steve White call a summit meeting. Mr. White needs to call an emergency meeting on the state of California Prisons. He should bring in Attorney Navarro, Steve Birdlebough, Peter Crysdale, Vickie Valine, Tim Newell, Richard Polanco, Willie Brown, Sheriff Mike Hennessey, Todd Clear, Michael Jacobson, the NAACP, ACLU and the ADL and devise a plan to be implemented immediately to disband the prison gangs, ameliorate the violence and cut recidivism in half within the next two years. Steve White needs to follow the advice of Attorney Navarro and bring inmates to the meeting. Mr. White should go to Oregon and find out how Steve J. Ickes implemented a program, which is transforming Oregon's prisons. Oregon prisons have a higher rate of GED completion than the seventeen community colleges in the state that offer the instruction. Oregon's plan is working. We must not forget that Oregon is not pampering prisoners. This is not about prisoners having swimming pools and golf courses. This is about people leaving prison and not committing more crimes. Please remember (and I will repeat) that Allen J. Beck of the Bureau of Justice statistics says about 614,000 people will be released from prison this year. Also recall that in California alone, Professor Jacobson said about seventy thousand people, seventy-five percent of the state's total number of parolees, are sent back to prison each year for a new crime. How much money is this costing taxpayers? How many lives are being lost at the hands of parolees who got out of the monster factory physically? But not mentally? How many women and children are raped each day of the week by a man who got out of prison sicker and slicker, meaner and tougher than he was when he went in? Parolees (who commit new crimes) take up over twenty-one percent of all the state prison beds each year, costing California 1.2 billion dollars according to Professor Jacobson. One point two billion dollars! The teachers on strike asking for an 11.7 percent raise? Couldn't we fund their raise with this money and have money left over to buy life-transforming books for kids in school?

Mr. White needs to be very pragmatic and analytical in his relatively new position as Attorney General. Any person, including Mr. White, Mr. Polanco, Mr. Burton or Mrs. Waters who can transform California's prisons, reduce recidivism and save taxpayer's money ought to run for Governor and will win. "The thing people need to know is that most of these folks in prison are eventually going to come out again. So we think it's smart policy to try to change them while they're locked up, so that when they return to society there will be fewer victims on the street". Remember that quote? By whom? Mr. Steve Doel, who is the president of Crime Victims United in Oregon. I challenge any reporter to dare the wardens at High Desert, Pelican Bay,

Lancaster or any of the thirty-three prisons in this state to allow you into their prisons and to let you talk with inmates and to point you to any programs that are helping change inmates and teaching them to become productive citizens. There is no rehabilitation in C.D.C. and I really don't think the work rehabilitate applies to many in CA prison system. Re - means again or to do over, etc. habilitate means to make capable, etc. Many inmates can't be rehabilitated because they were never habilitated in the first place. While we were spending our money getting tough on crime, building new prisons and hiring new prison guards, we shortchanged the teachers and schools, which were educating our children. We didn't fund youth activities, mentoring programs and leadership training for our youth. Ipso facto, many guys here never did anything except steal, sell drugs or gang bang. They know no other way. And the only way to have a chance at reaching, teaching and transforming them is gonna be to teach them how to read, how to write, how to think, how to control, channel and redirect their anger. And how to get a damn job. We ought to have communication skills taught in prison because men with no or low self esteem are at a loss when it comes to communicating. They only know one way to say "You disrespected me" and that is by physical attack. They don't know how to express their concerns, gripes, complaints, etc. in a rational humane and non-violent way. But it's hard to concentrate on communication skills when you have the threat of death hanging over your head every single minute of the day. It's hard to think about learning how to read or write or pray when you are capriciously thrown into solitary confinement by a racist prison lieutenant. Difficult to focus on spiritual restoration when you are here and you know you are innocent, but may never get out. It is very difficult to achieve self-empowerment when you go to bed every night wondering who will stick, stab, and rape or murder you tomorrow. The situation in C.D.C. looks mighty, mighty bad. It is horrible that state sanctioned slavery, murders, segregation and rapes are running rampant in California's prison system. And very few people on the outside (you) know what's transpiring on the inside. Were it not for the I.A.C., ACLU, the ADL, the Quakers and a few other groups the prison system would have already exploded. The challenge is to try to get these groups that often are effective individually, to come together and work collectively to transform the CA prison system and prison systems across our nation. Cleaning up the prisons will in effect, reduce recidivism and lower the crime rate dramatically. I urge organizations across America to put aside our differences in philosophies, strategies and beliefs and to *focus* like a *laser* beam on the issues we agree on and to clean up the monster factory. We can no longer allow the fate of the people to rest in the dirty hands of our politicians. If taxpayer's in California are waiting on Gray Davis to admit that the problems are as bad as they really are, we'll be waiting for hell to freeze over. It took a courageous judge on June 21, 2001 to put the governor in his place in another example of Mr. Davis' beliefs that warehousing here in prison forever is the only available option. A judge struck down Gray Davis' policy of blocking parole in murder cases, and ordered the prompt release of a Calabasas man who has attracted support from legislators, law enforcement and church leaders. Davis has said he would never allow a murderer to be paroled and has vetoed paroles across the board since he was elected in 1999. "This bias against an entire class has caused him to violate *due process* rights," stated L.A. Superior Court Judge Paul Gutman. Judge Gutman ordered the release of Robert Rosenkrantz, who in 1985 fired ten shots from an Uzi into seventeen-year-old Steven Redman after Steven exposed him (Rosenkrantz-then eighteen) as a homosexual. Judge Gutman stated that Gray Davis must act on the basis of "Reason and Justice". The permissible factors are those in state law, relating to the crime, prison conduct, and likely *future behavior.* The judge stated, "While the governor is entitled to express his own opinion, the opinion itself must be factually supported, and it is not" in the Rosenkrantz's case, Gutman wrote. The governor is appealing this decision. "He's a very happy man and wants to get out of prison," stated Attorney Donald Specter, who called Gutman's ruling "a courageous act that respects the governor's power but also the role of the judiciary to check the chief executive when he goes too far".

In a stunning move former Parole Board Chairman Albert Leddy, the CA Council of Churches, The Board of Rabbi's of Northern CA and the CA Province of the Society of Jesus (the Jesuits) entered the case as Friends of the Court, urging parole for Rosenkrantz. That is awesome. A former parole board chairman, a man who was on the inside and a part of the bureaucracy, joining with righteous leaders and telling old Pharaoh to "Let my people go". That's exactly the kind of unity we need in America if we are going to free innocent men in prison. Albert Leddy, the Board of Rabbis', the Jesuits, etc. are a model of the type of unity which is required in order to obtain justice and due process. If we want to stop prison rapes, murders and stop the authorities from warehousing men as animals so that when they get free, they won't kill, maim, rape and molest. We must work together. What if Murray Janus, Barry Tarlow, Gerry Spence, Mr. Uelmen and Mike Snedeker combined their legal brilliance and filed Friends of the

Courts briefs seeking my release from this wrongful conviction? I would be home in less than six months.

What if Al Sharpton, Jesse Jackson, Billy Graham, Richard Polanco, Maxine Waters, etc. called a summit meeting in the set of prisons in CA and across the nation? What if they worked with the Quakers, Amnesty International, CA Prison Focus, the IAC and penologists to come up with a plan to stop the monster factory from producing, schooling and facilitating murderers, rapists and predators? If those people came together they could force California to clean up the monster factory. Then, all of these seventeen, eighteen and nineteen-year-old boys in prisons would not have to sacrifice their bodies, blood and minds and succumb to the pressures of the California prison gang. We can clean up the prisons, not only in California but all across the nation. It's time for governors to listen to the voice of the people. Allow me to digress and ramble a bit. Earlier, I wrote of a great, brilliant attorney who has represented a man on death row pro bono for many years. She cares! At that juncture, I was uncertain of the correct spelling of her last name. Thanks, however, to help from Elisabeth Semel and Judy Gallant I now have it. Her name (forgive the previous error) but I've already mailed that portion of this tome to the typist) is Katherine Puzone of Paul, Weiss, Rifkind, Wharton and Garrison. She is a prominent New York Attorney. Tonight I'm writing Steve Birdlebough to ask that he undertake the task of sending me data, every study etc. with which the Quakers and his committee are familiar on prisons. I want to know what has failed across America and what has worked across the world. I shall assemble this material and deposit the contents in my next tome. Perhaps I'll title the book "The Monster Factory" or maybe "Warehouse Animals". I hope to have that book published before Christmas 2001. I'm gonna attempt to send hundreds of books to churches, the ACLU, IAC, the Innocence Project, the Friends Committee on Legislation, CA Prison Focus and to colleges so that they can get the book into the hands of people who need to read it. Joe Volk, Shirley Price, Vickie Valine, Steve, Peter Crysdale, Kenneth Larsen, Mary Ratcliff, Spike Lee, etc. I need you all to help me to distribute this book en masse. I need help. I do not expect for every single reader to close this book and believe I'm innocent. I can live with that. Yet, even if you don't like me, my case and if you don't give a damn about me, I would hope and pray that you will (do) give a damn about others. It would be foolish and preposterous to assume there is not a single person at New Folsom Prison who is innocent. There are thousands across America sitting in these cages that are innocent. And I encourage you to help them to get free.  Not only that but I encourage you to help even those who are guilty to be treated as human beings while they are caged in prison. Even if you speak out with a vested interest.  Even if you only do it because you don't want men coming out of prisons as monsters.  If you only do it because you want the next man who walks free to have a shot at being non-violent and productive members of society, etc.  Just do it!  Six hundred and fourteen thousand prisoners will come to join you this year.  They will be free.  And for the sake of my daughter, my family and my friends, I don't want predators walking the streets of our cities.  And many prisons across this great nation are producing mass murderers, serial rapists and child predators.  What else can these guys become?  In prison with diminished privileges, with family (conjugal) visits stripped away, no educational or transformational opportunities, living in ultimate was zones, etc.  What do we expect?  There is a sickening stench running through the gray walls of most prisons. There is also the development of the attitudes of hopelessness, void and depression, which is escalating behind these walls.  And when we do arrest the right man for the right crime, I think he should do his time.   He should be locked away.    But we cannot contrive to dehumanize, degrade and deprive him.  I've seen the results of this foolish approach.  It creates monsters, literally.

Michael Gorman?  He was murdered here at New Folsom Prison by his cell partner in ad-seg.  I listened for hours as Mike banged on his door yelling and crying.  He pleaded with prison staff to move me out of this cell.  My cellie is gonna kill me.  Staff laughed at him and dismissed his pleas as out of hand.  I still see Mike who was a tall, thin, young White guy in my mind's eye.  I still hear the voice of his cries echoing down the sound tunnel of my memory.  That night, Mike's celly choked him to death.  He sodomized him and stuffed a TV guide up his anus.  This is real life.  Not a war story but a true story. I believe with my heart and mind that each prison official who ignored Mike's pleas ought to be charged with accessory to murder, deliberate indifference and willful negligence.  Mike was scheduled to be released from prison within a year.  But instead, he is dead and the puddle of blood lies on the hands of C.D.C.  This is wrong.  This is wrong!  This is not supposed to happen in America.  Not in America!

I shall engage in tautology and again urge Steve White and prison directors across the country to study what does work and change the system.  Steve needs to talk to inmates.  Steve needs to talk to Dr. Gilligan, Mr. Jacobson, the Quakers and the IAC and the taxpayers must demand a change in the system.  C.D.C. is busting open at its seams!  We need to come together collectively as Americans and change this. We have got to get over our differences, idiosyncrasies and all our divisions and work together to transform those prisons that are dungeons of despair and hopelessness. We must come together and liberate every innocent prisoner who is trapped in the bowels of these monster factories and we have to come together and inject the soul of the youth of America with the juice of hope, the milk of human kindness and the fruits of love. Love hides a multitude of sins. We must be genuine, sincere and authentic in our efforts. It's time to rise up and unite. I'm gonna tell y'all quite clearly that there may be a lot of organizations which may find different paragraphs in this tome with which they disagree. There may be several traditions, practices and particulars within the policies of some of these organizations (even some I've supported in this book) that I disagree with. So be it. It is not about agreeing on every issue. It's not about seeing eye to eye on everything. It's about fording what we agree on and unifying our efforts toward making a difference. I want great organizations such as Friends Committee on Legislation of California, and Amnesty International, the ACLU, the ADL and the IAC to come together and network. The day that somebody at the IAC will call somebody at FCL or vice versa. The day that Gerry Spence will call Barry Scheck or vice versa. The day that the ADL will call the NAACO or vice versa and say "Let's come together and change C.D.C. , lets call Richard Polanco, John Burton, Mr. Vasconcellos, McPherson and Karnette and call a summit meeting, etc." That's the day of transformation within C.D.C. we must get into Emergency Mode and we got to do whatever we got to do to stop these rapes, killings, gangs and racism in these prisons. We got to do whatever we must to weed and seed out innocent men who are in prison. We must put this pretty stuff back in the closet. Forget protocol and the bylaws of our diverse groups, etc. and utilize and exercise the power of togetherness. The day that Murray Janus, or Roy Black, Willie Gary or somebody will call Gerry Uelmen, Ephraim Margolin or Barry Tarlow, etc. and say "I need you to go get Sherman Manning out of prison." That's the way of transformation and liberation for me. The day that (even if you happen to be unsure of my innocence) you will begin to call your congressmen, senators, media, newspapers, youth groups, etc. and say "I don't know whether this guy is really innocent or a fraud, but here is some powerful stuff in this book that the public needs to read, etc." That's the day we will reach people. That's the day some young person on their way to prison may get this book and decide "I did not know prison was like that. This ain't the way the media portrays it. I'm getting out of this gang, off these drugs and I'm gonna change. I do not want to end up in prison!!" If we unite our efforts against poverty, homelessness, hatred, racism, wrongful convictions and prison abuse etc. That's the day that time and purpose will slap their hands together and the universe shall render exactly what we need! We need to come on out of our corners, our cliques, our traditions and rise above our divisions and work together. God will judge America if one does not return to compassion and love for others. We have become so greedy, so selfish, so vindictive, and so judgmental in this country that even some churches are preaching borderline messages of hatred. This is wrong. Come out of your corner and come on out to the center and let's find common ground. Common ground. God can bring us from the background into the forefront. I have learned that all my life God has been preparing me for where I am now in order to get me to this place that He wants me to be and even as you read these words you are at the right place at the right time. God is leaving us a breadcrumb trail and we must keep on coming. Keep moving and keep on going. Somebody reading is in prison and it all seems hopeless. I can identify with that feeling in a very intimate sense. But don't you dare give up. This ain't the time to quit. This is not the time to give up. This is no time to commit suicide. I know you are writing and people won't write back. I know you are praying and it seems that God does not hear you. I know you may feel abandoned, alone and lonely. But hold up your head and know that you are not alone. God is with you. Your breakthrough will come. You can change your whole life. You can transform you life. You're at a destiny point. Don't sit there and wallow in hatred, don't wallow in hopelessness, violence, anger, racism or foolishness. Don't reach out to drugs, alcohol, hooch, and all the other foolishness. Reach *in* not *out*. Reach inside yourself. Reach in you and read the spirit of God. That's the tool that will be used to bring you to the brink of your destiny. God is not asleep! God is not dead! He is alive and well. He is on the case and on the job. Don't you ever, ever give up. I pray and hope that just maybe something I write in these pages will cause your family, your friends, some group, lawyer, law professor or student to decide to be used as a tool to help you who are in prison. This book is bigger than me. It's bigger than my personal situation.

God is ready to move. He can and He will. God can do the Almighty through the least likely. I want prisoner, lawyers, housewives and professionals alike to get up, get active and let's work together. The problems in this country are many and I can't cover them all within these pages. My focus within these pages has been on issues relating to (mainly) wrongly convicted guys in prison and to the failure of the prison systems across America to prevent, deter and reduce crime. But I think we've touched on a multiplicity of issues. I would hope that some young man who is abusing drugs, carrying a gun or contemplating dropping out of school, etc. will read this book and decide he does not want to come to the monster factory. I cannot overemphasize the fact that this book is not all about me. I tell you with probity that if you read this book and decide you want to help me, I will consider it a Godsend. You! I've had people call and say "I'm gonna help you Sherman" and the next week they walk out on me. But I know somebody, someday is gonna free me. But even if you don't help me, I want you to help somebody. I want you to mentor a teen. Mold and shape their lives. Help some teen live and lead a better life. Help somebody! Find some prisoner in whose innocence you do believe and reach out to them. I want to motivate Eric Dane, Judge Gary Ransom, Atty. Jerry Singer, Linda Phipps, M. Gerald Schwartzbach, Seth Bray, Andrew Heyman, Tommy Goss, Tony Brown, Doug Banks and Max Bonner to keep on following your hearts and the leading of your spirit. Max Bonner has almost performed the Scheck-effect for Michael McCormick in Tennessee. Mike has the death penalty for allegedly murdering Donna Jean Nichols. But Max has won him a new trial. I hope justice prevails and if he is innocent, he should be acquitted. By a jury or his peers. Every lawyer who handles appeals or tells you that to overturn a conviction a court must first find error and then decide that error was prejudicial. A very small number of appeals have cleared those hurdles in the CA Supreme Court. This court has found an extraordinary range of trial court errors to be harmless in the past five years. Errors such as egregious examples of improper admission or the exclusion of evidence, prosecutorial misconduct, ineffective assistance of counsel, jury misconduct and faulty instructions!!

The CA Supreme Court is asleep. Seemingly prosecutors in California can say or do anything and get away with it. The courts in CA will excuse the courts need to do justice and punish prosecutors and trial judges who don't play by the rules what happened to "We believe that it is better for ten guilty people to be set free, than for one innocent man to be unjustly imprisoned?" Did this ideal die with Justice J. Marshall? "There is no way that judges who know that their careers are on the line when they rule on a case can be impartial, they simply don't have the insulation that a federal judge has," states Stephen Bright of the Southern Center for Human Rights. Many inmates are indigent and can't afford a private lawyer - who can they turn to? What's the *price* of *justice*? Most have nowhere to turn to. A study by the National Association of Legislative Review discovered that over ninety percent of California's incarcerated prisoners suffer from a lack of free community advocate assistance. Need I remind you to help Barry Scheck? "As long as the world shall last, there will be wrongs, and if no man objected and no man rebelled, those wrongs would last forever," stated Clarence Darrow in 1930. "Injustice anywhere is a threat to justice everywhere", stated Dr. martin Luther King, Jr. When inmates are being abused, beaten, wrongfully punished and arbitrarily thrown into the holes in all thirty-three of California's prisons, *something is wrong*. Somebody needs to call Steve White, Gray Davis and Richard Polanco when I'm receiving U. S. Mail that is twenty-five and thirty days old in C.D.C. something is wrong. When inmates are arbitrarily transferred, etc. because somebody does not like them, somebody needs to step in. (Why are you transferring Brandon Martinez and Sherman Manning? Where is Charlie Badakker? Where is inmate Christopher Parker who was in LA County Jail in 1995? Why isn't he in P.C.? What's going on?). This nation is becoming so vindictive and so cold. We kill people who kill people to show that killing is wrong. The USA is the only western industrialized nation that still has the death penalty. Y'all gotta come together and fight the death penalty. I pray may Bishop T.D. Jakes, Bishop Carlton Pearson, Paul Crouch and others who *know the word* will tell their president that we would love a grant from you for our Faith Based Program. But we must also inform you while you write us a check that Jesus Christ did not support the death penalty!

Are y'all reading? All that it takes for evil to rage is for *good men* to remain silent. Jakes says, "When the church remains silent people *die*." I want to (again) plead with my readers (you) to send this book to George Soros, Jason Ziedenberg, John Lott (Yale University), to Senators, pastors and to the media across this country. If these people get this book it may stir something in their spirits and cause them to make a change. Change is what we need in America. How many times must I tell you that even if you forget Sherman Manning do not forget America. Don't forget that it is more *blessed* to *give* than it is to receive. Yes - if I can get a lawyer I'll prove I'm innocent. I need help and you can write me today. I'm waiting on you. You can also help Barry Scheck, the IAC, Amnesty International, the Friends Committee on Legislation, the NALR, etc. These are legitimate organizations that are fighting for human rights. Some of you pastors who are reading my words should sit down today and write a check for fifty dollars, five hundred or five thousand dollars and send it to David

Protess' Center on wrongful convictions, Scheck's innocence project, the NALR and/or the NAACP.

Your money, your life, your prayers and your activism can *make a difference*. You ought to remember that *books change lives* and people in prison *read more* than anybody else. If you help even guilty guys in prison to read something more than *Playboy* you might help them to transform themselves into productive members of society. God and good books transformed Malcolm while he was in prison. So on behalf of all prisoners, I'm asking you to help *me* to get this book to men in prison. Send me twenty dollars, two hundred or two thousand dollars, etc. and help me to help prisoners call Amazon.com and order "Actual Innocence" by Barry Scheck and have it mailed to a prisoner. Send a check to Books Through Bars (4722 Baltimore Avenue, Philadelphia, PA 19143) and they'll send a book to a prisoner. Support Centurion Ministries in Princeton, New Jersey. Send a check to America's Promise, the YMCA, etc. There is no limit to what you can do to make America better for all people and please remember the words inscribed above the U.S. Supreme Court's entrance "*Equal Justice Under the Law*". I'm here to tell you I did not get *Equal Justice* under the law nor did Brandon Martinez, Nathan Hanson and thousand of others. Your help your prayers, your calls, letters, money and compassion can make a difference. As I close I must remind you once again that prisons across this country are failing to do what they were designed to do. I'll use the California prison system as my example. Once again, I want to tell every taxpayer, citizen, preacher, layman, housewife and businessman that if anyone you know of ever comes to C.D.C. they will be forced to join a prison gang! They may (very likely) be assaulted, stabbed, raped or even killed. C.D.C. does not protect non-racist, non-gang affiliated and non-violent inmates. C.D.C. is a complete disaster. It is a monster factory. It needs a catharsis. It should be dismantled from the top down. You the people need to know C.D.C. is *producing* predators, rapists, killers and gang members. C.D.C. is fomenting violence within these walls. Every prison warden needs to be told by the voters to clean it up or close it down. Six hundred and fourteen thousand! Six hundred and fourteen thousand people *will get out of prison this year*. They are coming to your community, your neighborhood and your city. What will they do when they get there? If you're in Oregon, chances are likely that they will get a job, pay taxes and go to church. In California chances are likely they will rob, steal, rape and kill. This is wrong! I get so sick and tired of folks seeing injustice and just kicking back and doing nothing about the wrongs that they see. Damn! Earlier, I mentioned

Attorney Van Jones. Well I got a letter from Van today and I am very excited about it. In a few minutes I will tell you some more specifics about Van and what he's doing to help change America. Remember I talked a lot about police brutality and inadequately trained police officers, etc. well that will coincide quite clearly with Van's story, as you will see very soon. But let me ask you to consider contacting and supporting the following organizations: The Center for Constitutional Rights in New York City - call them at (212) 614-6464. Soul/School of Unity and Liberation in Oakland, CA - call them at (510) 451-5466. The National Congress for Puerto Rican Rights in New York - call (212) 614-5355. We Interrupt This Message in San Francisco, CA - call (415) 537-9437. The Criminal Division of the Legal and Society in New York - call (212) 577-3387. COPA/Purple Berets in Santa Rosa - call (707) 528-9043. Coalition on homelessness in San Francisco - call information in San Francisco. Berkeley Corporation in Berkeley - call information in Berkeley. The October 22$^{nd}$ Coalition - call (415) 864-5153. Human Right Solidarity Committee - call (415) 543-9444. Please contact the above mention organizations and help them. They need your time, prayers, talent and your money. Send them five, ten, a hundred or a thousand dollar check to help them. Tithe to them and use your money in a benevolent fashion to help them to help others. Don't delay - call them today! In fact, I care so deeply about tome of the thugs that some of these groups are doing that I want to put my money where my mouth is. This book is selling for twenty-four dollars and I want to (here and now) give my written permission to any of the organizations I have mentioned in this book (including the IAC, Friends Committee on Legislation, NALR, Ella Baker Center, Bishop T. D. Jakes etc.) to use this book as a fundraising tool. For every book you (non-profit organizations) sell at twenty-four dollars each - your organization may retain ten dollars. Take the order, keep ten dollars and send me fourteen dollars. I was listening to T. D. Jakes again today and Jakes was talking about "stumbling onto the place". It was ironic that I stumbled upon Van Jones today via the mail. I'm telling y'all that God is real. God will see to it that you get what you need, when you need it. If you will ever love people and do the very best you can to keep it real and do good, God will bless you. Paul Crouch almost didn't tell about the personal details of his life. But Paul heard Jakes preaching about "Show me your wounds", etc. and Paul decided to tell it all.

But God said, "keep it real and people will identify. Show them your wounds, your scars, your sins and you life. Tell the truth." And so I did. And sometimes I have to remind myself of what I been called and anointed to do. I may be similar to Sampson and David and Joseph in the Bible. But God called me to do a work and I got to do it. No matter where I am. I'm in the belly of a whale. But I'm still in His will. My work will be done, one of these ole days! Van Jones graduated from Yale Law School in 1993 and founded Bay Area Police Watch, which Van says is the "First civil rights organization created completely by the hip hop generation". They hold rallies, run police violence hotlines and connect victims of police abuse with lawyers. Van opposes the use of pepper spray. I would hope C.D.C. would stop *using pepper spray* on inmates. Bay Area Police Watch has grabbed national attention, opened a New York office and found innovative ways to fight the age-old problems of police misconduct and brutality. Van Jones is a street lawyer. He is very young, energetic and ambitious. At one policy rally, Van Jones commented to a large crowd, "The fact that we're all here together - Black, Brown, Yellow, Red, White, poor, rich, students, etc. is a shock to the system." And Van is correct. When people of different backgrounds and diverse races, etc. come together and stand in unity, the system (be it C.D.C., police departments, etc.) gets scared.

Van Jones grew up in rural Tennessee, and never imaged he would dedicate his life to fighting police abuse. And that's how God works. Many of the Barry Schecks, David Protess, Robert Clings, Willie Browns and Willie Gary's never imagined they'd be fighting the system, freeing the innocent or suing corporate America. But they needed their callings and some of you reading my words right now have a calling that you are not answering. That's why you are so unhappy. You are not doing what you are called to do. This book is a wake up call to action. At Yale while his classmates angled for six figure jobs on Wall Street and clerkships with U. S. Supreme Court Justices, Van Jones fine-tuned his organizing skills. He organized a national campus hunger strike when Bill Clinton refused to stop detaining Haitian refugees at Guantanimo Bay in 1993. His personal awakening transpired when Rodney King was beat by police in 1992. When Jones saw people setting fires and looting he became distressed. "The whole country knows the court system is bullshit and the best we can come up with is to steal sneakers?" Van asks today. "I went home and cried for a long time. I thought there's got to be something else we can do besides just explode." And Van Jones found *something else to do*. He has used his life and law degree to help somebody else. As executive director of the Ella Baker Center on Human Rights Van has gotten in the mix. He has not limited himself and/or his service. He won a pact with S. F. Sheriffs Department on the heels of an inmate hunger strike he supported. In mate Martin "Benzo" Reed called the ACLU from jail. ACLU Attorney Michelle Alexander (a brilliant young lawyer) who is the director of the ACLU's new racial justice project, called to see if Van wanted to get involved. Van Jones went to the jail to visit Mr. Reed and the rest is history. I told you about David Moreno in Book One. Remember he was wrongfully convicted, etc.? There's more to David Moren's story. *"We Interrupt This Message"* and Van Jones orchestrated a humongously successful media campaign around the Moreno/Pacheco murder trial. The media campaign generated global news coverage and led to a major human rights victory. They highlighted racism in the criminal justice system, the scapegoat of youth through "anti-gang" laws, and the prosecutorial misconduct engendered by granting prosecutors wide discretion.

Moreno, Pacheco and Alvarez English were Latino youths who in 1997 fought a group of six White youths. A White youth named Chad O'Connell repeatedly stabbed Alvarez-English in the back; Alvarez-English died in the hospital. The district attorney freed the White youth after he confessed to the crime and charged Moreno and Pacheco with murder instead. He claimed the Latino youths committed a "provocative act" by aiding their friend in the fight and so they were responsible for his death. Moreno and Pacheco stood trial twice. First trial was completely ignored by the media outside of Solana County, CA and Moreno and Pacheco were found guilty. The *Third Eye Movement* (youth group) and EBC provided support and technical assistance to the families and others against this injustice. EBC organized rallies and brought in the media. A judge ordered a new trial for Moreno and Pacheco. EBC and *We Interrupt This Message*, a top-notch media advocacy and training group brought the spotlight on this case. Moreno and Pacheco were found innocent. The more I think about it the more I realize that I may need Michelle Alexander, Van Jones and Kim Deterline. I've been so afraid of media's coverage of my wrongful conviction. I just didn't want the media to focus on the paper trail of my past. I knew that if you look at my past and believed fifty percent of it; you'd fail to see that this case for which I'm in prison here and now is a case in which I am innocent. I've just hoped that a Gerry Spence, a Johnnie Cochran or a law professor, etc. could come to my rescue and work behind the scenes to get me equal justice. Equal justice would fully exonerate me in this case. I did not want my name, my life and my past (ninety percent of which is bogus and duplications) to be aired over the televisions of America. But just maybe a Kim Deterline can help me get the whole story told. I'll have to show the world my wounds. But I am extremely excited about Van Jones, Kim Deterline, Jasmin De La Rosa, J. Imani, Steven Francisco, Chris Zamani and Eva Owens. I hope they will help me get this book to all the youth and student activists across the nation. I need Van Jones, Atty. Michelle Alexander, We Interrupt This Message and Steve Birdlebough, etc. to help me. I want the world to read about what's transpiring in courtrooms across this country every day. Noted San Francisco Attorney Dennis Riordan states, "State courts are now stocked with people who believe their function is to see all convictions upheld. There are more and more criminal cases coming through the state system that . . . by any intellectual measure involves gross violations of constitutional rights and indisputable prejudice." I can relate to Mr. Riordan's beliefs. If I could get Mr. Riordan to see all the errors and violations which transpired in my trial in Santa Monica Superior Court, I know Dennis could get me out of here. Hell, a dedicated first year law student could perhaps at minimum win me a new trial. But I still don't have all the full transcripts of my trial. Altman sealed a lot of the transcripts of my trial. Perhaps he didn't want a Dennis Riordan, a Gerald Uelmen, a Michelle Alexander or a Stanley Greenbert to read the transcripts and to see how they railroaded me. And here I sit in a subhuman environment called prison. I'll flat out tell you I think the California prison system is the most racist, violent abusive prison system in America. It is the worst. "C.D.C. is rotten at its very core," stated FBI Special Agent James Mattocks. It is past time for taxpayers to realize what a threat to public safety and a risk to our children these volatile prisons in America are. I was talking to a nineteen-year-old inmate today. He has a seven-year prison sentence. He is housed in the cell with a forty-eight -year-old inmate serving life without parole. "Where you from?" he asked me. "Atlanta, GA," I said. "You got any speed?" he asked me. "I don't do any drugs," I told him. He went on to explain why he came to prison. He told me how his ex-celly turned him on to drugs and *turned him out* (raped him). He explained that he had been trying to get captains and wardens to put him on a protective custody yard for a year. He was forced to slice (cut/stab) another inmate because that inmate was in prison for a sex crime. He barely escaped being charged and having to stand trial for the stabbing. Then the gang told him to do another hit and he refused. So his celly (owner) beat him up and stabbed him. Older inmates serving life sentences in C.D.C. own any inmate under twenty years of age. It's called *slavery* and C. D. C. is *well aware* of it. This kid will be out of prison in four few years. And he will more than likely become a rapist, murdered and continue using drugs upon his release. And after he molests your child, burglarizes your home, shoots you or kills you - he'll come back to prison and be a hero. He'll return with some war and hero stories to tell. And he will be welcomed back to the hood. In here, he is learning *helplessness*. He's learning anger, racism, violence and rape.

Dr. Seligman, of the University of Pennsylvania, in his book "Learned Optimism" wrote this: "we measured the depression level . . . of male prisoners before and after incarceration. Because suicide in prison is such a prevalent problem, we wanted to try to predict who was at most risk for becoming depressed. To our surprise, no one was seriously depressed upon entering prison. To our dismay, almost everyone was depressed on leaving. Some might say this means the prisons are doing their job, but it seems to be something deeply disturbing is happening during imprisonment."

I think the demoralizing of prisoners is a tough issue, which is epidemic in California's thirty-three prisons. It's a problem in prisons across the country. In the midst of being demoralized, mistreated, abused and beaten; inmates become disobedient and also turn to drugs, alcohol and violence. Any human being who has no influence over his environment will become depressed. In California prisons inmates have no influence over their privileges, release or environment. No incentive to learn, study, follow the rules or improve their conduct. If a guy knows he'll never get out, why obey the rules? If a guy knows he'll be tossed about and arbitrarily transferred by C.D.C. Anyway, then why try to do good? Even housing (celling in general is a mass problem in C.D.C. Inmates are sent packing to the hole at the stroke of a pen. Piss off a racist, authoritarian sergeant, lieutenant, captain or warden and they will invent a reason to put you in isolation (Ad-seg). Stand up (non-violently) for your rights and they will transfer you on a whim. California prisoners are systematically trained to believe that constructive and positive behavior has absolutely no effect on their environment. And they get depressed, frustrated and angry. The one's who don't kill themselves (suicide) instantly, do so slowly (via drugs, alcohol, etc.) and those who kill not themselves kill others. The lucky 614,000 who will come to meet you in your neighborhood this year will carry their learned pessimism, anger, depression and violence to civilian life with them. Again I submit that Gray Davis' prisons are producing predators, killers and rapists. Gray Davis' prisons house them, feed them and breed them to steal, kill and rape! Mr. Davis is totally disinterested in discussing rehabilitation and education, etc. because he is politically ambitious. He's afraid he might appear soft on criminals. He's afraid he might appear too compassionate and too human. Rush Limbaugh might find out that Gray Davis is transforming men's lives behind these walls. And Rush will make it appear as if Mr. Davis was/is coddling prisoners. So Davis allows morals, ethics, compassion, gumption and public safety to go out the window. All he is driven by is his politics, desire to either be re-elected or to run for governor. "Keep those animals trapped in their cages. Give 'em a lil food, let 'em get weapons and drugs, etc. And do not allow the media in my prisons. Keep 'em trapped. Screw education, transformation or rehabilitation. Must lock 'em up and call my speechwriter and tell him to give me some good sound bites to make me appear tough on crime. Get me another three strokes type law and don't let Polanco, Burton or Vasconcellas know what we're doing. I gotta appease the right wing. I gotta raise some more money for my next campaign." Governor (presidential candidate) Gray Davis??

Steve White needs to come see this mess and talk to the inmates who are living in these racist, violent, drug infested war zones.

But my main hope is that young hip-hop activists such as those in the Third Eye Movement, (3EM) Concord and Beyond, Critical Resistance Youth Force, the Human Right Solidarity Committee, etc. will take up the cause of making prisons work and reducing recidivism. I hope "We Interrupt This Message" will inundate the media with *this book* so the real deal message will finally be told (read). I hope young people will rise up and challenge the evils of C.D.C., wrongful convictions and prison violence. I believe it's gonna take the youth. We need a coalition in prisons. We need an oversight committee, which investigates prison guards. One of the reasons prison guards get away with murder, smuggling drugs and abuse of inmates is because C.D.C. covers for them. The thin blue line is a powerful act of silence. They sweep abuse, misconduct and staff racism under the rug everyday. There is a C.O. Woffrey (partial pseudonym) here on ad-seg who is racist, evil, violent and a threat to the safety and security of any prison. You think his captain does not know it? Of course they are cognizant of the fact that this guard who works in seven block (Ad-seg) at New Folsom is abusive and out of control. Yet, he remains in power, in control and on the payroll. A sergeant (R.S.) told me yesterday, "If you were a real man, you'd be on B-yard fighting with the Blacks and putting work in. But you're a P.C. Rat. But your day is coming. When you transfer to Corcoran, SATIF or Lancaster the Blacks are gonna have you for lunch." This guy works on B-yard but does overtime on A-yard once in a while. And this is why even an innovative ladder type system would be stymied in

C.D.C. because with racist, small-minded and renegade cops write false reports everyday in prison. So they would take a carrot and stick program and abuse it. They would use it to oppress and distress inmates whom they dislike. Point blank. I'm sorry to sound pessimistic (because usually I'm an incurable optimist) but even if Steve White had the will to clean up C.D.C. I doubt (very seriously) if he would have the power to do so with the present staff members running rampant throughout C.D.C. It needs a catharsis! And for you guys reading right now who thought I was in prison for attempted murder, I don't apologize. I had to tell you that prison is a terrible place and I should not be here. I am unambiguously, categorically innocent. But a lot of people in prison are narrow-minded, unwilling to think and unintelligent. Some of the very people who know that is Attorney Van Jones who says, "The court system is bullshit," they won't allow for the *fact* that I might be innocent. And as corrupted as C.D.C. is they may transfer me any day, anywhere and I would be killed in certain prisons. So I had to *lie* about my instant offense. The only difference in C.D.C. officials and me is I am bothered when I lie. I feel bad if I lie and I'll come clean. But these officials will tell a lie forever and sleep well at night, no matter what. The sad part of the story is that for those people who are sick, evil, perverted and vicious enough to actually commit rape. For guys who really did rape a woman or man we are not doing a damn thing to change them while they are here. There are child molesters on this yard. And they are just as freaky now, just as sick and perverted now as they were when they came here. One guy collects news clippings and ads out of newspapers of babies in diapers. He cuts out any pictures he can get of any child in underwear, etc. Children!! I'm talking about one, two, three and four-year-old children. And he apparently masturbates looking at these pictures. How sick can you be? But he will be released from the monster factory in two years!!! He'll go home. He is coming to your neighborhood and your community. He should not be abused or killed in prison. But he should be serving a long prison sentence for his horrible crimes. And he should be getting psychological treatment for his perverted treatment. What in the hell do we think we are changing by giving a man a five-year sentence in prison to do nothing except gang bang when he is sick? Shouldn't we punish him and try to cure him while we punish him? Don't our children deserve that from our tax dollars? I have absolutely no sympathy for any adult who harms, abuses or molests God's children. I have a zero tolerance for them. But I know that pragmatically we can't lock them up for an eternity, nor should we abuse or kill them. And pragmatism tells me that most abusers were abused. And simply warehousing them in prison for a few years where they will be re-abused is nothing but recycling child molesters. It does not take a rocket scientist to see this. But Mr. Gray Davis has no time to analyze the roots of these illnesses because he is trying to position himself for higher office. But don't you know the blood of the children is on Mr. Davis' hands for not trying to prevent the revictimization of children. God only knows our children need left and right wing politicians to come together and cut recidivism in half. And this won't happen as long as politicians are concerned about public opinion polls and do nothing to mold public opinion. If Mr. Davis sincerely went to the taxpayers and told them the truth, they would support him: "Ladies and gentlemen, I love politics. I do not want to lose my career. I'm politically ambitious and if I appear soft on crime the right wing will use it to defeat and unseat me the next time I run for office. So I need my supporters to wake up and take note. We have a sixty-four percent recidivism rate in California; our prisons are not working. Guys are getting out in worse shape than they were when they went in. We are warehousing them. Your tax dollars are supporting racist segregation, abuse, rapes and schools on how to commit more crime. We can't lock up everybody forever. We have due process in America. We have equal justice under the law for all citizens. We have laws against cruel and unusual punishment in America. Locking 'em up and throwing away the key ain't working. We have failed miserably. Beginning today every man convicted of a sex crime will undergo intensive therapy, counseling, treatment, etc. While we punish him. Every inmate in my prison will get the opportunity to better himself. If he wants to go to school, church, get counseling, read books that will transform him, etc. we are gonna make it available to him. If he wants to get out of the gangs, stop being violent, live in an interracial setting, etc., we will facilitate and accommodate him safely. If he acts a fool, is violent, does nothing to better himself, won't accept treatment for his sexual perversions, etc., he will never get out. We will make room for violent sexual predators who refuse to get help in prison by paroling non-violent offenders. We will make room by paroling some of these inmates who have been in prison for eighteen and nineteen years with no end in sight. We are gonna model the program in the state of Oregon, etc. We are not going to coddle prisoners. We are not going to treat them as if they were at the Waldorf Astoria. But they will be treated as human beings. As governor I am pledging this day to do everything I can to make prisons effective punishment and a deterrent to crime. I will pledge this day to *reduce* recidivism by a minimum of twenty percent once the next four years in California. By effective, innovative and humane punishment, rehabilitation, education and safe housing. We are disbanding every prison gang including the gang of rogue, racist and renegade cops *working* in the prisons. You deserve a better return on your 4.5 billion dollar investment." If Gray Davis went to the people in this way, help would come out of the woodwork. Van Jones, Dr. Gilligan, Steve Birdlebough, Steve Riggs, T. D. Jakes, Mr. Newell, the Quakers and pastors all across this state would help him. And if Gray Davis cleaned up the prison system and effectively reduced recidivating in this state by a mere fifteen percent he could point to his record on a recidivism decrease next time he forms an exploratory committee on whether or not to run for office. But I have little faith in Mr. Davis' desire to change the system. My faith is in Jasmin De La Rosa, American Friends Service Committees, Youth Making A Change, 3EM, Aaron Bentley, Van Jones, Richard Polanco, John Burton, Marcia Cordero, J. Imani, Sara Greer, Kathryn Galbraith and student activists all over America. I know that Kim Deterline is brilliant enough and savvy enough to cause this book to spark a revolution. Kim Deterline can make sure Spike Lee, Bill Cosby, Sean "Puffy" Combs, Queen Latifah and Chris Gardner hear about this book. Kim Deterline can find Scott Andry at the Center for Coastal Studies, Trevor Loflin, etc. and Kim can get them this book. Kim has the skills and contacts to make sure that every youth activist, every 3EM member, every law school student gets a copy of this book and these teens will mobilize! They will go to Steve White, Richard Polanco and say we are ready to work with you to change the monster factory and reduce crime. I am asking Kim to help me to get the word out about this tome. I want it read by every youth activist in America. And I want it to at minimum cause them to never come to an awful place like this. And again I challenge every reader to support organizations such as Friends Committee on Legislation, Innocence Projects, and Ella Baker Center for Human Rights, etc. with your money. They need help. Somebody needs to get this book to Paul Orfalea (Founder of Kinko's) the copy King and I guarantee you that Paul will help some of the organizations. Paul has almost two thousand Kinko's copy centers and he is a great, altruistic and caring man. He will contribute. Dr. Fred Allman, Jr. will contribute. I know Dr. Allman would give a thousand dollars or so to 3EM, or Friend on Legislation, etc. There are still some compassionate and caring Christians in this country who are *givers*. And to anybody that reads this book and *gives* at least five hundred dollars to any organization I mention in this book I will mention you (unless you choose to remain anonymous) and your gift in the *next book*. I'm *unsure* about the title of my next book, but whatever it is it will pick up where this one leaves off. Again, I need (you) Kim, Van, Imani, Michelle Alexander, etc. to get this tome to the people. Tell Jennifer Gonnerman about this book. Mobilize the Black pros. Call Tony Brown, Susan Taylor, Source Magazine, Earl Graves, BET and all the vocal and national Black pros and tell them to put the word out about this book. And to all my young readers I remind you to stay off drugs. Stay off alcohol. Stay in school use your mind as a sponge to soak up all the knowledge you can find a cause you believe in and fight to make America better. *Use your life to help somebody else.* Call Van Jones and say how can I get involved because I'm bored. Ask Van how you can help to free an innocent prisoner. Ask Van, Kim, or Steve Birdlebough how can I fight crime by reducing prison violence. How can I start an Internet, fax or letter writing campaign to make a difference? When is the next protest, how can I volunteer, etc. There is *work to be done* and we need *you*. I know that Diana Frappier, Jose Badillo, Erica Ballinger, Vincent Ferri, Robert Haaland, Dave Quezada, Michael Snedeker, Dennis Riordan, John Crew, Spike, Sean and Latifah can help me to get out of here. I know you can help Brandon Martinez, Victor C., Johnnie W. and others who should not be here to get out of prison. If Sean, Latifah, Spike, etc. would help us or if Magic Johnson would help us, we would not die here. I need you to help me. Send me your letters, data, finances, etc. directly here at the prison. I am waiting for your letter. I am waiting for your check or money order. If I had a hundred grand, I could hire Gerry, Barry, Dennis or Mr. Cochran to come and get me back home to my family. So I am pleading with you to help me. I am pleading with you to help others. I want my young readers to feed the hungry, clothe the naked, and hold workshops and seminars on leadership, activism and youth empowerment. Even if you choose not to help me, there are thousands of people whom you can choose to help. Be a Good Samaritan. Do the work of a citizen. Don't let Dr. Martin Luther King's dream die. *Revive the Dream! Revive the Dream! Revive the Dream!* You can do it! I want my young readers to put these feeble, corrupted, lackadaisical and phony politicians out of office. Write in, protest in, sit in, pray in, sleep in and vote in to get them *out of office*.

You young people have so much power. I feel like the Apostle Paul as I write to you in the book. I want to encourage you to use your youth power to change America. Use your power! Develop a passion, energy, and a soul force within your being that causes you to change the country. If you don't like something organize and stop it. Get in touch with Van Jones, Michelle Alexander, Gery Armsby and

Steve Birdlebough and say, "I'm ready to serve." This is your country and I know you are sick and tired of the bullshit! Bullshit galore! I do not support teenage drinking at all. So I don't want my words twisted. But I do agree with the young man who wrote me the other day and stated, "At seventeen years of age I was old enough to fight a war. I can join the marines and operate bombs at seventeen years old. But I can't buy a beer 'til I'm twenty-one. This is Bullshit." I know your frustrations. But don't break the law or commit a crime. You just organize and change the law and pool your dimes. Raise money. Do your car washes, fish fries, T-shirt sales or whatever. And take your money to 3EM, or Youth Against Crime, or wherever and let them use it to elevate, educate, inspire and transform. Let's get together and make America better. Get online and hookup with teens, students and youths all across this country. Tell your Internet buddies about this book. Tell your Internet buddies, "Let's use teen power like David Protess' students do out at Northwestern University. Let's organize and strategically, legally help force innocent prisoners. Let's make our communities safe by cleaning up the monster factories. Let's campaign against these foolish laws that don't reduce crime. Let's protect our innocence by making sure that real predators go to jail. And when they get there they are punished, treated, analyzed, educated and they get better. Presently our system is making them vicious, violent, angry, sicker, slicker and (when they get out) they return quicker." You have the power. Every teen, every law student, everybody reading this book must get involved today. We can transform America. But we must temper justice with mercy. We must put up or shut up. Hip-hop generation, I'm calling on you. Rise up and take the country back. It begins with you. You matter. You young White boy in the suburbs, you young Black boy, you young Latino, etc., you are the power brokers. You got the power! I want you to use it now. With the click of your mouse in that computer you can spark a revolution. You can change laws. You can organize, strategize and rebuild the cities, the states and the entire nation. This is your time and this is your beacon call. This is your draft notice. I want you to rise up and get involved. "You must be a dope dealer!!" I was in Richmond, Virginia in 1994. I was driving a signature edition, Lincoln Towncar. I had on a Rolex and a two thousand dollar suit. I pulled up in front of a Gospel Record Store on Broad Street. Two lil Black girls looked up at me and said, "Mister, you must be a dope dealer," need I say more? When eight, nine, and ten-year-old children of any ethnicity have been programmed to believe that if you're Black or Brown and you have money - you must be a drug dealer. You know we are in trouble. I'll leave that alone because that's a subject for another book . . . Again I want to remind you that if you doubt anything I've written within these pages. You can double-check my facts. Steve Riggs can attest to these facts. Every time I call Andrew Young or some of the other folks I used to work with and tell them about the celling and living arrangements and policies within C.D.C. They are mesmerized. "Are you really telling me Reverend that if I came to prison and I wanted to live in the cell with my White buddy whom I've known for twenty years he would be stabbed and so would I?" a Black pastor asked me. I told him that of thirty-three prisons in California and more than ninety different facilities within those prisons there is only one facility that he could cell interracially in. I explained that even if the inmates wanted to allow it staff (the good ole boys) who've worked in the system for fifteen years plus) would foment a riot. Staff poses more racism and threats than inmates. There are many, many White and Mexican inmates who are nowhere near being racist. And many who would have absolutely no problem living in the cell with a person of another color. But they are scared. They know the shot callers will kill them. And they know hard-nosed prison guards will scandalize, abuse and set them up. I told this preacher that C. D.C. is asinine in its policies. If inmates refuse to work, refuse to obey an order, etc. They will lock down the entire institution. Yet, when it comes to segregated celling, they'll tell you, "we can't force inmates to cell interracially." This is a game. Nobody wants them to force integration. What thousands of us want is safe housing. Prison is a microcosm of civilian life. And hell, interracial marriages have some problems in civilian life. Some people look at them funny. Some call their houses and make threats over the telephone. But by and large if I choose to marry a White or Mexican woman, I won't be stabbed or killed for loving with her. In C.D.C. they allow this. So the pragmatic thing to do would be weed and seed. Gangs are illegal. Racism is illegal. So anybody who poses a threat to non-gang members and non-racists must be punished, separated and treated. There is a way to do it.

As I stated earlier, these prisons are getting more and more violent everyday. And there is absolutely nothing being done to make them safe. And even when you can get a politician to discuss reducing prison violence, increases rehabilitation, and reducing recidivism; they want to come up with some asinine plan to diminish inmate's privileges. They want to build programs that say if you don't stab another inmate "I'll give you a telephone call. And they want to bill the taxpayer another eight million dollars. I could be wrong but I think one of the most desperate problems most inmates face is a lack of communications skills. Most of the violence I've seen, heard and read about in prison could be rooted (in someway or another) on the lack of the ability of the inmate to communicate effectively. If you take any man or woman and pump fear into them on a daily basis, etc. and if that person feels like he can't talk to you because he is intimidated or he can't talk to you because he does not speak your language, vernacular or lingo, etc. that person will lash out violently. "Better safe than sorry." And we need to teach communication skills in every prison in C.D.C. Innovative, self-help and self-transformation courses can be taught beginning tomorrow. Guess how much it would cost taxpayers? Zero! Nothing! I was a motivational speaker in civilian life. I'd bill C.D.C. zero for my experience. And guess what? Steve Covey, author of "The Seven Habits of Highly Effective People" will *donate free* materials and books to C.D.C. if we want to begin self-help programs. How do I know this? I wrote him and asked him. But guess what? C.D.C. says *no*. We won't allow inmates to teach any workshops in prison. Why not? Hell, ask *them* not me. We can start a band. We can run our gangs. We can rape each other, murder, stab and do dope. But we can't teach hope. We can't share of our knowledge, etc. Not in C.D.C. Tony Robbins, Zig Zigler, Steve Covey, Iyanla Vanzant, Les Brown and many others would be *more than happy* to send resource materials, videos, tapes and books in if C.D.C. wanted to start a pilot program at New Folsom Prison that transforms prisoners from the *inside out*. We could pilot it for one year at no cost to taxpayers. We could do so and keep statistics on the increase or decrease in violence stabbings, disciplinary reports, etc. And let the numbers speak for themselves. I know Urban Poole, Sheriff Mike Hennessey, Ed Sluss, etc. would help us. I believe Van Jones would help us but it is next to impossible to do anything innovative with old school, vicious, renegade and racist staff members running these prisons. "The Bottom Line is we want inmates practicing on the inside what works on the outside," said Steven J. Ickes who (as I told you) is an Assistant Director of the Oregon Department of Corrections. I guess C.D.C. thinks that racism, segregation, stabbing, rapes, arbitrary and capricious transfers, etc. works on the outside. It's a joke. It is so sad and foolish that I laugh to keep from crying.

"What was your *first* fear the moment you stepped in prison," I asked a twenty-four-year-old inmate today. "I feared surviving. How was I gonna make it? I knew I didn't run with gangs. I knew I was no killer. I feared what would happen to me. Being raped, stabbed or killed. And here are my stab marks. I was stabbed four times before they finally gave me P-C," he told me. Ain't that a **shame**? It is shameful and cruel that Gray Davis has allowed this. I want Van Jones to track the number of suicides, homicides and stabbings in California's thirty-three prisons over just the last two years. And then ask Mr. Davis to point to one program in these prisons that prevent, rape, assaults, murders and racism. I want Steve White to go to Oregon and meet with Mr. Ickes and let's model their program, which is reducing recidivism. I am not asking anybody to just open up the jails and release violent offenders. I'm not advocating that we allow rapists to get weekend furloughs. I do not suggest we pass out condoms in the prisons and have weekend parties for convicts. Hell no! I'm not soft on crime. But we need to be smart on crime and effective on crime. Think about it my brothers, those inmates in isolation units across this state. Those even at New Folsom's ad-seg get no help. They are left there in their cells for twenty-four hours per day. They can't go to church. They get no counseling, no telephone calls, and mail comes twenty-five and thirty days late. And they are consistently harassed by C.O.s like Woffrey (partial pseudonym) every day. Do we really think sitting in a cell twenty-four hours a day with *no* church, *no* books, *no* interaction, *no* counseling, etc. is gonna make an inmate better? And thousands of the 614 thousand who will get out of prison this year will be paroled directly from ad-seg. Picture this - I'm in solitary confinement. I have to beg, kick and bang just to shave or shower. I have not been to church in two years. I have not had a telephone call in two years. I have guards coming by and spitting on my door. I get pepper sprayed every other week. I sit in my cell twenty-four hours per day swapping war stories with my cell partner. Old folks said an idle mind is the devils work shop. I am allowed to go to yard once per week for an hour and a half. And prior to going to yard I have to show the prison guard my anus. Price to returning from yard I again show prison guards my anus. It is now June 5th and I'm going home. Going to the streets. Prison guards arrive at my door at 7:30 a.m. to see my anus and testicles again. They shackle me, cuff me and put a chain around my waist at 7:15 a.m. They march me over to the Release Center. And after fingerprinting me they release me with a two hundred dollars check. That's it! I'm gone! I'm out of prison. Well keep my bed warm because I'll be back. One minute in chains and showing my anus, one minute at the bus station going out to conquer the world. What in the hell would you expect me to do? A seven-year-old child would tell you that you could bet money I'm gonna violate parole. And you will pay (by default) for my re-arrest and re-incarceration. You will pay with your life, liberty or with your child. You may be my newest victim. I may kill, rob or assault you. Again Steve Doel in Oregon who is a victim's rights activist. This man is not a liberal. This man is not a prison rights activist, quite the contrary. But even he says clearly, "The thing people need to know is that most of these folks in prison are eventually going to come out again. So we think it's smart policy to try to change them while they're locked up, so that when they return to society there will be fewer victims on the street." This is a public safety issue. Not a prisoner's rights issue. This is about stopping future rapes, molestations, murders and crime. Can't you see? Can't you see? We need to bring a fresh approach. Steve White needs to call in businesses in the communities. Call the pastors, churches, the Quakers, 3EM, T.D. James, the NAACP, criminologists, penologists and psychiatrists and say, "What do you suggest? Will you help us model Oregon State and reduce crime, reduce recidivism, reduce prison violence and save the taxpayers money? Will you help us change and save lives?" I can hear T. D. Jakes, Chris Gardner, the NAACP, Van Jones, and Steve Birdlebough saying, "We thought you'd never ask us. If you're serious we are more than willing to help you."

My God from in Zion! We can do this! But in the meantime I want to tell inmates not to wait on transformational programs to come from your prison warden. Don't wait on King Pharaoh to soften his heart and offer you help. I want *you* to turn your jail cells into classrooms. I want you to read like crazy. Read, study, pray and save yourselves. You can do it. Yes you can! And I want to remind Van Jones, Steve, Michelle Alexander and J. Imani to help me. I want ya'll to call C.D.C. headquarters once per week to check up on me. Make sure I'm not transferred, in the hole or dead. Check up on me and don't you dare forget that I am innocent. I should not be here. I need help. Dennis Riordan, Ephraim Margolin, Gerald Uelmen, Barry Tarlow or any appellate specialist could exonerate me. Paul Ciolini, Laura Lawhon or my seasoned investigator could dig into my all White jury and find juror misconduct. An investigation could prove prosecutorial misconduct, judicial over reach, perjured testimony and lies. Evidence is waiting to be discovered. I need help. This is not a complicated case. Lome Aseron, Jose Badillo, Robert Haaland, Greg Johnson, Dave Quezada, Van, Kim Deterline, Andrew Shue and Diana Frappier can free me. I need help today. And I want to tell all *inmates* to do for self and kind. If you want change you must change. Change your habits of complaining and inactivity. You can hustle up pruno, drugs, pornography, etc., well hustle up some money, stamps, etc. and send it to Brenda Miller, Van Jones, Steve Birdlebough, etc. These groups are ready and willing to fight for us. But they need more money. They won't get any grants from George W. Bush or even Gray Davis, etc. But you and me our families and friends, etc. can help them financially. Quit complaining and do something. Send that dollar, twenty dollars, one hundred bucks or whatever you can to these groups that can help us fight the good fight. It's time to make a change. And change comes from within. Let's transform *self* and ipso facto, we will transform the world . . .. Lenore Anderson, Jasmin De La Rosa, Steven Francisco, Chris Zamani, Doug Anderson, Patti Boyle, Maria Codero, Brother Reed, Sammi Short and all y'all at 3EM. I need you to spread this book like wildfire. "You know the system is bullshit," says Attorney Van Jones. And I want the world to know it. This book is the untold story of innocent and wrongfully convicted men trapped in prison. This book is the well-kept secret of C.D.C.'s monster factory. This book is interactive and you can help me get it on the Internet. Get it reviewed and written about in newspapers across this country. You can get Doug Banks, Tommy Goss, Susan Taylor, John Johnson, Earl Graves and Tony Brown to give it some play. You can take it to our people who'll read it and do something about what they read. If you need more copies of this book, if you need a thousand copies or a couple hundred, etc. write me a letter today. And we'll get them to you at a reduced rate. Drop me a line. I need to hear from every *soul* intern, YMAC Leaders, and student activists across our country. I need you and to all of you who received this book free of charge, send me my money. Send me twenty-four dollars plus three bucks for postage. I can't make it without your help and I need you to send the money today. Thank you in advance. There are two great speakers of antiquity, Demosthenes and Cicero. When Cicero would finish a speech, people would approve and say "what a great speech." When Demosthenes would finish speaking, people would stand up and declare, "Let us march." I need this book to motivate you to march! Take action on what you have read within those pages. Do the right thing. *Do something today*. I want to send a shout out to Attorney Gary Diamond and William Schmidt. These lawyers are fighting for *lifers* in prison. They head a prison legal clinic in Rocklin, California Senators Polanco, Burton and McPherson also deserve to be thanked....

> *Just a prayer*:
> Most Holy, Eternal God our Father. Lord I come into thy presence with praise and thanksgiving. I thankYou for all thatYou have done. You've been so good. Thank you Lord for the many

blessings that You have given. Oh dear God, I bring Governor Gray Davis before your throne tonight. I bring governors all over America before the sacred bar. I bring George W. Bush before the altar of prayer. Our senators and our congressmen need You. This nation is in trouble tonight. We have become callous, cold and careless. Our greed, hunger for power and our political ambitions have corrupted us. So many of us say that we are born again Christians. So many of us are simply going through the motions. We have men and women in political offices who have blood on their hands. There is spiritual wickedness in high places. We have lost our compassion, love and concern for the least of these our brethren. Lord, even some of our pastors have lost focus on the message and ministry of Jesus Christ. We continuously wait on the great revival of the church and we keep missing and overlooking the message of Isaiah Chapter 58. We keep forgetting what Jesus said to those who wanted to kill the woman who had been caught in adultery. We have lost focus. Oh my God, we need Thee. We need You now. We have stored up our treasures on earth. We have cast our pearls to feed swine and snakes. We have become so materialistic and so vain in our lives. Lord we need You. We need You to deliver us from our greed, hatred and our foolish ways. I call on You to touch our so-called leaders. Help them to stop following opinion polls. Help them to begin to lead, mold and shape opinions. God I pray for men in prisons all across this country. Please transform the lives of those who are guilty. Please send help, lawyers and releases to those of us who are innocent. Touch lawyers all across America and inspire them to help free the innocent in prison. Lord, I pray for the homeless, the left out and the forgotten about. They need food, clothing and shelter. God I pray for our youth. Your word says suffer the little children and let them come unto me. Please protect and bless our youth. Shield them from predators, molesters, abusers and murderers. God help them to choose hope instead of dope. Help them to stay in school, obey their parents and use their lives for good. Lord I pray for the people who are in the trenches doing Your work. I pray for organizations, programs and projects that reach out and touch the less fortunate of our country. I pray that Bill Gates, Jeff Bezos, Chris Gardner, Oprah Winfrey, George Soros, Ted Turner and all those who have wealth will use some of their money to help others. Touch wealthy men and women and inspire them to give love and to invest in the futures, hopes and dreams of the least of these our brethren. America needs You Lord. We need You in the White House, in The Senate, in The Congress, in the schools, in the juveniles, jails, prisons and in our homes. We need your power, grace and mercy. If we have ever needed the power of God before; we do need You now. I pray oh God for victims of crime as well as criminals. I pray for defense lawyers as well as prosecutors. I pray for judges and juries. I pray that You will raise up men and women who will temper justice with love. Raise up men and women who will do justice, have mercy, and walk humbly with our God. Lord I also pray that You will use this book to touch lives. Let somebody get inspiration, encouragement and hope from something within these pages. Don't allow this writing to have been in vain. Use this book for good. I pray for peace, justice, righteousness and mercy. Lord have mercy on the soul of America. Lead us and guide us in the way that You would have us go. It is in Jesus Christ's name I pray oh Lord. Thank you. Amen.

I felt led to do that. I'm not sure why. I want to strenuously suggest that you read "No Equal Justice" by Professor David Cole, "The Debt" by Randall Robinson and "Race Matters" by Professor Cornel West. "There can be no equal justice where the kind of trial a man gets depends on the amount of money he has," stated Justice Hugo Black and I want to tell you that I have pointed out that there are (indeed) hundreds of poor White people behind bars for crimes which they did not commit. It is not always about color. Yet one cannot overlook the fact that this judicial system and its prisons are racist - racist - racist. Politicians sidestep and pussyfoot around the issue all the time. And Governor Gray Davis has failed (specifically) not only to deal with but also even to acknowledge and address his racist prison and judicial system in California. California prisons and its good ole boy wardens and guards remind me of Hitler's Berlin, Stalin's Moscow, and White Supremacist South Africa. The perception and reality of racism contribute to the crime problem in America by eroding the legitimacy of our criminal law and undermining my cohesive sense of community. Blacks and Latinos don't trust or accept many police policies and practices. Their faith and confidence has been destroyed by the double standards they see everyday. When a community accepts social rules as legitimate, those rules are largely self-enforcing. Numerous (sound) studies have proven that most people obey the law not because they are afraid of punishment - the risk of being apprehended and locked up is infinitesimal for any crime except murder - but because they and their friends have accepted and internalized the rules, and they don't want to fail or shame their community. But the rules are ineffective and community pressure to conform is ineffective because minority communities do *not* believe the rules are *just* and that the authority imposing them is fair. This racism and classism in our judicial system actually undermines the system's legitimacy and *increases* crime and its attendant costs minorities today feel less compelled to cooperate with the system whether by giving leads to police, testifying for prosecutors, or entering guilty verdicts as jurors. We need to rethink American (so called) justice. The United States has the second highest incarceration rate of all the developed nations in the world. We need to restore legitimacy to our system. But even more we must endeavor to restore communications, which have been doubly ravaged by crime and the criminal justice system. We must reinforce and support community-building organizations in the inner cities (such as 3EM) and transform the way we respond to crime itself. Our present crime policies have robbed inner city neighborhoods of entire generations of young men. Our present response to crime today is a self-defeating ploy. By stigmatizing criminals, cutting them off from their communities and fostering criminal subcultures that encourage further criminal activity we fail. If we want to reduce recidivism, we need to adopt measures that seek to reintegrate offenders into the community, and that reinforce social ties within and across neighborhoods. Unless all Americans begin to see the problem of bias and racism in the justice system as their own, and unless we take responsible measures to respond to it, America's crime problem and racial divide will eventually explode! And what the hell is Gray Davis doing to restore confidence in the justice system amongst Blacks, Hispanics and poor Whites? Not a damn thing except building more prisons, fewer schools, locking them up and throwing away the key. Again, "As long as the world shall last there will be wrongs, and if no man objected and no man rebelled, those wrongs would be lost forever," stated Attorney Clarence Darrow. That's why Murray Janus, Gerry Spence, Bobby Lee Cook and Mike Snedeker, etc. must continue to object. How can we explain away unequal justice in America? How in the hell does Clarence Thomas or Ward Connerly sleep at night? Was Thurgood Marshall's work in vain? I say to Mr. Clarence Thomas (I hope y'all get this damn book to him. Send him a copy) that Dr. Martin Luther King, Jr. would roll over in his grave if he saw the way you have conducted yourself in the Supreme Court. I am not in the least perturbed by the fact that you married a White woman. I believe that love is colorblind and so should justice be colorblind. But you (Mr. Clarence Thomas) know darn well justice in America is not colorblind and you have not done a damn thing to rectify the bias, the prejudice and the racism in the justice system since you were appointed as a house (n -----) Supreme Court Judge. You can't (nor can anybody) explain away the fact that politicians impose the severest criminal sanctions on conduct which they and their constituents are least likely to engage in a majority White congress has mandated tough prison sentences for the possession and distribution of crack cocaine one hundred times more severe than the penalties meted out for powder cocaine. Blacks comprise more than ninety-one percent of those found guilty of crimes involving crack, but only twenty-one percent of those found guilty of powder cocaine crimes. By comparison, when young Whites began smoking weed in large numbers in the mid 1960's and 1970's, state legislators responded by reducing penalties and in some states decriminalizing marijuana possession. If the Black/White incarceration rates were reversed and Whites were locked up at seven times the rate of Blacks, the heavy reliance on incarceration would not be tolerated. "The White majority can afford the costs associated with mass incarceration because the incarcerated mass is disproportionately non-White", stated Dr. Akbar. "When Black people in LA see a police car approaching they don't know whether justice will be meted out or whether judge, jury and executioners is pulling up behind them," stated California Assemblyman Curtis Tucker. Those same fears apply in Cincinnati, New York, Philadelphia etc. Those same fears apply in prison when eight prison guards walk up in front of your cell carrying batons, pepper spray and guns. New Folsom's Ad-seg Officers routinely "tune up" (beat down) inmates. And these tune-ups, beatings and brutal attacks transpire at Corcoran, SATF, San Quentin, Lancaster, Mule Creek, and High Desert and in every prison in the State of California. Statistics show most inmate complaints of brutality are dismissed out of hand. And C.D.C. merely transfers complaining inmates from one monster factory to another. Who can prisoners turn to? Gray Davis? Who can poor Whites, Blacks and Hispanics in the inner city turn to? John Ashcroft? The Supremely White Court? Black Uncle Clarence Thomas and his White brethren have immunized a wide range of law enforcement from any Fourth Amendment review. This is wrong! But these people are politicians. Just as Gray Davis is a politician. If brother Gray had any true interest in justice, he would clean up and clean out his prisons. Why won't he appoint a Stan Simrin, George Kendall or a Michael Snedeker to represent me on appeal? It's a pipe dream. In Gray Davis' state I was tried and convicted by an all White jury. (Jasmin De La Rosa - I know you're reading. Don't let me preach to the choir; get this book to Mr. Davis!) I want Clarence Thomas, George W. Bush and Gray Davis to explain this nightmare to me. I am open-minded. George W. is (according to his profession to purportedly be born again) my Christian Brother. He (George W. Bush) says he is not a racist. And I know damn well I'm no racist. So can't we have a dialogue on statistics? Can't one of you reading ask our president who promises to leave no child behind to explain this to me? Let's consider this: In 1992 the U.S. Public Health Service estimated, seventy-six percent of illicit drug users were White, fourteen percent Black and eight percent Hispanic. Yet Blacks make up nearly forty-two percent of all drug arrests, fifty-seven percent of all drug convictions, and seventy-six percent of all sentences for drug offenses. From 1986 to 1991, the number of White drug offenders incarcerated in state prisons increased by one hundred percent, but the number of Black drug offenders increased by four hundred and seventy percent. In New York ninety percent of those in prison for drugs are Black or Hispanic. And this same unequal, unfair and biased, racist, classicist pattern emerges in the treatment of juveniles. I can't even write about the racist, classicist treatment of our youth (our children) by the courts without tears welling up in my eyes. Let me move on. Jerry Dewayne Williams received twenty-five years to life in prison for stealing a slice of pizza in Gray Davis' state. I've already told you of my White friend Alan Stark doing twenty-five to life for *theft of cigarettes*. CA three strikes getting *violent* offenders off the streets? Malarkey! In it's first two years, California's three strikes law led to life sentences for twice as many marijuana users as murderers, rapists and kidnappers combined. Ask Gray Davis to explain this. Taxpayers in a Democratic Governor's state paying more money to have marijuana smokers, pizza and cigarette thieves with life sentences, than for murderers, kidnappers and rapists combined. Mr. Davis? These draconian, expensive foolish laws make police work more dangerous, because a repeat offender facing a life sentence, in the words of LAPD Spokesman Anthony Alba, is like "a cornered animal". "If he know he is going to get life in jail, he is definitely going to up the ante in eluding his captors." Two years into the California laws existence, an auditor estimated that it had cost Los Angeles County alone an extra $170 million. California has built seventeen new jails in the last fifteen years. Almost twelve percent of California entire budget is spent on prisons. California (Mr. Davis) spends more on corrections than it does on higher education! Damn! Damn! Damn! I need to digress and revisit a few issues. Today I journeyed to Sacramento Superior Court. En route I conversed with a Black inmate who is housed on B-yard at New Folsom. After exchanging pleasantries, he began to tell me about the riots which broke out on B-yard in 1996. "The cops set us up. They keep Blacks and Mexicans divided in prison because they know if we unite they'll have a problem. It's all politics. I was there in the riots. I know for sure that cops set the riot up. And when they decide to stop the riots they shot all the Blacks. The only non-Black who was shot received a lethal shot. And C.D.C. internal affairs swept the set up under the rug." As we continued he states that all inmates on B-facility are on lock down. He says they are receiving only two hours yard recreation time per week. The requirement is ten hours weekly. I asked this Black inmate point blank, "What would happen if you moved in the cell with a White guy tomorrow?" He reacted abruptly, "Brother are you out of your mind?" I (candidly) said, "are you racist?" He replied, "Hell no! Some of my best buddies on the stroll (in the streets) are woods (prison slang for White). But if I moved in the cell with a White boy the White boys would kill him and the brothers would kill me. That's real. That's what's up in California state prison. You know what I'm saying. But in the federal system, I would hook up (cell up) with a wood with no problem. Matter-of-fact one of the few people who writes me and sends me coins (sends him money) is a wood!"

That's the story of C.D.C. and I don't care what any prison representative claims; the good ole boys (prison authorities) *set it up* this way. Let me move on. I went to court today for a hearing on this case I have pending. The one in which if convicted I'll receive an automatic seventy-five years to life term. This is, as you know, a case in which my life will be taken for two pieces of paper. Mary Hanlon stone is seeking to finish me off. She alleges that she received a threatening type letter in the mail from me. But wait; unlike most prosecutors, I won't withhold anything. I'll tell you the rest of the story. There was an additional missive. The other letter was apparently mailed to a Sheriff in Clayton County, Georgia. Here's what it says: "Unless you release all Black men from your jail within a week you will be killed." The sheriff says he does not know who I am. He says he has no idea who I am. He indicates the letter did not frighten him, nor did he take it seriously. He says he thought it was a prank, a political statement or someone who had gone "crazy". Yet Deputy District Attorney Debbie Glynn at the urging of D.A. Mary Hanlon Stone is gonna try the case. The two letters were allegedly written three and one half years ago. The Sheriff did not release (no pun intended) any Blacks and he was not killed. A prison lieutenant stated, "Jan Scully should be ashamed. They should dismiss this bullshit case. I think it is your handwriting. But I saw you during the time those letters were supposedly written. You were a nut! You had been in solitary confinement for thirteen months. That hole drove you crazy. And I told them if I heard the 115 (Rules Violation Report) on those two letters I would dismiss them due to your mental state point blank."

I'm simply giving you the facts and you may interpret them, as you will. Can Judge Jane Ure dismiss the case? Sure she can. Will she? No way! Jan Scully's office receives extra funding for every prison case they try. And the DA's conviction record goes up because it is so easy to convict a person who is already in prison. If I had the wealth, which I had in 1994, there would be no way the case would go to trial. Paul Comiskey, Don Heller, Tony Serra, Dennis Riordin or Shawn Chapman would totally exonerate me. But Jane Ure initially appointed Jon Paul Lippsmeyer to represent me. Mr. Lippsmeyer is known for loving the sound of his own voice. I heard he loses nine out of ten trials. He withdrew because his caseload was too heavy. Then K. Druliner was appointed. Her husband is a Chief prosecutor in the attorney general's office. I asked her was there a conflict of interest and she became livid. She strolled into court and told the judge she was withdrawing. She allowed the judge to read my confidential correspondence to her. I told her about the fact that Robert Clancy (who was the initial D.A. in my new case) had discussed this case with me here at the prison. I told her how seventy-five percent of my legal mail was opened and read by the man who used to screen my mail when he was a S&I Officer. I told her how the case was compromised, biased etc. and she told all of this to the judge and Debbie Glynn. Now comes Donald Dorfman. Mr. Dorfman is a complete loser. He may have an I.Q. of seventy-five. I'm being too hard on the guy. Perhaps he means well but I don't trust him. I do not trust him at all. He has asked me to do legal research for him. And he brags about how much Judge Ure likes him, etc. Judge Ure is not going to appoint any lawyer to my case who can/will win it. But don't blame Ure. This kind of inadequate appointing occurs system wide. Had Brandon Martinez been able to afford a private lawyer, Brandon would not be in prison serving twenty-five to life. He would not be in prison. He was barely seventeen years old when he was arrested. If Alan Stark had Barry Tarlow, Alan would not have gone to prison for cartons of cigarettes. And I am not selfish or self-centered in my quest for freedom and justice. I encourage any law student and lawyer to please look into Brandon Martinez' case. He is a young man. A Christian and he is not a murderer. Look into Alan Stark's case. He needs help.

I've already told you how little money they pay public defenders. But let's take a closer look. I want to elucidate this issue for fair, unbiased politicians who are reading such as Maxine Waters, Richard Polanco and John Burton. Let's go back in time. Clarence Earl Gideon we an indigent man in Florida. He was charged with a crime and couldn't afford a lawyer. Clarence claimed that he had a constitutional right to have a lawyer appointed by the state to defend him. A Florida trial judge denied him and he represented himself and got convicted. In prison he sent a handwritten note to the Supreme Court asking it to hear his case. The Supreme Court appointed Abe Fortas, who was one of the most highly respected lawyers in the country, to argue Clarence Gideon's case and he won. The Supreme Court rules that the sixth amendment guaranteed indigent defendants the assistance of a lawyer in all serious criminal trials. Upon retrial, with an attorney paid for by the state, Clarence Gideon was acquitted. Henry Fonda played Gideon in the movie adaptation. This right, which Gideon secured, is central to realizing equal justice under the law because without an attorney a defendant has virtually no chance at vindicating his or her constitutional rights and obtaining a fair trial. But America has failed miserably to realize the promise represented by Gideon's precedent. The decision was handed down in 1963. In today's court our judges simply rubber stamp the issue. These judges need only to provide a warm body with a law degree to poor defendants. These people (such as B. Martinez' attorney) are overworked, underpaid and given insufficient resources to adequately investigate and prepare a defense. The Supreme Court has rubber stamped cases in which lawyers have gone to sleep during trial and come to court intoxicated. Across America we spend $98.4 billion annually on criminal justice. More than half of that goes to the police and prosecutors, who investigate, develop and try criminal cases. Indigent defense, receives only 1.2 percent total state and federal criminal justice expenditures. The courts rules ensure that the poor will get inadequate representation and then be punished for the ignorance of the attorneys the state has given them. The fact that state courts all over our country routinely appoint low skilled lawyers to represent the poor is not a mere error. It is the single most significant mechanism by which the courts and our society ensure a double standard in constitutional rights protection in criminal law! The vast majority of people in prison would not be here if they could afford private counsel. Johnnie Cochran, F. Lee Bailey, Gerry Spence, Barry Tarlow, etc. don't have many clients in prison. In 1992, eighty percent of defendants charged with felonies were indigent. Three quarters of all inmates in state prisons were represented by public defenders. This is not due process. This is fundamentally unfair. And most of the public thinks all inmates backlog the court systems with lengthy appeals, etc. Let me tell you a well-kept secret. States only provide appointed counsel for indigent defendants on their first level of appeal in a conviction on the first level. And wins at the first level. I was *lawyer-less* in my trial before an all White jury in Santa Monica. I found some money and hired private counsel to appeal at the first level. He lost and I ran out of money. He did not even send me all my trial transcripts. And the court has refused to assist me in getting the transcripts from my lawyer. In most state criminal cases, there are nine stages of review after the initial appeal, including two separate sets of appeals through the state system and a separate review process known as habeas corpus, in which a defendant is allowed to present his constitutional claims to the Federal Courts. Yet I cannot obtain a lawyer to represent me in any of those other eight levels. If Governor Davis was serious about justice and knew that I belong here - why not *appoint* Don Heller, Tonny Serra or any reputable lawyer to continue my appeal? Why does the right to counsel end after one appeal for the poor, but extend to nine levels of appeal for the rich? Equal Justice? Poor conviction representation is often more important than pre-conviction layering. How can an indigent defendant deal with matters such as the fairness of the trial judge, the prosecutor's failure to turn over exculpatory material, or the significance of newly discovered evident? We can't! How can we develop evidentiary hearings? We can't! This is a long, long way from equal protection and due process under the law. Richard Polanco, John Lewis, Joe Biden, Maxine Water, and John Burton: I'm telling you (politicians) I am one hundred percent innocent of my conviction. Why don't you appoint Van Jones, Michelle Alexander to obtain my transcripts and appeal my case?? This is America! Poor Blacks and Hispanics end up getting a Ron Click, or a John Frank Cannon to represent us at trial. They dump us into the monster factory and leave us here to die. Then we get here and staff plays us against each other. They keep us *at war*. And the public doesn't know, don't show or just don't give a damn. Prison officials routinely pin a prison murder on an inmate. The inmate gets a Donald Dorfman as lawyer. He interviews the inmate once (thirty minutes) before trial. And Jan Scully's conviction rate goes up, up, up and away. Better lawyers (Michelle Alexander, Tony Serra, Ephraim Margolin, Mike Snedeker, etc.) raise more issues, investigate and litigate more aggressively, and identify more constitutional errors. Alan Dershowitz, Steve Bright, Gerald Uelmen or David Coles would turn my case right side up if they read my trial transcripts. But B. Martinez, Alan Stark and *all* poor inmates get poorly funded, overburdened and often unqualified lawyers. And (remember) the right to a lawyer is the linchpin of equality in the criminal justice system, yet differences in the quality of legal assistance available to the rich and poor play the most *significant* systemic role in maintaining a *double standard* in criminal justice. These constitutional rights are only as good as the lawyer one has to assert those rights. Poor defendants who are according to the law presumed innocent do not get a fair shake. Something is wrong. "This shitty system is only covered in a veneer of legitimacy," states John Paul.

I must admit that prior to 1995 even I did not know that poor defendants did not get appellate attorneys after the first level of appeal. Even Oprah Winfrey was not cognizant of this fact. She asked Betty Ann Waters why she had to go to law school to get her brother out of prison. She said "Aren't there plenty lawyers out there?" She did not have a clue. And many of you (prior to this tome) absolutely had no clue that poor inmates get no free lawyer to represent them in the other eight levels of appeal after they lose the (rubberstamping) first appeal. Many of you had no clue about the racial segregation of inmates that transpires in every California prison. Many of you had no idea that there are members of racist militia's running the prison system right here in CA. If anybody wants to challenge that fact you can contact Attorney Morris Dees in Birmingham, Alabama. And have Morris contact me. I'll give him names and I guarantee that he will be able to track these people through his *Klan witch* database. Right here at New Folsom prison, which is right outside the State Capital, (I'll remind you) there is not a single Black program administrator at this prison. No (zero) Black captains. But I blame some of that on the Black staff that are here. Every Black lieutenant, sergeant and C.O. in the state ought to file a class action lawsuit against C.D.C. for racist discrimination. They should complain loudly to the State Department of Fair Employment and Housing. If enough of them complained, action would be taken. C.D.C. is an extremely political organization to work for. "Half of the captains, associate wardens, etc. in C.D.C. are unqualified. They got their bank in the good ole boy system," stated a twenty-three-year veteran of C.D.C. It's that way with the inmates also. The captains call the shots on who gets inmate jobs. You all have eighteen inmate clerk jobs on C-yard. Only two Blacks work those jobs. You see White inmates working in the watch office sixteen - eighteen hours per day. But if a Black inmate is assigned as a clerk they will *delete* the job before they give him the job. When C.O. - King (Black) and C.O. - Wheeler (Japanese) were assigned to S&I they *delete*d the jobs. The only Blacks or Browns they allow in S&I are the one's they can control and who won't think for themselves. I've undergone twenty-three years of being passed over. I have a *Master's Degree* and I can't make lieutenant or captain. None of the White captains at New Folsom graduated from a four-year college. These guys grew up in hick towns where they never interacted with any Blacks. They hunt, drink beer and fish and now they are running the prisons. Some of them *mean well* but they're just racist. Almost every C.D.C. lieutenant, captain, associate warden and warden I have met can be summed up in one word - *Duplicitous*!! Period. (I'm digressing). Senator Polanco, Burton and all of you who received this book free of charge; send me my money. There is nothing unethical about sending me twenty-four dollars (or more) for this book. And if you want to remain anonymous - just get a money order made out to *Sherman Manning J98796* (instead of a check) and utilize a pseudonym and no one has to know who sent it. It is entirely legal. Ask your lawyer. And I need everybody reading to tell somebody else about this book. If it has seemed that thunder is raging in my belly and lightning is flashing in my spirit as I have written this book; it is true. I can't stay here much longer. I need Rubin "Hurricane" Carter, law students, Michelle Alexander, Van Jones, Gerry Spence, We Interrupt, David Cole and Charles Ogletree, etc. to help me get *out of here*. I am *innocent*. I have not seen my family in more than six years. I am three thousand miles away from home. Get this book to Bishop T.D. Jakes, Spike Lee, Sean Combs, Deon Sanders, Michael Irvin, etc. and tell 'em I need *help*.

Solutions - we can free the innocent and set the captives free if we work together as one nation under God. If sincere politicians such as Richard Polanco, John Burton, Maxine Waters, Joseph Biden, Ted Kennedy, etc. will put politics aside and demand that the innocent be set free. If they would ally with Van Jones, Steve Birdlebough, California attorneys for criminal justice, the Innocence Project and law professors, etc., we could weed and seed the innocent out of prison. Judge Barry Loncke had an idea about establishing a committee similar to South Africa's Trust and Reconciliation Committee to get innocent offenders out of prison. Mr. Polanco, Mr. Burton, Mrs. Waters, Steve White etc. need to call Judge Loncke and *set it up*. I'd be willing to bet that Barry Scheck, Peter Neufeld, David Protess, Robert Cling and many professors and law students would be willing to help Governor Davis (and all governors) if they got serious about freeing innocent prisoners. Every inmate who was convicted by an *all White* or *all* anything jury ought to be seriously considered for at least a new *trial*. How difficult would it be for any governor to say to a *bipartisan* team of legal *experts*, "Look at these transcripts and report back to me. All I want to know is did he get a fair trial? Was he convicted fairly? Is he guilty beyond a reasonable doubt?" And these governors can't claim,

"I'm not going to interfere with the appeals process, etc." Why are there nine levels of appeals if the first eight never get it wrong? And if the rich can get a lawyer to carry their appeals through the entire nine levels - why should we abandon the indigent inmate's rights? How difficult would it be for Governor Davis to call Judge Barry Loncke and say, "Why do you feel we need a committee to determine who was wrongfully convicted and who should not be in prison?" For that matter (with all due respect, because I happen to admire these people) how difficult would it be for Senator's Polanco, Burton or Waters to call Professor Gerald Uelmen, Professor Chemerinsky or Dennis Riordan and say, "I want you to do me a favor. Please read Sherman Manning's trial transcripts and tell me three things: A. Did he get a fair trial? B. Was he convicted by the rules. C. Was he proven guilty beyond a reasonable doubt?" I believe with all my heart and soul that Yale Law School graduate Van Jones, or Attorney Barry Tarlow, Stanley Greenberg, Ms. Alexander, David Cole or some legal expert (unbiased) would read my transcripts if any senator asked them to. And let the chips fall where they may. I know I'm innocent and I know that there are others. Too many people are dying here for crimes they did *not* commit. They fit a *profile* or they had a prior *record* or they were poor, etc. But remember **Richard Jewell** (Atlanta, GA) fit the FBI *profile* of a *bomber* in the Olympic Bombing. But he was innocent. Racial profiling is illegal. Criminal (history/record) profiling should be banned. The question *must be* "Did he commit this crime?" Let us set the innocent free. I want the Black media to call Governor Davis and our senate and ask them "When will you ally with Judge Barry Loncke and set up a Blue Ribbon Task Force on wrongful convictions?" I want the Sacramento NAACP, ACLU and all of you to demand that we save the taxpayer's money by purging the system of innocent men and women. Let's clear up prisons all over this country; let us reduce recidivism. Let us disband prison gangs. Let us restore order and stop prison violence. We can (as I've advised) model Oregon State's prison system. Inspector Generals such as Steve White need to study Oregon, the Scandinavians and the Swiss. Taxpayers deserve a better (safe) return on their investment. Citizens deserve to be safe and more secure. They will never (ever) be safe when 614 thousand violent, vicious men who have lived in violent, racist and segregated prisons such as these in California are getting out or prison *this year*. We must study and implement systems which work. Governor Davis. We do not need any more expensive three-year studies. The Little Hoover Report pointed out some of the major problems with your prisons and you have done absolutely nothing about the data, which they provided, to you. Mr. Davis - how would you feel if one of your relatives came to prison and was serving a five year sentence. He called you to say "Gray I am scared out of my mind. I committed a crime and the judge sentenced me to five years in prison. The Loss of Freedom is my punishment. But I'm seeing Black folks mistreated by staff. I have been given one day to either join the Aryan Brotherhood, Nazi Low Riders, and Skinheads or get a *daddy*. What can I do? I went to the captain and he told me to be a man. Is being a man equated with being racist, belligerent, violent and evil? If I join these groups, I may never get out. You know Jan Scully loves to re-charge inmates in prison. Please, get me out of here. How did you allow these prisons to get like this?" America must stop relying on incarceration as our primary response to crime. We should be embarrassed that the *only* country in the world that incarcerates more of its people is *Russia*. We must rethink our approach of criminal justice and implement a community-based criminal justice system. We must take seriously the role that a cohesive community plays in deterring and preventing crime. This kind of police would strengthen rather than destroy communities and barrios. Rather than building more prisons, meting out longer sentences, and locking up more men, let us focus on reinforcing the community ties which prevent crime in the first place, reinvigorating neighborhood associations involving the community in punishment and rehabilitation, utilizing alternatives to prison and reintegrating offenders into society. Only if we take the community seriously will we break the vicious cycle in which crime and law enforcement disproportionately harm the poor. Mass incarceration radically severs ties between lawbreakers and their communities. Mass incarceration places men in a setting where the only *communities* available are criminal subcultures. We must organize youth activities that provide an alternative to gangs, guns, drugs and violence. We must manipulate, motivate and encourage teens to stay in school. School attendance prevents crime. A 1996 Rand Corporation study found that programs, which offered incentives to disadvantaged youth to finish high school, were far more cost effective in reducing crime than three strikes and you're out legislation. This study estimated that, dollar for dollar, such incentives programs reduce crime four times as effectively as Mr. Davis' three strikes and you're out legislation. We must keep kids in school and out of adult prisons. Throwing kids in prison is like poking out their eyes and then punishing them for not being able to see. When we simply remove a man from the law-abiding community and introduce them to a law-violating community in prison, we cripple them. Once convicted and sent to prison most can't vote, can't enter the military, etc., etc. They can't ever serve on a jury. They are limited, limited, limited. Upon being released we do nothing to reintegrate them into society. We should even consider reiterative shaming. Australian criminologist John Braithwaite advocates reiterative shaming. He points to Japan as a model for successful use of reiterative shaming. Japan is the only nation with a crime rate that is lower today than it was during World War II. Japan has one of the lowest crime rates in the entire world. In 1995, there were only thirty-two gun murders in Japan and 13,673 gun murders in America. We have only two times Japan's population, yet we have more than four hundred times as many murders! Japan also *solves* more of its reported crime than America does. Japan's justice system relies more on informal processes such as apology, confession and forgiveness rather than formal conviction and incarceration. Less than six percent of those convicted of crime in Japan serve jail time, compared to thirty-five percent of those convicted in the U.S. Japan focuses on extensive voluntary community networks dedicated to crime prevention and rehabilitation. In 1970 Japan had 541,000 local *crime* prevention associations, 10,825 vocational unions for crime prevention, 127,000 volunteers engaged in street work with juveniles, 8,500 big brothers and sisters for delinquents, 320,000 volunteers in the women associations for rehab. 80,000 volunteer probation officers, 1,640 volunteer prison visitors, 1,500 employers willing to provide jobs for probationers and ex-cons and 2,030 police school liaison councils. At every level of Japan's justice system officials are required to be lenient for the purpose of facilitating reintegration into the community. America's system of justice via new laws and massive incarceration is very different from Japans. We need to study Japan and the Centro Sister Isolina Ferre, a Catholic Organization in La Playa, Puerto Rico. I am well cognizant of the fact that appearing soft on crime is the kiss of death in today's politics. But there are limits to our unrelentingly tough on crime approach. One is economics. Two is the failure to work. Three is public safety. Incarceration is hideously expansive. It costs more to send a man (yearly) to jail than it does to send him to Yale. Even former federal drug czar Lee Brown stated, "You can't incarcerate your way out of the drug problem" and crime in the streets. It is time for innovative and creative leadership. Community based justice is not soft on crime. The preventive elements of this policy, community policing, the incentives to stay in school, youth activities - seek to prevent crime before it occurs. The reactive part stresses the importance of public support. We must come together and save the nation. "We must delight in each other, make others conditions our own, rejoice together, mourn together, labor and suffer together, always having before our eyes our community as members of the same body," stated John Winthrop, the first Governor of Massachusetts. Some of the most successful community-based anti-crime and reiterative efforts today are operated by the Nation of Islam, which actively recruits converts in the jails and prisons and offers strong social networks to help them stay clean and straight after they get out of jail. I believe that since we are well cognizant of the fact that it is politics as usual in Washington, etc. Every church, every pastor, every bishop ought to reach out to prisoners. Not just with a Bible and a prayer. But also with a lawyer, a job, workshops and reiterative programs. Since we know that it is our people in these prisons we ought to save them. Governors obviously don't give a damn. They will have to answer to God for much of what they are doing. Remember that many of them claim to be *born again Christians*. How can a Christian have no mercy and no compassion? When you rob a man of his freedom you are not only punishing him. You punish his family. I'm in a California prison. California refuses to transfer me to a Georgia prison. I have no family, no visitors, nobody in California. It is barbaric and draconian for Governor Davis to allow my family in Atlanta, Georgia to never see my face again when there are many prisons in Georgia where I could serve time for this wrongful conviction. If my mother or grandmother (God forbid) were to have a heart attack and die because they love, miss and worry about me and because they have not seen my face in six years. Then their hurt, their pain, their tears, their blood would be on Gray Davis' hands. I call on Ron Sanders of the Sacramento NAACP. I call on Catherine Henry, Van Jones, Michelle Alexander, etc. to investigate and sue C.D.C. I call on every law professor in this country to do something to save our youth. Get the innocent out of prison and create programs to rehabilitate them in prison. If David Protess and Robert Cling can do it, I know damn well David Cole Charles Ogletree, Willie Gary, Gerald Uelmen can take on two pro bono cases per year. It's a sin and a shame that I can't find *one* prominent attorney, law professor nowhere in America who will just obtain (I can't get them) and review my trial transcripts. It is not supposed to be this way in America. *Not in America*. I need help somebody please help me. Use the WWW and find Brian Haley in Modesto, CA and get his address to *me*. I'll send him this book. Maybe he'll start a letter writing campaign to Mr. Uelmen, Gary, Cochran, Neufeld, Cling, Tarlow, Polanco, Burton, etc. to get me free. Please take action on what you read in this book. This is not a novel and it is not fiction. This is real. I am begging you to support (financially) those groups that are trying to do good. Van Jones could help me if you all donated more money to the Ella Baker Human Rights Center. Steve Birdlebough might be willing to help me find a law professor to review my case if you all supported the Friends Committee on Legislation. "Though I speak with the tongues of men and of angels and have not charity (love), I am become as sounding brass, or tinkling cymbal", I Corinthians Chapter 13, verse 1. I suggest Mr. Davis, Mr. Bush and all politicians read the entire 13th Chapter of I Corinthians and read the 8th Chapter of St. John. They wanted our Lord to allow them to stone a woman who had been caught in the very act of breaking the rules. She broke the law. They wanted to condemn her according to the rules. What did Jesus do? What did he say? Mr. Bush you say you are born again. Are you spiritually blind? Mr. Davis, are you spiritually blind? Don't you see something evil, racist, immoral, wicked and demonic about the death penalty, spending more on prisons than schools and allowing idle wickedness to run rampant in your prisons? Mr. Davis are you going to be like Mr. Bush was when he was Governor of Texas and *ignored* letters from Christopher claiming innocence? Yet, this Governor (George W. Bush) knows our Bible says, "Ye shall know the *truth* and the *truth* shall set you free". But Mr. Bush ignored the truth and it took Barry Scheck to set the wrongly convicted prisoner free. Mr. Davis, you've been served notice that I am *innocent*. No matter what *they* say about my record, profile, history, etc. I did *not* commit the crime for which I am doing time. I am unequivocally innocent. What will *you* do? Ignore me? *God* will hold you accountable.

Attorney Van Jones, Attorney Alexander, 3EM, Mr. Birdlebough, F. Lee Bailey, Gerry Spence, Johnnie Cochran, Willie Gary - *Please help me*. I am in a racist, evil monster factory and I am innocent. I have sinned. I've done wrong before. I've made many mistakes. But I did *not* commit this crime. David Cole, Charles Ogletree, Morris Dees, Steve Bright, Stanley Greenberg, Michael Snedeker, Lisa Short - please get me equal protection under the law. Shaquille O'Neal; I love you bro. I need less than you (Shaq) earn in one game to get Dennis Riordin, Mr. Snedeker, or Mr. Spence to get me out. Denzel Washington, Magic Johnson, Edward James Olmos, Ramsey Clark, Earl Graves, Susan Taylor, y'all please *help me*. Whatever you do, do it with love and never forget our children. Please save the children. They are *our* tomorrow. Let us come together and transmogrify the youth of our world. Save the children. *Save the children*.

Nelson Mandela became an activist and a leader at a young age. You young people can follow in the footsteps of great leaders like Nelson Mandela, Mahatma Gandhi, Dr. Martin Luther King, Jr. and do something to make the world better. Put down the guns, stay away from drugs and violence and use your life to make the world better. You are somebody. You have been called to dream bold, bodacious, hopeful and majestic dreams. You can make those dreams become reality. *Yes you can*! Let me also challenge prisoners to get up and do something to *change your lives*. Every prison ought to have a *reading institute*. You can organize it. Reading is not only a great escape, but reading is empowering enlightening and it is the greatest source of inspiration know to mankind. Use your *time* to learn, to grow and to develop your mental capacity. Get "long walk to Freedom" by Nelson Mandela. Read "Mean Justice" by Edward Humes. Read "No Equal Justice" by David Cole. Get "Journey to Justice" by Johnnie Cochran. Exercise your mind and spark your intellect. Stop laying around complaining and do something for yourself. Go read "Makes Me Wanna Holler" by Nathan McCall.

You don't need permission from the warden to read. It will free your mind and help you to find hope, a way out of no way and to transform yourself while you are incarcerated. Your mind need not be incarcerated. If y'all would ever organize your families, we could transform the system. Tell your family to contact Van Jones, Brenda Miller, Steve Birdlebough or the Friends Committee on Legislation. Pool your resources and organize our people. Write the NAACP, Jesse, Al Sharpton, ACLU, etc. and tell them we want jail and prison chapters of their groups. Ask the NAACP, ACLU, etc. to send books to your prison so you can begin a reading institute. Write local pastors and instead of begging for a handout - ask for a hand up. Ask for books. Organize think tanks, workshops, etc. for self-improvement. Let's elevate our minds and get ourselves together. Let me encourage, also rich lawyers, entrepreneurs, physicians, etc. to send a book to a prisoner. Write me and I'll send this book to any jail or prison in the nation. I'll ask Van Jones, Ms. De La Rosa, Imani, Brenda Miller, Steve Birdlebough, etc. to help me get this book to prisoners. So please send me some funds and send me the name of any prisoner you want this book to go to. If you don't know anyone, specifically, in prison but would still like to help, etc. just send me a check. I will ask Ron Sanders at the NAACP, Van at Ella Baker Human Rights Center, Brenda Miller, the I.A.C., etc to give me a list of prisoners to send this book to. Prisoners write the I.A.C., Brenda Miller, ACLU, Van Jones, etc. all the time and these guys need this book.

Last but not least, let's get this book into law schools. I want law students to *read this book*. I'll end the challenge where it began, Youth! Youth! Youth! I need my young folks to set fire to this book and spread it around the nation. Put the word out! Get on the Internet and find everybody I mentioned in this book and tell 'em, "You better go get it. If it doesn't fit, you must acquit Part II." Remember to read everything you get your hands on. Read! Especially non-fiction books. Let your mind become a sponge for knowledge.

Let me ramble a moment; I want to thank Pat Clark and all of the Quakers at American Friends Service Committee out in Philadelphia. I encourage all prisoners, prisoners' family's lawyers, activities and politicians to read "The Fortress Economy" which explains the economic role of the U. S. Prison System. It is a *must* read handbook and you may obtain it by calling the American Friend Service Committee in Philadelphia. Let me also state (re-state) emphatically that I am totally innocent of the crime for which I'm serving time. I have absolutely no interest in local, yellow journalistic type media interviews. If they want to dig up my past and paint me up as a madman that is not difficult to do. I have sinned. Period. Yet, in 1995, nobody was the victim of any crime committed by Sherman D. Manning. There was no crime. Period!!! "Black (and Brown and poor White) men born in the U.S. and fortunate enough to live past the age of eighteen are conditioned to accept the inevitability of prison. For most of us, it simply looms as the next phase in a sequence of humiliations," stated George Jackson in 1970. I really don't know what to expect next. I do know that I should not be here. And I know for a fact that these prisons (especially in California) are producing killers, rapists and predators. I am also well cognizant of the fact that prisons are big business. They are slave plantations and the American taxpayers are boxing the bill. Someway, somehow the Richard Polanco's, the John Burton's and the people must rise up and spark a catharsis. C.D.C. needs a catharsis. I spoke today with an eighteen-year-old boy who is trapped here for five years. There is absolutely no way he should be here in prison. No way! But if you (the reader) remain silent the epidemic of wrongful convictions, prison violence, renegade cops, high recidivism, etc. will continue to spread like wildfire. But you, the people, have the right and the chance to wake up and change it. Transformational and changing power is in your hands. I want you to go back and reread "The trial lawyer of the century in this book" and I want you to ask yourself "what can I do to change this disastrous problem?" You can get the word out. I am telling you this is a well-kept, well-hidden secret. This book let's the *cat out of the bag*. I don't need you to make the *issue* about me. Yes, I need *help*. Yes, I *know* that any good lawyer, law professor, etc. *can get me out of here*. Yes, I know that financial contributions from Sean, Queen, Spike Lee, Chris Gardner, or anybody could/can/would/will afford me the opportunity to get a Gerry, a F. Lee, a Mike Snedeker, an Uelmen and/or a Dershowitz to vindicate my rights. I know I can get out of here on the evidence alone and I pray that somebody, somewhere is writing me a check today. I also know this is bigger than *me*. This is about the masses of men, caged here like animals and receiving absolutely no help to prepare them to become better people upon their release. This is about children being deprived superior educations in Watts, Nickerson Gardens and in rural areas because all the tax money goes to lock up and warehouse prisoners. This is about a system designed to fail. This is about a bad investment. It is about poverty, hatred, inequity, classism and bigotry. We must change the system for the safety of our children. I don't want my mother or my sister raped by an ex-con who learned rape in prison. I don't want my brother or my sister killed by a former resident of Gray Davis' plantation. I don't want children preyed upon by some of these guys who collect photos of babies in prison. I want to make America better. I want to make our street safe. We can do it! Farrah Gray, Steve Rigg, Michael Taketa, David Quindt, Susan Taylor, Earl Graves, James Shelby, Doug Banks, Eric Dane, Judge Gary Ransom, Judge Barry Loncke, Al Sharpton, George Soros, Larry Holmes, Bill Zimmerman, John Lott, Van Jones, Michelle Alexander, Trevor Loflin, Gerry Spence, etc. etc. Y'all got the power. Use it! Ain't nothing gonna change 'til we unite and take action. We must work together. Each of you reading must get on that telephone, get on the WWW, fax and write letters to every person named in this book and propagate. How hard could it be: "Trevor Loflin (Senora County) I saw your name in a book. Have you read it?" And "Mr. Tony Brown (New York) you were mentioned in a book . . ." It's easy y'all if you'll just take the time to care and act. I love y'all so much. All of *you*. I love you with God's love. Oh, how I wish I could sit down with each of you and tell you my story. You can pull my criminal file (profile) and read *their* story and theories. But I can tell you where it is spurious, prevarication, mendacity and (quite candidly) where it is bullshit. I can tell you the Atlanta story, the Richmond, Virginia story and the California story. Where we end up will still be left with the fact that I did not commit this crime. Ipso facto, I do not belong here in prison. "What about this? What about that?" A conviction of a crime is not about this or that. It's about the facts. Just the facts. Here are the facts: I *did not commit the crime* for which I was convicted in *no way*, shape, form or fashion.

I am innocent! My heart goes out to the family of celebrity Attorney Barry Levin who apparently committed suicide a few weeks ago. It appears that Attorney Levin received some very distressing data about his health from his doctors. It seems he took his own life. To every lawyer who is perusing my tome today, I want you to reach out to Barry's former clients. God bless his family and friends . . . David Broder shook up the media a few weeks ago when discussing Chandra Levy. "If she had been Black or Latino the press would not be all over it as they are". Wow! I send my heartfelt condolences out to the Levy family. I pray for some good to come out of this awful and suspicious situation. I know the parents are hurting. I don't blame them for using their resources to bring the media's focus on this case. I also agree with David Broder. I am well cognizant of the fact that we must use our resources to dramatize the plight of thousands of innocent men in prisons across this country. We must also use our resources to attract attention to the *monster factory* (California's thirty-three prisons) called *prison*. We have power. We must write columnists such as Arianna Huffington, Clarence Page; call the media, etc. and send them a copy of this book. They will respond. We want them to know that the *Energy Crisis* is not the only problem, which Gray Davis has ignored. We want them to know that the billions of dollars Mr. Davis *wasted* on a failed Energy Plan are not the only billion dollar failures he has been a part of. We must let Doug Banks, Spike Lee, Sean "Puffy" Combs, Tony Brown, Susan Taylor and Clarence Page, etc. know that C.D.C. operates on a quid pro quo system, which is out of the 19th century. This "letting them know" can be accomplished through the A.F.C., Ella Baker Human Rights System, and groups such as "*We Interrupt This Message*". But we must press the issue. That is why I'm telling prisoners to organize, strategize and galvanize. We can't do it if we have the shackles of racism, hate and wickedness on our minds. We cannot do it with the chains of violence, ignorance and illiteracy holding us back. There is nothing worse that I've ever seen than an *incarcerated mind* and an *incarcerated spirit*. When we take the chains from around our brains, intellects and our spirits; we will empower ourselves to obtain justice. We will, in fact, mobilize toward liberty and justice for all. I cannot overemphasize the need for innocent men in prison to pass *this tome around*. To read, study, write and grow as an individual. Nor can I overemphasize the need for *every* person (guilty or innocent) in prison to transform yourself from *inside out*. To reform, develop and to acquire life coping skills right where you are now. There is a purpose for your pain. And your ridiculous and awful past (history) is only a set up for a victorious and glorious future. You must aspire to rise up at least as high as you went down or fell down. The lower down you have fallen (guilty men) or have been knocked (innocent men) the higher up God can raise you if you'll only be sincere and work to get your freedom. You must *crave* freedom. It must consume your being. You're got to want it and to work for it. God can do the almighty through the least likely....

In 1996 Sheila Bryan was charged with first-degree murder and arson in Omega, Georgia. She stood accused of murdering her own mother. District Attorney J. David Miller stated the state's case was airtight. Sheila fit the profile of a woman capable of committing fratricide. "She set the car on fire and killed Freida Weeks," stated D.A. Miller. He was successful in selling his theory to the jury. Sheila was convicted and sentenced to life in prison. But not so fast, the Georgia Supreme Court reversed the conviction. The state's high court ruled that the prosecutor mislead the jury. Sheila was released from prison pending a new trial. She got what few innocent and wrongfully convicted men ever get, a second chance. "If you think that because you're innocent that things can't go wrong - you're wrong," Sheila stated. Sheila's community came together and raised money for a new defense. They held bake sales, car washes, prayer vigils, etc. and they retained Attorney J. Converse Bright of Valdosta, Georgia. Mr. Bright is notorious for caring about his clients. Sheila's friends stated, "We've got to prepare her for the next round." Prayer is an important part of Sheila's family. They prayed up on some unexpected help. An expert named Gerald Hurst from Austin, Texas agreed to review the case and testify pro bono. Gerald even paid for his own flight to Georgia to attend the trial. He conducted experiments and pooled empirical data to demolish the prosecutor's theory of the case. Gerald Hurst stated, "I'm interested in cases that use junk science to persecute people. I'm a scientist and their (prosecutor's) experts are full of prunes. Truth and justice don't always prevail at trial." The new trial was indeed a trial by fire. The D.A. refused to let up. He insisted on retrying this woman and sending her away for life no matter what the state's high court thought. His anger raged furiously and it was a sight to behold. The similarity in his rage to that of Mary Hanlon was remarkably obvious. At the new trial Converse Bright confronted the prosecution's expert with earth-shattering evidence of his bias. Gerald Hurst shred the prosecutor to pieces. It took the jury only three hours. It didn't fit and they did acquit. One day Sheila was serving life in prison. A few years later she was free. "There's an awful amount of randomness in our court system. It is frightening," stated Gerald. "To God be the Glory. The Lord Reigns," stated Sheila's supporters after the acquittal.

"People need to realize just how easily this could have happened; even to them," Sheila said.

I salute and commend the community for coming together to help Sheila. If we can get "We Interrupt This Message", Kim Deterline, and 3EM, etc. to help those of us who are here and innocent to tell the world of the shame of our conviction, etc. If we got Kim to help us tell California taxpayers about the conditions of these prisons, etc., I believe that law professors, Uelmen, Spence, Dershowitz, etc. would help some of us pro bono to even the scales of justice. I will remind lawyer, preachers, prisoners, etc. to send financial donations to "We Interrupt This Message" so that they can have adequate resources to help expose C.D.C., my case, my tome and many injustices that are transpiring in courtrooms everyday. I am confident that if we help these organizations, they can help justice to roll down like waters and righteousness like a mighty stream.

We have got to get the word out about what is transpiring in these courtrooms and in these prisons. If Robert Register (Sacramento), Andrew Heyman, Gerry Spence, Ida (NAACP in Sacramento), Tommy Goss and Ron Sanders knew what transpired in my case, they would stand with me. But they don't know because the racist, sensational media won't tell them. If they told my story they would not focus on the evidence in this case. They would simply lambaste my past. But I hope somebody reading can realize that the depth of your history is indicative of the height of your future. No matter how bad a person may become or how low he may sink he is still entitled to Equal Justice under the law. He should not be allowed to spend his life in prison for a crime he did not commit. Bishop Jakes, Mr. Mfume, Jesse, Mr. Polanco, Mr. Kennedy are you reading my words? This place is absolutely intolerable. Prison: "steal a pair of shoes and go to prison; steal a railroad and go to the U.S. Senate," stated Mother Jones. "If you go back in history and plot the population of all prisons.... and compare it to all the other variables you can think of, you will find a positive correlation only with unemployment. The higher the rate of joblessness, the higher the rate of prison commitments. There is no question about it," state d Norman Carlson, Director, U.S. Bureau of Prisons. Jail over Yale? "For every person who goes to prison, two people don't go to college. For every day a person is in jail, twenty children eat starch instead of protein," stated in

American Prisons and Jails, 1978 Vol. 1. Did you know that? "Kids sell drugs to get money, it's that simple. We need to take the millions (billions) of dollars slated for construction and operation of prisons and at least match it with job training and placement programs. If we, as a nation, tried as hard to create job opportunities for unemployed youth as the drug sellers try to sell drugs, the battle would be more than half won," stated Sheriff Mike Hennessey. This is law and order sheriff. Not a liberal. "It is unrealistic to expect (ex-cons) to function as autonomous and independent individuals in society after their release," stated a New York Attorney. "Just think what a catastrophe it would cause if every con across the country decided never to commit another crime. Think of how many different hands I go through from the time I'm arrested. Lots of dollars and lots of jobs. *We* are your *bread* and *butter*," stated Henry Abernathy in a Texas prison. "Prisoners are commodities and a profit must be realized from commodities. A lot of "good guys" make an easy living off the misery of us "bad guys" - Norman Nusser in a Pennsylvania prison for burglary. "We are all chickens for the colonel. Wake up before you find yourself and your kind on someone's menu," states Larry Smith a former C.D.C. prisoner. Governor Davis? These young people in prison learn new criminal skills. All thirty-three California prisons are violent institutions, which breed violent individuals. Dr. Seymour Halleck stated, "*If one had systematically and diabolically tried to create mental illness. One could probably have constructed no better system than the American prison system.*" Y'all better call these politicians and tell 'em "alternatives (to prison) will inevitably fail to become true alternative without explicit policies for reduction in the use of incarceration, becoming instead merely supplementary programs to continue prison and jail expansion" William Nagel, Former prison warden. Wait, I know who Mr. Davis will listen to; a Judge! "The real roots of crime are associated with a constellation of suffering so hideous that, as a society, we cannot bear to look it in the face. So we hand our casualties over to a system that will keep them out of our sight," stated U.S. Federal Judge David Bazelon. "Crime, in most instances, is the product of desperation - despair born out of poverty, community decay, and the sense that the future is merely a continuation of the past, and certainly no ground for hope." U.S. Representative John Conyers stated. Prisons do not protect society from crime. They avoid the more challenging solution of economic justice by reinforcing patterns of economic and social inequality. We need to refocus on making our communities vibrant and safe places to live. America has failed miserably on the social order. Communities are torn apart. But I encourage communities to come together as did Sheila Bryan's did for her. Come together and raise holy hell until politicians stop robbing communities of your children and putting them in monster factories. Raise hell and demand a better return on your billion dollar investments into a failing prison system. If you don't know what to do or how to organize, call Attorney Van Jones in San Francisco. Call "We Interrupt This Message" in Frisco. Call your pastor and the local NAACP and say "I want to help get innocent men out of prison." Tell them "I want to change the prison system and save tax dollars". You can make a difference. Find Matt Hammond at U.C. Berkeley, Tim O'Brien at U.C. Santa Cruz, etc. E-mail every person I have named in this book and say, "Let's get busy". I'm very serious. Don't close the book and do nothing. Close the book and take action. Fax each and every politician I have named and tell them "we want to have a town hall meeting to discuss the contents of this book". If they refuse to meet with you, write nasty letters about them to newspapers and notify the media! Take action today. Not only for me but for every teenage boy trapped here being raped, assaulted and forced to segregate and joining gangs. Call Attorney Eva Patterson and Michelle Alexander in Frisco and say, "We want to sue C.D.C." Get active! Call Rev. Leroy Elliott, Rev. Gilbert Patterson, Bishops and priests and ask them to raise money and help the least of these. Tell them to make Isaiah 58 come alive. You the people can change the world. This is still America. Not communist China or Russia. Not South Africa in the 1950's. You have the power. Exercise your power today. Eighty percent of the facts within these pages will never and definitely have never appeared in the major media. The media paints a Black or Brown face on crime and drugs. The real deal is more White kids in suburbia do drugs than Black and Browns combined. But you won't discover that from the local news. Call American friends Committee in Philadelphia and get the real figures. Not so we can scandalize White people. But so that we can conduct a real war on crime and redirect our efforts to leave no child behind and Mr. Bush can leave no child high on drugs. We, the people can do something. To every teenager reading my words and doing speed, cocaine, heroine (you know who you are) I want you to get help. Drugs are a dead end street. They kill, destroy, disempower and deform. Get some help today. Don't wait another second. Somebody gives a damn. You don't have to be bound by drugs and alcohol.

**_Get help today! Rise above it!_**

"We strenuously encourage the reader to fax, E-mail and telephone the following people: Michael Mallo (Washington, DC), Attorney Don Heller, Hiker Eric Tucker (Bay Area), Charles Whitaker, Ted Shaw (NAACP), Attorney John Payton (Washington DC), Attorney Jeffrey Lehman (Univ. of Michigan Law School), Lee Ballinger (Univ. of Michigan), Rev. Michael Beckwith (Culver City, Agape Int. Center of Truth), Quincy Jones, Laila Ali, Rev. Kenneth Ulmer (Faithful Central Bible Church, Inglewood), Denzel Washington, Magic Johnson, Bishop Charles Blake, Della Rees, Marilyn McCoo, Mason Betha, Frank Wilson, Ollie Brown, Sister Peer, Donnie McClurkin, Dave Hollister and tell them to get this book".

***Publisher's Note***

# For teens and taxpayers only!

"A nation should not be judged by how it treats its highest citizens, but its lowest ones.... (America treats it's prisoners like animals)," stated President Nelson Mandela. "The way a society treats people convicted of crimes is an indicator of the human values of that society," states Marc Mauer of AFSC. I want all y'all who are perusing this tome to grab you a cup of coffee, kick off your shoes and read with caution. I aim to force you to feel the issues of crime and punishment in this section.

I assure you that if you will read with a halfway open mind your view of the prison system will be altered in a dramatic fashion. All along the course of our journey (together) throughout the pages of this book I have alleged and contended that I am absolutely, categorically, and unequivocally innocent of the crime for which I am doing time. However, if you feel that my cry is one of mendacity, prevarication or spurious, etc. I can live with that. Yet, I want you to forget about Sherman Manning (for a moment) and focus on the millions. I want you to make (very) sure that you share this chapter with movers and shakers. Share this chapter with politicians, pastors, parents, teens and every newspaper editor that you can locate. You have my permission (Ella Baker Human Rights Center, Quakers, prison activists, ACLU, NAACP, SCLC, Operation Push, etc.) to put this chapter on the Internet on your Website, run copies of it and send it to jails, prisons and to anybody you want. This is the bombshell. If George W. Bush is a God-fearing Christian, this brother needs to re-read the Bible. If lil bro' Gray Davis has a heart he needs to check his pulse and visit a psychiatrist. No American (liberal or conservative) can walk through any prison in California and leave out without tears in their eyes. These prisons are in a shameful, embarrassing, devastating and detrimental state of emergency. We must get John Lewis, Joseph Biden, Richard      Polanco, John Burton, Willie Brown, Jesse and Al into these prisons. Having seen the truth they can't turn their backs on us! I respect the leadership and legally of Senator Ted Kennedy, Joe Biden and a few others. I am well cognizant of the fact that a few old school politicians are still committed to justice for all! I have faith with all my soul and being that if you help me put this book in their hands - they will take action on the contents. I believe with certainty that Doug Banks in Dallas, Texas, Tommy Goss, the Ratcliffs, Van Jones and Kim Deterline can help this book to rock the nation and create a firestorm. I need you to help me to do better than preach to the choir. Taxpayers have been hoodwinked, lied to and cheated out of their money. Monies, which could be utilized to empower neighborhoods, transform inner city schools, empower churches and uplift our youth. Taxpayers have been robbed while high-level bureaucrats have poured hundreds of billions of our tax dollars into asinine prisons that don't work. Record rates of high incarceration have had very little impact on crime. A disproportionate amount of crimes are committed by sixteen to twenty-four-year-old males. Until (Mr. Bush, Gray Davis, Rush Limbaugh, et.) we address the life circumstances and options of these youth, our pool of potential offenders entering these crime-prone years shall continue to replace and exceed the relatively few who are incarcerated. We cannot build our way out of a prison-overcrowding crisis. We must reconsider alternative responses to crime and punishment. We must realize that prisons do not exist in isolation from society. Social, political and economic factors play major roles in determining a society's utilization of prisons as part of it's overall social policy, contrary to media lies, there is very little relationship between street crime rates and rates of incarceration. Mr. Bush, Mr. Davis, Steve White and the rest of us would do well to consult with Nahjee Ali, Naim Akbar, Mr. Farrakhan and all Muslims because they have been successful at intervening in the lives of prisoners and transforming their lifes. Yet, I doubt Mr. Bush will ever suggest giving Farrakhan any of his faith based dollars! Obviously we need to turn to somebody because what we are presently doing is not working. Prisons across the country are modeling the former Alcatraz and Marion (Illinois), by utilizing revised editions of control units. These are the ultimate places of punishment and sensory deprivation. In these units, prisoners endure "lockdown", solitary confinement and beatings. They are kept in their cells twenty-four hours a day. They have almost no access to recreational or cultural activities, and live in primitive conditions. Prisoners right in California spend months and years in this type isolation and not only in Pelican Bay or in Corcoran. Even New Folsom Prison's Ad-seg is a mere disguise for a control unit. These ad-segs do not only house violent inmates etc. they house any inmate whom staff arbitrarily decides to place there. They house any inmate whom informants decide need to go there. Tonight I could utilize the same ink pen with which I'm scribbling this tome to send any inmate to Ad-seg that I choose. All I need to do is write a letter to S&I alleging that an inmate's life is in danger or that an inmate is going to assault staff. I need not sign the letter. To do so anonymously is considered (by staff) sophisticated. Upon receipt of this baseless, factless, unsigned missive the inmate will be put in the hole. He will lose his job, activities and all the small privileges that come from being in general population. He will be placed in the control unit. I can get his job, cell and even steal his property while he goes off to the hole. "Why won't staff implement a tracking system to verify who sends each letter, or merely suspend the inmates activities temporarily and investigate before uprooting him and throwing him into a control unit?" Good question, ask C.D.C. Rehabilitation is not even an issue for maximum-security institutions. If we want to avoid tragedies such as more prisoners assaulting and killing guards, we must re-examine prisons. Tensions and violence between prisoners and staff can be exacerbated or alleviated by the structure and dynamics of the institution itself.

"True I killed a guard, but no one has ever bothered to ask me why. They only slammed me in my own prison; go out of their way to make it as tough as possible in the name of security and justice and now what? I never thought of killing anything before I came to prison or H-Unit (Control Unit). Although I was sent to H-Unit behind a murder in Leavenworth, it has been reversed. Because the "rat", who said it was me, later confessed he lied to get a transfer to a sweeter joint so he could escape, which he succeeded in doing. So I entered H-unit with a life sentence I didn't deserve and I am mad about it. It has been a nightmare ever since. I'd like to see a better way for all, because murder isn't pretty in any language or moral sense. I'm also an example of how prisons avoid dealing with their own backyards. Not only hasn't anyone ever bothered to rap with me, they don't want to deal with it so they have locked me up indefinitely. They have turned Marion into a concentration camp, hurting innocent men and their families with their oscillated 'get tough' policies, which is what got me where I am today. Not all dogs put their tails between their legs when their masters beat them constantly. Some eventually bite back - men, especially innocent men going through hell for no other reason than being subjected to others overpowering vindictiveness and paranoia will also bite back so how many more bodies will fall and how many more individual 'special housing units' like mine, before they face up to the jobs they get paid well for? More bars and guards are hardly the answer, because I am a living example of what the cage and that way of thinking causes," stated Tom Silverstein, a prisoner. I suggest you go back and re-read his statement. I also suggest you remember that "There but for the grace of God go I". That could have been written by Sean P. Diddy (Jay you better make sure Sean reads this book). It could have been your son or your daughter. Keep in mind that Tom was sent to the control unit charged with a murder, which he did not commit. Innocence means nothing when one is in prison. Prison staffs are well cognizant of the fact that nobody in society gives a damn about the guys and gals who are confined in prison. But if they knew that Susan Taylor, Magic Johnson, Bishop Jakes, Rev. Hezekiah Walker, Chris Gardner, Johnnie Cochran, Willie Ratcliff or the NAACP would show up when a man was arbitrarily punished; they would take note.

"I was completely and utterly isolated. I did not see the face or hear the voice of another prisoner. I was locked up for twenty-three hours a day . . .and every hour seemed like a year. ... . I had nothing to read, nothing to write on or with, and no one to talk to. The mind begins to turn in on itself, and one desperately wants something outside oneself on which to fix one's attention. . After a time in solitary, I relished the company even of the insects in my cell, and found myself on the verge of initiating conversations with a cockroach . . . Nothing is more dehumanizing than the absence of human companionship," stated President Nelson Mandela. He speaks of Robben Island, a prison in South Africa. But there is a striking resemblance to Robben Island and Pelican Bay, Corcoran, Lancaster, High Desert, all thirty-three California prisons and prisons across America. In prison and "in politics one can never be surprised or underestimate how little people (really know about a situation . . . A few hours later . . A captain came to our cell and commanded the four of us to pack our belonging. In prison, one counts oneself lucky to be able to wave good-bye to one's comrades. One can be in extraordinarily intimate circumstances with someone for months and then never see the person again. It is dehumanizing, for it forces one to adapt by becoming more self-contained and self insulated . . . I was taken back to Pretoria. The Department of Prisons released a statement to the press that I had been removed from the island for my own safety because PAC prisoners were planning to assault me. This was patently false; they had brought (transferred) me back to Pretoria for their own motives . . ." stated Mr. (President) Mandela. And all of the above is exactly the manner in which C.D.C. operates. If they think I'm getting along too well with my cell partner (B.G.M.) or settled in too well, they will (and do) arbitrarily transfer me or the other person. They lie and invent an excuse. They specialize in reminding us that they are in charge and they can do what they want, when they wish. And they recognize that nobody (before this tome) in the public gives a damn.

"What is happening here should not be allowed to exist, or be portrayed as the panacea to society's ills. Shorter sentences, and the incentives inherent in a program aimed at self-improvement and rehabilitation, should be the trend and not the exception with education, and not dehumanization, as the rule. The debilitating effects of this Orwellian program can only result in a further departure from society of those already alienated by virtue of their incarceration and economic backgrounds. The consequences of these effects would be the likes of nothing yet seen in American society," stated another American (Marion) prisoner.

"The warden (Governor Gray Davis, Mr. George W. Bush, etc.) has overlooked the logic that until prisons are first supervised in fairness, everyone - prisoners, activists, and prison administrators - sense a feeling of hopelessness and despair as far as accomplishing any of their goals. However, the Bureau of Prisons fails to acknowledge that the situations that presently exist in this prison is a sign or mark left by a gross enological error and should act as a warning to the decision makers of prisons that they must rely on sound judgment and not their emotional feelings in making decisions that eventually affect many lives including their own. The public must begin to examine whether or not alternatives are being utilized to the fullest extent possible to bring about more humane conditions inside the nation's prisons. One thing is for sure, the repression that is constantly being invoked inside prisons cannot be contained just to the inside of these walls and will eventually overflow into the outside society and should be of concern to the public," stated a prisoner in "The Lessons of Marion" published by the A.F.S.C. Former Governor George W. Bush's Texas Prison System created the killer who dragged Jimmy Lee Byrd to death.

"I know that most of us will agree that society as a whole is largely caught up in its own struggle to survive, with the world as it is today. But society must never lose track of the thought that prisons are today's thermometers that measure its repression tomorrow. Marion can and will only spill back into society. As the slain guard's wife cries out in anguish, so does the wife and loved ones of the tormented convict weep their tears as they experience his psychological and physical torture. Death and cruelty are no strangers to those who live and work within these cages, as every action delivers a reaction. When one finds himself chained and beaten up against he wall, his actions and thoughts manifest into total madness. This is the situation Marion (C.D.C.) finds itself in and this view is shared by both the kept and the keeper. No deed is too vile, as all reason and humanity ceased to exist," a prisoner wrote.

Isolation, the hole, Ad-seg, etc. does not work. Repressive incarceration does not provide safety or a positive environment for prisoners or staff. And when men are locked away and dehumanized etc. They rage and they snap and once released into society our citizen's become the victims of their anger. Society must rethink prisons. We must finally look behind the media's depiction of the crime and analyze the social and personal events that contributed to the immoral, illegal and antisocial behavior. We should insist that the offender take responsibility but we must punish inhumane, sensible and pragmatic ways. Society must demand an end to brutality. The only way the brutality will end is when the public speaks out. We must tell our congress to exercise congressional oversight and use their authority to clean up the prisons. Y'all know damn well that you can't cage people like animals in a zoo, remove educational programs and treatment programs and then expect them to exist in prison and obey the law. Education is the most potent weapon and engine of personal development. But because of and through education, the son of a peasant can become a doctor, the daughter of a garbage man can become a scientist and an ex-con can become a youth leader. Any society, which eliminates the opportunity for mental and intellectual growth, is a society that shall soon see its demise. Prisons have done away with the Pell Grant, college courses, etc. and they limit the amount of books inmates can receive. Hell, you can't ever receive hard cover non-fiction books in prisons in California. The more I think about it, the more I become cognizant of the fact that the prison guards need to be re-educated and re-trained. Some of them are doing the best they know how. They have not been adequately trained. I am a compassionate human being. But I cannot swear to you that I would know how to treat (fairly an inmate whom I knew was a convicted child molester. That is a sick, evil, horrendous crime. Would I as a guard remember that he might have been falsely convicted? Would I remember that he was probably raped as a child? Would I remember that no normal human being simply wakes up one morning and arbitrarily develops a sexual affinity for children? Or would I kick his ass and abuse him maliciously? Would I think of my kids and imagine him raping my kids? It's not difficult to comprehend that we need to train cops on how to treat those men with equal protection under the law. I have no sympathy for child molesters. Yet, they are still human beings. This is a country (supposedly) founded on the principles of liberty, justice and equality.

We're gonna have to join forces and shine the light on these prisons. We need to call on Al Sharpton, Jesse Jackson, Ted Kennedy, Joseph Biden, etc. to speak up and to speak out. There is modern day slavery taking place in America's prisons. I believe Al Sharpton can do something about it. Al has grown tremendously. I believe Al Sharpton has matured as a fighter. Al started preaching when he was a kid as I did. Al had to stand on a box to see over the pulpit as I did when I was a boy preacher. They called Al "Wonder Boy" preacher and they called me "Boy Wonder". I need Al Sharpton. Al's "House of Justice" needs to fight to free innocent men and end brutality in prisons. Al can bring (New York Attorney) Alton H. Maddox, John Conyers and Jesse Jackson to California and turn C.D.C. right side up. Al understands the media and the games the media plays. The media tries to tell Black folks to choose between Al and Jesse. "I wouldn't even be in a position to ever consider national leadership if it wasn't for Jesse. I've been a student of Jesse's for thirty-two years. So what I do is not to compete with him, but to complement him and to give a return in the investment he gave me over all these years." Al understands what happened to King and Malcolm and how even some preachers weakened the movement by not putting *egos* aside and coming together. "Anytime a Black leader emerges, who will question racism in this country, he or she better get ready to be hammered by what is called mainstream media'." Al knows that our youth have become disconnected to the struggle. But if we can get Al, Van Jones, Jesse, Richard Polanco, Willie Brown, Earl Graves, John Johnson, Greg Baranco, Herman Russell, Chris Gardner, Sean Combs and Oprah on the same team and begin to rebuild the youth (Black and White) he would see a transformation in America.

"After I'm gone, my hairstyle won't matter and my jogging suits won't matter. But what I do about racial profiling, police brutality and the international fight against slavery will matter. Because when you are no longer there as a personality, they have to look at your work. The people who study you will study you because of substance, not style. I don't know what kind of suits Dr. King wore. I don't care. I don't know what kind of hairstyle Marcus Garvey wore. That didn't matter with them and it's not going to matter with me," stated Rev. Al Sharpton.

And I say Amen; you're right, Let's fight. This is my public call to Rev. Al Sharpton: I need you (Rev. Sharpton) to come and see about me. They want me to die here for a crime I did not commit. And I also call on every leader (Black, White, Mexican, other) to come and see about the least of these thy brethren. They are languishing in the bowels of violent prisons all across America. An investment in them (us) today, will pay off in safer communities, neighborhoods and cities tomorrow. Sean P. Diddy Combs could have been sitting in Rikers Island being abused by ignorant and bigoted authorities. Sean came very close to going to prison. It is sickening what they tried to do to Sean. Sean said of the trial that he became truly scared and for the first time in his life, felt there was nothing he could do to control his own destiny. It is not difficult to imagine that Sean can relate to how prisoners feel, especially innocent prisoners.

"I know these cats were serious from the get go, but I still had trouble understanding how big of a deal the prosecutors were making out of what they claimed I had done," stated P. Diddy.

And prisons are running over with men who were indigent and had no idea prosecutors were gonna send them away for twenty, thirty and forty years on bullshit cases.

"I always kept my faith in God. I never panicked. I kept my faith in God and I believed that He was going to work it out. No matter the outcome, you have to keep your faith strong. I give all the glory to God for this situation with my life and everything. I said that after the trial and I repeat it. No matter how good my lawyers were, how much money I had, how much fame or success, the only thing that pulled me out of this situation was God," said Sean. He learned very valuable lessons in almost losing his freedom. I say to Sean keep on making money. Continue to dream, to hope, to strategize and visualize. Don't ever forget about the least of these thy brethren. I say to Doug Banks, Tony Brown, Oprah, Earl Graves, Susan Taylor and all of our leaders that we need you. We need you now. Stop letting the media, prosecutors and police reports decide for you who you should help and who is a lost cause. Stop allowing the media to divide us and conquer us. Feed the hungry, clothe the naked and visit those in prison. Decide to never let it happen to somebody else. Use your life to make the world better. Be careful how you treat the homeless, the downtrodden, the prisoners, the least of these. It just might be Joseph, Paul or Silas. It could be a Malcolm in the making. Dave Hollister, Denzel Washington, Magic Johnson, Queen Latifah. You can make a difference. Read on...

Albert J. Strickland graduated from Whitney Young Magnet High School in Chicago. He is going to Harvard and wants to become a Chris Gardner. Y'all get Albert this tome and invest in his future. The children are our tomorrow!!!

Yes they are! I want (anyone reading) you all to find people (who are in this book) like David Hannon (D. Hannon live somewhere in Sacramento, CA) and get this book to him. Francisco Grine, Christopher Day, Kim Randolph, Suzanne Goldstein, etc. need to read this book. Every law student at Georgetown University Law Center, Brooklyn Law School and at Harvard needs this book. Ron Goldman (the new press in New York) Stephen Bright, George Kendall, Johnathan Greenberg and F. Lee need to read this book. You've got to find them and let them know that C.D.C.'s best-kept secrets are within these pages. Put the word out. I had a meeting the other day with representatives from the Inspector Genera's (Steve White) office. One of the guys was an ex-police officer. I was quite reluctant to divulge any confidential matters to this guy. Perhaps he meant well but I could sense that he is pro-C.D.C. and I'm not unmindful of the fact that Steve himself is a former District Attorney. Yet the Tomas Garcia guy seemed a bit more receptive. But Tomas too seems pro-establishment. He used to work in the Attorney General's office. Yet, I don't expect them to clean up C.D.C. my issue was mail. Legal mail. It is ludicrous to assure that my pending case in Sacramento is un-compromised when prison staff (all over the state) routinely opens my (and many other inmates) confidential mail. They know my defense. They feed this to the D.A. they even steal mail. It is sickening. I also learned the other day that the public information officer (Lt. B.M.) called a young man who was interested in helping me; "What kind of character does Manning have?" he asked the P.I.O. "He's a predator. He etc. etc….," the Lt. told the guy. This is a blatant violation of C.D.C. policy. Yet, I'm angrier with the young man than I am with the P.I.O. The young man should know that my keepers would do everything they can to paint me in a bad light. These people are wicked, racist and corrupted. In Book One I wrote (in the Book) "send me a photo and I may use it in the next book". Guess what C.D.C. says? "Manning is trying to get porn in the prison". How/why in the hell can you misconstrue an author's public request, in print to "send me a photo" and allege that means, "send porno?" It's preposterous! So I'll rub it in. Here and now I want everybody reading to send me a photo! Sean P. Diddy, Jay, Don King, Kim Deterline, Valencia, Wendy Pizarro, David Hannon, Professor David Cole, Greg Johnson, Professor Protess, professor Robert Cling, Morris Dees, etc. Send me a photo today!! I support Human Rights for all people. I do not bash gays, lesbians, Blacks or Whites. I believe we here all created equal. Having said that, I was to tell you (another C.D.C. secret, and a well kept prison secret around the country) that C.D.C. promotes homosexuality, violence, racism and deviant behavior (again I am not in anyway dehumanizing, defaming or despising anyone who is gay. You are human too and deserve to be treated equally as all other human beings). It is (usually) natural for a man to want to be with a woman. Yet C.D.C. has systematically (virtually) eliminated    family visits across the state. Those guys serving life in prison have nothing to look forward to.  Since they know they will never, ever (unless they rape a C.D.C. employee and that does happen) have the opportunity to be intimate with their wives or women (in general) again.  So what do they do?  They become perverts, bi-sexual, rapists, predators, etc.  They reach out (in very obsessive ways) to pornography, fantasy, violence and drugs.  C.D.C. perpetrates and facilitates this kind of epidemic.  The guys who will get out (and move to your hood) have been raped, forcefully sodomized, associated, affiliated and assimilated to this epidemic abnormal behavior etc. so that when they get out; they go rape, molest, steal and kill.  C.D.C. rips men from their family and harasses even the few people who do visit us.

"I was horrified that I was going to be viewed naked. I cried for days.  I considered not visiting my husband anymore.  I love my husband and I'm not ashamed of him... I, on the other hand, have done nothing wrong. .  Imagine your wife or daughter coming to see you, and she's crying because the security guard downstairs x-rayed her and saw that she was having her period," stated Ms. Elizabeth Eradabaugh at a C.D.C. hearing in which David Tristan tried to justify C.D.C. viewings visitors' tampons and forcing them (visitors) to prove they were on their period.

Mr. Tristan said it's all done to keep drugs out of prison.  Senator Cathie Wright was livid upon hearing this. "What the devil are you fellows doing?" Sen. Wright asked David Tristan. "I'll be honest, I'm a little callused about the fact that we pay so many dollars out in settling claims and court cases that we should be using on... programs," stated Senator Wright.  Attorney Monica Knox who also made David Tristan look like a fool at that meeting.  Within the past eight years, C.D.C. has undone all of the prison reforms which inmates at San Quentin and Folsom rioted and killed staff to attain in the 60's and 70's.  Will the rioting and the killing of guards begin again?  I hope not (to all inmates read my words, please unify.  Use the courts, the media, prayer and non-violence to win your rights.  Do not use violence!)  But it is almost inevitable if C.D.C. continues to say to inmates "we do what we want because the public does not care".  They repealed the inmates Bill of Rights.  They've engaged in takeaways and restrictions from family visiting and eliminated weight equipment.  They're proposing to eliminate law libraries in prison.  So you tell me what will an inmate wrongfully convicted in prison do without a law library?  You can't afford Ephraim Margolin, Gerry Spence, Mr. Cochran, Mr. Uelmen, Mr. Serra, Mr. Riordan or Don Heller, etc.  The court will not appoint you a lawyer (only through the first appeal.  But there are eight other levels.)  C.D.C. takes the law library?  That's a

331

threat to public safety. Escapes will take place. Guards will be murdered. Staff will be taken hostage, etc. Wait and see. It is almost inevitable. They have restricted inmate's personal property and virtually eliminated vocational and educational programs. They've built humongous prisons capable of housing seven thousand prisoners with *visiting* rooms that hold only one hundred people. They routinely terminate visiting due to overcrowding. They discourage written communication by branding mail. They discourage telephonic communication by charging astronomical fees, which include a forty-eight percent kickback to the state. C.D.C. constantly restrict, modify and eliminate. They approach problems with little or no knowledge of the scope of the issues. In effect, their monster factories merely warehouse, frustrate, aggravate and create predators, helpless, horrible and ignorant inmates to return to society prepared to explode. This is asinine, ludicrous and quite frankly ridiculous! Inmates across this country lose all decision-making authority like when to eat, sleep and talk. They are commanded in Hitler-type environments by guards who are angry, racist and ignorant. I spoke to a C.D.C. officer today who earned $114,000 last year. Not a warden, captain, lieutenant or even a sergeant. A C.O.! How? Overtime pay! He works ninety - one hundred hours per week. He is a threat to the safety and security of all institutions and the public. But C.D.C. allows him to come to work (handling firearms, etc.) sluggish, fatigued and agitated. Instead of x-raying visitors for drugs and contraband they need to x-ray guards!! Ninety-five percent of the inmates in prison in Florida today will get out of prison. But how long will they stay out? Who will be raped, molested, sodomized, robbed and killed while they are out? This system of warehousing will bust at its seams if we don't restore order. Stop building more prisons than schools and libraries. Mentioning prison buildings etc., I want to commend California's youth (that's who we must tap into if we want to win the war on crime; the youth. Some guys like George W. Gray Davis and John Ashcroft etc. are so biased, ambitious, greedy and bigoted that they will never become innovative or creative. They simply want to lock up the poor and throw away the key) for their recent victory. What did the youth do? They kicked butt! (Read "Shades of Power" by Julie Brown) waving, chanting and raising over seventy clenched fists in the air, a colorful throng of youth and their posse marched into the belly of C.D.C. They overflowed and overwhelmed the stuffy confines of a California Board of Corrections meeting in San Francisco, CA on May 17th. The youngster's mission was to convince the Boc to deny $2.3 million in state funds for Alameda County's effort to build the biggest (per capita) Juvenile Hall in the country. As these youth looked at the all White panel of stone-faced "suits" who make up the Boc, a body which has presided over the largest *prison boom* in the world - even the lead (according to Julie Brown) organizers doubted that the youth could pull it off. But these youth spoke passionately about the need for schools for youth and not jails. Our youths even serenaded the Boc with a "Freedom Song" about Harriet Tubman rescuing youth through the Underground Railroad. The Boc panel listened, argued, debated among themselves and then stunned Alameda County officials by voting ten - two to reject the $2.3 million funding request. Formerly smug county officials then scurried out a side door without comment while the youths and their allies exploded into wild cheering.

"We have witnessed the first solid victory in California for what is clearly a growing youth led movement against the prison industry nationwide," stated Rachel Jackson. Rachel works on the Books Not Bars campaign associated with the Ella Baker Human Rights Center. "Once again, youth activists have upset the set up and set up the upset?" said an exuberant Fela Thomas of the Youth Force Coalition, "People are gonna have to learn that you can't mess with California's youth, ya'll," he said. "I've never seen anything like this one kid with a magic marker and a poster board just blew away all the county's experts and statistics and double-talk. Our youths had done their homework. They left these big-time county official stammering," said Attorney Van Jones. This was a group of Black, White and Brown, kids. This is Dr. King's dream come true. I'm so excited about what Van, Rachel, Omani, Imani, etc. are doing. They came together. This youth force coalition included over thirty Bay Area Organizations. Aypai/Asian Pacific Islander Youth promoting advocacy and leadership, Jewish Youth for Community Action, Let's Get Free 510, Young Women United for Oakland, YMAC (Rachel, I want you to help me get this book to all these youths so they'll know that although Tom Brokaw didn't mention them - that we do *recognize*) etc. All joined together. Annie E. Casey Foundations, Bart Lubow and the Youth Law Center's James Bell, etc. All helped! I hope Fran Beal and Rory Caygill are reading now. If you are: God Bless Y'all! Keep on motivating our young people to stay off drugs, in school and to fight (non-violently) for justice. Julie Brown's article had me near tears when I saw those kids standing up for what is right. Hell (Rachel and Julie) I may write a book entitled "Books No Bars" and donate the proceeds to all these youth groups. On that note, I want Murray Janus, Gerald Uelmen, Barry, Doug Banks (all ya'll) to contribute money to these youth groups. Even if it is only forty or fifty dollars, write a check to help these groups today!! Don't y'all know that even Dr. Martin Luther King, Jr. became cognizant of the fact that if you mobilize the youth for any cause they are unstoppable? Ain't no stopping what can't be stopped! But the American media does not do feature stories on the positive things our youth does. They'll show us gangs, guns and youth violence. But they rarely show us young Black, White, Latino and Asian people who are fronting for social justice, human rights and worker's rights. That is why I (redundantly) call on the Bayview newspaper, African-American News, BET, Ebony, Source Magazine, Tommy Goss, Doug Banks, Tony Brown, Susan Taylor, Latifah, WWW, newspapers, etc. to give our youth the props that ABC, NBC and CBS won't give them. Talk about 'em! Write about 'em. Sing about 'em! Preach and teach about them. This is one of the reasons I've told the best-kept secrets of C.D.C. in this tome. I want this book to scare them straight and to motivate them not to come to prison. I have guys who wanted me to write only about family visiting, etc. Some guys wanted me to only write about MCI and how the prison system extorts our families with these outrageous telephone charges, etc. They (convicts) have vested interests and I too (I'm just a radical, sincere, unique and crazy author. This is what scares a lot of big publishers away from me) have a rooted interest also. I'd much rather write only about innocent men in prison who have had our freedom stolen from us unjustly. I want Van Jones, Barry Tarlow, Gerald Uelmen, Law professors, law Students, David Cole, Robert Cling, Kim Deterline, Sean P. Diddy, etc. to help me. But I must also be a voice for the voiceless. I must not be selfish and that is the biggest problem in America. We prisoners, we Americans, we politicians, we are all into self. How can I (only) help me? How can I get another vote to get elected? How can I make more money? How can I? But each of us are breathing the same air and drinking the same water. We need to realize that we all need *each other*. "Injustice anywhere is a threat to justice everywhere," Dr. Martin Luther King, Jr. said. We must stop allowing the media and slick politicians to fool us. They thrive off of ratings and good news gets no ratings. Hell, if we could get just forty percent of American youth to do a one-week television (boycott) blackout, we would bring the media to its knees and they'd stop telling the *bad* and *ugly* only. They would tell us the good, the bad and the ugly. They won't tell us the rest of the story. They even eviscerate the message and meaning of Dr. King's "I Have A Dream" speech. They don't play the part about a demand for the reshuffling of America's economic deck! They don't play up the similarities in *Malcolm* and *Martin*. They give you bits and pieces and they are very selective. Hell, I am not convinced that most people in this great country are racist. No! I do not believe most of us are evil, mean and vicious. I can't, won't and don't accept that. Perhaps I'm an incurable optimist, but I try to be realistic also. I do believe with my heart and soul. That if the average, taxpaying citizen (Black, White and Brown) knew what is transpiring in these prisons, they would force politicians to change the system. Ipso facto, you are now reading the real deal. I refuse to believe that churchgoing White folks, lil old ladies in the Black hood, deacons, teachers, etc. would support prioritizing jails over schools and bars over books. You can't convince me that the average citizen would support sending sixteen, seventeen, eighteen, and nineteen-year-olds to prison for five years to be schooled by murderers serving life sentences. They would not support it if they knew that every day of the week in prisons in California, Texas, etc. Those young men are being sodomized, abused and living in fear, etc. Forced to join gangs that C.D.C. won't disband, etc. That they wouldn't be able to figure it out, "we are creating killers, molesters and predators. It's a rush to judgment and we need to focus on prevention instead of punishment. Books not Bars! When they commit a crime, we need to commit to teaching them alternatives to crime", I can hear our citizens saying if they *knew* the *truth*. So here (in this tome) is the truth. I've simply put it out here for you to analyze. Figure it out for yourself. Poor Whites are also the victims of this warehousing for profit and the breeding of a new class of humans; young, untaught, un-fathered, uninspired and guilty of committing minor infractions yet sent to prison. Viciously brutalized by seasoned convicts, these young boys grow up (physically) in prison. But their mental, analytical and spiritual selves are stunted by arrested development. In prison they learn disrespect, hate, rage, intolerance, anarchy, exploitation and blind revenge. Seventeen-year-old boys sent to prison to earn bachelor's degrees in prison political science and master's degrees in prison subculture. We must change now. Change the way we (and the reasons why) send boys to prison! Change the inside culture of the prisons so that when we must send a person to prison they can correct themselves and have a decent chance at getting out and not re-offending again. We need Yuri Kochiyama, California prison focus, the Fortune Society, Critical Resistance, Prisoner's Rights Coalition, 3EM, etc. to tell our citizens the real deal. We must write columns, letters to editors, publish our own newsletters, books, sponsor town hall meetings, etc. to get the word out. Let's save the children! Elizabeith "Benita" Martinez, Andrea Smith, Van Jones, Christopher Day, Al Sharpton and Jesse are ready to rumble but they can't do it alone. That's why this book must be put in the hands of our politicians, the Black media, activists, youths, etc. and you young people must tell everybody (WWW, school, papers, teachers, politicians, etc.) about this book. Not just for me young people, but for Mumia Abu Jamali, David Wong, Brandon Martinez and all wrongfully convicted or political prisoners. Are you familiar with Geronimo Pratt? Co intel pro? The war on poor communities being waged by criminal justice is a formulated counter insurgency tactic to crush the spirit of resistance. Remember the Black, Puerto Rican, Native, Chicano and Asian communities in the 60's and 70's? They don't want a resurrection of those powerful moments. It's deeper than you think. Mass incarceration terrorizes whole communities. Slam (Student Liberation Action Movement) out at Hunter College, Just Act, 3EM, NAACP, S.C.L.C., etc. needs to mobilize the youth. I suggest you read "Global Links", which is published by Just Act in San Francisco. Augustin Avila, Marcela Olivera, Van, Al, Jesse, Naim-all y'all come together and recruit the youth. The drug dealers and pimps are gonna recruit them if you don't. What to do about the prisons? Gimme a break! You know the damn answers! Transform them. Prisoners ought to be required to participate in intensive education, antiviolence, self-help and tolerance programs. Bring in volunteers from Just Act, 3 EM, BNB, churches, foundations and businesses, etc. to teach prisoners *how to live*. Every prison ought to have a turn around program for drug addicts, thieves, sexual predators, violent men, etc. We can implement these weekly and daily workshops and seminars immediately and change lives. T. D. Jakes did a series of sermons called "Nothing just happens". I am telling you for a fact that every prison Chaplain ought to get that video and set up a turn around program and let every prisoner view it. Thousands of men have been for their way to welfare lines, and soup lines but got saved by the U. S. Military. There is something about the uniform, drill and ceremonies, etc. which just instills discipline, confidence and pride in a man. Why not do it in prisons? Not this abusive, bull crap boot camp stuff some judges are sending prisoner to. But we can base it on the same strategies and curriculum utilized by JROTC Departments in high schools and colleges across the country. Give men a uniform. Teach them drill, ceremonies, marching, etc. Teach leadership, discipline, self esteem, public speaking, diversity and tolerance. Let them earn rank like Private First Class all the way through Command Sergeant Major. Lieutenant all the way to General. Are you with me? I can look at your preparation and accurately predict your destination. So the ultimate reason most of the 614,000 inmates who are getting out of prison this year are gonna come back to prison is because they are prepared psychologically, spiritually, physically and emotionally to return to prison. Evil preparation/evil destination! What parent would prevent and discourage their child from going to school, reading, socializing and going to church, etc. and expect that uneducated, untrained, untaught and undisciplined child to go out and magically become a doctor? Garbage in, garbage out! You know guys are not gonna live in idle, shameful and abusive environments where they have nothing to look forward to for years, etc. and leave a barbed wired fence setting and go out and conquer the world. Their pasts will pollute their futures! You don't need to pamper them in order to prepare them. Bring any psychiatrist into the prisons and let them see the slave labor, gangs, rapes, violence and lack of familial involvement, etc. Ask them is there anyway any man can live like this for sustained amounts of time and leave and be successful? If you drop out of school, abuse drugs and start stealing to support your habit, we can easily predict that "He's gonna end up in prison." So it does not take a rocket scientist to figure out if you go to prison and continue doing drugs, join a gang, live in fear for your safety, get raped, victimized by older cons, brutalized by staff, no visits, few books and no education, etc. You will end up becoming a murderer!! The system is corrupt, it is dangerous and it is set up to fail. Don't wait on your governor or government to change the system. Some of them are oppressors and freedom ain't given voluntarily by the oppressor. It must be demanded by the oppressed. Parents, teachers, students and lawyers must demand a change. We must not only exonerate and liberate the innocent. We must emancipate men who are innocent! And educate, turn around and empower men who are guilty.

Global education, literacy (intensive), skills, community living, self-esteem, anti-racism training, pray-ins, teach-ins, preach-ins, read-ins and love-ins. Preparation determines destination...

Tommy Goss was Christian enough to respond to a letter I wrote him. On air (KBMB The Bomb - Gospel Express) "I received a letter from Rev. Sherman Manning . . .. This song "Hold On" by Rev. Clay Evans is dedicated to Brandon Martinez, Rev. Sherman Manning and all the guys at New Folsom Prison", Tommy stated on July 15, 2001. I want to thank him for his prayers and his ministry in song. I want all the Tommy Goss', Doug Banks, etc. to help put the word out about this book. "I'm reading a book by Sherman Manning. You need to get it," they can say. I want the world to know the facts contained herein. Oaz Nir (Duke University), Reid Barton (Boston, Massachusetts), David Hannon, and youth across the nation must read this book. I want them to join Just Act, 3 EM, Books Not Bars, and Youth Activists, etc. we've got to come together here and now. I hope and pray that this book will move Jesse Jackson, Billy Graham, Jay Bakker, Al Sharpton, Richard Polanco, Ted Kennedy, John Lewis, Spike Lee, Sean P. Diddy, etc. to action. I hope Kim Deterline, Van Jones, Rachel, Just Act, etc. will use this book as a mobilization tool. I hope they'll send it to colleges, professors, lawyers, prisoners and politicians. But if I fail, I tried. I sincerely gave this the best I have. If my time has come I can push and get a delivery. I still have a dream. It's time for our dreams to become a collage and a rainbow. We must love one another. We must prepare our youth. We must pray for our leaders. Books Not Bars. Love not hate. Schools not jails. Colleges not prisons. Please write me today. If you received this tome free of charge, please forward twenty-four dollars to me so I can send it to somebody else. Keep love alive! Stay tuned, I'll be writing another book again soon (last time). Youth: Use the Internet to spread this book like wildfire....

*Just a reminder*. If we get teens on college campuses, high schools, Elizabeth "Betita" Martinez, Faviana Rodriquez, Ana Bertha Campa, Rachel Jackson, Margaretta Lin, Mark Ran, Colin Rajah, Lily Wang, 3EM, Just Act, We Interrupt This Message etc. to use those telephones, fax machines and the Internet to call Mr. Spike Lee and ask, "Have you read, 'If It Doesn't Fit You Must Acquit Parts One and Two?'" "Richard Polanco, have you read Sherman's book?" If we get young people to go on the web and find every person whom I've named in this book to talk about this book, etc. what would happen? What would happen? We could motivate a David Cole, David Protess, Billy Martin, Gerald Uelmen, Johnnie Cochran, Robert Cling, Barry Tarlow, Tony Serra or a Dennis Riordan to get me out of here. We don't need armchair revolutionaries! We need active cadres and committed grassroots organizers. I'm sick of rhetoric. Let's do something other than preach, talk, profile and analyze. Let's strategize and mobilize. Write me for more books. Send me advice, support and prayers. Fax John Lewis, Ted Kennedy, Joe Biden, Maxine Waters, Polanco, and John Burton and tell them the cat is out of the bag. You know the truth! I am innocent! The profile tricks must fail. The paperwork tricks must fail. The criminal profiling, etc. must fail. We must look at the facts of this case and if you do you'll know I do not belong here. What if Billy Martin, Charles Ogletree, Abbe Lowell, Ellis Rubin would spin my case the way Martin spins the Levy case? I'd be at home now. Mary Hanlon Stone utilized past sins, embellished pleas, racist police profiling, lies, perjured an illegal testimony to convict me of a crime that didn't transpire. If you want to scrutinize my past (in a sensational and biased fashion) I lose hands down. If, however you want to look at this case, the evidence, the testimony - you will conclude it does not fit!!

Liberty and justice should be for all! The Black, White, dark and light. The people who have criminal histories and those with lily white backgrounds. Latinos in the barrios as well as Whites in the suburbs. If I had gotten the kids gloves treatment that Gary Condit got there would have been no trial. But instead I got a hanging (a modern day lynching). I gotta stop writing for now. Pass this book around. Order (write me) more copies today. Pray for me and get active! Get on that Internet and locate Bryan Robles in Ceres, California, Oaz Nir at Duke and Reid Barton, etc. Tell them to get this book and join us in the human rights struggle. We need you now!!!

* * * *

Senators, Polanco, Burton, waters, NAACP, ACLU, etc. you all should demand a change! We cannot do it with outdated techniques. We must involve the youth. The youth ought to have a say in how these prisons are run. Don't give me that "they're too young" bullshit. At seventeen years of age you're old enough to join our fighting forces. Army, Navy, Air Force and Marines. Old enough to throw a hand grenade and operate weapons for mass destruction. Why should we deem you too young to have a voice in transforming the prison system? Why should we deem it inappropriate for you to have a say in crime and punishment? We the people will try a twelve, thirteen and fourteen-year-old boy as an adult in a court of law. We (yet) will have an old judge, old prosecutor and an old jury. What is a thirteen-year-old being tried as an adult asked for a jury panel of thirteen-year-olds? "They are too young to understand the jury process, courtroom procedures and the rules of evidence," some judge would exclaim. But isn't that a judicial oxy-moron? A thirteen-year-old kid can be tried as a man because, etc. etc. and we claim he'll understand and be mature enough to assist his attorney in his defense. Yet, his peers (other kids) are not old enough to decide his fate? It is preposterous and John Ashcroft knows it. If we try a thirteen-year-old his jury should be his peers. It is also preposterous to assume that seventeen and eighteen-year-old high school graduates ought not be considered mature enough to advise us on how to run prisons more effectively. I want to see a Youth Blue Ribbon Committee on crime and punishment. I want to see a Youth Truth and Reconciliation Task Force under the direction of Judge Barry Loncke in place to decide who does not need to be in prison. It's time out for vesting the power of the people in the hands of (only) old gray headed, hillbilly, rednecks, cowboys and uncle toms. What do they know? In all seriousness, I can remember a long conversation I had with former Ambassador Andrew Young. Andrew Young was a trusted aide to Dr. Martin Luther King, Jr. He went on to be elected congressman and appointed a U.N. Ambassador. Later he became Mayor of Atlanta. We used to talk all the time. He was very patient with me. When he became Mayor of Atlanta, I asked him "who teaches you how to be a mayor? How to run a city, govern, etc.?" I thought there must be a school you must go to (and perhaps there should be) which teaches you how to be a politician. I figured there must be a manual that all mayors had to read, etc. "Nobody teaches you," he told me. He explained that absolutely nobody teaches, trains, instructs or schools you on how to be a mayor. I was mesmerized. Andy explained that there is no book even on how to be a governor, senator, president, etc. These guys just (supposedly) raise a lot of money, give a lot of speeches (sound bites) and the richest man wins! They are catapulted into powerful positions with all kinds of responsibilities with no training. They go on experience. So when we look at it realistically Governor Gary Davis has no more (specific, detailed, intensive) specialized knowledge in how to run a prison than the youth at 3EM does. You won't hear politicians openly divulging this information. But it is true. Most politicians don't have a clue. We need to remember this. There is no six-month training program to teach people how to be senators or presidents, etc. Supposedly, "I'll cut taxes and protect the American people. I'll leave no child behind", etc. But really, "I am lost. I have no special training. My dad was a president who didn't know what the hell he was doing. An oil man, we are wealthy. We can't relate to poor people, homeless, inner city kids, etc. we are narrow-minded. I ran for Governor in Texas and tried to grow into my position. I had absolutely no idea (and no concern) about how to run a prison, reduce recidivism, stop prison violence, stop prison rapes, gangs, etc." That's a fact! So if an untrained man can campaign (sell out) for public office and have the lives of the masses under his auspices then why can't young people advise senators, governors and mayors on how to stop wrongful convictions and how to transform prisons? I want our youth to get involved here and now. Don't be intimidated by politics! Don't be intimidated by old age. Love your elders! Be nice, considerate and respectful to our seniors. But also let your ideas, innovation, ideals, etc. be known. I don't need to give you a step-by-step approach. You do it. My job (aim) is just to stir up the fire in your belly. I didn't tell Craig Kielburger (when he was only thirteen years old) how to start

"Free the Children". He just got some kids together and started and International Movement. Read his book entitled "Free the Children" and take notes. Start a movement or join one. Start an Internet campaign. Start a letter writing campaign. Start a newsletter. Get ten thousand teens to write or sign a petition on an issue that concerns you. Find your passion and go for it. Call Van Jones, Rachel or Diana at the Ella Baker Center in San Francisco. "Attorney Jones we're gonna do a fundraiser for 3EM. We're gonna sell one thousand copies of Sherman's book and donate the proceeds to the movement. We need structure".

Or call Just Act "we're gonna do a book-a-thon" or "we're gonna get ten thousand signatures on a petition and submit it to the governor" or "we want to help free innocent men from prison" or "we want to start a pen pal service for prisoners" or "we want to start diversity, tolerance and leadership workshops", etc.

Young folks *your* potential is unlimited and *we the people need you* to take a stand and get involved. Mr. Bush says (a lie) he's all of our president. So you need to let our president know how you (in mass numbers) feel about crime and punishment, prison violence, recidivism, foolish three-strikes laws, etc. If he won't listen, you know how to march. You know how to raise money and write a newsletter. Write the New York Times, Washington Post, etc. Raise ten grand and take out a full-page ad in the Washington Post. Buy radio time and talk about him. Sit-in, pray-in, camp-in and march-in, etc. Just mobilize and do something. When I look at Craig Kielburger, I get so inspired. Craig has freed more exploited children than anybody I know. And (I repeat) he built his organization from the ground up when he was only thirteen years old. I want to ask my readers to send this book to Craig. Also send him a check to help his group. (Free the Children International: 1750 Steeles Ave., West, Suite 218, Concord, Ontario, L4K-2L7 - Canada. Call (905) 760-9382). Craig has received the Roosevelt Freedom Medal and the State World Forum Award. He's young, creative, motivated and innovative. If you will help me get this book to people like Craig, Jimmy Dougherty, (Davis CA at "The Paragon") Michael Holt (teacher at Middle School in Rural, CA)), Joseph Shalaby and Jonathan Peck (U. C. Barbara), Josh Tifton (Salto, CA), Darrell Steinberg (assemblyman) and to everybody you know; we will spark a (non-violent) revolution! How many times must I ask you to use the World Wide Web? If you need more copies of this book, just write to me. One Morehouse College student wrote to me, "I'm getting three copies of Part II. I'll write in our college paper about the book. I'll send one copy to my chief of police and one to our governor. I'll stir up debate in this city about your book. Prisons per se and your wrongful conviction." That's what I need each of you to do. Discuss this book with your fraternity and sorority brothers and sisters. Write open letters to the New York Times, Washington Post, LA Times and the Atlanta Constitution about this book. The media will zero in on my checkered past. That's inevitable. They will slam me! But they slam Jesse, Al, Louis, Jim, Jimmy, etc. so it's all right. But when all is said and done, the question you must ask is did Sherman Manning commit the crime for which he is doing time? That's all we want to know. And we want to know does warehousing poor men in prison, with no lawyer, no education, no intervention, no preparation and no rehabilitation work? Can we make a change? You damn right we can. Fight the power! Fight spiritual wickedness in high places. Can I (once again) engage in tautology and redundancy? Since it's my book, I think I can! I want to remind you to get "Nothing Just Happens" by T. D. Jakes at Potter's House in Dallas, Texas. I care less how old or young you are. Your nationality, ethnicity, gender, denomination and occupation are irrelevant. Get "Nothing Just Happens" either on video or cassette tapes. These are life-changing messages. Get them! People are writing me about my speech entitled "Keep on Dreaming" which I gave before thousands of youth in Atlanta, Georgia at the Bethel Mission Youth Convention in 1994. I don't have the tape. My mother has the only video. However, I am sure if you call (404) 284-1410, Dr. W. J. Stafford or Pastor Jean Barber can get it on tape for you. I want to hear it also!!! God blessed us in that convention.

I need y'all to go back and review this tome. I want you to review it analytically. I'd like Just Act, 3EM, Books Not Bars, Youth Making A change, NAACP Youth, S.C.L.C. Youth, Jewish Youth, etc. teens to sit down and hold discussions on the ideas, quotes and statistics which are contained herein. I want you rich old millionaires who received this tome free of charge to send me my money for this tome. Help get it to our youth and I want you young people to pick yourself up. Find you a purpose and a mission in life. Reach for the stars. You can make it. Your life may be broken. Dreams Busted! Parents divorced. Not doing well in school. You may be hurting and it may seem like all hope is gone. But no matter how bad it seems, all hope is never gone. Get up out of your depression and clean yourself off. Wash your face and go to your destiny! Find your calling and your passion. The work and area, which you choose to utilize your energy, is up to you. The problems, challenges and difficulties are many. But one thang (to my hip hop partners) I know there is power in unity. We must stop allowing our differences (of opinions, colors, ethnicities, etc.) to divide us. We must simply find that common ground and create that beloved community. My God, my God, there is power in people. When Martin Luther King, Jr. pulled together two hundred and fifty thousand people (Black and White people) at the Mall in D.C. not all of those people agreed on every issue. Come on y'all. Some of those in attendance were Atheists, Agnostics, Jews, Christians, Muslims, etc. You name it. Some had communist views and some had democratic or capitalistic views. Some thought interracial marriage was sinful and some knew that love was blind. But they united in one cause for one march. You young folks must be hip enough to hop along and unite yourselves in the cause for liberty and justice for all. You must be independent and intelligent enough to think for yourself.

When these bastards at C.D.C. call you to attempt to turn you against me or any person convicted of a crime, you must decide for yourself. "He was locked up in 1900 for this. He pled guilty in 1977 of that. He was accused in 1987 of this and suspected in 1997 of that," they will tell you. The media will hammer the accusations, convictions, speculation and the prosecutor's theories about the accused. But you must be single-minded enough to say (for example), "That's well and good. But my concern is this case for which he is presently incarcerated. I want to know the facts of this case. Was the alleged victim credible? Did he have adequate counsel? Was their D.N.A.? Was the judge fair? Was the jury made up of their peers? Is he really guilty? If so what is he evidence which proves guilt beyond reasonable doubt?" These are the questions the D.A. (Mary Hanlon Stone) does not want you to ask. She does not want you to question her or Robert Altman's motives. "Why did Judge Robert Altman call a Deputy Sheriff over the telephone (outside the presence of the defense, lawyers, the jury, etc.) and tell him not to testify on Manning's behalf?" What's really going on?

Now for all y'all who are interested in making Isaiah 58 come alive read on. For you who are unfamiliar with prisons and how they operate, I want you to imagine a Black Hole. C.D.C. is certainly a black deep hole. Please understand it is a trap. The challenge for each person in prison is how to survive intact, and how to emerge from this hellhole undiminished. How to conserve and replenish one's belief system. Governor Davis' prisons (and most prisons across the U.S.A.) are designed to break a person's spirits and to ruin one's resolve. Prison authorities accomplish this by demolishing our initiatives, exploiting every weakness and negating all individuality. They strive

343

to put out the spark that makes each of us human. For those of us who are here and innocent of the crimes for which we were convicted we must continue to hope, to fight, to write, to strive to prove our innocence. While we are here, we have got to understand what the authorities are trying to do and to share that understanding with each other. We must support each other and gain knowledge, strength and a sense of family from each other. Each of us has different capacities and reactions to stress. But the stronger ones of us must teach, reach and raise up the weaker ones of us. All of us shall become stronger in the process. We must create our own lives in prison. We must be very cognizant of the fact that most so-called leaders don't give a damn about us. Either they don't know (after this book they can't claim ignorance anymore), don't show or just don't care about us. Our governors (most of them such as Gray Davis) and senators, etc. don't understand what a true leader is. A real leader (John F. Kennedy, Jimmy Carter, Gandhi, Dr. King, President Mandela) must often do things which are unpopular, or whose effects shall not be seen for years to come. There are successes whose glory lies only in the fact that they are known to the people who win them. Leaders are supposed to find consolation in being true to their ideals, even if don't nobody (lingo intended) else knows about it. All too often when I consider the actions of George W., Gray Davis, John Ashcroft and many others; I wish they would study Dr. King, Hosea Williams, John F. Kennedy, Andrew Young and Maynard Jackson. These guys shape their policies (and sound bites) by the results of the latest public opinion poll. So guys in prison must learn to regard our struggle in prison as a microcosm of the struggle in the streets. The racism and repression are the same. They are simply intensified in prison. Prisons and its guards attempt to rob you of your dignity. You must be unwilling to lose your dignity at any price. You must keep your feet moving and keep your head tilted upward. There are many dark and lonely moments in prison and your faith in humanity can be surely tested, but never give yourself up to the awful despair that is all around you. That's the recipe for death and defeat. You must strive to out think your oppressors. In many instances, this won't be too difficult a task. I was talking last week with a C.D.C. captain. I think he's a bit deceptive, perhaps even a racist. But I happen to like the guy. Yet, our conversation reinforced my belief that most of the senior prison officials are not too intelligent. Get this: C.D.C. claims (a blatant lie) it does everything possible to maintain the ties between inmates and their families and friends. Okay, we are allowed fifteen minute telephone calls daily to anyone who will accept our call. However, our automated telephones are not capable of telephoning internationally my best friend, Christian brother and (he also runs my company) close associate who resides in Switzerland. I can't call him. He can't fly over and visit me every week as he could if he resided in the U.S.A. So I asked the captain, "Can Peter call the institution (at his expense) and speak to me for fifteen minutes on the telephone in the presence of staff. We'd like to do it once every thirty days." Here was his reply, "I'm uncomfortable because staff won't be able to hear what Peter is saying. They can only hear you." Now this captain meant no harm. His thinking tools are just limited. (Keep reading) I said, "Captain - the telephones are speaker phones. All they have to do is put us on speaker phone and staff can hear him and me." (Wow - it took a rocket scientist?!?!) He called the warden and he approved. But guess what? Even without a speakerphone there would be no breach of security. In the waiting room, no staff goes around listening to conversations. With one hundred inmates, one hundred family members, kids yelling, a television blasting and three guards sitting up front at a desk, couldn't we discuss an escape? Couldn't we discuss overthrowing the government uncensored in the visiting room? And he (this captain) is one of the smartest one's around here. Most captains, AW's and even wardens are simply old prison guards who earned rank by kicking ass and taking names later. Their formal education is limited, suspect and elementary. They are intimidated by any of us who are educated. They have it set up so that indigent inmates can't study. Higher learning is discouraged. You get punished for knowing too much. I'm not gonna make the reach and say it's all a planned conspiracy. But I will tell you that somebody, somewhere has figured out how to get rich building prisons and how to create slaves out of inmates. Guys willing to work their normal shift plus. I see guys everyday who earn less than twenty cents per hour. They go to work at 6:30 a.m. and although they're not due until 8:00 a.m., they work from 6:30 a.m. until 9:30 p.m. seven days per week. They receive no overtime pay. They get no extra compensation. When asked why they work eighteen plus hour per day for little more than twenty bucks per month, "It's better than sitting in my cell." I reply, "Are ya crazy? You are being exploited, used, slaved and raped by C.D.C. You ought to be in your cell praying, reading studying and writing people to try to get the hell out of here. Nelson Mandela earned his postgraduate degree in prison. Malcolm read the entire dictionary in prison. Get a life. Fight for your freedom. You owe it to yourself to improve and strengthen yourself. You can't do it slaving for the system." But many guys here are under the inadvertent impression that they are the system. They mean well

345

but are misguided. As I've told you some are trying to get staff to begin a latter system where you earn your privileges. But it will only be utilized as a weapon to punish litigious guys who are considered troublemakers. It is well intentioned and wrongheaded. I can think of many inmates who would never (ever) receive a telephone call, visit the canteen or receive a visit if it were left up to certain staff members. Any carrot and stick type program will be used against unpopular inmates. It shouldn't take a brain surgeon to see this. When staff discover two inmates getting along too well, cellies who read, study, pray and are not a part of any cliques (like my celly and I) etc. staff will arbitrarily, capriciously separate them. "Pack your stuff Martinez, you're transferring" or "pack it up Manning, you're going to Ad-seg". So I'm sorry to tell my brothers (who really mean well) that no program such as a latter system will work. It will be used as another weapon in the arsenal of our enemies. If y'all want to fight, fight (non-violently) to get the Pell Grant back. Fight to get workshops, seminars, teach-ins, read-ins, revivals, anti-violence and communication clinics in prison. Fight to reduce the amount of money our families are being charged for these collect telephone calls. Fight to create a public referendum in prisons. Tell our politicians to require all C.D.C. employees to undergo intensive psychological testing and advanced diversity training. Screen staff better and educate them better. Don't be around here begging the Inspector General to implement a program that gives staff more power. They (staff) already treat us like slaves! If every working inmate refused to go to work tomorrow they'd bring the Pell Grant back. If we all absolutely refused to clean, build, supply and run their job force, etc., they would be forced to change. I don't want the Governor to get worried. I am not adulating an inmate strike. I'm not attempting to advance that idea. (Even if I were in favor of a strike it would fail because most prisoners are so brainwashed and disorganized that they would not quit their job for a thousand dollars.) No you don't need to strike. There are certainly many other ways to accomplish the goals of advancement other than striking. I'm simply saying we need to unite and utilize our energy (via the court system, writing activists and politicians) to cause prisons to be more humane. We should write the American Red Cross, Amnesty International, Judges, Politicians, the media and churches and tell them that we want a change. Newspapers, books, magazines (not the porno crap) ought to be more valuable to us in here than gold or diamonds. People in the public ought to voluntarily purchase newspaper subscriptions and send them to prisoners. Newspaper companies ought to discount rates (fees) for prisoners. C.D.C. has (another) a repressive policy, which is designed to keep indigent inmates from reading. If I have a newspaper subscription and I find a story, which I want to share with other inmates, etc. C.D.C. will not allow me to make a copy of any articles. We are not allowed to make copies of any newspaper articles, books, etc. - Nothing.

That is why we must fight to save, restore and rebuild ourselves from the inside out. "There is no prospect about prison which pleases - with the possible exception of one. One has time to think . . .. Prison provided the time - more than enough time - to reflect on what one had done and not done," stated President Mandela.

Men in prison ought to do time (constructively, non-violently) and not allow time to do them. Again - there are a few organizations out there willing to help us and to fight for us. But they need money. You ought to help them. You who are in civilian life must help them. Even guys in prison can send stamps, money orders, etc. to help their groups who help us. Prison ain't no joke. But if does not have to be violent, racist, sexist and corrupted. You politicians, pastors, doctors, lawyers and activists must get involved today. You can't protect your neighborhood or ensure the safety of the public by locking men up and throwing away the keys. You cannot expect men who are idle, mistreated, disrespected and abused to exit these racist prisons and obey the laws of the land. We the people must revisit crime and punishment in this great nation. The time is now. I want Murray Janus, Johnnie Cochran, Michael Snedeker, Barry Scheck, Don Heller, Gerry Spence, etc. to fight the powers. I want every innocent man (including me) in prison to get help. Help from law professors, law students, pastors, lawyers and politicians. I want wrongful convictions to stop. I want all men in prison to be given tools for change so they can leave out and stay out. I want every young person to live life to the fullest. Dream, hope, yearn, strive, study and use your life to help somebody else. Don't waste your time on bullshit. Get up each morning with a goal in mind. You must develop a goal and a strategy for attaining that goal. Build a life. People who are not doing anything with their lives go around trying to investigate other people's lives. They are so idle, so bored and so miserable that they watch other people's life as if it were a soap opera. Even in prison (and certainly out there). I'm too busy to worry about who's in prison for what or he said, she said - or I heard on the grapevine. Don't you know that I'm too occupied trying to figure out how to get you to take action on this book? I'm so busy trying to figure out how to spark a fire in your belly for justice. I'm trying to figure out how to reach Doug Banks, Christopher Gardner, Susan Taylor and Bill Cosby that I don't have time (literally) for prison gossip. Don't you know I spend so much time in prayer, reading, studying, visualizing, hoping and yearning that I have no time to investigate rumors. You ought to be busy. Never allow yourself to be idle. Young people join gangs because they feel powerless, idle, lonely and angry. But if you hook up with a good church, hook up with Just Act, 3EM, Boys and Girls clubs or youth making a change. If you get on your computers and fax politicians, write, read, study, pray, get a plan and roll with the plan, you won't have time for mess in your life. You won't tease and mistreat your classmates or outcasts. You'll leave the freaks, geeks and nerds alone. You'll be so busy trying to make the world better and preparing yourself for the future. That you won't have time for negativity. Get a life! Build a life. Get you a dream and chase it. I don't care where you are, who you are or where you came from; there is something deep down inside of you that if you tap it you will revolutionize your whole life! You will find your calling, your purpose, your destiny and your passion. But you gotta look for it. It's inside you. Open up your mind and find it. Reach inside your spirit and your soul and tap it. You cannot allow your history to limit your destiny. You have got to find a way to believe in yourself and prepare yourself for the future. You have got to know that there is greatness all down in the marrow of your bones. You can make it. I know . . . I must be crazy. I'm supposed to be writing about wrongful convictions and the judicial system. I'm supposed to be giving this vicious, violent prison system hell, but here I am giving a motivational speech. I must be crazy!

Yes I may seem crazy but they thought Martin Luther King, Jr. was crazy when he talked about his dream. Some thought Joseph was crazy when he articulated the dream that he had in Genesis. But the truth is they probably *hoped* Joseph was crazy more than they thought he was. I'm sure Bull Conner *hoped* King, Jr. was crazy more than they really thought so. I'm sure it *seems* crazy for a man in prison to be reaching out to our youth and telling them (you) to change. But there is something down in my heart, my soul and my spirit that even prison can't contain. I want to reach Brian Stanton (First Covenant Church), Christopher Day, Michael Novick, Ron Jones, (Rock Start) Bono, Michael Hardt (at Duke University), Attorney Donald K. Wilson and Dion-Cherie Raymond (D.C.) and encourage them to work together to free the innocent from prison. I am crazy enough to believe that someway, somehow some youth group such as the Youth Against Community Injustice (YACIN) out at Castlemont High School in Oakland is gonna mess around and get this book. Somebody like Jamil Posey, Mrs. Fuchs, Massanda D. Johns, or The Veneya Camp is gonna get this book and use it as a tool for mobilizing. I'm not stupid, crazy or foolish enough to believe that God has allowed this wrongful conviction to transpire in my life without a reason (purpose) for the season. Something is about to happen. I believe it will ultimately be Yacin, 3EM, BNB, Youth Making A Change, etc. Our young college students, young law students and young church groups that end up freeing Mumia Abu Jamal, Sherman Manning, Brandon Martinez, David Wong and many others who should not be here. I thank punk rock activists like Rob Middaugh, Scott Gibson and Ron are gonna mess around and unify with Black, White and Brown youth and figure out how to (legally and legitimately) exonerate me, exonerate Mumia and even Leonard Peltier. I believe somebody is gonna fool around and get Karen Murphy Smith, Gloria La Riva, Monica Moorehead, Attorney Ramsey Clark, etc. to unify with Willie Gary, Al, Jesse, Johnnie Cochran, Barry Scheck, Judge Barry Loncke and to formulate a truth and reconciliation committee to see who should not be in prison. Young folks like Jamil are gonna mess around and bombard the WWW with new postings about this tome! I'm telling y'all something is about to happen in America. Young people are angry, neglected, rejected and tired. Rather than rioting out in the streets, killing and robbing, I call on our youth to come together and organize. Fight Prop 21. Fight the criminalization of our youth in schools, barrios and neighborhoods. Fight the power! Did y'all see the movie "One Last Dance"? How about "Searching for Forrester"? It was (in a sense) the youth of South Africa which freed Nelson Mandela. It was the youth that filled up the jails in Alabama with King and defeated Bull Connor. You can do it! You young people can transform L.A. County Jail. You can transform these racist prisons. You can write in, call in, fax in and march in a protest, which will force prisons to focus on rehabilitation. I'm telling y'all if you want to change racial profiling, stop false arrests and the warehousing of humans, etc. we must demand a re-training of all police officers and prison guards. We must **demand** that these people who control the lives of millions of Black, Brown and poor Whites in prison everyday be retrained. *Jane Elliott* needs to be called into C.D.C. and prisons across the country to conduct her race reactions seminars. Oprah did a show with Jane Elliott in 1992. She re-aired the show on July 20, 2001. Jane Elliott could help these evil, racist, corrupted, biased and belligerent prison guards in C.D.C.. Call Jane Elliott. Ain't no power like the power of our youth. I call on you today. Organize! Unite! Come together and fight the power! I want young people to begin to focus more than once on your communication skills. Learn to listen and not just hear. Learn to communicate and not just talk. I want you to join debating teams and learn to become master negotiators. If you want to penetrate a corrupted power structure, you must learn to think, to rationalize and to analyze. You must never be exclusive. Always be inclusive. You must realize that all men, even the most cold-blooded, have a core of decency. Decency may be diminished, hidden or obscured but if a person's heart is touched, the person is capable of change and transformation. Don't shut out any person. Don't overlook anybody. I want my young people not to tolerate diversity. Nobody just wants to be tolerated or put up with. I want you to celebrate diversity. Celebrate, honor, encourage and motivate people to show you who they are and what their culture is all about. I want you to form visiting committees. Yes - I want you to visit prisoners, as did Lesra Martin. I also want you to visit older people in convalescent homes. Don't overlook our elders who are lonely, depressed and many of whom die from a broken heart.

I want each one to reach one. We need mass mobilization and mass organization and I want to remind you that the world media, the power structure and my keepers don't want this book to come out. But if you're reading this we did it. It is out! Now I want you to put flame to the spark. I want you to write me for more copies. I want you to talk about this book on the radio, in school assemblies, at the shopping malls. I want y'all to sponsor car washes, bake sales, garage sale, etc. to raise money to send me for more books. It is our job to get this tome to every high school in Frisco, Oakland, Sacto, Atlanta and New York. We must get it to politicians, lawyers and judges. We must make this book force a system change. Unless we do they're gonna keep on looking up our babies, boys and girls. They're gonna keep on brutalizing and dehumanizing prisoners. They're gonna keep passing new laws and building new prisons. Yet they'll stop building youth centers, schools and libraries. Call your governor and ask, "How many new jails and prisons have we built in the past ten years?" Then ask, "How many libraries and schools"? What in the hell is going on? I'm telling you we have a leadership deficit in America! Bush is not a leader. He is a slick politician. Nelson Mandela (in his autobiography "Long Walk to Freedom") says "A leader must ... tend his garden; he, too, plants seeds, and then watches, cultivates, and harvests the results." A leader must be a promoter of unity, an honest broker, a peacemaker, etc. He can't be a poll follower and it is impossible to lead people whom you don't understand. You can't understand people whom you don't know. Could I fly to Russia tomorrow and lead the country? No way. I don't know enough about their history, culture, dreams or hopes. Mr. Bush is the rich man's president. He does not understand the poor or the working class the way John F. Kennedy or Jimmy Carter did. Even Bill Clinton (at least) understood the working class. Bush was born with a silver spoon in his mouth and with golden slippers. He'll never understand teens out in Nickerson Gardens, Nancy Lane, Perry Homes, or Watts. Bush can't understand the poor and downtrodden. It would help if he (George W.) and Dick Cheney went to a Jane Elliott workshop. Bush should read Mandela's biography. Bush should hole up for six weeks in Kennebunkport and receive lectures from Dr. Naim Akbar, Cornel West and Charles Ogletree. If Bush wants to leave no child (does that include poor Whites, Black, Mexicans and Asians?) behind he needs to know their history, hopes, feelings, dreams and desires. I challenge Bush to show America (not rich America - but all America) to show us you're serious!! Bring Jane Elliott, Naim Akbar, Cornel West, etc. to you home and let them lecture you. Don't get on TV and say, "I don't think these protestors represent poor people" when you don't know a damn thing about poor people. Sit down with Ramsey Clark, Gloria La Riva, and Al Sharpton, Jewish and Hispanic leaders. Listen to them. I want my youth to fax and E-mail Mr. Bush, Cheney and Colin Powell and tell him of this challenge. We desperately need to change the good ole boy politics as usual. Boys will be boys as long as you allow them. Boys will be men if you (Yacin, 3EM, Just Act, etc) educate them. Call these prison wardens and tell them "614,000 are getting out of prison this year. What have you taught them? Are they studying, learning and prepared to re-enter society?" You should demand a change. I've begged C.D.C. to order T.D. Jakes video "Nothing Just Happens" and put them on our TV's or in a big screen so men can watch them and transform their lives. The answer? Hell no! You young folks are the victims of rapes, molestations, gang violence and kidnapping. You have a vested interest in every releasable inmate in prison. Inundate the telephone lines and fax machines of governors, senators, courts, judges, prosecutors and lawyers demanding that the innocent be set free and the guilty be punished and rehabilitated. Young people you can motivate that retired (Professor Gerald Uelmen) law professor or big shot lawyer (Billy Martin, Johnnie, Tarlow, Greenberg, Margolin) to "read Manning's transcripts and tell us if he got a fair trial". You have so much power. The power to hurt (gangs, guns, drugs and violence) and the power to heal. Do not wait on mercy; you must force the hand of the enemy. Don't rest until Abu Jamal and all political prisoners are free. Don't rest until the Angola 3 gets free. Fight for Alan Stark, B.G. Martinez, David Wong, etc.

Fight the Power! Rise up! "Johnnie Cochran is a sell out! He only fights for the rich and powerful. He's all about money now," a brother told me the other day. I strenuously disagree. I have nothing except love, respect and admiration for Mr. Cochran. Period! "Why haven't you organized prisoners yourself?" The same brother asked me. Simple answer; the authorities will not allow me! Ipso facto, I have not tried to organize any group in prison and I never intend to organize any prison group. Yet, this tome alone will spur people on the outside to organize prisoners. I've pragmatically decided I'd rather be a kingmaker than a king. I don't care if I don't get recognition, awards or esteem. Those so-called important things are unimportant to me now. After more than five years of agony, hurt, pain, loneliness and racism I've learned what truly matters. My driving force is not accolades on applause. My motivation is not to be seen but heard. I'd rather the listener have no idea who I am and yet transform their life, than to know its Rev. Sherman Manning, praise my name yet remain the same. I'm tired of the same old games, rhetoric, lies and finger pointing. It's revolution time now. It is time for people to come together and unite for the cause of justice, love and equality. We need to be revived and restored and I'm quite cognizant of the fact that I need not lead this revolution. My baggage, the stigma attached to being an accused rapist is too much for many people to handle, especially when the media weighs in with past accusations, etc. Yet, I can and will encourage the Black media to tell the whole story. I do not play games with myself. I'm not delusional. I'm quite cognizant to the fact that Ward Connerly will not read this book. He's not open-minded enough to want to read anything that he knows collides with his subsequent beliefs. Some folks don't want to see, hear, study or read anything, which does not paint a picture that, coincides with their paradigm. "Oh, that prisoner is a rapist". They said the same thing about Joseph. In modern times it was said about Rolando Cruz also. Yet, Rolando was in worse shape than me for Rolando's alleged victim was a child. But Rolando was innocent. But while he was in prison, Dan Rather, Oprah, Montel didn't want to hear anything this prisoner had to say or write. So I'm cognizant of the fact that my audience may never include Rush Limbaugh. But I don't need Rush! People like Rush are bigots at best and racist at worse. They are narrow-minded, biased and classist. They believe in profiles of what criminals are supposed to look like. They'll look at your past (police record) and try to predict your future. But Justin Weinburger's past didn't matter. Even after this twenty-year-old male was caught with child pornography, etc. psychologist indicated, "He will adjust well and is not likely to commit any crime in the future." That was a couple of years ago. Well Justin just got arrested for raping and murdering twelve-year-old Courtney Sconce (an innocent child). But guess what? Justin's father is a prosecutor! Of course, the D.A. influenced the profile which clearly stated Justin was not likely to commit any crimes. So should we continue to be persuaded by profiles in the media and profiles by so-called experts who are (at best) biased, engaging in conjecture and predictions?

Gary Condit? He may not have killed Chandra, but with just the lies and obstruction of justice alone he'd be in jail if he were poor, Black, Mexican, etc. You know I'm right. I'm not trying to reach Gary Condit. I'm trying to reach Christopher Day, Jamil Posey, Dr. Cornel West, Tony Brown, Spike Lee, Chris Gardner, Gerry Spence, Alan Dershowitz, Ramsey Clark and Gerald Uelmen. I want to reach Kim Randolph, Steve Birdlebough, Jay Harris, Ron Jones, Ed Gordon (B.E.T.), Mark Rand, Clemente "Ibe" Wilson, Mrs. Fuchs, human rights groups, Mr. Nelson Mandela, YEC (Oakland), Jewish Youth for community action, YMAC and James Bell. I'm quite cognizant of the fact that when just one or two of our young people decide to put the word out about this book they will invent ways to do so. They will make sure that Jimmy Santiago Baca (Jimmy taught at Yale, yet gave up the prestige and now teaches at the Youth Detention Center in China) and his students find out about this book. They (my young readers) will inundate chat lines, the web and newsrooms, etc. talking, writing and arguing about this book. No, I'm not depending on Ward Connerly or Clarence Thomas. But I want my youth to come together and never give up 'til we get justice." I want you young people to take over jails and prison reform. Call John Burton. Fax Richard Polanco, Tom Daschle, John Lewis, Maxine Waters, Joseph Biden, Ted Kennedy, the NAACP and the ACLU and tell them we want to investigate and transform L.A. County Jail, Dekalb County Jail and prisons all over America. Get on it young folks. Tell Governor Davis that the "cat is out of the bag" because you read it right here in this book. Tell Davis to prove his prisons are not monster factories. Tell him to prove his prisons don't foment violence, racism, segregation and predatory behavior. Go to L.A. County Jail and ask why Blacks and Mexicans are allowed to rape, beat and enslave any (all) White boys who enters L.A. County Jail. Send in the NAACP and interview every White inmate there and ask how many have been assaulted, had their shoes taken and been sexually abused by inmates of color with deputies looking on. Tell the governor to prove via empirical data that prisons, profiles and C.D.C. works. Tell him to show you one single reply he has written to me when I told him I was wrongfully accused. We want empirical data. We are not interested in profiles, rap sheets, etc. We don't care about any police speculation that Mumia Abu Jamal was supposedly violent. We will not be swayed by media depictions of our people as rapists, predators and thugs. We want Mumia out of prison. And if Sherman Manning did not commit this crime, we want him out of prison. This is what you must tell the power structure. You must be strong and firm in your efforts. Don't let the power structure hoodwink you on Mumia, David or me. We want the truth, the whole truth and nothing but the truth. We can't be interested dismayed or hoodwinked by the media, innuendo or criminal profiles. I read my police profile a few years ago and I was livid. It was so bad, biased and one-sided that it was almost comical. These are the field reports that FBI experts read to come up with these profiles. I could not believe some of the bull shit they included in these profiles. It said, "Mr. Manning was in Chesterfield, Virginia riding in a limousine. He turned his head and blew a kiss at a pedestrian". Blew a kiss? This is used to determine I'm a predator?

And C.D.C.? My God they'll fill up your C-file with innuendo, propaganda and biased lies. "Manning is highly manipulative" they say and then they allow lieutenant B.M. to get on the telephone with David, schools, etc. "You don't want to write or visit Manning. He is vicious, a killer, predator, etc." Yet, this is allowed by the folks downtown of C.D.C. "File a 602, grievance or talk to the media and I'll put you in the hole. Then I'll transfer you to Corcoran (SATIF) or Lancaster. I'll transfer your celly also," they tell me. Yet drug addicts, alcoholics and belligerent inmates never get transferred or thrown into the hole. Young people (Just Act, 3EM, MAC, Yacin) I want you to *just act*. Take action on this book, with your power. Get with Van Jones, Ron Sanders, 3EM etc. and strategize. Call C.D.C. (Sacramento) in shifts. Call Gray Davis in shifts. Call radio talk shows and steal the show.

Use your energy! Use your youth! Use your power for good. You are somebody. You are worth greatness, power and potential all down in the marrow of your bones. Don't let anybody stop you from dreaming, hoping, visualizing, imaging, reading, learning and taking action. Use your life. Use your power! You are somebody.

Once upon a time (to my youth I write this) an eagle lost an egg and the tiny lil eagle egg was discovered by a hen. She carried the egg home to the chicken coop and sat on it with all the loving patience of an incipient mother. Shortly thereafter the egg was hatched and out stepped a tiny lil eagle. This tiny bird had an eagle history, eagle genes, eagle chromosomes, eagle power and marvelous eagle potential. Yet, because he was born in a chicken environment, he grew up thinking he was a chicken. He grew up thinking chicken thoughts, dreaming chicken dreams, scheming chicken schemes praying chicken prayers, playing chicken games and behaving like a chicken. He was even made to feel inferior and ashamed of his eagle features. He didn't know who he was, but the other birds in the barnyard did. They said to each other, "We must keep this bird thinking he's a chicken, because if he finds out that he's an eagle, he will lord over us."

The other birds made fun of his mighty eagle beak, because they had little thin, narrow, weak chicken beaks. They joked about his eagle talons, because they had weak, tiny scrawny chicken feet. The bird became ashamed of the richness of his deep, dark eagle feathers. At this juncture, he even considered plastic surgery. He thought about cutting off half of his eagle beak and dyeing his dark eagle feathers so he could look more like the chickens. His greatest ambition in life was to one day hop, skip and jump up on the fence post to cockle-doodle-do at daybreak like the rooster. But one day, when this confused bird was playing in the barnyard, he saw the deep, dark contours of a mighty shadow swim across the ground. For the first time in his life, this little lost bird *looked higher* than the fence post, *higher* than the tree line and saw the remarkable sight of an adult eagle in full flight - with all of it's majesty, grace and power. This little lost bird was transfixed. He said to himself, "I wish I could be like that." The big eagle perceived the dilemma of the little lost bird and swooped down from the stratospheric heights and said, "Boy, you ain't no chicken. *You're an eagle*! Your mighty talons were not meant to rake and scrape on the ground for worms and feed, but to snatch the side of yonder mountain of achievement. Boy, you ain't no chicken. You're an eagle! Your eagle eye was not meant to be limited to the narrow confines of the barnyard but to seek out the distant horizon of your own unfulfilled potential and spread your wings as you catch the lofty winds of your immeasurable genius. You ain't no chicken - you're an eagle! Each of you reading can take a lesson from this study. I'm writing to you the poor and downtrodden. *You,* the rich and uppity. *You*, the Black, Brown or White kid. *You*, who have been poor into poverty and raised in misery. *You*, who have been programmed to fail and live in conditions worse than hell. *You*, who see pain, problems, death, hurt and misery all around you. *You*, who have wealthy parents but know how to use a computer or has a nanny instead of a mother and a father. *You*, students at Castlemont High School, Heritage, Columbine, Archer/Harper, in Atlanta, Chicago, New York, Oakland

and Los Angeles. I want you to know you are not a chicken. You are not a loser. You are not a nigger, a faggot, a nobody or a nothing. You are an eagle. You (Jamil Posey and all *youths* are somebody! You must raise the angle of your vision. Look higher than the fence post. Look higher than welfare. Look higher than poverty, honorable mention, and failure. Look higher than the ghetto. Look higher than juveniles, jail cells and prison cells. Raise your vision and rise above your circumstances. You are a human being. You have potential. You have worth. I want you teens to begin to call Tallahassee, Florida and hook up with Dr. Naim Akbar's folks. I want you to read Naim Akbar's book, "Breaking the Chains of Psychological Slavery". I want you to get his tapes such as "Maleness to Manhood". Read, "Makes Me Wanna Holler" by Nathan McCall. I want you to inundate your mind with all sorts of data, which reminds you of who you are. I want all you reading to read "Long Walk to Freedom" by Nelson Mandela. I'm sick and tired of us waiting 'til people are dead and gone to celebrate their greatness. Malcolm, Martin, Mahatma and Medgar never got their props while they were alive. Neither did John F. Kennedy or Reuben Salazar. And we are not giving our people (Black, White or other) props while they (we) are alive. Let's celebrate great Black men (Naim Akbar, Earl Graves, Willie Gary, Jesse, Al, Louis, Chris Gardner, Bill Cosby, P. Diddy, Oprah, you! Me?) and women now! Let's celebrate great White, Jewish, Mexican, Pacific Islanders who are contributing to the betterment of mankind here and now. Don't wait 'til we die. I want young people to study the "Free The Children" movement. Study and analyze how Chris put this organization internationally when he was only a kid. He took action! (I'll remind you) read "Free The Children". "The Youth at Castlemont, 3EM, Just Act, etc. need to unite globally. They need an immediate victory under their belts. They need to work vigorously to free Mumia. They must work to free Leonard and David Wong. They must work to free the Angola 3. These cases will no doubt take awhile to win. Your case (Sherman Manning) can be won within six months with the right lawyer. Pragmatically, if you can get youth to inundate Johnnie Cochran, Barry Scheck, Barry Tarlow, Gerry Spence, Professor Uelmen, Professor David Cole, Professor David Cole, Professor Dershowitz, etc. with requests to take your case - you will be freed soon. No way your case can stand legal scrutiny. It's a bullshit case. But if you can get help and get out you can't forget others. "God will punish you if you get out and forget others who don't belong here," stated Lonnie Young to me. So I appeal to Jamil Posey, Massanda D. Johns, Just Act, 3EM, We Interrupt This Message, etc. to come to my rescue. Help me to get out of here. I won't ever stop fighting for justice for the innocent. I want y'all to hook up with Anthony Porter, Rubin "Hurricane" Carter, Atty. Steve Bright and Peter Neufeld. Tell them I need help. Find Rolando Cruz and I'm sure he'll relate to what I'm going through in an intimate way. Hook up with Al Sharpton, Jesse Jackson, F. Lee Bailey and members of our Senate. Shine the light of the judicial system on my case. But don't dare believe I can get any help from the media. No way. They will sensationalize my case and paint me with the predatorily strokes of a profile. I need y'all to put work in now. Perhaps I can serve as an umbrella to youth groups all over the world. If some of you youth activists want to hook up with my (confidante, business associate and the best Christian friend I have in the world) friend Peter Andrist and talk about reviving I-may and organizing a youth summit you can E-mail him at HalloPeter@yahoo.com and maybe I need to get Peter to fly over here to Sacramento in November of this year. Let's talk about it. I want to remind anyone reading that you can send contributions (from one dollar to one million dollars) directly to me here at the prison. Nobody is authorized to receive money for me. So if some of you begin taking up offerings at church, clubs, meetings, etc. for me and you need to know where to send it; send it directly to me.

Again I want to encourage our youth to takeover the streets. Take over politics and take over the hoods. I want you to get busy not only for me but for Mumia, Leonard, David and all political prisoners. Get busy (also) for yourselves. I want you to maximize your mental powers. You need to start mastering, reading, writing, math, poetry, economics, science and psychology, turn your little hoods into universities! Let's get it on! Bush lied and is leaving many children behind. But I want my young people to begin to meet once or twice per week and hold study groups. Read out loud to the entire group. Get you some soda (no alcohol) and popcorn or chips and sit around for a couple hours and debate Nathan McCall's book. Debate "The Debt", my tome, "Long Walk to Freedom", etc. put your thinking caps on and organize. Hold little public speaking contests and critique one another on how to improve your speeches. Get busy. Get active!! Y'all got the power to fight the power! I want you to develop your potential and nurture your minds. Do it now! You need to begin having youth leadership training groups. Develop your leadership skills. Aren't you burnt out on reactionary, sound bite snake oil salesmen? We need some Kings, Kennedys, Ghandis and some Mother Teresas. Sometimes a leader must move out ahead of the flock, go in a new direction, confident that he is leading his people to the

Promised Land. I'm sorry but I can't even fathom Bush as a unifier. I can't imagine energy crisis Gray Davis as a leader. These guys are ambitious they are controlled by polls and motivated by money.

They are on the wrong side of history. Every time I look into the eyes of eighteen and nineteen-year-old boys (in prison) who were raped, sodomized, stabbed and beat in Davis' prisons, I know Davis is no leader. Every time I see all White wardens, abuse, staff corruption and racism all over the state, Davis is no leader. He and Bush and many more are followers. But we the people can shame them. We the people can demand a change. A change in these prisons. A change in these courts. A change in this racial profiling and police shootings. A change is gonna come if and when, *you the youth,* organize, galvanize and unite. I cherish my own freedom dearly, but I care even more for your freedom. Too many have been gunned down by police officers, set up by vicious prosecutors and imprisoned since I came here. Too much blood has been shed. Too many of our youths are dying, some even at the hands of their own brothers and sisters (in here and out there). These prisons are systematic apartheid. David allows this. The ghettos and barrios in the streets are havens of despair. It's time to transform them. I want my youths to come together. I want you to vote in record numbers when you turn eighteen. I want you to lobby congress and demand a change in these prisons. Demand a change in police, jails and trials. Tell our congress that the rioting in Cincinnati can happen again. But we don't want it to happen. We want equal justice. We want Mumia, David and Leonard free. We want more schools and fewer jails. We want racist police officers fired. We want education to take priority over incarceration. We demand a change.

I want my young folks to write Bishop Desmond Tutu and Fmr. President Mandela and tell them we want their help, prayers and suggestions. Send them this book. Become active, strategic and disciplined. Stop rioting and tearing up your own neighborhoods. Rich life goes on in the suburbs when you riot in the hood. Sign petitions, march (non-violently) to the offices and homes of mayors, governors, senators and prisons and let your voice be heard. President Bush was a no-show at the NAACP convention this year. He sent a video! "Watch me! Hear me! Listen to my sound bite! I don't need to hear you. Hear me". He's dictating. This is not Russia nor communist China. This is America! Tell Bush we want to be heard. We, the children, he promised not to leave behind. Come on y'all, let's get it on! Use your energy, your mind, and your brains to transform life for the working class. Call Governor Gray Davis and tell him you don't want to hear excuses. We don't want another three-year study. We want change in these prisons. We want the rapes, abuse, beatings, killings, and violence to stop. We want the gangs disbanded. We want L.A. County Jail and Sacramento County jail cleaned up.

We want people in prison to receive books, visits, education and transformation. We want the innocent set free. We want the wrongfully convicted released. We want more libraries, schools and better pay for our teachers. We want Jane Elliott to train C.D.C. officials and police officers. We want corrupted D.A.'s fired. Call him, fax him. Call Richard Polanco, John Burton and ask them to help us get innocent men out of prison. Call! Write! Fax! Contact brilliant, powerful, caring warriors of the courtrooms such as Mr. Bailey, Mr. Spence, Mr. Tarlow, Uelmen, Roy Black, etc. and tell them that we need help. Call Michael Snedeker, etc. Get active!

I want Christopher Gardner, P. Diddy, Don King, Spike, Snoop Dogg, Shaq, etc. to help me. Help us. Send me some help so I can get my freedom. Donate money to 3EM, Yani, Just Act, the NAACP and SCLC.

I saw many at the Essence Awards talking a good talk. Let's come together and walk the walk. We are our brother's keepers! I want all adults to start giving back to our youths and help them develop controlled intelligence and self-discipline. We must invest in our youth. Help! Help! Help! Help to save our chillen!! (Chillen?) - Children! All children! Black one's, White one's, Mexicans, all of them. Give them the resources they need to save themselves. Maybe you still don't give a damn about me, my wrongful conviction, etc. Okay. I can't lose what I never had. But P. Diddy, Christopher Gardner, Bishop Jakes, John Johnson, Earl Craves, Susan Taylor y'all help young people. Put some money into buying books (non-fiction) into inner city schools. That's a start. Contact the Partnership for the Homeless (New York City) and find the address to Richard Lattimore. I'll send Richard's program a check. You all must save the children. Pat Anderson (The Crescent Ninth Ward, Sandy Utah/The Ensign), Monica Moorehead, etc. can tell you what guys like me are going through. Please get involved. I want my youth to contact New York Times reporter Lena Williams, the Washington Post, etc. and write them open letters. Contact Richard Terzian, Judge Gary Ransom, Senator John Vasconcellas, Diane Martinez, and Darrell Steinberg and tell them we want to discuss "If it doesn't fit, you must acquit, Part II". Find Josh Tipton (Sacramento computer wizard) David Hannon, etc. and ask them to join us in fighting wrong and evil. Let me tell my young activists something else; yes you must use our power to free Mumia Abu Jamal, repeal Prop 21, and restore rehabilitation and family visiting to prisons. Transform your schools and hoods, etc. I want you to unite, get together, right now. Call Attorney Michelle Alexander, Van Jones, Barry Scheck, etc. and say, "How can we get together". Contact Al Sharpton, Jesse Jackson, Louis Farrakhan, Friends Committee on Legislation, Jewish Youth activists, etc. "How can we get youths together? We do not see eye to eye on many issues but a lot of our short-term objectives are very similar. How can we get our youths together?!! Call Martin Luther King, III in Atlanta, Coretta Scott King, Julian Bond, the NAACP, SCLC. The ADL and tell them we want to unite our youth against hate. Many of these old organizations seem a little outdated and behind the times but they need help. They need your energy, youth, street power, innovation and money. We gotta do this y'all use youth power. If the big media attempts to eviscerate the motives of your unity, etc. - forget them. Call and write the Worker's World Newspaper. Call Mr. Ratcliff at the San Francisco Bayview Newspaper. Call Michael Novick at "Turning the Tide" (310) 495-0299. Call the Afro-American newspapers, Atlanta Daily World, Atlanta Voice and tell them we need coverage. Tell Mike, Ratcliff, Diedre, etc. "We want you to pump up 'If it doesn't fit, you must acquit, Part II'". Tell them, "We are holding a rally outside C.D.C. headquarters and we need you to cover it." Put your news on the Internet, print flyers and make your voice heard. And (innovative) raise money to help these newspapers that give you exposure. WW paper, P.A.R.T., the Bayview, etc. and a few others routinely send papers free of charge to inmates! They need help. I want the Bayview, WW, Turning the Tide, etc. to increase their circulations and they will do it if you (my young posse) help them. Do a bake sale, car wash, etc. once per week and send the proceeds to these papers. Write your own book review, newsletter, talking points and memos, etc. and mail them to every senate member and the House of Representatives. Use your power. Are y'all (really) ready to rumble? Call Attorney Murray J. Janus, Charles Ogletree, Stephen Bright, Barry Scheck, and Gerry Spence and ask them to explain how prosecutors are getting more power. Tell them to explain the new limits on appeals, etc. Ask them to explain how indigent inmates get robbed of a fair trial. Murray, David Cole, Samuel Dash, Alan Dershowitz will explain it to you. Call Ephraim Margolin, Gerald Uelmen (at Santa Clara) and tell 'em "We are going to the Senate and demanding equal protection under the law for all people. We need to know what we are talking about. Can you explain to us, etc. etc.?" Get on it! Fight the power! March to C.D.C. and demand that inmate rapes, abuse, prison gangs, etc. be stopped. "Mr. Davis we demand that you clean up the monster factory which is sending (training and teaching) predators, frustrated, angry and hopeless men to our communities every day". Correspond with guys in prison. Write us many men here who never get a letter. (If you are under the age of eighteen, get your parents permission before writing prisoners. Let no prisoner play you. Be careful! I don't discourage you to write. I encourage you to reach out to prisoners. They are human beings. But be cautious, prayerful, and realistic and don't believe everything somebody tells you). Fight the power! Fight. Contact Ed Gordon at B.E.T. and tell him "We want an hour on TV". Call Ebony Magazine and get with Mr. John Johnson and Lerine Bennett "We want you to do a story on Yacin, Just Act and 3EM and a review on Sherman's book, please". Call Susan Taylor "Review Sherman's book in Essence". Call Earl Graves, Queen Latifah, Tony Brown. Get moving y'all. It's revolution time. But don't talk about it do something about it!!!

Call Bishop T.D. Jakes and tell him to pray about it and preach about it. Call Gilbert Patterson. Get on the telephone and call Bishop Paul Morton (St. Stephens Full Gospel Church in New Orleans) and tell Bishop Morton we need help. Call Doug Banks, Cathy Hughes (in D.C.) and tell 'em help. We must bring our youth together. Let's do it! And I want to tell all police officers and Chiefs of police, etc. stop crying! Ain't nobody telling you not to be proactive. I want you to do your job. I join with Rev. Damon Lynch at New Prospect Baptist Church (in Cincinnati) by telling you to do your job. I want my youth to respect your (police) authority. Obey the law. No one is advocating bombing or beating the police. Yet, we want you to police in the hood the same way you police in the suburbs. Come to Perry Homes, Watts, and The Barrios with the same courtesy, niceties and respect that you carry to Buckhead, Beverly Hills and Malibu. You don't want us to treat and view all police as being racist or corrupt? I respect that. Then stop the silence. Disrupt and break then time blue line. Stop turning your head when you see abuse, excessive force, etc. Tell your coworkers "If I see you do wrong I will report it". Then we all can get along. Let's come together. I am making a national call (here and now) to stop the violence in Cincinnati, Atlanta, and Los Angeles and all over America. I make a national call to begin bringing communities and police together. I make a national call for churches, entrepreneurs and the government to fight poverty, hunger, illiteracy, and racism all over America. I make a national call to end police brutality, prosecutorial misconduct, etc. Obviously Mr. Bush is too busy giving tax cuts to the rich and he does not care. He only throws some words (which are usually mispronounced) at social problems.

Youth, students, lawyers, doctors, Blacks, Latinos, Asians, Whites, the working class, etc. Let us come together and rebuild America. Rebuild our schools, libraries, communities and churches. We need Jamie Bakker, Jesse Jackson, Al Sharpton, Rev. Damon Lynch III, Julian Bond, etc. we need pastors to come out of retirement and wage a war on social problems. We should be embarrassed by the fact that more than two million men are in prison in this great country. People in Switzerland, Sweden and Spain are shocked at the sheer number of inmates in prison in America. The sheer numbers of new three strike laws, etc. that have been passed in the get tough on crime policies era of American politics. It is time to call out the dogs! Time to come out of retirement. Time to groom the youth and let them lead! Bush led one hundred and fifty-two to the death chamber in Texas. He seems only to lead the poor to death row and the rich to the bank. We must pull ourselves out of this mess. Let's revive ourselves. America needs revival. Revival.

We cannot forget to revive our court system. There are too many back room deals being made in which innocent people's freedom are being stolen. "Rape is the one crime in which proof of guilt of the offender depends upon proof of innocence of the victim . . . She (he) must prove herself (himself) to be free of precipitating the attack, of consenting to it and of falsely accusing the defendant," states F. Lee Bailey and Henry B. Rothblatt. Judge Altman disallowed us to prove Ricardo Calvario was a prostitute. He disallowed us to prove there was not a rape. States Lord Chief Justice Hale, "Rape is a charge which is easy to make, difficult to prove and even more difficult to defend". Yet Robert Altman made it impossible to defend. "The court should fine the prosecutor for prosecutorial misconduct and reverse and remand your case Sherman," stated Atty. M.J.

"If the witness tumbled, appeared confused or simply rambled in a virtually incoherent fashion, the jury (of your peers) will probably disregard his testimony," stated Atty. F. L. Bailey. Ricardo Calvario? He took inconsistency, fabrication and fantastic mendacity to another level. Then why am I here? Judge Altman sustained and made his own objections any time we pointed out a lie. The jury had not a single Black person on the jury. "Elicit contradictions between the witness's testimony at trial and his prior testimony or statements," states Lee Bailey but Altman crippled the defense by yelling, shouting and berating the defense in front of the jury when we pointed out Ricardo's inconsistencies.

And here I sit, three thousand miles away from home. I am innocent - totally, unequivocally, factually and fully innocent of these crimes. Rubin "Hurricane" Carter told his supporters "Y'all gotta get me out of here." I say to my youths, P. Diddy, Chris Gardner, Cochran, Scheck, Lee Bailey, Tarlow, Janus, Snedeker, Uelmen and Margolin - Please get me outta here. This place is absolutely intolerable. Mr. G. Davis allows his thirty-three prisons to enslave, rape, beat and murder inmates. To allow forced homosexual relationships in prison constitutes cruel and unusual punishment. Davis allows arbitrary, capricious, irrational and abusive punishment to be inflicted upon his inmates. This is wrong! Here and now I am asking somebody (anybody reading) to send a copy of this tome to Fmr. President Nelson Mandela and one to Bishop Desmond Tutu. I'm rushing to press and I don't have the time to obtain their addresses. Please (if you do nothing else) help me get this book to Mr. Mandela and Bishop Tutu. I want them to read about the embarrassing, humiliating and apartheid like conditions of the American prison system and our judicial system. I want them to know what's going on. Just a few months ago Jose Morales was freed after serving twelve long years in prison for a crime he (too) did not commit and Reuben Montello (in the same case) is likewise to be released in a few days also. His mother (Senorita Maria Montalvo) stated, "My son has wasted twenty years of his life in prison." "Another man came forth and admitted to the crime before the trial. The D.A., court and police would not listen to him," states Rand Maher (lawyer for both Morales and Montalvo). He got railroaded. A man confessed to the crime to father Joseph Towl and the prosecutors are arguing that it was a religious confession and should be inadmissible in a court of law. Why? To save face. They don't want to let a man walk free after they've stolen twenty years of his life. This is politics. They would rather let the wrong man do the time for the crime than to say "we were wrong". Don't you know if they thought I committed a murder and they discovered I confessed it to a priest they (Mary Hanlon Stone or Debbie Glynn) would argue strenuously that the confession be allowed in court so that a murderer would not go free on mere technicality.

But if the technicality is exculpatory in results they wish to disallow it. This is what Gray Davis, John Ashcroft and George Bush call "Tough on Crime". Montalvo is just a "casualty" and shit happens.

Stuff (injustice, wrongful convictions, judicial error, prosecutorial misconduct and police brutality) will happen as long as we the people allow it to happen. How much longer will we (the people) allow this? I tried but I cannot end this without quoting one of the greatest human beings who ever walked the planet. A Black man whose 640 page book I have been carrying around the prison for a week now. I have had Black inmates, Whites and Mexican's to say, "Can I read it when you finish?"

He said, "I always knew that deep down in every human heart, there is mercy and generosity. No one is born hating another person because of the color of his skin, or his background, or his religion. People must learn to hate, and if they can learn to hate, they can be taught to love, for love comes more naturally to the human heart than it's opposite. Even in the grimmest times in prison, when my comrades and I were pushed to our limits, I would see a glimmer of humanity in one of the guards, perhaps just for a second, but it was enough to reassure me and keep me going. Man's goodness is a flame that can be hidden but never extinguished!!!!" Nelson Mandela . . . Amen! Amen! Lord have mercy on us all! God Bless South Africa! God Bless America! Nkosi Sikelel' Iafrika!!

" . . . .I found that I could not . . .enjoy . . . Freedoms I was allowed when I knew my people were not free. Freedom is indivisible; the chains on any one of my people were the chains on all of them, the chains on all of my people were the chains on me . . .A man who takes away another man's' freedom is a prisoner of hatred, he is locked behind the bars of prejudice and narrow- mindedness . . . The oppressed and the oppressor alike are robbed of their humanity," stated Mr. Mandela in "Long Walk To

Freedom". I challenge my youth (all of you) to read Mr. Mandela's book. I also challenge every American politician who boasts and brags on having read Shakespeare, Tolstoy, etc. to read Mandela.

It is simply one of the best books ever written on earth. If you choose (I hope not) to put down my book and forget about me. I can live with that. But please read "Long Walk To Freedom". There is healing, hope, direction and reconciliation in that book. "I will go down on my knees to beg those who want to drag our country into bloodshed.... take your guns, your knives, and your pangas, and throw them into the sea! Close down the death factories. End this war now," stated Mr. Mandela. Has Bush, Limbaugh (no way), Davis or Ashcroft read it?

I'm not simply demoralizing Bush and Davis. I really, really wish we could get these men to open up their minds and hearts and do justice, love, mercy and walk humbly with God. Mr. Davis needs to clean up his prisons. His guards make (as I stated) the L. A. Rampart cops look like stealing characters. The L.A. Rampart scandal was not about cops who became criminals, it's about criminals who became cops. C.D.C. is not about prison guards who became corrupted/racist; it's about corrupted/racist people who became prison guards. Californians (and the entire country) have been played by corrupted officials and hustled by political hacks. C.D.C. likes to hide the truth by getting Internal Affairs to sweep allegations of misconduct under the rug. Officers get protected because C.D.C. wants to avoid scandal and publicity. We need ferociously intense lawyers such as David Kenner, Barry Tarlow, Stanley Greenberg and Tony Serra to take on C.D.C. we need Stephen Yagman, and Milton Grimes to sue the hell out of C.D.C. men who have some status such as Suge Knight ought to expose C.D.C. in the media. And Suge ought to reach back and help somebody else. Steve Cooley ought to clean up the LAPD by charging and trying rogue, racist and renegade cops when they commit crimes. The Attorney General ought to charge and try C.D.C. officers when they commit crimes. But too often we give Carte Blanche status to officers of the law. We need to get fierce, ferocious investigators such as Sergio Robleto, Russell Poole, etc. to investigate C.D.C. I know damn well that Sergio and Russell are cognizant of the fact that many peace and police officers are rogue, racist and corrupted. In fact, Sergio or any investigator out at Kroll Investigations could take one look at my case and discover that "Sherman Manning does not belong in prison". I wish people would come forward. We need help.

"No greater honor will ever be bestowed on an officer or a more profound duty imposed on him than when he is entrusted with the investigation of the death of a human being. It is his duty to find the facts regardless of color or creed without prejudice, and to let no power on earth deter him from presenting those facts to the court" is the Homicide Officer's creed! How many take it seriously?

There are more backroom deals being made to sweep murders under the carpet than you can imagine. How many murders of Black, Hispanic and poor Whites are unsolved in L.A., Cincinnati, Oakland, and San Francisco? And how often does staff (within California's thirty-three prisons) have inmates to kill other inmates and sweep the murders under the carpet? The public must rise up. C.D.C.'s mostly White management is like a country club for the good ole boys. Go to any prison in California and say "show me the Black wardens and captains" and you'll come up practically empty. Talk to the inmates and you'll discover abuse, bigotry, racism and corruption. Abuse? These people feel untouchable. They beat, pepper spray and forcefully extract mentally retarded inmates from their cells on a daily basis. When they conduct a cell extraction they turn all ventilation off in all cells in two hundred and forty cells (two separate buildings which have the same ventilation systems attached). Inmates are forced to sit in hot windowless cells for two and three hours per day with absolutely no (zero) ventilation while cops pepper spray and extract inmates for the most trivial infractions on a daily basis. This is a health risk for all inmates. Several physicians have advised C.D.C. that forcing inmates to sit in hot cells with no windows or ventilation is cruel, unusual and unhealthy. C.D.C. continues to pepper spray and cut off the vents day after day. I want Richard Polanco, John Burton, Maxine Waters and the Feds to totally revamp these prisons. C.D.C. needs a judicial laxative, because it is full of defecation. I want Ted Kennedy, Joe Biden, Al, Jesse, Van, the ACLU, etc. to call a summit meeting on crime and punishment. We really need to revisit crime and punishment in this country. Some laws have been the results of rushes to judgment. They are not smart, well thought out laws. They simply need to be repealed. We need to wipe them off the books. We also need to offer better protection for the true victims of crime. It is a sin and a shame that a man could kidnap, commit rape and even kill a person. He can go to prison, do his time, get out and return to the same community. Is it fair for a man to molest a child in Petaluma, go to prison and serve five years - get out and return to Petaluma? There is no law prohibiting it. What does it do to the sixteen-year-old girl to see the man who molested her while she's out shopping in the mall? If the little girl was your daughter and you saw the guy who raped her while you were in the mall wouldn't that trigger something inside you? Rather than try to prevent vigilantism and crime our laws provoke and promote crime. "You rape a baby and we'll send you to prison. When you get out we want you to parole to the same (exact) county in which you were arrested. We will put you on the Internet as a sex offender and when the victim (or the victim's friends and family) locates you they may burn down your house or kill you. Then we will lock them up in our prison for arson, assault or murder. It appears to be a set up to keep the prisons full. Somebody (our slick, ambitious politicians) is not thinking or are they conspiring? It is difficult (always has been) for me to believe in broad scale conspiracies. But when I look at how we have set up crime, punishment and corrections in America, it makes me wonder are we that dumb or does somebody have a vested interest in keeping the prisons full? Jason Wade (life house), David Hannon, Michael Taketa and Farrah Grey could see through this once they are presented with the facts. I want America presented with the facts in this book. The cat is out the bag. Steve White can change these prisons. But the public must demand the change. It won't/can't come easily. We - Van Jones! We - Michelle Alexander! We-Rachel

Jackson! We - I.A.C.! We - Elizabeth Birch! We - the youth must take action. We need legislative action, political action, grass-roots action and public education. I want my youths to hold Town Hall meetings on crime and punishment. Educate taxpayers on the need for rehabilitation in prisons as a matter of public safety. Use this time to provide them with empirical data. We need to orchestrate thousands of telephone calls, letters, E-mails and faxes to governors, senators, and the President and to our congress members about truth and innocence, wrongful convictions and the prison monster factory. I want this book to bring people together. Support the Human Rights Campaign in D.C. Call Elizabeth Birch out at H.R.C. Send money to the SCLC in Atlanta, Georgia. Help Jews for Justice, 3EM, NAACP and any organization that is making a real difference.

And I want to remind my young readers not to wait on Gray Davis, George Bush, or anybody else. Be like Craig Kielburger and Farrah Grey. Start your own group. Do your own thing. I need my youths out at Castlemont High School; I need Rachel Jackson, etc. to help me find Father Greg Boyle in East Los Angeles, Gus Mojica and (criminals and gang members anonymous) C. G. A. and get this book to them. Pump it up and tell them to read this. Use your telephone, the Internet, the ink pen word of mouth, etc. and put the word out. I want y'all to organize. What would happen if 3EM, Youth Making a Change and hundreds of other youths decided to come together and fight to get innocent men out of prison? What if C.D.C. received one thousand telephone calls and faxes about me tomorrow? If Tony Serra, Gerald Uelmen, Alan Dershowitz, Dennis Riordin or F. Lee Bailey got ten thousand letters asking them to get me out of here - don't you think they would reply? If you go to Van, we can win this. David Kenneth, Gerson Horn, Barry Tarlow or Don Heller can free me. But I need action minded people.

Don't you dare put this book down and do nothing. Organize, strategize and galvanize. Don't wait! Do it now! And (tautology but this is dear to my heart) if you are in a gang - get out! If you are using drugs stop now. Obey the laws of the land. Don't come here! Prison is awful. Prison is a cold, evil, racist and vicious place to be, especially in states such as California where Mr. Davis turns a deaf ear to prisoner's complaints. Mr. Davis closes his eyes to prison (staff) corruption, rapes, drugs and racism. But he opens his eyes to public opinion polls! Hell, perhaps we need to call on Fmr. President Bill Clinton, Senator Hillary Clinton and Jimmy Carter to help us.

Young people use your life, energy, talents and your mind, to rebuild America! You can do it! There is a somebody in you. You are worth more than precious gold. You are an eagle not a chicken. Raise your thinking, dreaming, hoping and your spirit. Get up and go to your destiny. Don't let anybody cause you to abort your dreams and your hopes. Turn you life around and pick up the broken pieces right now.

Murray Janus, Johnnie Cochran, David Boies, Roy Black, Gerry Spence, F. Lee Bailey and all of you warriors of the court mean a lot to me. I want every true lawyer to know I appreciate you from the bottom of my heart. Lawyer's you can give yourself some chicken soup for your soul if you'll just keep fighting! Help Barry Scheck, the ACLU, prisoner, the ADL and church groups. Give something back to our youths. Lawyers are great, strong and terrific role models. Don't forget the least of these thy brethren. We need you Brandon G. Martinez, Mumia Abu Jamal, Leonard Peltier, and so many others need your help. P. Diddy, Chris Gardner, Earl Graves, Bernard Browner Susan Taylor, John Johnson, Al and Jess, Don, Dr. Allman, Michael Morchower, etc. let me hear from you soon. Thank you...

I want to sincerely thank Gerry Spence for his encouragement and resourcefulness. I must also thank Patricia Lee for her typing expertise. I'm encouraged by the fact that I learned that Chris Gardner has given away over a half million dollars in the past four years to public education. Chris Gardner (Gardner Rich and Co. in Chicago) says, "Equal opportunity also means equal responsibility." Yes, I'd be free in less than one year if Chris, P. Diddy, Shaq, etc. etc. would donate, loan or give fifty thousand dollars each toward my defense. That would be a miracle. Yet, if nothing else I wish, hope and pray that Chris, Dr. Allman, Murray, etc. will fund thousands of copies of this tome so we can get it to the people who can be helped by it. I want teens in high school, college and law schools to have this book. Perhaps Mr. Gardner will put two or three thousand copies in Chicago. Maybe he'll help me get it to Professor Robert Cling and his students at Chicago Law School and David Protess at Northwestern University. Remember you (the reader) can help me with a donation (from one dollar to a million dollars) by sending a check or money order directly to me. I want my youth to never forget the importance of study, education, spirituality and action. I want Matt Hammond out at U.C. Berkeley, Trevor Loflin, Jamil Posey, etc. to stay up and get active. Use your life. Read! Read! Read! There is a book called "The Little Boy In Me" by Bishop Bloomer which is a must read for all teens! Get that book today! Remember I need teens to use your computer wizardry to put the word out (to schools, activists, lawyers, politicians, media, churches) about this book. Reach and contact people who are written about within these pages. Folks like Melvin Beckwith out in

Omaha Nebraska needs this tome. Mr. Beckwith has a newsletter aimed at reforming American prisoners. Youth use your wit to find him and get this book to him. I gotta remind y'all (young folks) not to give up. Keep faith in God and in yourself. You are somebody! No matter how bad it seems at times, you must rise above it. Never quit! Never give up! Never, never, never quit! You got to keep on walking! Life will hand you some things, which are perplexing, confusing and mind boggling sometimes. But I promise you that it will get better. It won't be like that always. You must keep hope, faith and love alive. People will let you down. People will deceive, abandon and mistreat you at times. But don't allow the wrongs of others to cause you to lose hope! You can make it! Yes - you can!!!

**To** David Kenner, Suge Knight, Barry Tarlow, Oprah, Mr. Graves, Jesse, Al, Louis, preachers, lawyers, professors, students, sinners, saints, atheists, Christians, etc. anybody, please help me. Before you turn another page sit down and write me today:

> **Sherman Manning J98796**
> **Mule Creek, FA2-240**
> **P.O. Box 409099**
> **Ione,Ca. 95640-9099 USA**

I ask you today - how can we forget that this is America? It is America and we cannot allow this great nation to continue building entire communities around prisons. Nor can we continue to allow this nation to continue destroying entire communities around prisoner! We must make a change. Prison has got to become a last resort and when guys go to prison, we can't let them be abused, raped, humiliated and forced into gangs. Come on, there must be another way. I think that when lawyers (the great one's like Murray J. Janus, Ephraim Margolin, Morris Dees, F. Lee Bailey, Snedeker, Scheck and Cochran) begin to sue Gray Davis and various other governors for their abominable prisons they'll bankrupt the system. Mr. Davis and others will be forced to pay attention to their prisons and clean them up. We can begin to model the State of Oregon and other systems that work. Steve White can meet with Willie Brown, Sheriff Mike Hennessy, Van Jones, etc. and meet with prisoners; and devise a strategy to correct corrections. Inmates want power! Why not call Warden Leland Linahan at Valdosta State Prison and model his program? Why not call Joe Clark at Essex County in New Jersey and get his input? Prisons can consider starting J-ROTC programs inside prisons. Give inmates rank, uniforms, stripes and teach drill and ceremonies (as I've mentioned). Drill and ceremonies instills discipline. Start J-ROTC right here at New Folsom. Hell, we already wear uniforms anyway. Why not add stripes for inmate leaders? Why not teach discipline, leadership, ethics and communication skills within prison? It's all about making better human beings so that when people return to civilian life they'll have a better start. I'm tired of parolees raping, molesting, robbing, stealing and killing. But people can change if we provide them with the resources. Let's make a change today. We can do it! I want y'all to call Ephraim Margolin, David Kenner, Barry Tarlow and F. Lee Bailey and beg them to help get me free. Ephraim Margolin and Gerald Uelmen could have me home within six - twelve months. Murray Janus (Richmond, Virginia) has part of my transcripts. He'll be glad to send them. Much of my transcripts (for some strange reason) are still under seal. How can I appeal when I can't get the transcripts? Mr. Margolin, Gerry Spence, F. Lee Bailey could demand them! I need you to help me get outta here. *God bless you and use your life...*

*Author's Reminder:* I want to tell Jesse Jackson, Al Sharpton, Billy Graham, Charles Rangel, John Lewis and all who are in positions of leadership to be a careful, powerful, corrupted people will (I know from experience) set you up, with a man, woman, etc. They will have people to falsely accuse you etc. in order to discredit you. They use drugs, sex, money and media to bring powerful people down and once you (like me) have been falsely accused it's almost over for you. The data in your record will haunt you for the rest of you life . . .. This just in: Governor Davis and his administration are in the midst of scandal. This administration (Davis himself?) is accused of insider trading. They, apparently, invested in Cal Pine while simultaneously lambasting them publicly. That's only half of the story! C.D.C. (under Davis' auspices) allows prisoners to purchase (books, watches, shoes, televisions, etc.) items from a select few companies. Companies such as Walkenhorst, Access and Pack Central make millions off California prisoners. Are these publicly owned companies? Does C.D.C. wardens, the director and the governor, etc. get any kickbacks from these monopolies? C.D.C. certainly receives kickbacks from MCI for the exorbitant calling rates they charge us. What's really going on? I encourage the NAACP, ACLU, CA Prison focus, etc. to open an investigation into the financial arrangements of MCI, Walkenhorst, Access, Pack Central and C.D.C. Find out where the money is going. If Grey Davis were Marion Barry (Black Fmr. D.C. Mayor), they'd be calling for his resignation by now . . ..

I counted eighty-nine new C.D.C. recruits (officer in training today. Of eighty-nine, all were White. Not a single Black face. Is C.D.C. really an equal opportunity employer? It is a country club! A hood! A racist, corrupt, biased, asinine, duplicitous and backwards department. Morris Dees, Willie Gary, Stephen Yagman, Johnnie, F. Lee, Milton Grimes, anybody, let's sue C.D.C. and the Black media must expose C.D.C. I want story after story to appear in the Bayview, P.A.R.T., WW publishers, Black Voice, etc. We must expose this sham of a system!

* * * *

Johnnie Cochran, Gerry Spence, Willie Gary and Isaac Byrd flew in to Richmond, Virginia and arrived (late) at the law offices of Attorney Murray J. Janus at 1:27 p.m. on a Saturday. Barry Tarlow, Blair Berk, James Brosnahan, Gerry Uelmen, Ephraim Margolin and Dennis Riordin were already in the conference room waiting. "We must find a way to exonerate Sherman Manning from prison," Mr. Janus stated. "Guys, I've never seen a weaker case than this one. It is riddled with incredible, inconsistent and impossible testimony, which was given by Ricardo Calvario. Quite frankly, I cannot fathom or imagine how/why this jury convicted Rev. Manning on that testimony. I've called you here today to ask each of you to help me help Rev. Sherman Manning get out of prison. With all of these brilliant minds in the same room and under the same roof, I cannot believe that we can't find a way to get him out of there.

So let us strategize and come up with a pragmatic plan, which will secure his freedom by any legal means, which are necessary.

He's been in there too long and he's losing hope. We've got to get him out before he breaks.

Now, I'm in the process of getting letters of recommendation for Sherman's release from prosecutors David Hicks and Aubrey Davis. In fact, Michael Morchower is playing golf today with Aubrey Davis. Hicks is definitely on board and we're trying to get a few senators and congressmen to help us also.

I need help. Everybody in this room knows Rev. Manning is innocent in this case. We must now decide whether or not to ask for a pardon, a new trial or some type of special circumstances release. If we're gonna get him home this year, we must be pragmatic, strategic and we must play politics. It is time to *get him out* of prison. He's no saint and he is no angel but Rev. Manning did not commit this crime . . ."

The aforementioned (beginning with the names Johnnie Cochran and Gerry Spence) is fiction. I believe life must imitate art if I'm going to obtain justice. We call on Edwin Spencer Matthew, Jr., Lynn Stewart, the National Lawyers Guild, Peter Sussman and all legal thespians to come and *get me out*. I did not commit this crime. I'm innocent . . .

# Kobe Bryant and False Accusations

"I've been falsely accused . . . I'm innocent," came the words out of the mouth of NBA Superstar Kobe Bryant on Friday, July 18th at a press conference. Kobe was responding to allegations that he raped a nineteen-year-old female in Eagle County, Colorado. Rape is a horrible, sinister and vicious act. Any man or woman (although women are rarely charged, tried or convicted of rape) who is low, evil, sick, perverted and wicked enough to force any human being to have any kind of sex ought to be prosecuted to the full extent of the law. They ought to go to jail. They should be sentenced to serve time in prison and while we punish them for their awful crime, we must force them to get treatment in prison. Pragmatically, with the way our laws are set up in the American system of justice, we don't usually send sexual offenders to prison for life. They get out everyday of the week and more often than not they re-offend again. So we must wake up to the fact that doing time, serving a prison sentence, does *not* cause a sexual predator to wake up one morning and *decide* not to rape again. With that indisputable fact in mind, it is high time that we restructure our laws and insist upon treatment while punishing the rapist.

Kobe Bryant must go to prison! Kobe must also be enrolled in a treatment program for sexual deviants while he serves his prison time. We must demand that Kobe Bryant be sent to prison, if he committed this horrendous act of violence. If he is innocent, he must be exonerated and vindicated. This writer was not in that hotel room. Nobody reading this tome (with the exception of Mr. Bryant and his accuser) was in that room that night. So, in spite of media hype, sensationalism and yellow journalism, we must follow the law and according to the law, Mr. Bryant is presumed innocent. He must be considered innocent until or unless he is proven guilty beyond a reasonable doubt to a moral certainty. That is the law no matter who says differently. I have absolutely no vested interest in the outcome of Kobe's case. I have no bias either pro or con in this case. My only demand is a demand for justice. I spent too many years being tutored, taught and schooled by the late Rev. Hosea Williams, former Ambassador Andrew Young and others who helped shape my paradigm of justice in America. Too much has been invested in me for me to be biased, prejudiced or vindictive. They taught me to follow the law of the land and since the law is clear, we must give Kobe the presumption of innocence. Everybody is talking about this case and this case is a clear example of how easily a story can become twisted and people can hear things, which have never been stated and see things, which have never been shown.

I spoke with a man tonight who was convinced Kobe is guilty. This man has tried and convicted Kobe even before Kobe made a single court appearance. Kobe has not even been read his rights and this guy said, "I ain't got no respect for no man charged with rape." I felt Johnnie Cochran, Murray J. Janus, Gerry Spence and Anthony Brooklier coming up in my mind. "What would Johnnie, Murray or Gerry say?" I asked myself. And so I replied to this guy, "You're ignorant. You're absolutely brainwashed. You say you have no respect for any man charged with rape. Yet, you told me you're innocent of the three strikes case you are now serving time in prison for. You told me that the cops set you up and planted the drugs on you. You want me to believe *you*! You expect the courts to believe that sworn peace officers, who wear badges and uniforms, would stoop low enough to lie, deceive and commit perjury to set you (who?) up. Yet there is no way a woman can lie and say he raped her. That is one of the most ridiculous, preposterous and selfish statements I've ever heard come out of your mouth." Then he decided to remind me that, at first, Kobe Bryant said he did not have sex with her at all. But when the DNA came back proving he did, now he (changed his story) is saying he did but it was consensual. This was another absolutely foolish statement and what's worse is I've heard no less than ten people make that same false statement today. Kobe never (ever) stated that he did not have any sex with this woman. He absolutely did not ever say that. What he did say was he was innocent and that when everything comes clean, it would all be fine and we would see he is innocent. There is nothing contradictory (per se) in that statement and it is entirely compatible with, "I did commit adultery".

We now come upon the problem with jurors, prosecutors, judges and police officers in this country today. The problem? We are all human beings and human beings make mistakes. I submit that there is absolutely nothing I could say or do to convince these people that Kobe didn't say that but he didn't. And so when jurors hold the lives, freedom and futures of the accused in their hands, they often make mistakes. They think they heard a witness say this or do that. "When I saw tears coming down her cheeks, I knew she was telling the truth" a juror will say. But when we go back and review the tape, we see absolutely no tears coming down her cheeks. As I write this (this very moment) Attorney Billy Martin just reminded a nightline correspondent that Kobe did not change his story. The question was "Doesn't Kobe look bad since, in a sense, he has changed his story?"

That loaded question was a deceptive question. "Kobe never said he didn't have sex. He said, "I would never do something like that, meaning rape" - came the answer to the question.

When we see how clearly, how quickly and how easily people can add, delete, embellish and soften their memories of events, which transpired (or didn't transpire) in less than a week, it should not be difficult to comprehend why Johnnie, Scheck and Spence so adamantly oppose the final judgment, which is the death penalty. Johnnie Cochran knows how often humans actually mean well but make mistakes. We can't allow people to hold the power of life and death in their hands when we clearly often get it wrong.

One of the defense lawyer's nightmares is a lying witness. And even more terrifying for the Janus, Billy Martins and Barry Tarlows of the legal profession is the lying witness who believes he or she is telling the truth. Most of the people I talked with about Kobe actually believe they heard him say that he did not have sex with that woman. They are lying. They are absolutely mistaken but they don't know it and one of the challenges for law students as well as law professors today is to learn and to teach lawyers how to adequately and effectively deal with the lying witness who believes they're telling the truth. Countless cases have been lost because the defense lawyer did not know how to effectively challenge cross-examine and deal with this kind of witness. Ipso facto, there are men and women who are innocent but convicted because somebody lied on them and their lawyer was ill equipped and ill-prepared to cross-examine the lying witness. It takes a certain stomach and a unique kind of guts, willpower, skill power and instinct to successfully cross-examine the lying witness.

We all have our biases and our life experience is never left outside the doors of the courtroom. We have opinions and jurors, judges, lawyers and witnesses carry those opinions in the room. I personally have an opinion. I do not believe Kobe raped that woman. I could be wrong and if I am wrong, he should go to jail, period. I do know something about human behavior, behavioral science, body language, facial expressions and truth telling. And I must interject that I don't give a darn about Kobe's celebrity. It is irrelevant to me. When I saw that twenty-four-year-old young man say, "I am innocent," every fiber of my being believed he was telling the truth. And if I'm correct, I want him to receive a fair trial. And if he gets a fair trial, I believe he will be acquitted plain and simple.

But will he receive a fair trial? Let's look at it. I know some will consider this the race card but it is in the deck of life. And I didn't invent the deck. Kobe is Black and his accuser is White. What kind of jury will he get in Eagle County? The jury pool in Eagle is all White and no Black man should ever be tried by an all White jury. Ipso facto, no White man should be tried by an all Black jury. Perhaps it is time for us to wake up in America and admit this is still a racist country. Justice must strive to be blind. In the process of looking for blindness, one must not be ignorant. And it is quite frankly ignorant to assume race doesn't matter in the room of a criminal courthouse. I challenge any person reading my words to call Tom Mesereau, Gerry Spence, Roy Black or Gerald Uelmen and ask them if race matters in a *trial by fire*. It matters and we must deal with it adequately. Again, I was not with Kobe Bryant. He very well could have raped this woman and if he raped her he should go to jail and be punished.

I do believe he is not guilty. I do believe the charges are mendacity. I believe that the so-called rape shield laws are well-intentioned and wrong-headed.

If there is a jury trial, Kobe's lawyers must be allowed to confront his accuser. And in that confrontational process, the victim's (alleged victim) past and present sex life, drug use and abuse, the fact that she attempted to commit suicide, etc. must be brought out. A fair jury ought to be able to weigh all the evidence and make a judgment based upon the facts of the case. This will not happen if the judge disallows the defense to divulge relevant details of her past.

One must remember that the potential consequences of the outcome of a trial can be life-altering. Anytime a person stands to lose their income, freedom, family and future, we must allow the jury trial to be open, honest and there should be an authentic search for justice. "Have you ever accused another person of rape or assault?" Is a question Spence would ask. "How many different sex partners have you had?" Janus would ask. "Do you enjoy or have you ever engaged in rough sex?" Roy Black would ask.

"Did you try out for American Teen Idol?" Uelmen would ask. "Isn't it a fact that the sheriff who filed these charges without consulting with the D.A. is a friend of yours and your family?" Maurice Bennett would ask.

The answers to these questions are entirely relevant when a man faces life in prison on a he said/she said case.

And I must caution young law students who are perusing the contents of this book that you must be bold, be confident, be tough and be precise when cross-examining a witness.

You must try to ask only questions to which you know the answers prior to trial. You cannot know these things unless you prepare. "Preparation, preparation, preparation and more preparation is how you win trials," said famed lawyer Willie Gary. And I'll add that you must prepare some more if you want to win.

I encourage law students to begin early to study public speaking and study what makes the great, great. You should study Dr. Martin Luther King, Jr., Anthony Robbins, Zig Zigler, Johnnie Cochran, Jesse Jackson and all great speakers. This will enable you to develop a speaking style, which will make people want to listen to you. Along with mastering public speaking, a lawyer must learn to *listen* and not just *hear*.

Listening is an art, which is overlooked by many in this day and age. But great psychiatrists, doctors, pastors, lawyers and counselors are great listeners. You must learn to read body language and develop as a sixth sense the ability to look at a person and notice what they are not saying. You can develop these skills by modeling other great listeners.

One of the reasons the judicial system here in America is so messed up and complicated is because there are so few listeners and so many talkers. It would behoove us as a society to shut up and listen to one another.

Something is wrong . . . I understand politics and I understand the "drum major instinct". I know many of us want to be first; we want to be out front and to be seen and heard. The desire to lead is not evil per se but we must listen, study and strive to be fair.

The bottom line is that many of our politicians are not listening to their constituents. They are passing draconian laws, which fill up the jails and prisons with boys who never became men and these boys go to prison and become rougher, meaner, sicker and tougher. When they get out they bring their regional demons, territorial perversions and distorted mental apparatus with them to the streets. When they leave prison they are pregnant with evil. They are pregnant with anger, hurt, pain and fear. Then they lash out at society, commit more crimes, demonstrate, destroy and annihilate more victims before they re-enter prison.

We must begin anew to protect the public from criminals and lawlessness and the way to do it is to fix our broken system.

We need three strikes. We need to be tough on crime. We need to be strict on criminals. Yet, we must balance toughness, strictness and justice with fairness, equality and mercy.

When a poor boy robs the corner grocery store, we know exactly what to do with him. We put him in prison. But when you have a white collar, a college degree and you rob Enron, we lose focus.

All of a sudden congress needs to meet and the judicial system is in an uproar because we don't know what to do about corporate theft and scandals.

Robbery is robbery and theft is theft. It should make no difference the color, attire or education of the thief, killer or rapist. We must be just, fair, equal and consistent.

Young people (by and large) don't vote in America. They don't vote because they feel they don't count. They don't think they matter. "People are going to do what they want to do whether I vote or not," they think.

We must change this erroneous thinking. We need our youth to vote, run for office and play an important roll in our democracy in America.

I believe if we had more youth in office, in the voting booths, in the church and in the movement, we would prosper, grow and get better as a country.

Young people are energetic, idealistic and hungry to make waves. They want to make a difference and one needs only look at what happened to Rolando Cruz, Anthony Porter and David Quindt to know we need difference. We need to immediately enact some changes in our judicial system, our courts and the way we do justice in America.

We must transform the system. Adrian Lamo, Donny Bezemer, Scott Yates and Kevin Shelton can make a difference. This is 2004 and we live in a constantly changing society. America and Americans are constantly reinventing itself and ourselves. And we need to bring our laws up to speed.

We need not become soft on crime in order to bring laws up to the times. We must change our system.

I encourage young people to vote. If you don't vote, you don't count. Vote as you please but please vote.

And while we are voting and transforming our judicial system, etc., we must also transform self.

There is a stinginess and self-centeredness, which seems epidemic in and among our youth. We need to get a handle on it and begin to give, to care, to love and to help.

How much money has Kobe given to help some innocent man pay for a lawyer? Has Shaquille given to anybody in prison?

We've got to look within ourselves and ask the question, "What have I done to help somebody else?" This must become the question of the day.

Innocent men are dying in prison and living everyday of your life trapped in prison for crimes you did not commit is horrible. It can suck the very life out of you. It can drain, frustrate and aggravate you. A person can become bitter, depressed and despondent when trapped here for crimes he/she did not commit. I would encourage columnists, writers and reporters to do follow-up columns and stories on Rubin "Hurricane" Carter, David Quindt, Anthony Porter and Anthony Faizon to discover what the pressures of prison did to them. America needs to know that there is a segment of the prison population who should not be in prison. We can't rubber-stamp it. We can't overlook it or try to justify it. We must rectify it. Attorney Edwin Spencer Matthews, Jr. who is a powerful civil lawyer at a prestigious New York law firm can attest to the fact that there are innocents trapped in prison. Attorney Matthews took on a case pro bono and got a wrongly convicted man out of prison. Men such as E. S. Matthews, Jr. give us hope and faith that things can and will get better. Mr. Matthews is not a criminal lawyer but he was moved by injustice and touched by innocence. He went out of his way spending millions of his own dollars to help free a stranger on the road and we hope that the Willie Garys, Isaac Byrds, Floyd Abrams and the Ephraim Margolins will likewise get in the ring and fight to free the wrongly convicted.

If Kobe Bryant is not guilty, I would hope he, along with P. Diddy Combs and others, will begin to contribute (even if they do so anonymously) to help exonerate others who went to prison for crimes they did not commit.

When men are represented by public defenders, they usually don't get justice. It's not only because many public defenders are not good lawyers. Sometimes they are great lawyers who care about their clients but they don't have the time or resources to successfully vindicate the rights of the falsely accused.

Public defenders are underpaid and their offices are underrated. Many California prison guards earn more money than public defenders. The altruistic philanthropy of the Bryants, Gardners, Garys and Combs could help level the playing field for some of the poor who are wrongly charged with crimes.

Let us never, ever forget the fact that public safety must be our main objective as a society as it relates to law and order. And each time we send the *wrong man* to prison for murder, rape or robbery, the right man is left on the streets and the right man is still out in our neighborhoods committing more and more crimes. This must be stopped.

On Thursday, September 25, 2003 a civil trial began for California prison guards in a prison rape case. Inmate Eddie Webb Dillard alleges prison guards punished him by setting him up and getting him raped by a convicted murderer known (as published in the Sacramento Bee newspaper) by the name "Booty Bandit".

Mr. Dillard states three prison officers violated his human and civil rights by setting up the rapes over two days in March 1993 to retaliate against him for kicking a guard at another prison. I have stated for years that prison authorities routinely transfer inmates in retaliation and that once we arrive at the new prison, the guards abuse, mistreat and punish us for whatever reason we were transferred. I fully expect to be transferred soon and to be punished at the new prison. Mr. Dillard alleges the guards - C.O. Joe Sanchez, C.O. Anthony Sylva, C.O. Robert Decker and now retired prison medical officer Kathy Horton-Plant then orchestrated a cover-up by refusing to take him to a hospital/infirmary and by not filling out medical reports.

"As a result, Mr. Dillard never received medical care," Attorney Marina Dini, Dillard's lawyer, said in the courtroom. "There is nothing in the file to document even an allegation. The evidence will show this was merely swept under the rug."

Dini stated Dillard complained to guards on a number of occasions that he was in danger.

Prison records indicated "Booty Bandit" Wayne Robertson was a sexual predator. Robertson has acknowledged raping and torturing Dillard and said the guards intentionally put Dillard in his cell. "They knew what would happen to him," Robertson said at trial.

Ex-guard Roscoe "Bonecrusher" Pondexter, who testified at a criminal trial under a grant of immunity, is also testifying. He said his fellow cohorts (officers) knew they were endangering Dillard when they left him in a cell with Robertson, who is serving a life sentence for murder and weighed twice as much as Dillard. Dillard's lawyer, Robert L. Bastian, Jr., did not state how much he is seeking but a state official said Dillard wants millions of dollars in damages.

C.D.C., which would be responsible for all compensatory damages awarded to Dillard, contends it is the guards and not the agency that were at fault.

C.D.C. lawyer Barbara Sheldon concluded in a 2001 affidavit that the guards had acted . . . with actual malice. Investigators also stated in affidavits that Robertson was listed in prison records as an enemy of Dillard. It is against department policy to house documented enemies in the same prison yard, much less in the same cell. Still so unbelievable that prison authorities refuse to document certain enemies and plan to transfer me to a prison where I have enemies?

They put this man (Dillard) on the yard and in the cell with a documented enemy! They put him in the cell with a documented enemy who had a history of raping and torturing cell partners. C.D.C. records document more than twenty-five instances in which Robertson assaulted and raped cellmates from 1983 to 1997, earning him the nickname "Booty Bandit".

Can you believe what you are reading now? Prison! The Department of Corrections. This is supposed to be a place where we send only the dregs of society, lawbreakers and these lawbreakers are supposed to be watched and guarded by law abiding citizens who are sworn peace officers. Very often, as can be observed in Dillard's case, the keepers are as corrupted, thuggish and evil as those whom they keep kept. Prison authorities not only swept this vicious rape under the rug in March 1993, but they contracted to place inmates in the cell with the "Booty Bandit" for at least four years after Dillard was raped. It is awful enough that they set the man up to be raped. It's horrible that they covered up the rape. But to cover up a crime and then knowingly continue to send young men in to be sodomized and traumatized for years is terrorism in the prisons. Where was the warden, the captains, S&I, counselors, and the chaplain, etc.?

C.D.C. initially *withdrew* its defense of the guards in the civil case but later agreed to pay for their lawyers. By withdrawing they were saying, "You're on your own. You're guilty. You did it and we are not going to be part of this." By later rejoining, they were saying, "You're still one of ours so we'll stand by your side and pay for your lawyers." This is another example of C.D.C. flip-flopping on issues and changing their positions on regulations, issues, inmates and staff on a whim. Do you still wonder why I state that C.D.C. is a monster factory?

A lawyer told me the other day that Sergeant Scarcella and Sgt. R. N. Saunders have been fired for allegedly beating a Black inmate nearly to death. The attorney states that Sgt. Elsberry was a witness and she "told the truth".

Yet, I've heard C.D.C. flip-flopped and decided not to fire Saunders and Scarcella. I have no personal knowledge of the incident but I am familiar with both Saunders and Scarcella. It has always been my opinion and belief that Sgt. Saunders was an evil, wicked and perhaps racist man. It is our hope that more lawyers will come forward and agree to take on C.D.C. and sue them, sue them, sue them.

I say to my adversaries to "Do what you want to me. Kill me if you want. Send me to Mule Creek, Corcoran, Salinas, High Desert or throw me into ad-seg again. Trump up a new charge but in the end we will win. Someway, somehow, I will expose the corruption within C.D.C.

I use to spend a lot of time being nervous and anxious about what they would do to me next but I'm coming to a new place in my life and God is helping me to learn how to have peace. I've learned that I am not my mind, I can rise above thought. Circumstances come and go. Life can seem good one moment and bad the next moment and very often we find ourselves planning to be happy when . . . I get out of prison, when . . . I get a billion dollars, a new car, a new wife, a new boat, etc.

But we ought to strive to be content where we are now. Celebrate now. Allow a deeper dimension of consciousness to flourish in your life. Shut out the voices. Block out the noise and look beyond your conditions and be happy.

Don't kill your present by seeking future fulfillment. We must work, strive, think, pray, plan and envision our futures and we ought to learn how to be happy *now* exactly where, how and who we are. On a daily basis, I'm learning how to take time out to enjoy life. I'm finding joy in my soul, in the present time. Most of us are much too wound up. We are so busy and our minds are running so fast that sleep doesn't even give us rest. We must *be still* and know who God is. God is not just future. God is now! God is present . . . I've found out how to be still. To be quiet. To celebrate now and I have decided not to die angry, nervous, uptight or sad.

All I have at this moment is *this moment.* So do you?

Deborah Saffell sent Peter (Andrist) an email the other day, which was quite inspiring. Apparently Deborah logged on to one of our web sites and decided to get involved . . . Thank God for Deborah!

Today is November 3, 2003 and I am being placed in (again) administrative segregation . . . I lost my cell, my job and my entire program! I'll be transferred and I guarantee you I'll be killed wherever they transfer me to. I was set up. Plain and simple! Jeff? Jeff? How could you? I sent him money! I got his brother a web site! I helped him and he lied! This is wrong! I'm not even angry. I feel sorry for Jeff. He's scared! Somebody got to him and forced him to lie. I can't finish this book. They are coming to extract me. Somebody get this book to Governor Arnold Schwarzennegger and Arianna Huffington. Pray for me . . .

**November 3, 2003**

# How You Can Help

1. Call 1-800-Bishop2 and order tapes and video's by Bishop Jakes.

2. Log on to www.outlawsonline.com/ShermanManning.htm and www.thepamperedprisoner.com/smanningca.htm, e-mail to hallopeter@freesurf.ch and pledge $100.00 or more to help exonerate Sherman Manning. (We pray that the La Van Hawkins, Cathy Hughes, P. Diddy and John Johnson's will *help*)

3. Call in to the Doug Banks Radio Show, Larry King, Radio One, Tommy Goss and Tom Joyner and discuss this book.

4. Call C.D.C. (Headquarters in Downtown Sacramento Ca.) and Warden Pliler and check (916-985-8610) up on Sherman.

5. Read and support Justice Denied Magazine.

6. Tell every lawyer, politician and pastor you know to get this book.

7. Order a copy of this book for a prisoner.

8. Discuss this tome on the internet and in debates.

9. Support Barry Scheck and the Innocence project in New York City.

10. Write to Sherman Manning at Mule Creek Ione, Ca.

To order more copies of this and other books, t-shirts, mugs, caps, hats, cards etc. visit *www.cafeshops.com/manning* or call *877-809-1659*. If you received this tome *gratis* please forward twenty five dollars to Sherman Manning at the Mule Creek address in One California.

"If you really want to become *great*; you must be willing to make another man great. If you have not been motivated to help me achieve justice, (for *me*) so be it. But I pray that *you* will help make other men (and women) great. You police officers, prison guards, lawyers and judges who have just finished reading this book need to make men great. I call on you to reach out to that bad boy (or girl) in your neighborhood and help them. Don't walk away from them. Look them in the eyes and tell them "I see *greatness* inside *you*." Take them under your wings and build them up. They need to know that you *care*. Take them to manpower and let them see T. D. Jakes, Eddie Long, Noel Jones and Paula White. Take them to the movies, a ballgame or to a concert.... Become innovative and creative and just *save our youth*. We can't give up on them. I love you and God be with you"....

**Closing Thought:**

Special thanks to Patricia Lee, "FHM" Magazine, Maxim, Ebony Jet, Details Magazine, President Mandela, etc.

I wish I could help Chuckie P., Jeremy Anthony L., E. J. Johnnie Willie and several others who are in prison. But some guys are hard to reach because of peer pressure etc. I do want to call on Tony Brown, George Soros, Mr. Jackson, Mr. Smiley, Steve Soboroff, FHM, Maxim, Mr. Jellinek, The Beat Within, David Deluz, Eric Nicholson, Jay Manuel, Esteban, Peter Camejo, Mr. Kucinich, etc. to put the word out about this book . . . Don't miss "Creating Monsters" - coming soon. Reserve your copy now . . . Contact me (via snail mail) in Ione, CA. Visit our online shop at www.cafeshops.com/manning or email us at hallopeter@freesurf.ch

I still believe in God for the intervention of Chris Heinz, Wendy at WBLS, Ed Schultz, Ted Kennedy, William Greaves, Mike Snedeker, Aaron Goodwin, moveon.org, George Soros and every pastor in America . . . God Bless my baby sister Shateecia (and Shanteeka) who lost her baby. And Mr. Ezell Moon . . . Rest in peace . . . Richard Simmons?? I'll leave the arguing to Gerry Spence . . . But I must tell Barney, Bobby G. (former AKA Ghost) Eric W. , Wayman B., etc.

*If* you all are ever going to "get out", we ***must*** get up, come together and work. Your oppressor will not volunteer freedom . . . K. C. Hunt, Jay Manuel, Tyra Banks, Mr. Nicholson at Jane Magazine and Esteban. We are waiting to hear from "you". . . Jim Higgins, Larry Ellison and Warren Buffet? Coming (soon) in "Creating Monsters" . . .

**Sherman Manning**
*Bestselling Author, Motivator, Peak Performance Coach, expert in the psychology of change, Entrepreneur, consultant, President, founder and CEO of the A&M Enterprises*

**March 2004**

www.ingramcontent.com/pod-product-compliance
Lightning Source LLC
Chambersburg PA
CBHW060115200326
41518CB00008B/831